The Art of the Watchdog

The Art of the Watchdog

Fighting Fraud, Waste, Abuse, and Corruption in Government

Daniel L. Feldman

and

David R. Eichenthal

excelsior editions

State University of New York Press
Albany, New York

Published by State University of New York Press, Albany

Excelsior Editions is an imprint of State University of New York Press

For information, contact State University of New York Press, Albany, NY
www.sunypress.edu

Production by Diane Ganeles
Marketing by Fran Keneston

Library of Congress Cataloging-in-Publication Data

Feldman, Daniel L.
   The art of the watchdog : fighting fraud, waste, abuse, and corruption in government / Daniel L. Feldman and David R. Eichenthal.
      pages cm. — (Excelsior editions)
   Includes bibliographical references and index.
   ISBN 978-1-4384-4929-6 (hardcover : alk. paper)
   1. Political corruption—United States—Prevention.   2. Misconduct in office—United States—Prevention.   3. Waste in government spending—United States—Prevention.   4. Legislative oversight—United States.   5. Public interest groups—United States.   I. Eichenthal, David R.   II. Title.

JF1081.F45 2014
364.1'323—dc23   2013002460

10 9 8 7 6 5 4 3 2 1

Contents

Contents

Acknowledgments

This book would not exist but for David Eichenthal. Even among the hundreds of fine public servants I have known, David stood out for his profound intelligence and integrity. For more than thirty years I have had the honor of calling him my dear friend. On the basis of his very kind estimation of a book I wrote not long after we first met, he thought an updated version would be warranted. I was smart enough to insist that he co-author it, and lucky enough to get him to agree. As a result, it reflects the vast experience and insight he acquired in those intervening decades. His contributions elevate it to an altogether higher league than that of its predecessor.

My academic home during the writing of this book has been John Jay College of Criminal Justice of the City University of New York, as I hope it will continue to be for many years to come, and a very fine home it is. For that I am deeply grateful to its president, Jeremy Travis, and to my Public Management Department chair, Ned Benton, each of whom has provided wonderful support and guidance. Fred Palm, recently retired as a member of our department, Jay Hamilton, chair of our Economics Department, and Frank Anechiarico, who visited as a professor with us from his permanent academic home at Hamilton College, each read through an earlier version of the manuscript and provided immensely valuable suggestions.

Some of our own experiences in fighting fraud, waste, abuse, and corruption in government enrich this book, and enhance its value to fellow practitioners, scholars, and general readers. Some noteworthy figures to whom I remain grateful gave me the platforms that enabled me to do such work. First and foremost, as is clearly reflected in the pages of this book, is Elizabeth Holtzman. Other than to say that she remains the ultimate role model for oversight professionals, I won't reiterate here the many debts we owe her: just check the index. A young member of the New York State Legislature hired me next to continue that kind of work, and whatever frictions may have colored our relationship thereafter, I must credit the current

senior senator for the State of New York, Chuck Schumer, for that. The
people of the 45th Assembly District of New York State gave me my next
job, succeeding Mr. Schumer, and six years later the then-Speaker of that
Assembly, Mel Miller, elevated me to chair of its Committee on Correction, significantly expanding and reinforcing my oversight powers for twelve
more years. After the public in its wisdom chose Anthony Weiner over
me to represent our district in Congress, then-Attorney General and now
my friend Eliot Spitzer chose me to direct the Legal Policy and Program
Development unit in New York's Law Department, once again empowering
me to pursue challenging, fascinating oversight targets for six years. After a
two-year stint running a trade association representing a genre of attorneys
who themselves engage in an important form of private-sector oversight, my
friend Tom DiNapoli, the comptroller of the State of New York, appointed
me as Special Counsel. From that vantage point I engaged in other kinds of
oversight for three years, until I left for full-time academic work at John Jay.

I incorporate by reference the thanks I have given individually to
family and friends in my other books. Please do not take this amiss; I do
occasionally need to spare other readers.

My final and greatest acknowledgment is to the United States—in the
words of Carl Schurz on the floor of the U.S. Senate in 1872, "My country,
right or wrong: if right, to be kept right; and if wrong, to be set right."

Dan Feldman

I often tell students, interns, and others starting out in a career in public
service that it really helps to have good people to work with and for . . . and
mentors . . . and friends . . . and, now, co-authors.

More than thirty years ago, I was introduced to a young legislative
aide who was running for the New York State Assembly. His name was Dan
Feldman. Dan won election to the legislature and eventually hired me, first
as an intern and then as a staff member. He has been a great friend and
colleague ever since. His 1981 book, *Reforming Government*, was an engaging and thoughtful take on the work of oversight that made me want to
pursue it as a career. Thirty years later, after Dan's book on his time in the
New York legislature was published, I told him that he really should update
Reforming Government. His challenge to me was, "I'll do it, but only if you
co-author it." My greatest hope is that there will be someone who reads
The Art of the Watchdog and feels the same way about the important work
of oversight that I did after reading *Reforming Government*.

During my first year of law school, I walked into a seminar on the criminal justice system led by Professor Jim Jacobs. Jim has been a friend, mentor and prod ever since. His work—along with Frank Anechiarico's—on *The Pursuit of Absolute Integrity* was incredibly thought provoking for me, both as a practitioner and—dare I say—now as a scholar. Jim was gracious enough to allow me to have an academic hook on which to hang my hat while writing this book as a senior fellow at the Center for Research in Crime and Justice. He also provided an appropriately tough critique of an early draft that I know made the final version immensely better.

After law school, I was fortunate to spend time at the Vera Institute of Justice, working at the Prosecuting Attorneys Research Council led by Dan Johnston. As discussed in the chapter on oversight of police misconduct, Dan greatly informed my thinking on that area. He was also the first person to tell me that sometimes "you can judge a person by their enemies"— important words to live by when you are in the oversight business.

Arnie Kriss also played an important role in my thinking on police oversight and oversight in general. I have known Arnie so long that I believe he is now the only person left who still refers to me as "kid." There are a lot of reasons why I pursued the Public Advocate investigation of police misconduct, but Arnie's influence may have been the most important.

I don't tell any of my Liz Holtzman oversight stories in this book—and I have a lot of them. The courage and commitment that Liz showed in the fight to bring Nazi war criminals to justice was regularly matched on a dozen other issues that I worked on with her in the comptroller's office. I learned so much from her and from others in that office—people like Tom Sanzillo, who was often my partner in oversight efforts and has remained a friend and great colleague to date, and Rhea Dignam, who helped me to think like a prosecutor without ever being one.

During my brief time at the School Construction Authority, I was lucky enough to get to work with people like Toby Thacher and Joe DeLuca—brilliant theorists and practitioners when it comes to the work of inspectors general.

Mark Green was a public advocate long before he was elected to the office. His willingness to take on the issue of police misconduct during the height of Rudy Giuliani's popularity was one of the gutsier uses of political capital that I have ever seen. I learned a lot from Mark and from other wonderful colleagues in the Office of Public Advocate.

At some point when I was considering the offer to come to work in Chattanooga, I asked Bob Corker's chief of staff how the mayor would handle it when I did something that stepped on important toes—almost inevitable in doing the work of a watchdog. The mayor's response was that "you should do what you think is right and we'll back you up." That's when I knew that Chattanooga was the place for me. Bob Corker stuck to his word and proved me right.

I thought that I had finally left the work of oversight when I joined what eventually was the Ochs Center. But then Tom Sanzillo—and another old friend, Larry Shapiro of the Rockefeller Family Fund—encouraged me to start to look at plans for new coal-fired power plants in places like Washington County, Georgia. I loved leading the Ochs Center and particularly loved the opportunity to work with smart young people, including two who contributed directly and indirectly to this book. Stacy Richardson was a bright and able researcher who worked with me on the issues related to Plant Washington—and also regularly prodded me on how the book was going. Shelby Kain had little to do with oversight while at Ochs, but she and former City of Chattanooga intern—Christian Montz—both helped me become smarter about the Government Accountability Office (GAO), where they both work. I should take pains to note that their involvement was a great dinner conversation—no secret GAO codes were revealed.

Unlike a lot of people who have spent their careers in government, I have always had a good relationship with the press. In part, I think that is because of lessons that I have learned from really talented press secretaries. Joe DePlasco, as a teacher of the role of the media in oversight, stands out in this regard. He was a great colleague in the Public Advocate's office and I learned more about the media by just sitting in his office and listening to his conversations with reporters than I ever could have from a four-year degree in communications.

Tom Griscom is a former reporter, congressional aide, White House communications director, and newspaper publisher. There might be some who could offer better advice on a book about oversight than Tom—I just don't think there actually are. Dan and I—and hopefully now you as readers—benefited from his comments on the book, especially on the role of the press and the decline of congressional oversight.

To all of these friends and colleagues, thank you for a lifetime of learning. All of your work made me better as I tried to practice the art of the watchdog and smarter as I help to explain it in this book.

To Bea and Seth and Emily, there is no way that I could have done this without you, so thanks. Your love and support are the best parts of my life. Thanks Bea for always listening to my latest idea in practicing the art of the watchdog over the past thirty years. Thanks Emily for laughing at my attempt at humorous stories that begin some of the chapters. And thanks Seth for your help on the manuscript and for introducing me to *The Wire*. I will always remember the day you called me to tell me that I had to watch the series and that you were buying it for me . . . with my credit card.

Finally, I want to thank my parents Bernice and Irving Eichenthal. Dan and I talk about the importance to effectiveness as a watchdog of having a low tolerance of injustice. I hope I have that and I know that if I do, it is because of my mom. If part of my thinking about the importance of oversight comes from wanting to see our nation do better, that comes from my father who served his country proudly in World War II. After my dad passed away a few years ago, I was going through his papers and found articles, speeches, and essays that I had written dating back nearly thirty years—many clearly read multiple times. I wish that he had been around to read this book. In many ways, it is for him.

David Eichenthal

Chapter 1

The Watchdog

Fraud, waste, abuse, and corruption retard and can destroy a nation's development. We understand the essential need to push back, to control, to resist those vices. More fundamentally, we fight back because those who steal the public's goods or waste our resources anger us. "Taxes are the price we pay for civilization," Oliver Wendell Holmes famously remarked. We pay the taxes, and we will fight those who would cheat us of the civilization we should get in return.

The immediate pages ahead summarize our experiences in government oversight, explain how those experiences fit into this book's mission of inspiring others, underscore the critical importance of that work, and introduce one model oversight effort and the model "watchdog" who undertook it. We offer the model as something of a template for the oversight efforts detailed in later chapters, as well as for those that lie in the future, to be conducted some day by our readers.

We don't fancy ourselves the very best watchdogs ever, but have spent most of our professional lifetimes in the effort. We have known each other for more than thirty years and during that time have spent countless hours talking through the practice of government oversight, both as practitioners and as teachers of the practice. Both of us have worked on or led oversight investigations in our respective careers as legislators and aides to legislators, prosecutors, auditors, mayors, and other elected officials. In his first book, *Reforming Government*, practitioner-scholar Dan Feldman wrote about his experience as a congressional and state legislative staffer conducting oversight investigations in New York City in the 1970s. Feldman then spent nearly two decades as a member of the New York State Assembly where he led legislative oversight efforts focused on the state's prison system. He also served in key leadership positions in the New York State Attorney General's office—under then Attorney General Eliot Spitzer—and in the office of the state's chief auditor, New York State Comptroller Tom DiNapoli.

David Eichenthal spent fifteen years in state and local government in the New York City Comptroller's office as an assistant to Liz Holtzman, as an Assistant Inspector General working to combat organized crime's influence on the construction industry, and as a top aide in the New York City Public Advocate's office (then run by former Nader Raider Mark Green) leading investigations of then-New York City Mayor Rudy Giuliani's administration. Eichenthal subsequently moved to Tennessee where he took on Wall Street's role in public pensions.

Although this book draws on cases from all over the United States, many of the case studies that we highlight in the chapters that follow are based on our own efforts to practice "the art of the watchdog." Those latter case studies make available to the reader the deeper level of knowledge and insight that should accrue from personal involvement.

If you are a practitioner, we will arm you with tools and techniques designed to combat fraud, waste, abuse, and corruption. If you are a student of government—but more importantly, if you care about the quality and integrity of government—we aim to provide you with a story of the good and the bad of current oversight, with an eye to improving our government.

Why an art? Why not a science? In part, it is because we believe that effectiveness as a watchdog depends at least as much on who you are as on what you know. If you are fatalistic, phlegmatic, and like to "go with the flow," don't make oversight your life's work.

The best public watchdogs combine a powerful indignation with relentless persistence. Public watchdogs need a low "boiling point"—an intolerance for abuse and injustice. So long as they share that burning need to fight abuse and injustice, a wide range of citizens can launch victorious oversight efforts as watchdogs: lawyers, legislators, auditors, investigators, journalists, staff for elected officials or civic groups, others. Still, success rarely comes quickly; almost always, it demands much more than David's slingshot conquest of Goliath. In this arena, Goliath revives and recovers a few times, so David needs to monitor his results and follow up on his efforts for a few months or years.

Why Oversight Matters

It is often said that people first decide, then justify; that is, they make decisions on a "gut" level, and afterward construct an intellectual rationale to justify their choice. On a day-to-day basis, we fight fraud, waste, abuse, and corruption because they infuriate us. But sound intellectual arguments justify a commitment to the practice of oversight.

Simply put, unchecked corruption can render a regime—or government—dysfunctional.

The author Thomas Friedman tells a great story of the Asian and African officials who visit each other's homes. The African wonders at the opulence of the Asian's home, so the Asian points to his beautiful picture window, and asks, "What do you see?" The African notes the large new bridge. The Asian points to himself, and says, "ten percent." Some years later, the Asian visits the African at home. Now the Asian is impressed: The African's home is far more opulent than his. The African says, "Look out the window." The Asian does so. The African asks, "What do you see?" Puzzled, the Asian says "nothing!" The African smiles, points to himself, and says, "one hundred percent."

Political conservatives may look at the effort to root out waste, fraud, and corruption as consistent with their goal to shrink the size of an inefficient government. For liberals who believe in an active government, there is an obligation to guarantee that the limited resources entrusted to the government for worthy purposes go to their intended use rather than to line the pockets of corrupt officials and that agents of government vested with power respect rather than abuse the public trust.

Our obvious enemies are those who would cheat and steal from the public and those who through inefficiency would waste valuable taxpayer dollars. We also have less obvious enemies. Those who suggest that all politicians are corrupt and all government is inefficient spread a lie that undermines our democracy and the integrity of our system of government. The more citizens who accept such a view, the fewer who will bother with oversight, or will react with outrage when they see fraud, waste, abuse, and corruption exposed. The more that apathy replaces outrage, the less that "watchdogs" will be able to generate pressure to force reform.

Moreover, that view leads us down a path where more and more Americans look to their government and simply say, "why bother." We believe that democracy is a participatory sport—and that the best way for democracy to succeed is for Americans to engage in it. Thus, the goal of oversight is not merely to make our government less wasteful and corrupt, but to build trust and confidence in our very system of government. Effective oversight that leads to more effective and efficient government is critical to maintaining the democratic values that we cherish. For us, in the participatory sport of democracy, we often root for the referee.

And that's why we wrote this book. Because at a time of tea parties on the right and Occupy Wall Street on the left, as the size of our national government has grown and fiscal pressure forces our state and local governments to shrink, as Republicans and Democrats in state capitols and city halls struggle to continue to deliver basic services to their constituents, effective oversight can play an extraordinary role in righting how government works.

Yet, in the past decades, the role of the government watchdog often has become more about the scandal of the day—or the hour—and what gets covered on CNN rather than the hard work necessary to investigate and expose scandal and convert it into reform. We write as the role of investigative journalism is being diminished, even as access to information has never been greater. We write in fervent hope that the "art of the watchdog" does not become a lost one.

Liz Holtzman's Efforts to Uncover Nazis in America

Both of us—at different times and in different roles—worked for one watchdog whose characteristics and accomplishments offer a model to be emulated by those who would serve the cause of justice—Elizabeth Holtzman. As a member of her congressional staff, Dan Feldman helped lead the investigation of the federally funded summer lunch program that led to felony convictions and program reform. As a member of her New York City Comptroller staff, David Eichenthal uncovered links between city contractors and organized crime and helped block more than $250 million in unnecessary construction projects. Those efforts fit within a more rigid and restricted conventional notion of the watchdog role. But the watchdog, in our view, more properly includes the broader range of targets encompassed by the somewhat amorphous term *abuse*, understood as the exercise of government authority for bad purposes. In that regard, Holtzman's work in challenging, exposing, and correcting the federal government's willingness to look the other way when it came to the presence of Nazi war criminals in the United States may be the best example we know of the art of the watchdog.

Liz Holtzman remains the youngest woman ever elected to Congress, the only woman ever elected as district attorney in New York City, and the only woman ever elected as chief auditor of the nation's largest city. Early on, Holtzman had taken on a leadership role in major issues before the Congress—ending the Vietnam War and promoting equal rights for women. At home, Holtzman also was hard at work building the kind of constituent services needed to win local support and re-election. She would also soon serve with distinction on the House Judiciary Committee in its impeachment proceedings of President Richard Nixon. In other words, she had quite a first term.

In 1973, Holtzman was still in her first year in Congress. Just a year earlier, she had defeated fifty-year incumbent and then-Chair of the House Judiciary Committee, Emanuel Celler, for his Brooklyn, New York seat.

Step 1: The Whistleblower

In the middle of 1973, that chaotic year of national turmoil, perhaps because of her outspokenness on other issues, a whistleblower from the Immigration and Naturalization Service (INS) approached Holtzman and asked to meet with her confidentially. At the meeting, he told her that the INS had a list of Nazi war criminals living in the United States but was doing nothing to bring them to justice.

These individuals had come here after World War II, in some cases on their own but also in some cases with the assistance of the U.S. government. For Holtzman, it was a shocking revelation. But at the time, no one within the federal government—or among outside organizations—was really focused on the issue.

As Holtzman notes, "Public interest in the Holocaust was not widespread at the time. The Simon Weisenthal Center didn't exist. Survivor groups had little political involvement, although the Jewish War Veterans sometimes spoke out. And obviously the U.S. government made almost no effort to take action against the Nazis."

Step 2: The First Hearing

Holtzman served as a member of the Congressional subcommittee with oversight over the INS. Several months after her meeting with the whistleblower, the commissioner of the INS appeared before the subcommittee during what Holtzman describes as a "relatively routine hearing." She used the opportunity, however, to begin asking questions about the issues raised by the whistleblower. When Holtzman asked if, in fact, the INS had a list of Nazi war criminals living in the United States, the INS commissioner testified that they did. Holtzman then elicited testimony that there were fifty-three alleged Nazi war criminals on the list. When Holtzman asked what the INS was doing about this, the INS commissioner could not provide an answer.

Step 3: Document Review

It would have been easy for Holtzman to leave things as they were—she had gotten the admission and surely the INS would begin to address the matter. Instead, she demanded to see the files of the fifty-three alleged war criminals who were living in the United States—and personally reviewed the material at the INS's New York office.

Step 4: Public Call for Action

After reviewing the documents, a month after the initial hearing Holtzman went public—blasting the INS for failing to conduct adequate investigations and proposing the creation of a War Crimes Strike Force within the INS.

Follow Up and Follow Through

These initial steps—and Holtzman's initial actions—led to an eight-year effort to translate oversight into action and results. She was the watchdog who, once she had the wrongdoer in her bite, would never let go. Her persistence turned what might have been just a good one-day story on federal inaction into a career-defining pursuit.

That was certainly the view from inside the INS. An internal Justice Department review of the history of the U.S. role in tracking down Nazi war criminals concluded that "Holtzman did not merely hector; she got down in the trenches. She met at her office with INS investigators to review the leading investigations; she visited INS' New York office and spent hours reviewing the files; and she sent the INS detailed critiques and analyses of the agency's work."

It took time, but Holtzman's continuous prodding started to produce results. In early 1977, Holtzman called for new Congressional hearings—this time focused on the INS and Nazi war criminals. At the hearing, the INS announced that it was changing procedures for investigating Nazis and would create a centralized task force, much as Holtzman had recommended several years earlier. The INS also ordered all closed cases involving alleged Nazi war criminals still living in the United States to be reopened for review.

Holtzman's oversight efforts also translated into legislative action. In 1978, Congress passed the Holtzman Amendment making it easier for the United States to both deport Nazi war criminals and exclude them from entry.

Even after the task force at the INS was created, Holtzman continued to follow up and monitor progress. The head of the so-called Special Litigation Unit, Martin Mendelsohn, "was a frequent visitor to Congresswoman Holtzman's office." And when funding for the effort became an issue, Holtzman proposed to move the unit to the Department of Justice main building to ensure higher exposure and adequate funding.

Both the Department of Justice and the INS initially opposed the proposed restructuring. Again, combining her oversight role with legislative authority, Holtzman proposed to mandate the shift by statute. Six years after Holtzman's first questions at a Congressional hearing, the Office of Special Investigations (OSI) was created in the Justice Department.

Still, even with the creation of OSI, Holtzman "remained vigilant about OSI matters, issuing press releases to announce OSI filings and victories; exhorting the State Department to work with OSI to update its Watchlist (they did); demanding that State modify its visa application form to take into account new legislation precluding the entry of Nazi persecutors (also done), and notifying OSI when she learned of a potential subject." According to the one-time head of OSI Allen Ryan, Holtzman "had the reputation in OSI . . . of being . . . Ghenghis Khan incarnate. You'd think going to see her was like climbing Mt. Everest to see the Dali Lama."

Even after leaving Congress—as a local elected official and private citizen—Holtzman remained a supporter and prod of OSI. As of 2006, eighty-three persecutors had been denaturalized; sixty-two have left the country permanently as a result of OSI's work, and more than 170 were prevented from entering the United States. There is a pretty clear case to be made that because of Holtzman's relentless efforts as a watchdog, hundreds of Nazis were brought to justice who otherwise would have gone unnoticed in our midst.

Conclusion: The Art of the Watchdog

With nearly forty years of hindsight, it is clear just how decisive Holtzman's role was in this important part of post-war American history. There is little question that but for Holtzman's pursuit of justice, there would not have been an OSI, the INS would have continued to allow Nazi war criminals to live in our midst, and hundreds of war criminals would not have faced accountability.

In the coming chapters, we discuss the art of the watchdog—what oversight is, how to do it, and how it is practiced every day at the federal, state, and local levels in the United States. We discuss a series of case studies—some involving our own work over the years—of the exercise of oversight. But the story of Elizabeth Holtzman and the creation of the OSI should tell the reader much in just these first pages of our discussion of the theory and practice of oversight in U.S. government.

First and foremost, Holtzman was deeply intolerant of abuse and injustice. Not everyone would view the same set of facts—the federal government's acceptance of war criminals in our midst—as an example of abuse. And, in fact, the federal government had taken no action—and was under no pressure to act—for almost three decades. Holtzman's deep sense of justice was part of what made her a good watchdog. Her "boiling point" when it came to injustice was lower than most people's and that pushed her to take on issues that others ignored.

Second, Holtzman understood the power—and her responsibility—to conduct meaningful oversight of an executive agency as a member of the legislative branch. Other legislators often focus primarily or exclusively on constituent service. Some deal only in the high-minded pursuit of policy through legislation. For Holtzman, asking tough questions and demanding accountability was a critical part of her work in Congress.

Third, she sought the type of information vital to performing the oversight role. We don't know why the INS mid-level officials—the whistleblowers—first came to Holtzman but it seems unlikely that it was by chance. Effective oversight starts with an understanding of the need to gather information from all possible sources.

Fourth, she seized every opportunity to discuss the issue. From questions at hearings to press conferences, Holtzman was able to take the issue of the government's inaction in response to Nazi war criminals to the public.

Fifth, she did the hard work necessary to get information and get results. Imagine a member of Congress personally slogging through agency files and offering detailed critiques of agency action and inaction. Oversight is not easy work and requires time and dedication of resources.

Sixth, she was absolutely relentless. Oversight is not for those who would yield to exhaustion, ennui, compromise or intransigence. Even after winning initial concessions and policy changes in response to her efforts, she continued to follow up and follow through—monitoring the progress of the effort, demanding structural changes, becoming a critical ally for budget issues and celebrating early successes.

For the local council member or state legislator, for the county auditor or state inspector general, for the watchdog situated at any level of power and authority from the highest to the lowest, the same tools that Liz Holtzman used to take on indifference to Nazi war criminals in the federal government can be used to take on more typical forms of fraud, waste, abuse and corruption at the state and local level.

Chapter 2

What is Oversight?

If men were angels, no government would be necessary. If angels were to govern men, neither external nor internal controls on government would be necessary.

—James Madison, Federalist #51, 1788

Accountability is a purifying element, a constant reminder that government and administration are not activities solely for the benefit of those who practice them—a simple fact, but one which heaven knows, it is easy to forget.

—E.L. Normanton, The Accountability and Audit of Government, 1966

"*Sed quis custodiet ipsos custodies?*," asked the Roman poet Juvenal: Who will guard the guardians?, anticipating Madison in Federalist #51. Those who skillfully oversee government practice the art of the watchdog.

In this chapter, we introduce answers to some basic questions. First, what do watchdogs watch for—in other words, what are the targets of a watchdog's oversight? Second, just who are the watchdogs?

Fraud, Waste, Abuse, and Corruption

When we "bungle" or miss something we should have noticed, we have committed an *oversight*. The word unfortunately has characteristics of both homonym and antonym: The process of oversight entails watching to catch and correct bungling and error. In this book, from here on, we use the word only in the second sense.

The foregoing makes it seem simple. But what are the "misdeeds" that the watchdog should monitor and expose? Often, they are described using the words *fraud, waste, abuse,* and *corruption.*

Fraud

Fraud is easily definable—and in fact is usually defined by criminal law—as intentionally deceiving others in a way that results in their sustaining a loss. There are, however, many different flavors of fraud. For example, one practitioner has identified two-dozen different devices used to commit fraud in the government procurement process alone, including:

- Bribe: a "thing of value" offered to or received by a procurement official to influence a pending decision.

- Gratuity: "a thing of value" received by a procurement official in appreciation for a decision.

- Kickback: a "thing of value" returned to a procurement official as a portion or reflecting a portion of the value of overcharge, nonconformance with requirements, or other advantage enjoyed by the supplier because of the cooperation of the procurement official.

- Leaked acquisition data: confidential pre-bid procurement information or information from competitors supplied to a favored bidder by a procurement officials to confer an unfair advantage in the bidding process.

- Change order abuse: changes from the initial order, at additional cost to government, assured secretly and in advance to be approved by the procurement official, enabling the favored supplier to win out over competitors by submitting an unjustifiably low initial bid.

- Bid manipulation: benefiting a favored contractor or supplier by any of a variety of methods, for example the acceptance of late bids or allowing a re-bid or a changed bid in response to competitors' bids.

Waste

Whereas fraud is often defined by statute, waste and abuse are often in the eyes of the beholder. A February 2010 survey by *ABC News* and *The Washington Post* found that, on average, Americans believe that 53 cents of every dollar they send to Washington is "wasted." Surely, if that were the case, it would suggest that the battle to combat waste in the federal government was an absolute failure.

For many Americans, every new weapon system—no matter how effective—is a waste of taxpayer dollars . . . just as for many other Americans, every dollar spent on Head Start or public health is wasted.

For the watchdog, the challenge is to determine waste from an ideologically and politically neutral perspective. A weapon system may be wasteful if it does not perform as required, if it costs more than originally estimated, or if the underlying policy rationale that led to its development is no longer relevant. For example, even a perfectly designed anti-Zeppelin weapon delivered on time and on budget would probably be deemed a wasteful expenditure of public resources. Similarly, a public health program that delivers even excellent health clinic services—but at twice the cost of all similar programs nationally with no better outcomes—would be regarded as wasteful.

Thus, unlike a determination of fraud that can often be made on a simple analysis of the facts, the determination of waste in government calls for a significant understanding of context—in terms of policy, cost, and performance.

Abuse

What do we mean by abuse? Here too, there is a need for substantial interpretation and analysis that go well beyond the facts of a particular situation. And, like waste, abuse can mean many different things.

Abuse can go to issues of injustice—when government acts, even lawful ones, result in what appear to be unjust or unfair results. In the case of oversight of the INS and its response to Nazi war criminals, there was no suggestion that the INS engaged in fraud or wasted funds or violated any law or regulation. Instead, the issue raised in the context of the oversight of the INS's operations was a policy failure as much as an administrative failure.

Thus, abuse can include broader issues of mismanagement beyond misappropriation or poor performance. As is common in the case of oversight of police and correctional agencies, it can go to issues of abuse of power and discretion under law. Failure by a police department to change policies and practices in the face of incidents of misconduct could constitute abuse of management authority.

Defining abuse, however, like defining waste, can be difficult, especially when relevant standards and the scope of discretion are vague or unclear.

Vagueness or ambiguity in statutory standards or statutory limits on discretion may be accidental. More often, a majority of legislators might reject a law that clearly set forth its objectives, but legislators who disagree on the important details of an issue might want to claim credit for supporting "public health." Thus, they may happily vote for a bill lacking in useful detail, thereby "passing the buck" for interpretation to the agency responsible for administering it, and, if irritated citizens challenge the agency's interpretations, pass it on to the courts.

Even when legislators did not prefer to enact an ambiguous bill, legislative intent may be difficult to ascertain. Conceivably, each legislator voting for a bill might have had a different view of what it entailed. Often, legislators vote for bills without *any* idea of what they entail. For that reason, experts in statutory interpretation generally disregard the floor comments of legislators who were not involved in the drafting of a bill, even if they saw fit to debate it.

So administrators do not necessarily have an easy time deciding how the legislature intended them to carry out the laws. And even clearly written laws do not ordinarily anticipate every circumstance in which they will be applied.

Those who carry out the law must inevitably be permitted discretion. A small-town police officer apprehending a teenager trespassing on private property may legitimately choose any of various options—arrest, scolding, informing the parents—depending on the circumstances, including the life circumstances of the perpetrator. Government employees attempting to follow the regulations of their agencies face the same problem. Regulations are rules formally adopted by government agencies to guide their employees in discharging the mission the statutory law authorizes the agencies to undertake. So, a correction officer finding an inmate committing an infraction of the rules may or may not "write up" the inmate. The police officer and the correction officer must use discretion to determine which course of action is most likely to improve the behavior of the offender and the safety of others.

Discretion comes into play at higher levels of administrative decision making as well. The federal Health and Human Services official who threatened an organization's tax-exempt status because it "violated" the civil rights law on gender discrimination by holding a mother–daughter luncheon, clearly failed to apply common sense in exercising his discretion.

Often, higher-level bureaucrats limit the discretion of lower-level personnel, so that the clerk at the Department of Motor Vehicles window may not be permitted to bend the rules even when common sense would so dictate. The higher-level officials may not trust the judgment of the clerk, but may reverse the clerk's decision on appeal—even if the clerk would have reversed his or her own decision, given the authority to do so.

The "watchdog" faces a difficult task before deciding that a government employee has improperly enforced the trespassing statute or the regulatory prohibition on prison contraband. The determination that the bureaucrat has engaged in an abuse of discretion requires, first, a judgment locating the limits or boundaries of that discretion.

Corruption

Finally, certain types of fraud, waste and abuse are forms of corruption. Corruption generally speaks to acts that may not just be fraudulent or wasteful or abusive, but are criminal as well. The standard for corruption—as opposed to just fraudulent, wasteful, or even unethical behavior—varies from nation to nation, state to state, or city to city. It also varies not just by place, but also by time.

For example, in Tennessee, it is illegal for members of the state senate to accept any campaign contributions during the legislative session and the maximum annual contribution allowed is $1,400 for an individual. In New York, no such limitation on the timing of contributions exists and the maximum contribution allowed is $16,800. In the hypothetical case of a legislator who steers a state contract to a poorly performing contractor who is a large campaign contributor, one could argue that it is wasteful (given the performance record of the contractor) and perhaps abusive (depending on the acts of the legislator) in both states. Add one more fact to the hypothetical—the contractor makes a $15,000 campaign contribution to the state senator during the legislative session. Arguably, the same act adds "corruption" to the mix in Tennessee, but not in New York.

The standard for corruption also changes in response to changes in law over time. Sometimes, these changes are in response to scandal or to new vulnerabilities to corruption. Public employees may be required to disclose their sources of outside income—often as a prophylactic response to scandals involving the abuse by public servants of their public power to benefit their private interest—for example, a regulatory decision that favors a business in which the public employee owns stock. The failure to fully disclose all such interests may arguably be a corrupt act, even if there is no evidence that the public servant sought to abuse power.

Accountability: Compliance and Performance

In preventing fraud, waste, abuse, and corruption, oversight seeks to ensure greater accountability. But just what type of accountability are we after?

Competing notions of accountability go back a long way into American history. One asks, "Are they following the rules?" and the other, "Are they getting the job done?" The first measures success by how much misfeasance it can nab, catch, "nail," "score"; the second, less dramatically, by how much its critiques, if adopted, can advance the target's mission. Although the two approaches can coexist, they can also clash, most vividly in those instances when breaking the rules gets the job done better.

So although most people today think of accountability in terms of making sure that taxpayer dollars are not stolen through contracts and corruption that violate specific laws or rules, accountability also—and, arguably more importantly—means getting the job done, when "the job" is effectuating the policies that the president or executives were elected to impose.

The bureaucrat who follows all the rules "honestly, efficiently, effectively, and at minimal cost," who thoroughly buys in to the "command-and-control" version of accountability, who follows Max Weber's ideal model of the bureaucracy and Frederick Taylor's principles of scientific management, may not, as Frederick Mosher said, indulge the "originality, experimentation, inventiveness, and risk-taking" necessary to advance a better policy alternative. On the other hand, the bureaucrat so compelled to achieve an end result may neglect the implication of the use of certain means—and the degree to which they violate laws and rules including the criminal law.

When Andrew Jackson threw out 10 percent of the federal bureaucracy in 1829 and replaced them with his own loyalists, he was accused—with some justice—of subverting the competence of that bureaucracy. However, he wanted a bureaucracy that was committed to implementing the policies he felt the American people had chosen by electing him. From that point of view, his changes made the federal bureaucracy more accountable to the public, not less. But after five decades, the need for a more efficient civil service had become so apparent that Woodrow Wilson urged, in his famous 1886 essay, adoption of the more professional European style of bureaucracy, despite the typical American resistance—even then—to European modes of government: "If I see a murderous fellow sharpening a knife cleverly," Wilson wrote, "I can borrow his way of sharpening a knife without borrowing his probable intent to commit murder."

To an extent, the essay reflected the passage, three years earlier, of the Pendleton Act, establishing the federal civil service on the basis of merit and competitive examination. The Pendleton Act itself reflected the widespread perception that the federal bureaucracy was too political and not competent enough to carry out the business of the public (and, by implication, the wishes of the public). But in 1939, after complaints from President Roosevelt (FDR) that once again, the president had too little control of the federal bureaucracy to implement the changes that the public wanted, Congress returned to the presidency a measure of control over the bureaucracy in the federal Reorganization Act, adopting the recommendations of FDR's Brownlow Commission. The 1978 Civil Service Reform Act, moving in the same direction, gave appointed agency heads more flexibility in inspiring the bureaucratic employees who work for them with performance pay and merit bonuses, arguably moving away from a rigid control environment toward a freer, more creative one.

In some ways, the current debate over teacher tenure at the state and local level reflects this tension between a focus on compliance and one on results. We want teachers—in many local governments, the single largest category of public employees—to be selected and retained independent of a political process. In other words, we want teachers who follow rules and are employed on that basis rather than because of their devotion to a candidate or political party. To protect that principle, they receive tenure after a set period of time, when they can no longer be fired, except under highly extraordinary circumstances. On the other hand, mayors and governors want to be able to deliver results on their promises of school reform and are increasingly demanding accountability based on performance. Such accountability entails empowering someone to fire teachers who fail to meet set standards, no matter how long they have been on the job.

Effective oversight embraces both concepts of accountability: rules and performance, control and creativity. In a vacuum, we cannot prescribe which should have primacy. As our discussion proceeds, the conditions favoring one or the other should become somewhat clearer, although, we regret to acknowledge, they will never become entirely clear.

Who Are the Watchdogs?

Government watchdogs are those who perform oversight to ensure accountability that reduces fraud, waste, abuse, and corruption in government. They expose and seek to remedy violations of the public trust. Often, exposure leads to other punishments as well, from demerits on the subject individual's personnel file to firings to criminal prosecutions and civil prosecutions. But for us, the key to being a "watchdog" is the responsibility for accountability and remedies that goes beyond an individual case.

Thus, we exclude law enforcement entities that exclusively focus on arrests and prosecutions as remedies, rather than larger efforts at reform. Clearly, when it comes to fraud and corruption, prosecutors and criminal investigators play an important role in identifying problems and imposing remedies that can incapacitate wrongdoers and deter future acts. Usually however, they do not seek—and are not charged with engaging in oversight that pursues—remedies beyond the immediate case. So, for example, we do not include special prosecutors at the federal level—who historically were charged with investigating and prosecuting specific allegations of criminal misconduct. We do, however, discuss the role of attorneys general who—

intentionally and unintentionally—engage in investigations that point to systemic reforms of government agencies and programs.

Similarly, we do not focus attention on—although we certainly refer to—the role of ethics and conflict of interest boards that deal with allegations of specific, limited violations of ethics rules by government employees, contractors, lobbyists, and others.

We also exclude from our purview those paid by government to exercise oversight only over exclusively private sector behavior. This excludes much of government's enormous regulatory sector—federal agencies such as the Securities and Exchange Commission, the Food and Drug Administration, the Internal Revenue Service; state agencies such as the state liquor commission, the department of motor vehicles, the state insurance department; or local agencies such as the taxi and limousine commission, the parking violations bureau, or the buildings department. They exercise "watchdog" functions too, of course, but they do not hold government employees accountable to the public; rather, they hold private citizens accountable for violating their duties to the law (and thus to their fellow citizens on behalf of whom their representatives have adopted such law). We do include government watchdogs, however, who oversee the interplay between government and the private sector (eg, investigations and oversight of public pension fund activity discussed in Chapter 12 and the congressionally mandated inspector general of the federal Troubled Assets Relief Program).

As we discuss throughout this book, oversight exists at all levels of government. Sometimes, the oversight role resides in the executive branch and sometimes in the legislative branch—and sometimes it resides in both. Some who engage in oversight are appointed and others are elected. In many respects, however, the concept of oversight is about a check on executive power. Thus, we focus almost exclusively on oversight of what would traditionally be treated as executive functions at the federal, state, and local levels. In most cases, oversight of the legislature deals mostly with the individual acts of legislators or staff—as opposed to how the legislature functions. The same is true for the judicial branch.

Not all government watchdogs are paid by the government. Thus, we include among their number investigative reporters and some private individuals and organizations.

Legislative Oversight

For Congress to know what laws are "necessary and proper for carrying into execution" the powers the Constitution gave it (Article I, Section 8), it had to know what the executive branch was doing, that is, it had to oversee its behavior. Thus, Woodrow Wilson wrote of the role of Congress, "Quite as important as lawmaking is vigilant oversight of administration." The same logic applies to the role of any legislature in the United States, thus making oversight a core legislative function.

At the federal level, legislative oversight comes in at least four categories: individual members, subcommittees and committees devoted to specific subject matters, oversight committees, and a special investigative arm. Individual members of Congress and senators have—at times quite usefully— "free-lanced," or investigated federal programs without special institutional authority to do so, like chairmanship of the committee with jurisdiction of the program in question. Chapter 5 includes a detailed description of one such investigation.

Legislative committees and subcommittees are expected to develop expertise in their subject matter. Their most prominent investigative tool is the legislative hearing, but standard investigative techniques, including the use of whistleblowers, underlie important findings at least as much. The committee or subcommittee chair ordinarily leads these efforts. The fiscal committees, House Ways and Means and Senate Finance, can exercise their oversight and review powers over an especially broad range of programs and issues.

In Congress, the House Committee on Oversight and Government Reform has operated under that name only since 2007, but under other names has played similar roles. The title of one of its subcommittees, Government Organization, Efficiency and Financial Management, signals its willingness to pursue investigations into virtually any area of federal government, which indeed (as the Committee on Government Reform) have ranged from the mistreatment of Iraqi military prisoners in the Abu Ghraib scandal of 2004 to the 2005 question of maintaining life support for Terry Schiavo, who had spent her last years in a vegetative mental state. The US Senate has no specific committee on oversight, but its normal standing committees exercise oversight functions as do the House standing committees.

As we discuss throughout the book, similar legislative oversight activity occurs at the state and local levels, as well.

Auditors

The Government Accountability Office (GAO) audits and investigates those federal programs that have aroused the interest of congressional members, subcommittees, or committees, and also at the instigation of its leader, the comptroller general.

The same audit responsibility carried out at the federal level by the GAO is carried out by a variety of elected and appointed auditors in state and local governments. Most states have treasurers, and most of them are elected; twenty-eight states have auditors, of which twenty are elected; of the states with comptrollers, the larger states are more likely to elect them. Although most of these officials perform many other important roles, they also usually exercise oversight. By definition, however, an "auditor" exercises oversight: The core function of a state auditor is to review the fiscal or managerial performance of other government entities within a state. State comptrollers, and many state treasurers, also count audit among their core functions.

State auditors and comptrollers annually produce thousands of audits exposing deficiencies in the operation of other state agencies. "Forty-three million in waste at the New Jersey Turnpike," "Improper and Wasteful Expenditures" by California State University; the Department of Corrections "cannot readily identify all transportation costs," (Colorado); "Audit Reveals Misappropriation of Funds from Gambling Tribes" (California) are typical examples. States also audit local governments, because local governments are, legally, creatures of the state. Thus, newspaper headlines read "Improper Spending by Garfield County School District," (Utah); or, "Audit Reveals How Sevier County Clerk Took $92,000," (Tennessee); or that Watertown "gave an improper $60,000 gift to a local development corporation" (New York).

Local governments may have officials with audit responsibility as well. The New York City comptroller issued sixty audits in 2010 alone, reviewing topics ranging from how well city agencies monitored the performance of their subcontractors to how well they complied with regulations requiring access to constituents with limited English proficiency. The comptroller of Houston, Texas in 2007 revealed that the city's police department was "unable to track police hours worked." Some local government auditors are elected, some are appointed and report to an executive, and others report—in a manner parallel to their federal GAO counterparts—to the local legislature.

Inspectors General

Federal inspectors general (IGs)—responsible for investigations and audits—notoriously suffer the most difficult balancing act. By federal statute, IGs must report to the heads of their agencies, as well as to Congress, when it is their assigned agencies that must be the focus of their scrutiny. Although in Chapter 7 we explain the special protections they enjoy, designed to foster their independence from those agency heads, IGs still face counterpressure when their responsibilities require them to issue public criticism. Some—although by no means all—state and local governments have IGs as well.

Other Appointed and Elected Watchdogs

Special committees or commissions—sometimes appointed by the executive, sometimes by the legislature and sometimes both—exercise oversight as well. At the state level, attorneys general—most often elected—also can play an oversight role beyond any role that they may have in the criminal prosecution of government corruption. At the local level, other elected officials—such as New York City's public advocate—also act as watchdogs.

Investigative Reporters

Not all government watchdogs work for the government. Investigative reporters are the best known of nongovernmental government watchdogs. Movies and books portrayed Bob Woodward and Carl Bernstein, whose dogged investigative work and reporting brought down the president of the United States. Seymour Hersh, who broke the Abu Ghraib story in 2004, the story of the My Lai massacre in Vietnam in 1968, and plenty of major stories in between, has done reasonably well. But the thin ranks of fine investigative reporters include more unsung heroes, like David Burnham, without whose 1970 stories in *The New York Times* John Lindsay would never have been forced to appoint the Knapp Commission to investigate police corruption, most likely; or Robert Parry, the Associated Press reporter who broke the Iran-contra story in 1986.

For-Profit and Not-for-Profit Government Watchdogs

Independent private-sector IGs (IPSIGs) are firms that include well-regarded personnel with legal, accounting, investigative, loss prevention, and management skills. Judges and prosecutors force companies with questionable records of integrity to hire IPSIGs as a condition of avoiding indictment or conviction. In that capacity, IPSIGs do not serve the watchdog function as we define it. However, a mayor can force companies to hire IPSIGs as a condition of being hired for public works projects. In the most highly publicized case, Mayor Rudolph Giuliani imposed IPSIGs on the companies hired by the city of New York to clean up the World Trade Center site after 9/11. There, the IPSIGs' direct responsibility was to assure integrity by the threat of exposing any corporate wrongdoing. But, as in that example, when government funds the corporations in question, the IPSIGs' role can also been seen as assuring the integrity of the government contract, and thus, as a government watchdog in the present sense of the phrase. Court-appointed monitors or trustees, usually prominent individual former prosecutors or judges with established reputations for integrity, may play similar roles.

The public, certainly in recent years, has not for the most part seen the private bar in a very sympathetic light. "Greedy trial lawyers," as they are generally known, represent individuals who allege personal injury resulting from the negligence of others. For the most part, those others have deep pockets; the plaintiffs don't; so these lawyers work on "contingency": They get paid if and only if their clients win. Sometimes, the defendant is the state: did negligent highway signage result in the accident causing plaintiff's injury? If so, the trial lawyer investigates and exposes the state's misfeasance when no one else would. Sometimes, the defendant is a private company. The federal Occupational Health and Safety Administration inspects perhaps 2 percent of construction sites. When the trial lawyer proves that the worker—often a penniless undocumented worker trying to support a family—died or was severely injured due to cost-cutting safety "shortcuts," the trial lawyer effectively exposes the inadequacy of the government response, and sometimes produces improvements in government regulation.

A less-prominent and thus less-vilified legal specialty within the bar represents citizens who have themselves identified culprits who cheat the government. *Qui tam* is short for the full Latin phrase that translates "who as well for the king as for himself." *Qui tam* actions enable private citizens to identify instances of fraud against the government and sue the perpetrators on behalf of the government, both for the cost of the fraud and damages. In effect, *qui tam* actions create a financial incentive for individuals and the bar to uncover waste and fraud.

Under the federal Civil False Claims Act, and now under some parallel state and local statutes, a citizen who brings such a case and wins will enjoy between 15 percent and 30 percent of the recovery as a reward, depending on whether the government (in the federal case, the Department of Justice) sees fit to support the action. Since 1986, when the original 1863 Act was modernized, *qui tam* actions have brought more than $30 billion in revenue to the federal government.

Not-for-profit organizations have provided immensely valuable "watchdog" services. At the local level in New York, for decades Gene Russianoff, of the New York Public Interest Research Group Straphangers Campaign, has spoken for subway and bus commuters, exposing management, finance, and service deficiencies, and forcing the New York City Transit Authority to respond to his revelations of service deficiencies. At the state level, the Brennan Center for Justice of New York University Law School in 2004 issued a blockbuster report that since then has cemented the word "dysfunctional" to the title "New York State Legislature," but in response to its revelations of gross deficiencies, has forced some legislative reforms. At the national level, Joan Claybrook has carried on Ralph Nader's pioneering work starting in the 1960s confronting the American auto industry with its grotesque indifference to driver safety, and has led Public Citizen to expose the failures of the National Highway Transportation Safety Administration. The Project on Government Oversight is probably at present the most vigorous and insightful non-for-profit watchdog of federal agencies across the board.

Citizen as Watchdog

The ascendance of the Internet in the late twentieth and early twenty-first century has enhanced the ability of individuals to play the role of watchdog. Individuals—from the whistleblower to the person who speaks at the town hall meeting—have always played a watchdog role. But with more and more information available from the Internet and the ability for almost anyone to create a blog or website, individuals now have an even greater opportunity to research and report on what they see as acts of fraud, waste, abuse, and corruption. Other technology—cell phone cameras, for example—have sometimes turned average citizens into citizen investigative journalists.

Oversight: Protective to Adversarial

We would hope that no "watchdog" could be protective in the sense of trying to hide any and all evidence of misbehavior. However, when catching and exposing malfeasance before prosecutors or the press discover it, watchdogs can present the revelations in a way that allows their employer to take credit for self-policing; and watchdogs can assiduously avoid exposing malfeasance when it cannot help but embarrass their employer. Thus, state inspectors general, hired by governors, often fall into the "protective" category. They will reveal misbehavior by commissioners and other state employees, but they will not blame their governors for hiring the personnel in question, or create the impression that their governors would tolerate such behavior until it appeared that other investigators were closing in.

A possible exception that proves the rule appeared in October 2010, when New York State Inspector General Joseph Fisch released a report sharply criticizing some legislative leaders but also including some milder criticism of then Governor David Paterson. Notably, however, Fisch issued the report two months before the lame-duck governor was to leave office, and included a footnote reporting that he had recused himself from the investigation and merely "reviewed the report prepared by staff to ensure that it met standards and to prepare him, as head of the office, to present the report to the public."

Federal IGs fall into a middle ground. If they unduly embarrass their agency heads, they may incur the displeasure of the president, who might regard the secretary of defense, say, as an important ally. On the other hand, the IG also reports to Congress. The 1978 Act creating the federal IG offices requires that they serve two masters, by keeping the agency head and the Congress fully and currently informed of problems in agency programs and operations. The president can fire the IG. If the IG can find nothing to criticize, Congress may well wonder why it needs the IG. So the federal IG has a difficult role, "straddling the barbed wire fence," in State Department IG Sherman Funk's 1988 phrase.

Federal IGs combine investigative and auditing functions. Pure auditors react in still another way. Because they function primarily to identify system strengths and weaknesses, they tend to see themselves as less adversarial than investigators. Auditors must allow their targets to respond to the weaknesses they identify, and to include any such responses in their audits. Very likely, they will return to their target agencies again sometime down the road. Therefore, financial officers such as comptrollers, auditors, and treasurers with audit responsibilities also tend toward the middle, although they are less likely to encounter the barbed wire.

Legislative committee chairs with specific substantive jurisdictions—transportation, defense, environmental protection—often advocate for the agencies in those fields. Chairs may have sought the committee in question because they share a commitment to the agency's mission, and if its constituencies lobby the chair, that commitment may deepen. When budget time comes around, the substantive committee chairs try to persuade their colleagues with fiscal responsibilities to favor their agencies. The committee chairs should also exercise oversight, and sometimes they do. But they may fall on the slightly more protective side of the protective/adversarial continuum.

Individual legislators, chairs of fiscal or oversight committees, investigative journalists, and private-sector watchdogs, whether for profit or not for profit, have little incentive to be protective. They tend toward the extremely adversarial side of the ledger. Really, so do IPSIGs. They make their reputations by being tough on clients, not by currying favor with them. Most clients don't hire them voluntarily. They must play to the audience of prosecutors, judges, and perhaps chief executives of governments. However, even these "outsider" watchdogs may sometimes play an inside role—a journalist who seeks to maintain a source, a committee chair or legislator who seeks the support of the executive, an IPSIG who wants to be hired for another assignment—and may thus have an interest in not burning certain bridges. In other words, few watchdogs are always as adversarial as possible all the time.

Conclusion

Watchdogs engage in oversight to reduce fraud, waste, abuse and corruption in government. Fraud and corruption speak to violations of law. As a result, different nations, states, and cities with different laws may have different definitions of what constitutes fraud and corruption—and, thus, the role of the government watchdog. What constitutes waste and abuse is more subjective—and often requires the watchdog to make judgments in a larger policy context and with a deeper understanding of the power and discretion of government officials that they are watching over.

Watchdogs seek accountability—both for compliance with laws and other standards and for overall performance and results.

Not all government actors who work on issues related to fraud, waste, abuse, and corruption are necessarily watchdogs engaged in oversight. Investigators and prosecutors of specific acts of corruption or fraud and regulators of purely private-sector activity are outside of our definition of government watchdogs. On the other hand, not all government watchdogs need to be a part of the government. Outside organizations, investigative reporters, and even individuals can play an important role in exposing fraud, waste, abuse, and corruption in ways that can lead to systemic remedies.

Chapter 3

Tools of the Watchdog

Follow the money.

—Mark Felt, a.k.a. "Deep Throat," Carl Bernstein and
Bob Woodward, *All the President's Men*, 1974

Always listen to experts. They'll tell you what you can't do, and why.
Then do it.

—Robert A. Heinlein, *Time Enough for Love*, 1973

We did not call this book *The Science of the Watchdog*. The methods of oversight often require excursions into territory with ill-defined boundaries and choices that can only be resolved by the use of discretion and intuition. The scientific method, at least as we learned it in high school, does not quite encompass such excursions and choices.

Watchdogs generally do their work through audits and investigations. Although there are important differences between the two, they are more similar than not. Both rely on the gathering and analysis of information leading to findings and recommendations for—when appropriate—reform. In this chapter, we discuss the standards applied to audits—and the general lack of standards applied to investigations. We outline some steps to take in conducting an investigation or an audit for the purpose of detecting and addressing malfeasance or misfeasance. We also summarize how the information and gathering processes work in practice—and throughout the book, we offer case studies that detail how the tools of oversight are used by its different practitioners.

Finally, the most important tools of the watchdog often are those used to promote their work and recommendations of reform. We close this chapter with a discussion of how different watchdogs approach that critical phase of their work.

Audits and Investigations: An Overview

Government audits are almost exclusively performed by auditors either employed or contracted by the government. Investigations are performed by internal governmental watchdogs (eg, IGs), external governmental watchdogs (eg, legislative oversight), or nongovernmental watchdogs (eg, journalists). Who performs an audit or investigation can greatly affect how it is performed.

Audits and investigations differ in approach in important ways. Auditors do not necessarily or ordinarily approach their task with the presumption that they will find something wrong. They must review the systems and processes of an agency or other entity, checking to ascertain that those systems and processes adequately safeguard the public goods and mission entrusted to the subject.

Investigators, in contrast, usually start with grounds for suspicion. They do not generally engage in full reviews of an entity's systems and processes, focusing instead on those particular aspects of the entity's operation that may reveal its flaws.

Standards for Government Audits and Investigations

Most government audits are conducted "according to generally accepted government auditing standards." Those standards appear in a document produced and from time to time revised by the GAO, colloquially called the "Yellow Book." Yellow Book standards speak to the auditor's independence, the completeness of the examination and the quality of the fieldwork, as well of other standards that constitute generally accepted government audit practice. The Yellow Book describes two types of audits—financial and performance. Either can identify fraud, waste, abuse, or corruption.

Whether engaged in a performance or a financial audit, auditors must first establish criteria. In the case of performance audits, auditors may ask: What are the purposes, goals, or measures of performance demanded by applicable statutes, regulations, grant or contract terms, agency policies or procedures, technically developed standards or norms, benchmarks defined by experts or by business practices, benchmarks based on prior period performance or on comparable entities' or sector performance? In the case of financial audits, they might look to whether funds were appropriately accounted for and whether they were used in a manner permitted by laws, regulations, or contract or grant provisions.

A performance audit should attempt to identify legal constraints on the programs, including statutes, regulations, contracts, and grant conditions; potential fraud and abuse; and the results of relevant previous audits and attestations. To be most useful, the audit should contemplate the public profile or need to avoid a public profile of the program in question; associated risks; age and/or changes in the conditions under which the program under audit operates; the affected budget, population, or other quantitative measures of the effect of the program in question; the type and extent of independent oversight available; the program's design, plan, objectives; and outside factors affecting the program.

Auditors may wish to use the agency officials' own stated goals as criteria for assessing performance, or develop other criteria. The audit may well compare "inputs" such as the size of the agency's budget, person-hours spent by employees, or office space assigned, with "outputs" such as the quantity of goods or services produced, or the quality of performance; and should also note positive and negative unintended consequences of agency performance.

Financial audits, at their core, must determine with reasonable assurance whether the financial statements of the audited entity "as a whole are free from material misstatements, whether from fraud or error." The treatment of issues of noncompliance, abuse, and deficiencies in internal controls roughly parallels their treatment in performance audits.

The next set of questions shapes the search for evidence. What kind of evidence do the auditors need to determine whether such criteria are met? If such evidence is not available, auditors may have to reshape the scope and objectives of the audit in line with available evidence. Of course, the unavailability of initially sought evidence may be an important audit finding itself. Auditors must determine whether that unavailability results from internal control weaknesses.

The target entity or program may have been audited previously. Auditors should not overlook the work of their predecessors. Even internal audits may corroborate findings and conclusions. Assuming that previous auditors were sufficiently qualified and capable, it will be important to determine if their findings warrant follow-up, and if the audited entity responded to weaknesses they identified. Sometimes, auditors may need to employ a specialist to evaluate the particular subject matter at hand.

An audit also may include a review of the entity's internal controls. In 1999, the GAO—then the General Accounting Office—published an entirely separate document providing guidance in this regard, *Standards for Internal Control in the Federal Government*, also known as the "Green Book." The GAO standards are used to determine whether internal controls at a given federal agency effectively assure that government assets are safeguarded against fraud, waste, and corruption; or, put differently, are sufficient to prevent and detect unauthorized acquisition, disposition, or use of government property or resources. Auditors also must determine whether such controls are updated appropriately.

Auditors must minimize the risk for the audit being wrong or incomplete. Such audit risk or observation error derives from insufficient or inappropriate evidence, weak audit process, or the auditor him or herself being misled, or overlooking something in the evidence. The methodology of the audit, the subsequent steps to be taken, the nature and extent of its procedures, must be designed to elicit the evidence needed to answer the questions, reduce audit risk, and assure the audience for the audit that the evidence supports its findings and conclusions sufficiently and appropriately.

Watchdog investigations are, unlike audits, generally not governed by any agreed on set of standards. Different watchdog entities may perform their investigative work under specific standards or none at all. For example, some governmental watchdogs—such as IGs—may conduct their work according to standards set forth in federal, state or local law with varying degrees of specificity. Nongovernmental investigations—such as those conducted by investigative journalists—may be conducted in accord with generally agreed on ethical standards. Still, other investigations, such as those conducted by individual elected officials may be completely unconstrained by standards.

The Audit and Investigative Process

Despite the rather stark difference between audits and investigations in the degree to which they are guided by standards, both audits and investigations involve essentially the same sort of tools and—generally—a similar process. Both involve the collection of information from different sources (eg, documents, data, and individual testimony or interviews), the analysis of that information and a report of findings and—most often—recommendations for reform.

The Audit Process

As noted earlier, not every audit is based on a suspicion of fraud, waste, abuse, or corruption. And, frequently, oversight audits can find that a program or government agency is in fact working well. As is discussed in greater detail in chapters that follow, auditors sometimes conduct audits not because of suspicion but because of mandates to regularly review agencies.

Once an audit subject is selected, however, the audit process is broken down into three main phases: planning, fieldwork, and reporting, where the proportion of time spent in each phase will vary by the scope and type of inquiry. A typical audit begins with a meeting of the audit team members and the officials managing the entity or program to be audited. During that meeting, the auditors explain the objectives of the audit.

For example, in one of its audits of the New York State Health Department, the New York State Comptroller's Office wanted to determine whether Medicaid payments for dental work on patients with dentures were made appropriately. The auditors then set forth the relevant time period. For example, they might want to examine documents reflecting relevant transactions between July 1, 2003 and June 31, 2008. The agency officials must be informed, if they are not already aware, that under state law they must make all records and files, even those designated as confidential or proprietary, available to the auditors. The auditors and the entity officials design procedures for making the requisite records and files available. The audit team questions entity officials and staff to make sure the auditors have the necessary understanding of entity's processes and their effect on the program or operation that is the focus of the audit.

The audit team then undertakes an exhaustive review of all records that bear on its objective. Sometimes these records are in the possession of the entity that is the subject of the audit. Other times, auditors use public records—budgets, court and property records—as part of their work as well. Even with computer assistance, this "fieldwork" phase takes the bulk of the time consumed by the audit. To find "21,752 questionable Medicaid claims totaling $2.9 million for dental services performed on patients with dentures," as auditors did in the 2008 New York audit example used here, they doubtless had to review hundreds—if not thousands—of claims in total, depending on whether all claims were reviewed or a statistical sample. Moreover, they undoubtedly had to assess the validity of the data and documents that were provided. Audits most often rely on disaggregate data rather than summary statistics or information generated by third parties.

Audits, however, involve more than just the collection of information. Auditors analyze the information to develop findings. Performance audits may examine operating data and apply analysis that puts the data into a relative context, examining changes in performance over time, by location or in relation to expenditure and revenue. During the analytic phase, auditors may apply the criteria identified consistent with audit standards: so, for example, they might seek to determine whether performance is consistent with statutory standards, best practices, or national norms.

The analytic phase of an audit is also especially important in the case of financial audits, particularly those that go beyond a mere accounting and seek to determine whether an agency or program has been infected by fraud or corruption. For example, financial analysis can include the detection of a pattern of activity that would only raise questions to the trained eye, such as:

- a coincidence of deposits and withdrawals from related bank accounts
- unexplained payments to third parties
- something as simple as consecutively numbered invoices from a single vendor over a long period of time
- multiple employees with similar social security numbers or addresses
- time sheets or vendor billings reflecting excessive time (eg, the contractor who bills a public agency for thirty hours of work on a single day)

Financial analysis can allow watchdogs to detect fraud through close review of financial statements. For example, to support a fraudulent balance sheet, a false expense item first needs "justification" in a journal entry. Managers rarely take such care in reviewing journals as they do in reviewing income statements or balance sheets. Symptoms of journal entry fraud include the absence of documentation for an item; unexplained adjustments to receivables, payables, revenues, or expenses; or an unbalanced entry (ie, the credit side of the ledger, showing the cash payment, should be balanced by the debit side, showing the goods or services for which it was made).

The Investigative Process

As noted previously, unlike audits, investigations are almost always the result of suspicion of wrongdoing. As a result, most investigations start with a lead—a piece of information that triggers a level of investigative interest by a watchdog, whether internal or external, governmental or nongovernmental. Leads come from watchdogs' own knowledge; from indignant citizens who have suffered from some abuse or mismanagement by government; or from "whistleblowers" who have lost confidence in their ability to persuade the management of the need for reform of the government agencies for which they work.

The lead could be in the form of a specific request from an agency head, a mayor, or another elected official based on suspicions. It could be based on information that comes through ongoing monitoring of certain processes—such as personnel decisions or the awarding of contracts. It could be through information provided by an internal or external source—a whistleblower who comes into an IG's office or an anonymous letter sent to a member of the city council.

Because investigators rarely have the kind of mandates for specific investigations that auditors may have and because—as we discuss throughout this book—investigators frequently have fewer resources, they must carefully analyze whether to pursue the lead. Given limited investigative resources of time, talent, and budget, watchdogs must ask whether the investigation will produce results significant enough to take away needed resources from other efforts.

Once there is a decision to investigate, there is a planning phase. But, depending on the nature of the investigation, the criteria may be more limited than those discussed in the audit process. The lead may be specific enough that the investigation can be narrowed to a single question—was there favoritism in the award of a contract or were payments diverted to the mayor's brother-in-law—or at least a narrower set of questions than would be entailed in an agency-wide performance audit.

Although virtually all government audits begin with a formal entrance conference, there is no similar requirement for investigations. Again, depending on the nature of the investigation, a considerable amount of what would be regarded as fieldwork in an audit—the gathering or analysis of information—may occur without an investigative target ever being informed that there is an investigation.

In fact, investigations often rely on secrecy as an essential component of the work—allowing investigative watchdogs to more easily cultivate sources of information and obtain data. Some investigations may involve surveillance as part of the process of obtaining certain information. In the case of nongovernmental investigations, such as those conducted by journalists or nonprofit organizations, the subjects of the investigation may never be informed of the investigation until its results are made public.

Although the basics of the investigative process—gathering and analyzing data—are similar to the audit process, the precise methods and standards may be very different. Whereas auditors may only rely on disaggregated data that they compile and then analyze, certain investigations may rely on "unaudited" data in reaching certain findings. So, for example, an investigation of local government performance may rely on the department's own aggregate data without doing an audit to verify the self-reporting.

Some audits and some investigations rely on legal tools for gathering information and data. Some auditors and some investigators have the power to subpoena documents and data and to compel certain testimony under oath. Clearly, not all investigative watchdogs have those powers. Although internal auditors and investigative watchdogs have the ability to gather data and documents through statutory powers, outside watchdogs engaged in investigations may rely more on public records or may need to rely on obtaining documents and data through freedom of information or open record requests.

Investigations ultimately use some of the same analytical tools as used by auditors when it comes to assessing performance and financial issues. Investigations that focus on corruption and abuse, however, may be more likely than audits to examine issues related to conflict of interest. So, for example, an investigation of a government department might be more likely to examine issues such as the business relationships of the department's key officials—disclosed through public financial disclosures or other public records—or the relationship between department contract awards and lobbying activity or political contributions than a performance audit would.

Achieving Reform

We have suggested that watchdogs don't just expose violations of the public trust. They seek to remedy those violations as well. Just as important as the tools of investigation and audit are the tools of achieving reform. They vary—sometimes between audits and investigations and sometimes based on who is performing the audit and investigation and whether they are engaged in adversarial and nonadversarial oversight.

For nonadversarial, internal watchdogs—such as inspectors general or internal auditors reporting to an executive or even a department head—the next step in the audit or investigative process is generally for the subject of the audit or investigation to have the opportunity to respond to the findings and investigations before they are finalized. This process allows for the investigator and auditor to assure the accuracy of their findings and can allow for subjects to comment on, reject or agree to—and, in the best case, begin implementing—recommended reforms.

In the case of most government audits, even if the auditor is independent, there usually is a similar requirement that gives the subject of the audit an opportunity to review and comment on the draft audit. In many cases, the final audit also must include the full written response to the draft.

In the case of investigations—especially those conducted by nongovernmental organizations—there is no similar required process that enables the subject to review or comment on the draft findings and recommendations of an investigation. In some cases, this may be made a condition of cooperation with the investigation. In other cases, the investigator may decide to share a draft as a courtesy or to identify points of disagreement before formal completion of the work.

Internal nonadversarial audits and investigations generally conclude with a presentation of findings and recommendations to the executive to whom the auditor or investigator may report. The likelihood that recommendations will result in action depends on a number of factors including the credibility of the auditor or investigator, the relative standing of the department head or heads or managers who may be the subject of the audit or investigation, the strength and seriousness of the findings and the commitment of the executive to change. Essentially, reform depends on a set of inside strategies common to any effort at change within a bureaucracy.

Thus, without a strong, credible and persuasive internal watchdog and—usually—without an executive willing to act, internal audits and investigations risk being filed away without action. That's because in most cases internal watchdogs lack access to the important tool of the external watchdog—"sunlight"—as in the famous advice Louis Brandeis gave to reformers a century ago, "Sunlight is the best disinfectant."

Independent auditors and investigators can use a fairly well-established template for taking their findings and working to convert them into reform. But the template provides an effective model only for the kind of problem that can be corrected by the credible threat of continued bad publicity for the malefactor.

Unlike internal efforts at reform that rely on the internal workings of a bureaucracy and the quality of the investigative or audit work, external efforts at reform rely at least as much on communication, and political strategies. That's because sunlight only works when it is accompanied by the glare of a TV camera or when it can be explained in a 140-character tweet. An investigation too complex or too focused on narrow findings will fail to attract the public attention and interest necessary for an outside investigator to gain traction and achieve reform.

While sunlight works for investigations by appointed independent auditors and investigators, and is the core premise of investigative journalism, it is a particularly effective strategy for elected officials who engage in oversight. For them, sunlight that exposes fraud, waste, abuse, and corruption and its potential remedies can also reflect on a political star.

One of the authors of this volume developed the principles and investigative format recommended herein in the course of twenty-two months in the late 1970s, when the investigating legislative subcommittee to which he was counsel spent a total of $60,000 on subcommittee staff salaries and saved about $3 million in government funds in 1970s dollars. The subcommittee staff worked for the subcommittee chair, then-New York Assemblyman

Charles Schumer. Schumer—now a US senator—was ambitious even then and clearly saw political opportunity and value in his focus on uncovering waste, fraud and abuse. He naturally attached the active verbs in the press releases to himself ("Legislator X Reveals _____"; "Legislator X Exposes _____," etc.). The principal investigator, the "watchdog," thus understood that good publicity can motivate politicians to underwrite this kind of work.

Similar motivation can be harnessed to drive other kinds of adversarial watchdogs. They may anticipate political careers, and even if they don't, favorable publicity enhances their prospects for later employment: newspapers or television stations will want to provide rewards sufficient to retain the services of reporters whose revelations are dramatic enough to draw readers and viewers.

The watchdog must insist on making the politician or news outlet understand the value of credibility. Credibility must not be wasted: Substantial proof is always required before publicizing accusations. The press release, and the news story, must avoid flimsy headlines. The good watchdog will not release even a true story if there is "less in it than meets the eye" (to paraphrase Tallulah Bankhead's famous line). A thin story will not lead to the necessary "credible threat of continuing bad publicity" noted previously. Without that kind of threat, the recalcitrant bureaucrat may be able to imagine that he or she can "weather the storm" of a few bad headlines. From the watchdog's point of view, press is a tool, not the goal, but the watchdog may have to resist pressure from above to see it differently.

Once a watchdog has completed an investigation or audit and formulated findings and recommendations, they can go to the press (or to go *to* press, if the investigator works for a news source): announce allegations plainly but colorfully; consider visual effects for television coverage and photos; use press advisories when possible.

The watchdog's work does not end with the initial spate of publicity. After a reasonable period of time—depending on the issue, a few days, a few weeks, a few months—it is time for follow-up. It is time to ask, were the changes implemented? Are they effective? The watchdog must now issue the follow-up press release or hold the follow-up press conference—and another and another until the solution is implemented.

Elected officials and others can also use public hearings to generate useful public outrage creating the political pressure to force reform. For investigators without the institutional resources with which to hold hearings, or when for any other reason hearings do not provide an appropriate vehicle, ordinary press conferences, press releases, and exclusive offers of stories to reporters can be equally effective.

Conclusion

The "art" of the watchdog depends on the ability to use the tools of audits and investigations as a means of exposing fraud, waste, abuse, and corruption and working to correct them. Although there are established standards for the conduct of government audits, investigations are far more subject to the discretion of investigators—especially those who are not part of the government.

In many ways, audits and investigations attempt to do the same things—collect and analyze information to identify specific findings and recommendations. But audits and investigations vary in significant ways—from their intent and approach to their process.

As noted in the prior chapter, the work of the watchdog is not just to expose misfeasance or malfeasance; it is to correct it. Depending on their independence and whether they are adversarial or nonadversarial watchdogs, there are real differences in how auditors and investigators engage in this aspect of the art. For internal watchdogs, success at reform depends on insider strategies that go to their own position within a bureaucracy. For external or more independent watchdogs, success depends on their ability to apply the disinfectant of sunlight to the problems identified and to use a combination of political and communication strategies to achieve reform.

Chapter 4

Limitations on Oversight

Managing government well is extremely difficult, even for the most accomplished civil servants. Yet far too frequently, we read about mistakes, missteps, actions or the absence of actions by the federal government that disappoint and frustrate us, and they inevitably raise the question: Shouldn't someone be watching the execution and implementation of these laws?

—Former Rep. Lee Hamilton, Director,
Center on Congress, June 9, 2010

When you control the mail, you control information.

—Newman, *Seinfeld*, "The Lip Reader"

As should be apparent, this book preaches the gospel of oversight. We practice it, we believe in it, and we hope and urge citizens to press for more vigorous oversight in the service of better government.

There are, however, both theoretical and practical limits to oversight.

We start this chapter by discussing a series of theoretical limits to oversight. As we noted earlier, particularly in the areas of waste and abuse, a lack of consensus over what constitutes wrongdoing subject to oversight can greatly limit the effectiveness of attempted oversight efforts. Others—most notably Samuel Huntington—have argued that some corruption may be the price we pay for economic development. Still others have suggested that in some cases too much oversight can do more harm than good. In particular, we focus on the goals of oversight and the distinction between oversight directed solely at uncovering and punishing wrongdoing and oversight more focused on prevention and systemic reform.

There are very real practical limits on oversight as well. Effective oversight depends on the ability to obtain information and the resources to use the tools of oversight discussed in the previous chapter. In a time of limits on public budgets, resources often are in short supply and watchdogs constantly engage in a battle for access to information—through data, documents, and first-hand accounts from individuals.

Finally, there are practical political limits to the oversight work of the watchdog. For some watchdogs, especially those who lack complete independence, there are political risks associated with the work that they do. Targets of oversight investigations—especially those who have political power—frequently fight back. Politics—both ideological and partisan—also can have the effect of limiting the scope and desire to conduct oversight or encouraging oversight activity that may be more political than meaningful.

An understanding of the limits on useful oversight should enable practitioners to use their time and energy more efficiently.

Tilting at Windmills

In the early 1970s, a reporter for local CBS-TV news in New York City, Steve Wilson, trailed after city government officials with his camera crew and microphone as they used their official vehicles to run personal errands. Shoving his microphone in a commissioner's face as he tried to escape, Wilson would ask, "Haven't you just used your official New York City government vehicle to pick up your laundry?" We do not recall whether any commissioner was reprimanded or punished for this abuse, but their embarrassment was apparent, and one may assume that use of official cars for personal errands decreased. Some years later, Wilson moved to California, and tried to recycle the same story line. City officials there reacted differently. They did not try to escape. They responded, in honest puzzlement, "Do you want me to take a taxi?" The political culture there simply did not regard as inappropriate the occasional use of a city vehicle for personal errands.

In the United States, trading ambassadorial appointments for campaign contributions is seen as the norm—not corrupt. The English think it is corrupt. On the other hand, they don't think trading peerages for political contributions is corrupt. But one might define corruption more broadly than we usually do, so as to include both such examples: as the transfer of money for political power (or political advantage), or of political power for money (or financial advantage).

Oversight will fail to correct conditions that the relevant political culture accepts. A Canadian scholar compared Israel and Ontario in their responses to revelations of scandalous misbehavior. Ontario responded to revelations of egregious failure in its water pollution control system by imposing dramatic reforms; Israel responded to revelations of egregious failure in its building construction industry code enforcement system by doing virtually nothing. In neither case did the problem industries—farmers whose pesticides and other chemicals caused the Ontario problem, or construction companies whose negligence caused the Israeli problem—"capture" the relevant oversight agencies or even resist reform. Instead, differences in political culture accounted for the opposite results. Canadian political culture places a particularly high value on integrity. In Israel, defense and foreign affairs occupy too much of the public agenda to leave much psychic space for issues of civil accountability.

In other words, what rises to the level of activity worthy of oversight varies greatly by culture and geography. Understanding these differences is crucial to the effectiveness of a watchdog—because the ability to drive reform so often depends on attracting public attention and outrage. But differences in the level of the bar for what is corrupt and what isn't does not mean that even in the most "tolerant" society that there isn't a certain level or type of activity that would be considered corrupt, the exposure of which would prompt reform.

"Greed is Good"

In the movie, *Wall Street*, the character Gordon Gecko argues that "greed is good." As perhaps a corollary, some scholars argue that certain levels of corruption are not just normal, they are good.

Samuel Huntington argued that, especially during periods of modernization, corruption facilitates the absorption of rising subcultures into the larger culture's power structure. So, as manufacturers rose to wealth in nineteenth-century England, the aristocracy resented and resisted their access to political power, but the manufacturers bought their way into power, just as the newly wealthy in developing nations today thus "become participants in the political system rather than alienated opponents of it." "Alienated opponents," clearly, create costs for a political system; participants benefit themselves as well as the system.

Huntington adduced more direct arguments for the value of corruption than its role as a less costly replacement for oppositional violence or other forms of opposition. Conservative politicians in mid-twentieth-century Brazil supported creative industrialists in return for bribes. In the United States in the late nineteenth century, railroad companies bribed legislatures and towns to allow their unlimited expansion, and to invest public moneys in them. Many such railroad companies failed and lost huge amounts of those public funds. But many succeeded, and built the transportation system that sped the explosive growth of the American economic in that period. Thus, Huntington saw some value in "moderate" amounts of corruption, as a means to "overcome unresponsive bureaucracy" in order to promote economic development." Shades of Huntington's forty-year-old argument still resonate in lobbying against anticorruption legislation like the federal Foreign Corrupt Practices Act, prohibiting US corporate executives from bribing foreign nationals.

Although norms as to corruption may vary from culture to culture, data suggest that corruption, far from a corrective, in fact goes hand in hand with "unresponsive bureaucracy." More corruption means less investment and economic growth, although of course at a certain point it becomes cost-ineffective to attempt to eliminate corruption entirely. Bribes benefit the recipient and the donor. Sometimes they also may enhance efficiency or fairness, but they do not usually do so. For those instances where they do, they would do so more effectively if they were replaced with legally adopted and openly publicized fees.

Tax evasion, pollution, certification of unqualified people for licenses or assistance, and carte blanche for organized crime do not generally enhance economic growth. Bribery encourages further corruption, such as incentives to create scarcity, delay, and red tape, false arrests and malicious prosecution, as well as a downward spiral, or vicious cycle, in which more and more people are pressed to engage in corruption. These entail serious systemic costs, among them undermining the legitimacy of government.

A World Bank survey in the mid-1990s found "more than 150 high-ranking public officials and top citizens from over 60 developing nations ranked corruption as the biggest impediment to economic development and growth in their countries." A comparison of certain representative cities in the United States also supports the conclusion that effective oversight in a culture that insists on government performance enhances economic growth, while a culture of corruption retards it. A persuasive proxy measure of corruption shows its steady decline in New York City from the 1980s through the early twenty-first century, a period when that city experienced a great resurgence in population and commerce. During the same period, corruption remained rampant in Cleveland, Ohio; New Orleans, Louisiana; and Birmingham, Alabama, while those cities suffered massive losses in population and commerce. Although this correlation does not definitively refute those who would defend some measure of corruption, it certainly supports the most consistent perception of the key factor in economic development reported in a survey of cities across the United States: effective local government free of corruption.

"The Pursuit of Absolute Integrity"

Two respected scholars (Frank Anechiarico and James Jacobs) sharply criticized the very emphasis on oversight and corruption prevention that we credit at least in part for New York City's resurgence in the decades since the 1970s. Anechiarico and Jacobs argue that, in the pursuit of what they describe as "absolute integrity," New York created a virtual "panopticon" (an all-seeing eye, taken from Jeremy Bentham's innovation in prison design) for its public servants and contractors doing business with the city—reducing efficient operation of government, thwarting innovation and actually creating incentives for more corrupt activity.

As an element of that commitment to oversight and corruption prevention, in 1983 New York City enacted a whistleblower law. To earn its protection, whistleblowers must report wrongdoing to the City's Department of Investigation (DOI) or the City Council. DOI central staff, not the IGs individually assigned to city agencies, investigate such allegations. If the employee alleges retaliation, DOI must investigate. Investigations can take months, the DOI issues a report to the agency head, and the agency head accepts or rejects the report (without the opportunity to review interview transcripts). If the agency commissioner rejects the report, is he or she perceived as soft on corruption, or corrupt?

Anechiarico and Jacobs offer as illustrative an example in which a so-called whistleblower accused co-workers of corruption just as he was about to be fired on the well-documented basis of his poor performance and obnoxious attitude. When he claimed that the anticipated firing was in retaliation, necessarily triggering DOI involvement, the disciplinary action had to be suspended. In principle and in fact, it is hard to prove that retaliation does not play a role, especially when the investigative agency operates on the contrary presumption. So DOI's four-year investigation, not surprisingly, took a huge toll on morale at the agency. The commissioner understandably hesitated to take further action. Only a handful of whistleblowers complain to DOI of retaliation each year, but even a few such cases can have an outsize negative effect on agency performance. Because we do not know how much useful information such whistleblowers have produced, Anechiarico and Jacobs argue that the costs might outweigh the benefits.

In the case of public contracting, Anechiarico and Jacobs point to a series of rules and procedures developed to prevent the award of public dollars to corrupt contractors. These rules were initially developed in response to a massive corruption scandal in the 1980s involving the New York City Parking Violations Bureau—and discussed in greater detail in Chapter 8. The city required prospective vendors to complete a detailed questionnaire—including questions related to its principals' past criminal record and allegations of criminal activity. All of this information populated a database called VENDEX, which city procurement officials were required to check before awarding contracts.

Anechiarico and Jacobs argue that this process—which cost time and resources for both the city and prospective contractors—actually reduced efficiency and increased the risk for corruption. Firms that the city would want to contract with—those that produced quality products or services and at a reasonable price—would be deterred from bidding, whereas unethical firms would merely create "straw" companies (with their identities disguised) to avoid disclosure of unfavorable facts.

Although Anechiarico and Jacobs correctly identified a serious problem, the way to address the ability of false whistleblowers to block disciplinary action is not to end whistleblower protection. It is to require more timely completion of investigations. Similarly, as we discuss in later chapters, the issues that VENDEX was created to address—the award of millions of dollars of city contracts to poor-performing or corrupt contractors—were quite real. The problem with that solution was that it didn't really add value. Disclosure requirements were easy to avoid because the accuracy of disclosures was only rarely checked and city officials frequently applied a Lake Wobegon-esque system of evaluating contractors—all of them were above average.

We believe that oversight is necessary and can be extremely valuable—but we also believe that watchdogs deserve the same scrutiny as the government entities that they are charged with monitoring. More oversight—with more rules and more regulations—is not a substitute for effective oversight.

Prevention versus Enforcement

The New York City DOI is—by far—the largest and most active municipal investigative oversight agency in the nation (we discuss local IGs in greater detail in Chapter 12). It now regularly releases "end-of-the-year" press releases summarizing its work. For the last several years, those press releases have had the following headlines:

- DOI ARRESTS 711 IN 2010—HALTING SIGNIFICANT CORRUPTION SCHEMES

- DOI ARRESTS 877 IN 2009, CONTINUING THE AGENCY'S RECORD HIGH TREND OF ARRESTS

- DOI RECORDS 848 ARRESTS IN 2008, MORE THAN
  DOUBLE THE NUMBER IN 2007, WITH FEWER STAFF
  MEMBERS

A consistent theme emerges. Although each of the press releases provides great detail in describing how the DOI's efforts also led to institutional reform, the focus is on stopping criminal activity through enforcement. For auditors, the focus is frequently on compliance—whether internal controls were ignored or rules violated.

In reality, oversight also—and, arguably more importantly—means making sure that officials are getting the job done, when "the job" is effectuating the policies that the public elected its representatives and executives to implement. This kind of oversight requires the monitor to gauge whether officials perform their function effectively and efficiently, or whether they have been provided the resources they need to do so.

Focusing on criminal activity or compliance can be in competition with a focus on performance. If a government is investing most of its oversight budget in compliance in order to catch wrongdoers, it won't have much money to spend on incentives and technologies that might prevent wrongdoing. Similarly, compliance oversight focuses its efforts on individual wrongdoers, while performance oversight focuses more on institutional operation and capacity-building. The bureaucrat that follows all the rules may not be creative enough, or may not have the tools, to advance an ambitious policy agenda.

Whatever level of government—city, state, or federal—establishes an anticorruption system, its usefulness depends on staffing it with competent, ethical people truly dedicated to integrity, rather than to creating paperwork and the appearance of oversight. But even the best-designed and best-staffed oversight system cannot substitute for competent, ethical people truly dedicated to the front-line government service they are supposed to provide.

An influential private sector analyst, W. Edwards Deming, taught much of industry that monitoring is secondary, merely a tool for assessing performance; quality improvement comes only from investment in front-end, process improvement. Deming regarded the alternative approach as deeply detrimental on the private side.

Scholars and practitioners struggle with the hard choice of allocating resources to compliance or to performance oversight. Some, however, believe that all resources allocated to oversight would be better allocated to operational improvement.

This is a false choice. Oversight actors can frequently play an important role in demanding better performance and investments in institutional reforms that would prevent future corruption or waste. At the same time, compliance and criminal investigative efforts are necessary to create a real deterrent effect for potential wrongdoers. Moreover, as we illustrate in Chapter 9, the best oversight actors can use their work on compliance issues to inform broader systemic reforms.

The challenge for oversight actors is to maintain the balance between enforcement or compliance and prevention or reform. The public likes to blame its officials for wrongdoing. Several years ago, Kevin McReynolds—then an outfielder for the New York Mets—complained that fans in New York actually liked to watch highly paid athletes fail: We've often felt the same way about how people view political corruption scandals. They are a little like car wrecks—everyone likes to watch.

As a result, the media are far more willing to report stories of individual wrongdoing than analyses of systemic weaknesses: the latter is boring. Furthermore, Democrats and Republicans agree that wrongdoers should be punished. They don't usually agree on solutions to systemic problems, which often cost money.

So oversight actors may find it impossible to resist pressures to produce compliance results. Such results—revelations of individual wrongdoing—carry more innate drama than capacity monitoring: "how many times can an IG make the finding that an agency's financial system is antiquated or that government is underinvesting in training?"

But, as Paul Light has suggested, oversight systems should link their inevitably compliance-oriented oversight to performance and capacity-building efforts. Outside pressure will continue to force oversight to highlight compliance monitoring, so the optimal course would be to insist at least that the elected branches and the public support the systemic changes needed to assure the kind of performance that they claim to want from their government.

Light used some of the history of the federal Department of Housing and Urban Development (HUD) to illustrate his point. In 1981, Charles Dempsey, the IG at HUD, warned of many integrity weaknesses. He succeeded in getting HUD to discipline or fire several of its high-ranking officials between 1981 and 1984, but Congress seemed to pay no attention to his reports. This may have been because his reports kept listing hundreds of millions of dollars in savings and financial recoveries achieved, hundreds and hundreds of indictments and criminal convictions, and praise for the support he was getting from HUD management. The next HUD IG, Paul Adams, included in his 1985 testimony to Congress many ominous problems at HUD, but then reassured Congress that HUD was addressing these problems. HUD IG reports throughout were long, boring litanies, although after the fact, one could discern the emergence of very serious problems.

But while all this testimony and reporting was going on, "HUD was enveloped by influence peddling, favoritism, abuse, greed, fraud, embezzlement and theft. In many housing programs objective criteria gave way to political preference and cronyism, and favoritism supplanted fairness. 'Discretionary' became a buzzword for 'giveaway,'" said the 1990 report of the House Government Operations Committee, Abuse and Mismanagement at HUD.

What happened? In 1988, for example, the HUD IG urged the Secretary to suspend one of the Section 8 programs (moderate rehabilitation). The 1990 report noted that most of these scant funds went to "politically well-connected consultants and a cadre of ex-HUD officials. . . . Some people with little or no experience in housing made a lot of money for a very limited amount of work . . . former Interior Secretary James Watt received hundreds of thousands of dollars for talking to the 'right people' at HUD, including Secretary Pierce, to obtain mod rehab funds."

HUD Secretary Samuel Pierce refused to suspend the Section 8 program, relying on what he thought was the expertise of his highest-level appointees—counsel, under secretary, assistant secretary—and discounting the opinion of the IG. It wasn't only Pierce's fault. A Pierce assistant noted subsequently that the Reagan administration had forced too many political hires on HUD, some of whom had been confirmed by the Senate, so real housing experts were in short supply at HUD.

Light takes from this that monitoring cannot do the job that capacity-building needs to do: If HUD had been run by people who knew how to build housing and had the resources to work with, these problems would not have happened. He may well be right, but it seems clear that had Congress, the media, the secretary, the president, or even the IG done a better job, monitoring could very well have prevented at least some substantial part of the problems, even in the absence of optimal capacity. Thus, although compliance monitoring may in some ways and at some times get in the way of more effective forms of oversight, an overabundance of compliance monitoring is not a big-picture problem.

Practical Limitations on Oversight

Although the limitations discussed here go to the question of whether oversight always has value, there are sometimes practical reasons why oversight efforts are either hard to perform or limited.

Access to Information

Investigations and audits are essentially efforts to collect information—documents, data, testimony—and assess that information against standards—contract language, statutes, best practices. Thus, the greatest practical limitation on oversight is a limit on the access to information.

In an information age, where we all now carry small devices with us at all times that can access every obscure factoid or point of data ever, it is hard to conceive of limitations on access to information. But for watchdogs, getting access to the right types of information is almost always the difference between success and failure.

Different watchdogs have different tools. The federal government, state governments, and virtually all local governments have a version of freedom of information laws where any member of the public can get access to certain government documents. And "documents" now includes a wide array of electronic transmissions—from emails to texts—as long as they remain in the possession of the government.

Freedom of information laws, however, almost always have exceptions—and those exceptions are frequently relied on to limit or prevent government disclosure of information. For example, in some states, certain information about government contractors is considered proprietary and exempt from disclosure. Information that is part of a law enforcement investigation, even if that investigation never leads to any actual charges, can be withheld from disclosure. Finally, to protect individual privacy, many government personnel records also are not subject to disclosure.

Government officials seeking to limit access to information also can force watchdogs to sue for information. This can impose additional costs on watchdogs and will almost always delay disclosure. It may take years from the date of the first request for information to a watchdog actually obtaining the first document.

Some watchdogs may have subpoena power or other statutory guarantees of access to information. Still, government officials may force watchdogs to litigate their rights under those grants of access as well. Even Congress—and the GAO—has been stymied in its access to information and to individual testimony as a result of broad claims of executive privilege under the administration of George W. Bush. At the local level in New York, the mayoral administration of Rudolph Giuliani was notorious for prompting lawsuit after lawsuit by elected officials and others seeking information.

Finally, the problem with the Freedom of Information Act is that it is often impossible to know when information exists that is not being disclosed. The email "inadvertently" omitted from a freedom of information response may be the single most important piece of evidence in an investigation or an audit, yet it is hard to know that it exists if it isn't disclosed.

That's why, notwithstanding the importance of documentary information, information from interviews or testimony is often essential. Every document, every email has an author and usually one or more recipients. Watchdogs usually find undisclosed documents through the testimony of such individuals. Testimony and interviews can also provide context for written documents—and, of course, not everything is written, even in an age of one-word emails. Virtually every audit or investigation requires some level of cooperation or information from an individual—whether a subject of the investigation, a witness, or a whistleblower.

To the extent that government officials refuse to be interviewed by watchdogs or assert executive privilege, they limit access to information. Moreover, the fear that the identity of individuals with information—whistleblowers—will be disclosed and that they will face retaliation imposes limitations on watchdogs and oversight as important as any delay in response to a freedom of information request or an effort to quash a subpoena.

Cost

Although technology and greater access to information online has reduced the cost of oversight, the labor-intensive nature of audits and investigations comes with a high price tag. Obviously, cost varies with levels of complexity. Narrowly defined local audits can take relatively short periods of time and require little travel or other nonpersonnel costs. In contrast, an investigation of defense contractor fraud might require thousands of hours of research and extensive travel both domestic and foreign.

Audits and investigations require auditors, accountants, investigators, attorneys, and analysts, not to mention support personnel. Thus, not only does oversight require personnel, it requires skilled personnel with salaries that are frequently higher than the average for other government workers. And these government workers receive the same other standard benefits, such as health insurance and pensions, that frequently rise in cost faster than salary.

More complex investigations may have other costs related to surveillance technology or access to sophisticated software or proprietary databases.

How much does an investigation cost? Obviously, the cost of each investigation and audit varies greatly based on the level of complexity and the amount of staff time and other resources that need to be expended. Investigations and audits that recover substantial sums of money may actually have no net cost. But the following data may be instructive:

- Based on its most recent semi-annual report to Congress, the current HUD IG completed 78 audits and closed 524 investigations over a six-month period. The HUD IG budget for fiscal year (FY) 2011 was approximately $122 million. Thus, the cost per investigation and audit—recognizing that the IG performed other work—was roughly $100,000.

- In its most recent semi-annual report, the Defense Department IG reported on 64 audits and 714 closed investigations over a six-month period. The DOD IG budget for FY 2011 was approximately $297 million. Thus, the cost per investigation and audit—again, recognizing that the IG performed other work—was roughly $190,000.

- At the state level, according to its most recent annual report, the Illinois IG completed 304 investigations in FY 2011 on a budget of $6.9 million. The cost per investigation—and, again, the Illinois IG performed other activities—was approximately $23,000.

- Finally, at the local level, the Kansas City, Missouri auditor's office reported completing nine audit reports and five memoranda on a budget of $1.1 million. The cost per audit was approximately $79,000. The auditor's office tracks the amount of time spent on each report: In FY 2011, the average was just over 1,500 hours of personnel time per report. In FY 2010, Portland, Oregon's city auditor completed 13 audits on a budget—just for audit services—of $177,000 per report and a reported hourly rate of $110.

At all levels of government, watchdogs generally have to compete against all other programs and departments in the appropriation process. Thus, executives and legislators can choose between hiring another auditor or another teacher or police officer.

Moreover, the subjects of government investigations frequently have substantial say over the budgets of watchdogs. Sometimes hostile executives will try to eliminate or at least limit oversight by bleeding watchdog budgets. It is rare that government watchdog budgets are protected from this type of budgetary retaliation: There are a few cases where statute sets a minimum level of funding for watchdogs.

Cost is also a critical limit on the work of those watchdogs outside of the employ of government—especially those in the nonprofit sector and in the press. To the extent that limited budgets and other resources limit these watchdogs—who frequently partner with government watchdogs—it has an effect on government auditors and investigators as well.

Political risk

Although we have made the case that effective oversight can produce political rewards for elected officials who engage in it, there is political risk as well—both for elected overseers and appointed officials. Individuals or corporate entities that benefit from fraud, waste, abuse, or corruption have an interest in preventing oversight efforts that threaten to end those benefits. Additionally, appointed officials may be reluctant to undertake certain audits or investigations if they believe that their appointing officials have an interest in the status quo.

At the federal level and in most states and localities, there is virtually no prohibition on individuals who work for government contractors or corporate interests subject to government regulation from giving campaign contributions to elected officials. A notable exception is SEC Rule G-37, which effectively limits campaign contributions by individuals who work in key positions for firms that seek public finance work from states and municipalities.

Otherwise, campaign contributions flow freely from government contractors and the subjects of regulation. With the Supreme Court's 2010 decision in Citizens United, the potential for corporate political activity through independent campaign expenditures is virtually unlimited. The interests of campaign contributors can lead to legislative and other benefits—including protection against oversight.

For example, the Center for Public Integrity argues that one reason for lax oversight of Fannie Mae and Freddie Mac before the 2008 federal bailout was the more than $4.8 million its principals contributed to members of Congress over a two-decade period of time. Other special interests with campaign checkbooks can have a similar interest in thwarting oversight efforts. At the state and local levels, public employee unions in some states have exerted considerable influence over legislative issues—again including oversight.

This isn't a particularly new phenomenon. As Robert Caro explains in his biography of Lyndon Johnson, early in his career LBJ ingratiated himself with Brown & Root, the company that became Brown, Root & Kellogg, KBR, and eventually Halliburton. Brown and Root were oilmen, and Johnson always did everything he could to advance their oil interests in Washington, where he was their man. In 1941, the Navy awarded Brown

& Root a contract worth hundreds of millions of dollars to build ships—their first experience with shipbuilding. In return for Johnson's continued loyalty, they gave him as much money as he needed not only for his own campaigns, but to distribute among his colleagues for their campaign needs as he saw fit, thus funding his rise to majority leader of the Senate. Of course, Johnson had similar relationships with other oil companies, but Brown & Root were foremost. Later known as Halliburton, it became well known, among other reasons, for employing Dick Cheney as its chief executive officer prior to his vice presidency, so it surely cemented ties on the Republican side of the aisle as well. Consider whether its seven decades of intimate involvement with Congress may have influenced the vigor with which senators and representatives review the details of defense contracting.

What happens when elected officials take on—rather than support—these interests? Sometimes they pay the price with their seat. Oklahoma Congressman Michael Synar was an outspoken advocate of restrictions on the advertising of tobacco. He, along with Congressman Henry Waxman, led a series of oversight and investigative hearings on the issue during the 1980s. In 1994, the tobacco industry—along with other special interests that Synar had offended—invested $3 million in a successful campaign to defeat Synar in his Democratic primary.

At the local level, Elizabeth Holtzman lost her bid for reelection as comptroller of New York City in 1993—losing the Democratic nomination meant losing the job—to Alan Hevesi, who raised a large percentage of his campaign contributions from various contractors that Holtzman had criticized in her audits and investigations, from construction firms to school bus companies. After eventually winning election as state comptroller, Hevesi was forced to resign in a corruption scandal. In 2010, he pled guilty to a felony as part of a massive "pay-to-play" scandal involving his control of the state's pension fund.

Sometimes targets of oversight have tools other than campaign contributions to go after oversight actors—leading to a different kind of political risk. Few targets of oversight simply sit back and "take it": instead, they often fight back—not necessarily simply by rebutting the charges. U.S. Representative Jim Cooper prompted Henry Waxman, then chair of the House Committee on Government Oversight and Reform, to hold hearings to investigate abuses by rural electric cooperatives, whom he suspected of improperly withholding refund checks due customers. In response, the National Rural Electric Cooperatives Association falsely accused Cooper of hacking its website and demanded an FBI investigation. Although Waxman said, "We won't be intimidated and we will continue to try to protect the interests of co-op customers by looking into any credible allegations of misconduct by the co-op boards," in fact he held no more hearings on the subject, nor has anyone else since to date.

The political alliances of individuals who appoint certain watchdogs can also result in political risk. Although Rudolph Giuliani is known for his work as a crusading, corruption fighting US attorney before becoming New York City mayor, his first appointee to lead the DOI was a long-time friend and ally Howard Wilson—leading many to question DOI's independence and its ability to investigate the mayor and his supporters.

In Giuliani's first year in office, the city's Public Advocate Mark Green—an independently elected citywide official—released a report on the city contracting process that cited a series of problems with the award of millions of dollars in food contracts to a Brooklyn-based firm, Maramont. Although the contracts were competitively bid, in most cases Maramont was the sole bidder. Moreover, there had been a series of complaints that Maramont's food—largely provided to the city's homeless shelters—was often inedible or worse.

Green's allegations clearly stepped on some toes—shortly after he released his findings, an aide to Assembly Speaker Sheldon Silver, at the time arguably the state's most powerful Democrat, visited Green and his staff to express dismay at the investigation. That was only the beginning of Maramont's apparent political muscle.

Both authors worked with, are friends with and admire Elizabeth Lang. At the time, Ibby Lang was the IG assigned to the city's Housing Authority. One of us—David Eichenthal—worked for Green and led his office's investigation of Maramont. He turned over his findings to Lang when he learned that the firm also had contracts with the Housing Authority—which had a separate contracting process.

Eventually, Lang urged the Housing Authority to reject Maramont's bid for a new contract because although under the terms of its existing contract it was supposed to supply meals that had been prepared not more than a day before delivery, in fact its meals had been prepared between two weeks and two months before delivery. The New Jersey Education Department had earlier rejected Maramont as a contractor based on "the poor quality of its products." A few days after Lang registered her objections in a memorandum to Ruben Franco, the head of the authority, Franco announced that she had changed her mind.

Maramont apparently had the support not just of Assembly Speaker Silver, but also Assembly Member Dov Hikind, a Brooklyn Democrat who had helped elect Republican Giuliani. In fact, the Housing Authority had put Hikind's former staff member in charge of its awards process for food contracts. So with Hikind's help, Maramont got the contract anyway.

At about the same time, Lang warned the Housing Authority to avoid doing business with Jack's Insulation, a construction company that had submitted a dishonest VENDEX questionnaire that failed to disclose its dismal environmental record in disposing of asbestos, including federal Clean Air Act violations, fourteen negative citations from the city's Department of Environmental Protection, and two investigations by the city's Department of Sanitation. But the owner of Jack's Insulation had contributed several thousand dollars to Giuliani's campaigns.

Shortly after the Housing Authority overruled Lang on Maramont, her employment there ended. Lang, as an IG, had reported to Wilson, the commissioner of the city's DOI, Giuliani's close friend. Wilson and Giuliani publicly applauded Franco's rejection of Lang's position on Maramont.

Conclusion

Effective watchdogs need to understand the limits to the power of oversight—both in theory and in practice. Watchdogs need to be prepared to rebut claims that the corruption they seek to prevent may actually be beneficial and that the real problem with effective governance is too much oversight. The reality is that effective oversight can play a critical role in public well-being and government performance.

At least as important, watchdogs need to be prepared to overcome more practical limits to their work. Effective oversight requires access to information, often difficult as subjects of oversight seek to stonewall or otherwise make the cost of information too high. All watchdogs face the problem of limited resources and watchdogs who work for the government often must battle against other "essential" public functions in the budgeting process.

Finally, subjects of oversight can and do fight back. Thus, watchdogs frequently must prepare to address political risk and the role that it can play in limiting their work.

Chapter 5

Congressional Oversight

Quite as important as legislation is vigilant oversight of administration . . . the informing function [of Congress] should be preferred even to legislation.

—Woodrow Wilson, *Congressional Government*, 1885

The power of the Congress to conduct investigations is inherent in the legislative process.

—Chief Justice Earl Warren, *Watkins v. United States*, 1957

The notion of congressional oversight precedes the creation of the republic, both in reality and in film. The movie *1776*—based on the Broadway play—is a musical comedy about the Declaration of Independence. In one memorable song and dance, the characters playing John Adams, Benjamin Franklin, and Thomas Jefferson sing about the approval of the Declaration and compare it to waiting for an eaglet to be born.

Throughout the film, members of the Continental Congress regularly receive reports from Gen. George Washington—virtually always proclaiming just how dire the circumstances are within the Continental Army. These reports fuel skepticism among members of Congress as to whether the Army could ever possibly defeat the British. In one scene, Congress hears reports of "drinking and whoring" by the troops in New Brunswick. Desperate for support for independence, John Adams asks the Congress to form a War Committee—consisting of Adams, Franklin, and undecided delegate Samuel Chase—to visit the troops in New Brunswick.

During their visit, the troops—who are starving—see a flock of birds and commence shooting. As Adams reports, "As chairman of the war committee, I can assure you, never have training and discipline gone more smoothly! Never have soldiers been more cheerful!" Their pinpoint accuracy

53

persuades Chase that they might actually be able to defeat the British and on return to Philadelphia he pledges his support for independence.

Congressional oversight—like the eaglet and the Declaration—was born.

This chapter reviews the ways in which Congress carries out its oversight responsibilities. Congress—used here to mean the House and the Senate—practices oversight through a variety of vehicles. Subsequent chapters discuss how the GAO—an arm of the Congress—and the federal IG system—created by Congress—engage in oversight. This chapter, however, focuses on how the members of Congress, primarily through their own congressional staff, continue to engage in oversight activities directly, on their own. After discussing why and how Congress investigates, we look at the decline of congressional oversight over the last half century and highlight two case studies—a "how-to" step-by-step approach to congressional oversight by one member of Congress and a more recent example of how an effort at oversight led to a constitutional confrontation.

Why Congress Investigates

Historian Arthur Schlesinger wrote: "The Founding Fathers supposed that the Legislative branch would play its part in preserving the balance of the Constitution through its possession of three vital powers: the power to authorize war, the power of the purse, and the power of investigation." Thus, Congress' oversight role and powers are central to the system of checks and balances under the Constitution.

In reality, Congress' ability to investigate is essential to its ability to perform its other vital roles. Oversight and investigation provide Congress with needed information to legislate more generally, to make decisions regarding the allocation of funds and collection of revenues through the federal budget, and to make decisions related to the authorization and prosecution of war.

Yet Woodrow Wilson suggested that Congress' role in investigation goes beyond the ability to carry out these core functions. Wilson stated that "The chief use of such inquisition is, not the direction of those affairs in a way which the country will be satisfied (though that itself is of course all important), but the enlightenment of the people." Thus, even where Congress does not respond to investigative findings through legislation or appropriation, investigation and oversight can play a powerful role in forming public opinion about a public issue. This is truer today—in a time of twenty-four–hour news channels and the Internet—than when Wilson framed the importance of investigation as a means to "inform" more than a century ago.

Perhaps even more important than the power to inform, oversight supports the congressional power to persuade, as Douglas Kriner has pointed out, suggesting that Congress, much as the president, can help to drive public opinion on an issue. Highlighting the role of the media, Kriner notes that "many congressional hearings are made-for-television events and are consciously designed to generate conflict. Conflict, according to many journalistic norms, is inherently newsworthy, and thus the press may play an important role in amplifying the congressional challenge to administration policies and actions and in broadening the audience such congressional cues reach."

When Congress Investigates

If Congress investigates both to aid its exercise of core Constitutional responsibilities and to inform and help shape public opinion, when does it investigate?

Although Congress may have conducted earlier inquiries, the stunning defeat of the US Army in 1791 by the Miami tribe of Native Americans at the Wabash River in what is now Ohio sparked the first generally known exercise of congressional oversight in 1792. The House created a special committee to investigate. It found understaffing, training deficiencies, and mismanagement of supplies. In response, Congress expanded the Army and set into motion its professionalization. The reconstituted Army forces defeated the Miami in 1794.

Congressional oversight activity has been described as being either a "fire alarm" or a "police patrol." Fire alarm oversight occurs in response to a crisis—usually a very public one, like the defeat at Wabash River. Scandal in the Executive Branch almost always will prompt some level of congressional oversight. On the other hand, police patrols are a more routine form of oversight, where Congress pursues an investigation as part of considering legislation or appropriations. Congresswoman Elizabeth Holtzman's investigation of the response to Nazi War criminals in the United States, described in Chapter 1, began with rather routine questions during a congressional hearing on appropriations for what was then the INS.

How Congress Investigates

Congress has the power to subpoena documents and compel testimony under oath. Yet, it has far fewer rules than a court of law when it comes to the appropriateness or relevance of questions or evidence. Evidentiary standards and due process that apply to a criminal proceeding where liberty interests are at stake do not apply to a congressional investigation where the greatest risk may be public ridicule.

Unlike a criminal court proceeding, Congress can use its investigative power to shine a bright light on matters that do not rise to the level of criminality. When Justice Louis Brandeis famously wrote that "Sunlight is said to be the best of disinfectants; electric light the most efficient policeman," he was writing of the work of the Pujo Committee, a congressional investigation of Wall Street.

There is little if any constitutional limit to Congress' use of its investigative powers. A series of Supreme Court decisions have held that oversight is inherent in Congress's legislative power and that the scope of oversight extends to any matter upon which Congress may act. Moreover, to the extent that part of the oversight role is designed to allow Congress to "inform" the public on issues on which it may not act directly, the power is virtually unlimited. In *Watkins v. United States* (1957), the Court did hold that "investigations conducted solely for the personal aggrandizement of the investigators or to 'punish' those investigated are indefensible." Still, as long as Congress can show a legitimate connection to its legislative role no matter how tenuous, Congressional oversight is fair game.

Who Investigates

Congress sometimes investigates through committees, one in each House, established with the primary responsibility for oversight of the breadth of government activity. Sometimes, especially as unexpected crises arise, they do so through special temporary committees created with finite and limited investigative missions. On a more-or-less nonstop basis, standing committees with permanent jurisdiction over specific subject matter areas and agencies review the operations of the government entities they oversee. In the context of the budget process, the fiscal committees assess the performance of each government agency. The two Houses may also establish joint committees, with members from each House expected to work together, which on rare occasions are expected to oversee especially sensitive areas of government. Finally, any given member of Congress or US senator has the authority to investigate a government program independently, and some have done so to great effect.

Standing Committees on Oversight

The Senate Homeland Security and Governmental Affairs Committee had its origin in 1842 with the creation of the Committee on Retrenchment to review federal government spending. In a later incarnation, as the Committee on Investigation and Retrenchment, it investigated corruption in the federal Custom House in New York City, between 1871 and 1873. A version of it reappeared in 1899 as the Committee on Organization, Expenditures, and Conduct in Executive Agencies, and then as the Committee on Expenditures in the Executive Departments, established in 1921. It was renamed the Committee on Government Operations in 1952 and the Committee on Government Affairs in 1978. It was reorganized under its present title in 2005. Its first permanent subcommittee, on Investigations, came with its 1952 revision, and its Subcommittee on Oversight of Government Management with the 1978 revision.

Of all the committee chairs in the House of Representatives, only the chair of the Committee on Oversight and Government Reform, as it had been called since 2007, can issue subpoenas unilaterally, without a committee vote, although chairs in recent years have in fact gotten committee votes in support of such issuance. Six years after the Senate established a committee under the same name, the House in 1927 created its Committee on Expenditures in the Executive Departments, and again tracked the Senate in renaming it as the Committee on Government Operations, this time in the same year, 1952. In 1999, Congress reorganized it as the Committee on Government Reform, adding to its jurisdiction those of the former committees dealing with the post office, civil service, and the District of Columbia.

Fiscal Committees

Undersecretaries, IGs, and sometimes Cabinet officials themselves represent their agencies in testifying before the subcommittees of the House and Senate Appropriations Committees in support of their budget proposals. "For many agencies, this constitutes their only *regularly* scheduled review and supervision by Congress." When the testimony does not satisfy the doubts or concerns that senators or members of Congress have about the operation, usefulness, or efficiency of an agency program, staff will often investigate with follow-up questions.

Between June 15 and July 28, 2011, the Senate Appropriations Committee held hearings on budget requests for FY 2012 by the Department of Defense, the Department of Education, and the Federal Disaster Assistance Agency, as well as on Veterans Administration issues and something called "Light Small Water Modular Reactors." Even with a large number of subcommittees and considerable staff support, the enormous size of the federal budget makes it difficult for the Appropriations Subcommittee to make real its theoretical ability to review the smaller details of federal spending.

It is more likely to attack vulnerable targets within the more newsworthy agencies, as when the House Appropriations Committee cut $1.9 billion, or about 11 percent, out of the FY 2012 budget for the National Aeronautics and Space Administration.

Less commonly, the Appropriations Committee may complain that the administration has insufficiently funded a program. In 2008, the Senate Appropriations Committee criticized what it considered inadequate funding provided in the Bush administration's budget for support of UN peacekeeping programs.

Other Standing Committees

Standing committees with particular subject matter jurisdiction, as opposed to the committees explicitly devoted to oversight, also engage in oversight. Although Congress always implicitly assumed this responsibility, it made the assumption explicit with the Legislative Reorganization Act of 1946, with language that now provides that:

> to assist the Congress in (1) its analysis, appraisal, and evaluation of the application, administration, and execution of the laws enacted by the Congress, and (2) its formulation, consideration, and enactment of such modification of or changes in those laws, as of such additional legislation, as may be necessary or appropriate, each standing committee of the Senate and of the House of Representatives, shall review and study, on a continuing basis, the application, administration, and execution of those laws, or parts of laws, the subject matter of which is within the jurisdiction of that committee. Such committees may carry out the required analysis, appraisal, and evaluation themselves, or by contract, or may require a Government agency to do so and furnish a report thereon to the Congress. Such committees may rely on such techniques as pilot testing, analysis of costs in comparison with benefits, or provision for evaluation after a defined period of time.

The statute exempts the fiscal, oversight, and rules committees of each House from its requirements. House of Representatives Rule X(2.b1) tracks that language, although with more detail. The Senate appears to have amended the provision quoted above in 1979, under Section 2a of Senate Resolution 274, to exempt itself. The Senate Rules now set forth each committee's responsibilities, including oversight, individually. Senate Rule

XXV imposes "comprehensive policy oversight jurisdiction" on a number of standing committees.

Select Committees

From time to time, the House and Senate establish "select" or "special" committees, intended as temporary. Very infrequently, either house or both will eventually change the status of such a committee to permanent. For example, in 1975 the House appointed a Select Committee on Intelligence, which under its second chair, Otis Pike of New York, investigated abuses by the CIA and FBI. Although the leadership of Congress refused to publish the committee's report, it was leaked to Seymour Hersh of *The New York Times*, with great impact. In 1977, Congress changed its name to the Permanent Select Committee on Intelligence, making its status indistinguishable from that of a standing committee, except that members do not have unlimited tenure once appointed, but serve on a rotating basis.

Like the House, in 1975 the Senate also selected members, under the leadership of Sen. Frank Church of Idaho, to serve on a temporary committee to investigate illegal CIA activities, the Select Committee to Study Government Operations with Respect to Intelligence Activities. Unlike the House, the Senate did permit its Committee to publish reports on its findings, which revealed CIA attempts to assassinate foreign leaders such as the Dominican Republic's Rafael Trujillo and the Congo's Patrice Lumumba. In 1976, the Senate renamed it the Select Committee on Intelligence, which, like its House counterpart, has become permanent. Unlike the House, the Senate in 2008 rejected proposals to establish an Intelligence Subcommittee under its Appropriations Committee.

The Glory Days: Truman and Kefauver Committees

Although congressional oversight dates back to the beginnings of the republic, in many ways its glory days came during the 1940s and 1950s when oversight investigations regularly grabbed headlines and played a major role in shaping policy and political debate. The oversight investigations of Sen. Joseph McCarthy during that same period may be a model for the worst of congressional oversight. In many ways, however, models for the best of congressional oversight may be found in both the Truman Committee investigation of defense contracting during World War II and the later Kefauver Committee investigation of organized crime.

The Truman Committee

As the United States prepared for World War II in 1940, the Army was building training camps for draftees. Sen. Harry Truman began investigating because he suspected that the War Department was not giving Missouri its fair share of defense contracts. But as to the training camp it was indeed building in Missouri, some of Truman's constituents thought they saw evidence of waste and fraud. What Truman saw at the camp showed him that his constituents were right. Driving himself around throughout many other parts of the country, from Florida to Michigan, he found more of the same. The contracts issued by the War Departments guaranteed a percentage profit for the suppliers, so the more costs they piled up, the more money they made, and no one was monitoring whether the costs were legitimate. Defense costs seemed to be a sacred cow: No one questioned them.

When Truman, speaking on the floor of the Senate in February 1941, called for a special committee to review defense contracts, his fellow senators shared his enthusiasm for the notion that the War Department should be more responsive to requests from elected officials as to where such contracts should be awarded. After all, who would know more about the qualifications of their own home state companies? But Truman's efforts would far transcend the politics of the pork barrel.

Truman faced a bad precedent, of which he was well aware. The Joint Committee on the Conduct of the War had hindered and hamstrung Lincoln's effort to the point that Confederate Gen. Robert E. Lee explicitly expressed gratitude for its behavior. But Truman had a cordial relationship with President Roosevelt, and Rep. Eugene Cox of Georgia, although also a Democrat, did not. Cox sought an oversight role through a joint committee of the Senate and the House. Sen. Jimmy Byrnes of South Carolina, much closer to FDR than Truman was, and chair of the Senate Committee in charge of the Senate's own expenses, convinced Roosevelt to let Truman run the investigation.

Thus, in March 1941 the Senate established its Special Committee to Investigate the National Defense Program, with Harry Truman as its chair. Truman stated that the committee's goal was to act as a "watchdog, a 'benevolent policeman' to dig out the facts and present them to the American people." The focus was on potential fraud and waste among contractors—something Truman had experienced first-hand in county government. "I have had considerable experience in letting public contracts and I have never yet found a contractor who, if not watched, would not leave the Government holding the bag. We are not doing him a favor if we do not watch him."

At the beginning, the Senate only gave Truman enough funding to hire one employee, a lawyer, for $9,000. The Special Committee did not just hold hearings in Washington. As he had done on his own, Truman traveled again, although this time mostly by plane, visiting Army camps in California, Washington State, Texas, Maryland, Pennsylvania, and elsewhere, finding millions upon millions of dollars in waste, with costs five and ten times what they should have been. Again, the guaranteed percentage profit really guaranteed waste and fraud. Despite all the money already wasted, Army sources later estimated that Truman's work on the camps still prevented about a quarter of a billion dollars more in waste—in 1940s dollars.

With the value of his work undeniable, the Senate increased the committee's appropriation to $50,000, allowing Truman to hire the necessary number of investigators and secretaries. Truman moved on to more challenging aspects of the investigation. He now discovered that Standard Oil and Alcoa, for their own business reasons, had forced American airplane production to fall behind to further their own business relationship with I.G. Farben, the huge German manufacturer, operating under the orders of the Hitler regime. He discovered that despite Army Air Corps denials, Curtiss-Wright was selling them faulty airplanes. An Air Corps general went to prison for his role in the deal. Truman discovered that U.S. Steel included substandard steel in what it supplied to the Navy for shipbuilding, falsely labeling it as adequate. The faulty steel caused a US tanker, the *Schenectady*, to fall apart in the water in 1943. Glen Martin, of the Glen Martin Company, told Truman that the wings on the B-26 bombers it was building were too narrow and would therefore cause trouble, but because he already had the contract and had moved the project forward, they would have to stay that way. After Truman explained that in that case, the contract would be terminated, Martin changed his mind.

Throughout its work, the committee exercised great care in being critical of corruption without being critical of the war effort. Despite the potential for politicizing its work, "the committee attained such recognition and public acceptance that it became virtually invulnerable to political attack. Ironically, the committee's unique status largely stemmed from Truman's request that the committee's deliberations be conducted as impartially and reasonably as possible."

The millions that Truman's boot camp investigation saved the country now turned into billions that his industrial investigations saved. More important, his watchdog efforts prevented greedy corporations from supplying shoddy materials that risked and lost the lives of thousands of American military service personnel. David McCullough, from whose book *Truman* much of the foregoing has been gleaned, quoted former senator and congressman Claude Pepper of Florida: "The man from Missouri had dared to say 'show me' to the powerful military-industrial complex and he had caught many people in the act."

The Kefauver Committee

The 1950s brought congressional investigations into the television age. Although there had been televised congressional hearings before the Kefauver Committee, it became "one of the most famous congressional investigations" because of the attention that it received on television.

Much as Harry Truman was the driving force behind the creation of the investigative committee on defense spending during World War II, Tennessee Sen. Estes Kefauver led the effort that ultimately resulted in Senate approval of the Special Committee to Investigate Organized Crime in Interstate Commerce. Kefauver was acting in response to appeals by many of the nation's mayors. The American Municipal Association "asked the federal government to look into the influence that nationally organized racketeers had on municipal governments throughout the country."

Ironically, Kefauver generally opposed the creation of special committees. A series of circumstances—almost all political—led to the Senate leadership's decision to create a special committee and to pick Kefauver, a freshman senator, as its chair.

The committee had three specific charges:

1. Determine whether organized crime uses the facilities of interstate commerce

2. Investigate the manner and extent of such criminal operations

3. Determine if organized crime was leading to corruption

In 1950 and 1951, the committee held hearings in fourteen US cities in what was essentially the first effort to expose the growing role of organized crime and its connections to political power. "Kefauver's conception of the committee's task was that it should reveal and dramatize to the American people the extent to which organized crime had infiltrated the nation's economic and political life." Like Truman, Kefauver was widely credited both for the fairness of the investigation and the strength of the staff work that supported the effort. As its counsel, Kefauver tapped Rudolph Halley, a veteran of the Truman Committee staff who was later elected as New York City council president. The American Civil Liberties Union later commented that "The hearings were conducted, with one or two exceptions, in an atmosphere of fairness and sober fact-finding."

Most of what the committee's investigations revealed was not new. Kefauver frequently noted that local law enforcement usually knew much of what his committee found—but little effective action had been undertaken to combat the problem. As Kefauver's biographer notes, "Scandals that had been almost forgotten were rehashed, and questions unanswered from years before about political corruption and lax law enforcement were suddenly being asked again."

The committee took on issues and allegations that were unpopular in Kefauver's own Democratic Party. The role of organized crime was most prevalent in the nation's cities—where local government was frequently in the hands of Democratic mayors, supported by Democratic governors.

In Miami, hearings revealed that local law enforcement seemingly favored one branch of the local syndicate over the other, cracking down on one while leaving the other to prosper. Individuals and entities linked to the favored gambling operations had pumped more $100,000 in contributions into the governor's political fund.

President Truman's political roots were in the political machine that controlled Kansas City. Yet, the committee did not hesitate to investigate "an ugly case of political corruption and influence peddling that stretched from the headquarters of the First Ward Democratic Club possibly as far as the statehouse in Jefferson City." The committee found that Missouri political leaders had aided local gambling rings run by the Mafia.

Televised committee hearings were widely watched. Some of the hearings in other cities were broadcast locally. But the committee's hearings in New York attracted near-nationwide attention. During hearings in New York City, witnesses from the city's organized crime families routinely invoked their Fifth Amendment rights. Local city and union officials detailed the nexus between unions, the mob, and local government. Former New York Mayor William O'Dwyer admitted to placing friends of organized crime figures into city government jobs.

The New York hearings lasted for eight days and the televised coverage brought what for many Americans was their first glimpse into the workings of the Mafia. That year, coverage of the Kefauver hearings won an Emmy award.

In all, the committee heard from eight-hundred witnesses at the ninety-two hearings that Kefauver chaired. During the course of the hearings and investigations, he traveled more than 52,000 miles.

Some have suggested that the Kefauver Committee had little immediate impact—"Of some 221 legislative recommendations submitted to Congress as a result of the committee's activities, only a handful obtained a full hearing by standing committees of Congress"—but in many ways the Kefauver Committee's work was the precursor for both future investigations—such as the McClellan Committee's investigations of labor racketeering—and future legislation aimed at a greater role in federal prosecution of organized crime, such as the federal Racketeer Influenced and Corrupt Organizations (RICO) law, enacted in 1970.

Moreover, Kefauver's efforts led to an increase in enforcement activity by the Internal Revenue Service Special Rackets Squad. And some attribute the publicity of the Kefauver Committee to successful efforts to stop the legalization of gambling in other states.

The Model of the Senate Watergate Committee: Protecting the Constitution

For many, the last great effort at congressional oversight as practiced by a committee was the so-called Senate Watergate Committee. Watergate began with the June 1972 attempted burglary of the national headquarters of the Democratic Party. Several officials associated with President Nixon's re-election campaign were among those arrested when the burglary was interrupted by Washington, D.C. police—setting in motion an elaborate attempt to cover up the burglary by the president's campaign and the White House.

Nixon was re-elected in November 1972 in a landslide. By early 1973, however, investigative reporting suggested wrongdoing beyond the Watergate burglary. In January, by a unanimous vote of seventy to zero, the US Senate voted to create a select committee charged with investigating charges of corruption in the 1972 elections. The Senate Watergate Committee was born.

The committee conducted two sets of televised public hearings—between May 17 and August 1973 and then again between September 24 and November 15. As prosecutors and the press were unraveling the Watergate scandal and associated wrongdoing with the president's re-election campaign, the Watergate Committee played a critical role in providing daily and direct information to the American public to answer the key question posed by the ranking Republican member of the committee, Tennessee Sen. Howard Baker—"what did the president know and when did he know it?"

The committee's investigation did not take the place of criminal investigations eventually led by the special Watergate prosecutor and impeachment proceedings were ultimately the responsibility and jurisdiction of the House Committee on the Judiciary. Moreover, few of the committee's recommendations in its 1,250-page final report resulted in congressional action. Yet, the Senate Watergate Committee is widely hailed as having played a critical role in maintaining public confidence in the Constitution as investigations revealed the Nixon White House's abuse of executive power.

Throughout the process, despite the focus of allegations around the partisan process, the committee sought to maintain a "just the facts" approach to the evidence.

In many respects, Watergate was the high water mark of congressional oversight. For many, Watergate and the investigative role of the Congress—initially the Senate Watergate Committee and then the impeachment proceedings before the House Judiciary Committee—proved that, as Schlesinger suggested, "the investigative power may indeed be the sharpest legislative weapon against Executive aggrandizement."

Faded Glory

Between 1961 and 1977, Congress more than tripled the time and percentage of hearings it devoted to oversight. But, by the late 1970s, critics characterized congressional investigation as "the faded glory of Congress." More recently, over the past twenty years, Douglas Kriner has written that Congress has become "the most disparaged branch" in part because of its "frequent failure to engage in vigorous, sustained oversight of the executive branch."

Protective Partisanship and Less Oversight

In part, this failure to engage has been the result of a form of "protective partisanship"—where members of the president's party control Congress and are reluctant to engage in oversight that might damage the leader of their party. Kriner notes, "All too often, partisan incentives to support a President of the same party trump institutional incentives to defend Congress's institutional prerogatives by vigorously overseeing the actions of the executive branch."

Less oversight is evidenced by the lack of time devoted to the work. Norman J. Ornstein and Thomas E. Mann attribute the decline of effective oversight to the reduced amount of time and attention devoted by Congress to its pursuit. Citing Joel Aberbach, they note that the number of hearings in the House dropped from 782 during the first six months of 1983 to 287 during the first six months of 1997. In the Senate, it went from 429 to 175. This trend continued into the last decade: "examining reports of the House Government Reform Committee, the journalist Susan Milligan found just 37 hearings described as 'oversight' in 2003–4 . . . down from 135 in 1993–4. . . . The House Energy and Commerce Committee produced 117 pages of activity reports on oversight during the 1993–4 cycle, compared with 24 pages during 2003–4."

*The Consequences of Faded Glory: National Security and
Economic Collapse*

Critics note that Congress' failures in the area of oversight have had extraordinary consequences, particularly in the area of national security. The 9/11 Commission "bemoaned the lack of oversight in the pre-9/11 era"—referring to it as "dysfunctional"—and "emphasized the importance of legislative oversight of antiterrorism policy across levels of government." During the first six years of the Iraqi War, congressional oversight was extremely limited. In the case of other wars, Congress played a far more active role in oversight—including the Truman Committee's oversight of defense contracting during World War II and the Fulbright Committee's highly publicized hearings during the Vietnam War. That was not the case during the Iraqi War. As Ornstein and Mann note, "The House Armed Services Committee held only five hours of testimony on American abuses of prisoners at Abu Ghraib prison, compared to 140 hours of House testimony on whether Bill Clinton improperly used the White House Christmas card list." Journalist Thomas Ricks referred to the role of Congress in the Iraq war as "the silence of the lambs." He notes that "there were many failures in the American system that led to the war, but the failures in Congress were at once perhaps the most important and the least noticed. . . . There was little follow-up investigation or oversight. There were, for example, no hearings with returning division commanders."

Finally, Congress has failed to provide effective oversight on one of the most important challenges to face the nation in the first part of the twenty-first century—the financial collapse and the near depression of 2008. There was no congressional equivalent of the Pujo Committee that investigated the creation of trusts in the early part of the twentieth century or the Senate Banking Committee's Pecora hearings that probed the Great Depression in the 1930s.

The Senate Permanent Subcommittee on Investigations began an investigation of the financial crisis in November 2008. The subcommittee did not hold hearings until April 2010, when it held four days of public hearings. The subcommittee issued its 635-page report a year later. Notably, the subcommittee's hearings were held almost a half year after the landmark Dodd-Frank legislation had been introduced, and issued its final report almost a year after the bill was signed into law.

By comparison, the Pecora Commission—the Senate Banking Committee's investigation named after its chief counsel—conducted dozens of public hearings over the course of a year. As Donald Ritchie notes,

Pecora called many of the nation's most prestigious financiers before the public. Repeatedly, he elicited from them such startling admissions of wrongdoing that he stole headlines from even the masterful Franklin Roosevelt. Nevertheless, Roosevelt cheerfully supported the hearings, for their publicity helped counteract business opposition to his financial reforms and aided passage of such controversial measures as the Securities Act of 1933, the Securities and Exchange Act of 1934 and the Public Utilities Holding Company Act of 1935.

Rather than leading its own detailed investigation of the financial crisis, Congress farmed out the investigation by creating the Financial Crisis Inquiry Commission in 2009. The commission was charged "to examine the causes, domestic and global, of the current financial and economic crisis in the United States." The ten-member commission—including some members of Congress—held hearings, but no network saw fit to cover them on a daily basis other than CSPAN. Instead, one summary of a commission hearing noted that it was "critical but yawn inducing." In comparing the work of the commission with the Pecora investigation, historian Alan Brinkley noted that "it is an anemic copy, lacking anything like the tenacity and impact of Pecora's investigation; instead, showboating and modestly informed members of Congress berate witnesses without eliciting any useful disclosures—only self-serving apologies."

On March 15, 2013, the Senate Permanent Subcommittee on Investigations, chaired by retiring Senator Carl Levin, released a ferocious, scathing report on J. P. Morgan's loss of "at least $6.2 billion" in gambles on synthetic credit derivatives in 2012. A few days later, two members of Congress with substantial oversight experience, Jackie Speier, a California Democrat, and Mike Coffman, a Colorado Republican, created the Congressional Watchdog Caucus to protect and promote the work of government watchdogs of every kind, from whistleblowers to inspectors general to their own congressional investigators. Whether these developments presage a return to quality oversight by Congress or some of its members, or else merely reflects the unusual freedom of a retiring Senator and the initiative of two congressional outliers, time will tell.

"Politics by Other Means"

Less congressional oversight has been accompanied by an increase in the politicization of the congressional oversight process—in a sense, the corollary to protective partisanship. When the president's party does not control the Congress, there is both more oversight and more partisan oversight.

There is nothing inherently wrong with politics affecting a legislative oversight agenda—it is part of the democratic process. Just as elections help to determine Congress' legislative agenda, it is only to be expected that they would affect how and where Congress exercises its oversight authority.

More than thirty years ago, historian Arthur Schlesinger Jr. wrote, "The reputation of the investigative power has fluctuated wildly among both contemporaries and historians. For legislative passions, like Executive passions, are liable to abuse. The problem has been to encourage Congress to serve as the grand inquest of the nation without permitting it to become the grand inquisitor."

For Schlesinger—and for many others—Congress had on occasion gone too far, engaging in personal and often unfair political and personal attacks. In the 1920s, columnist Walter Lippman described congressional investigations as "legalized atrocity . . . in which congressmen, starved of their legitimate food for thought, go on a wild and feverish manhunt, and do not stop at cannibalism."

Congressman Robert Luce wrote of investigations in the 1930s and 1940s in which "Prosecution turned into persecution, the ruthless sacrifice of reputation, the vindictive display of prejudice, the mean debasement of partnership, the advancement of personal fortunes through the use of scurrilous publicity. . . ."

And of course, there were the investigative abuses of Sen. Joe McCarthy's investigation of communism. McCarthy bullied witnesses, threatened careers and demonized public servants in the name of a crusade to identify and root out communists in the US government.

McCarthy began his investigation because he needed an issue to define his re-election campaign for the US Senate. His inaugural speech in the effort came not in a committee hearing room or on the floor of the US Senate, but in a political speech for the Senate Republican Campaign Committee in Wheeling, West Virginia.

As Ornstein and Mann note, "An assertive Congress . . . can act in two ways: to use its power mainly to embarrass or hogtie a president, or to act to challenge and rectify both genuine malfeasance and shortcomings in policy and administration in an executive branch." Since Watergate, Congress appears more concerned with persecution than oversight, with politics rather than policy or reform.

With the advent of twenty-four–hour cable news stations, CSPAN coverage of Congress, talk radio from the left and right and news, opinion and advocacy blogs, there has been an exponential growth in the number of news or news-like outlets for information coming from investigations.

Investigative efforts that might not have merited live coverage in the 1980s are sure to show up at some hour of the day on CSPAN. Every allegation can lead to a Drudge Report or Politico or other blog story and in some cases will be the source for a new website or new online attack video.

Another reason for the growing politicization of congressional oversight may be the availability of alternatives. The rise of political oversight in the Congress has coincided with the growth in the number and staffing of inspectors general within the federal government. Congress now has a means of ensuring day-to-day oversight through the 13,000 federal employees in inspector general offices that did not exist at the time of Watergate forty years ago.

Two political scientists, Benjamin Ginsberg and Martin Shefter, argue that congressional oversight has in fact become all about politics—to use their phrase, it has become "politics by other means."

Ginsberg and Shefter argue that electoral deadlock—with no one party holding a clear mandate for its agenda—has produced a stalemate, rendering each party incapable of effectively governing. In other words, the increased politicization of congressional oversight is a reflection of heightened levels of partisanship. Having failed to win an outright victory through the ballot box, both parties have sought to win through a combination of RIP—revelation, investigation, and prosecution.

They posit a "formidable iron triangle of institutions—Congress, the national news media and the federal judiciary"—that uses investigative power to thwart the results of democratic elections. The approach is bipartisan. During the 1990s, Republicans used their takeover of the House and Senate to launch a series of investigations—from Travelgate to Whitewater and ultimately to an impeachment process—designed more to block the Clinton administration's policy agenda than to right wrongdoing or to reform government.

Shefter and Ginsberg argue that "Republicans saw the never ending investigative process as a means of harassing Clinton and preventing him from pursuing any serious legislative agenda."

In other words, the investigative process was used to diminish the political capital, time, and resources that would otherwise have been devoted to promoting the president's policy agenda. They argue that "whether or not the GOP was ultimately able to destroy Clinton through a tactic of RIP, a sustained political attack left the administration unable to focus on policy issues. After retaining control of Congress in 1996, Republicans promised to use their investigative powers to harass Clinton for the remainder of his presidency. 'Clinton will be debilitated,' predicted the former Bush White House Counsel C. Boyden Gray."

Shefter and Ginsberg, again noting the bipartisan nature of the RIP process, also discuss how it can be used to attack substantive political targets. For example, they cite a 1990s investigation of sexual harassment in the military by Democrats as a process to "stigmatize and delegitimize an institution that has become an important Republican bastion." They point to Democratic investigative attacks on fraud in military procurement as the "equivalent to the conservatives' crusades against welfare fraud. . . ."

As noted previously, the media plays a key—and increasing—role in the use of investigations for politics by other means. Shefter and Ginsberg argued that "the media came to have a stake in finding and revealing damaging information about prominent politicians." This stake has grown as media outlets—such as MSNBC and Fox—have come to depend on audiences attracted more by ideology than journalism. In reality, Shefter and Ginsberg suggest that the politicized nature of the oversight process has come to be what the public who elects members of Congress expect and demand. In the absence of a clear electoral mandate for either party, we are left with "institutional combat"—where the separation of powers has functioned as a near dual sovereignty.

The Practice of Congressional Oversight:
A "Lone Wolf" and A "Lame Duck"

We conclude this chapter with two very different case studies on congressional oversight. The first explores in depth the workings of a "lone wolf" investigation by a member of Congress conducted by Dan Feldman. The second case study explores the limits placed on oversight by an executive who sought to "wait out the clock" by declining to provide information to a congressional committee.

"Lone Wolf": Oversight of the Summer Food Program

Liz Holtzman, in her second term as a member of Congress, chaired no committee and did not serve on the Committee on Government Operations, with its general oversight responsibility, or on the Agriculture Committee, with subject-matter jurisdiction over the program in question. Like Harry Truman at the start of his investigation of waste and fraud in defense spending, Liz Holtzman began her investigation of the Summer Food Service Program (SFSP) for Children on her own, without the benefit of institutional support or authority, because her local constituents brought their suspicions to her attention. Although both she and Truman succeeded in exposing the problems and forcing the reforms they sought, unlike Truman she completed her investigation the same way—as a "lone-wolf" legislator, without institutional support.

Feldman served as executive assistant to Holtzman in the mid-1970s, in charge of her neighborhood office at 1452 Flatbush Avenue in Brooklyn. Ironically, he first became aware of the program when Sholom Ber Gorodetsky, a constituent who ran an organization called Hassidic Corporation for Urban Concerns (HCUC), called the office to complain that the Department of Agriculture's Food and Nutrition Service (FNS) had approved only 60,000 daily lunches for his organization, instead of the 200,000 for which he had applied. In response to Feldman's calls, the acting administrator for the Northeast Region of FNS sent Holtzman a letter explaining why he could not increase Gorodetsky's allocation. Earlier, he had told Feldman on the phone that contrary to Gorodetsky's assertions, his program was "not clearly superior in efficiency." Feldman would later learn that this was a considerable understatement.

Congress established the SFSP in 1968 to fill the nutritional gap faced by poor children when the school year ended and they no longer had access to the school lunch program. The SFSP served worthy goals, but by the early 1970s people like Gorodetsky saw it as a potential profit center for their "nonprofit" organizations. For summer 1976, the federal government had approved—and would pay for—1.4 million summer lunches a day. Only about 600,000 lunches were delivered for children each day, however, and much of that was inedible.

Step 1. Investigating the lead: ascertaining the meaning of reports of cartons of food left on streets—discovering that they emanated from not-for-profit participants in the US Department of Agriculture Food and Nutrition Service's SFSP for Children.

During summer 1975, a few constituents called to express puzzlement at seeing cartons of food in their streets, especially because the cartons bore the label "United States Department of Agriculture." Feldman called the department, seeking an explanation, but was refused one on the grounds that the matter was "under investigation." When constituent calls came in for the same reason in 1976, and the Agriculture Department stonewalled Feldman's inquiry again with the same excuse, Feldman got Holtzman's permission to pursue the matter himself.

The GAO had examined the SFSPs of 1971 to 1974 at the request of Congress member Charles A. Vanik (D-Ohio), and in a report dated February 14, 1975, had identified some of the same weaknesses that Feldman had found on Holtzman's behalf in the 1976 program. But, as is often the case with a GAO report when no elected official takes a personal interest in publicizing and championing its findings, no one paid attention. Even Feldman remained unaware of its existence until decades later.

Step 2. Finding the physical locations of the food drop-off sites: asking community residents where they had seen the main distribution sites.

Two other staff members, Elizabeth ("Ibby") Lang and Sylvia Lerner, helped Feldman get more information from constituents who knew some locations to which trucks would deliver these boxes of food. A quick inspection tour showed that whoever organized this affair seemed to prefer otherwise empty, broken glass-strewn lots for the food distribution. Clearly, this was part of the same SFSP for Children that involved Gorodetsky.

Step 3. Learning the regulations governing the distribution of food at those sites: reading the statutes and regulations that directed FNS to have state education departments administer the program; reading the New York State Education Department (SED) regulations governing distribution sites.

Step 4. Inspecting food drop-off sites: determining that otherwise abandoned lots, adults taking lunches, multiple lunches taken by individuals, violated program regulations.

Feldman and Lang determined that under contract, FNS had delegated administration of the program to the New York SED. From there, it was easy to find the federal rules supposedly regulating the program. Those rules did not contemplate empty, broken glass–strewn lots: local nonprofit sponsors, like HCUC, were supposed to distribute lunches to impoverished children in clean and safe buildings where they were to have run organized summer activities for the children, like sports or arts and crafts. All lunches were supposed to be eaten on site, by children. Instead, the Holtzman staff saw adults with shopping carts carrying off dozens of lunches from dangerous dumping grounds. Some food sites for which New York State had authorized payment for the delivery of five hundred lunches a day could not possibly have accommodated more than twenty children.

Step 5. Alerting the public to violations via press tours of sites: putting public pressure on SED to enforce its regulations against nonprofit sponsors.

Holtzman had Feldman organized a surprise inspection tour. The press was invited to meet Holtzman at her Flatbush Avenue office to avoid any possible advance notice to those responsible for the locations, which were kept secret until the tour began. Some television stations and the *Daily News* sent reporters and cameras. They got good pictures, with mostly black and Latino people taking the lunches. A New York *Post* reporter, on a follow-up, asked for and was given a case of milk himself. Over the weekend of August 7, 1976, 16,000 sandwiches for the SFSP were discovered abandoned in an out-of-the-way lot in the Bay Ridge section of Brooklyn.

Step 6. "Following the money": inspecting SED files of competitive bidding documents required to be submitted as evidence of fair and arms-length award of food supply contracts between nonprofit sponsors and their vendors, designed to assure highest-quality food at lowest prices.

On August 12, a newly formed organization, United Parents to Feed All Children, picketed 1452 Flatbush, with its all-black and Latino picketers carrying signs saying "Holtzman, I need food to grow," and "Miss Holtzman, are you poor with children to feed?" Feldman invited the picketers to use the office restroom, and offered water and coffee. As he chatted amiably, he asked individual picketers who had sent them. "East Harlem Community Corporation" and "Accion Civica Evangelica" were two of the answers—both nonprofit sponsors in the SFSP. When he gently mentioned this to the apparent leader of the group, she blurted "They shouldn't have told you that!"

But the implicit, and sometimes explicit, accusations of racism against Holtzman would soon be superseded by even more outrageous accusations of anti-Semitism, considering that Holtzman was Jewish. Feldman—having recently seen the movie *All the President's Men*, about the Watergate investigation, announced to Holtzman that "we should 'follow the money,'" as Deep Throat advised Woodward and Bernstein. He made an appointment to visit the SED's contract officer for the SFSP up at the World Trade Center.

Expecting to be met by a hostile and defensive bureaucrat, he was pleasantly surprised to encounter Wendy Cooper, who had just finished her first year at Fordham Law School. Likely the SED officials installed her in the position because her sister worked for a food vendor in the program, so that she would be protective, or because she was inexperienced, so that she would not understand the misbehavior she was supposed to monitor. They had misjudged her. Cooper, extremely bright and alert, immediately pointed Feldman to the contract records she had already identified as most damning.

In principle, the program's funding should have produced the best quality food for children at the lowest feasible price. In reality, every participant in the program, from the state to the vendor, had an incentive to inflate the number of lunches claimed to be distributed: FNS gave the states 2 percent of the total reimbursements for lunches for their administrative costs, the states gave the nonprofit sponsors a maximum of 88 cents per lunch, and the nonprofit sponsors were supposed to award contracts to food suppliers on the basis of competitive bidding. The sponsors were permitted to retain 6.5 cents per lunch to cover their administrative costs. Thus, in theory each competing vendor, alerted by notice from the sponsor to the availability of the contract, would submit a bid, presumably including the price at which it would supply the lunches and credentials attesting to the high quality of its products. On a date specified in the notice, the bids were to be opened in public, so that each vendor could see its competitors' bids, thus enabling a vendor to complain, or even sue, if the sponsor selected a bid clearly inferior in price and quality.

In fact, of the 134 contracts the nonprofit sponsors signed with vendors to supposedly to deliver food to New York City children that summer, 124 gave the vendors the maximum possible price.

Cooper showed Feldman that HCUC and another sponsor, the B'nai Torah Institute, had signed contracts with their vendors several days *before* their bid opening dates. This seemed to indicate that they had solicited bids from competing vendors just for show: They knew in advance which vendor they intended to select.

Step 7. Alerting public via press releases revealing "bid rigging": showing collusive practices by nonprofit sponsors and their vendors to evade fair and arms-length competition.

On August 9, 1976, Holtzman made this charge public. B'nai Torah's lunch program director called the matter "a clerical error," and because on the HCUC contract, only the vendors' signatures, but not Gorodetsky's, were dated, he also denied the charge. But now the SED took action, acknowledging irregularities, claiming to have closed hundreds of food distribution sites in the recent weeks, and pledging to investigate more. Cooper had led Feldman to other indicia of bid-rigging collusion, so in addition to B'nai Torah and HCUC, the SED announced investigations of several other sponsors. About ten days later, although there were no signs of forced entry, the SED reported that someone had stolen files from a Brooklyn office it was using to investigate violations at various other programs, including Colony-South Brooklyn Houses Inc. and the Red Hook Christian Methodist Episcopal Church, an entirely fictitious organization constructed only to defraud the government.

In the days that followed, Feldman carefully analyzed the bidding records of B'nai Torah. Actually, B'nai Torah included five ostensibly separate organizations that were, in reality, its subsidiaries. Feldman determined that four of the five subsidiaries only received bids from vendors with whom it had less than arms-length relationships. All of the vendors submitted bids at the 88-cent level: They did not even try, or pretend, to compete with each other on price. And each vendor received a contract from one of the subsidiaries, at that maximum price. Only the Queens subsidiary, Queens Assistance Program, paid less than the maximum to its vendor. Why? Only for the Queens contract had a couple of vendors not connected to B'nai Torah managed to submit bids. In order to underbid those vendors, Food

Service Dynamics, one of B'nai Torah's usual vendors came in, this time only, with a lower bid. Of course, as Holtzman asked in her press release, in what is supposed to be a secret bidding process, "how did Food Service Dynamics know that it would be necessary to bid low in the case of Queens Assistance Program when it bid the usual maximum for the other 4 Pinter sponsors?" (Lieb Pinter ran B'nai Torah.) She also asked, "How can the Pinter group justify accepting the highest possible price from a vendor which had previously bid at a lower price?"

Step 8. Investigating the new national lead: ascertaining the meaning of nonprofit sponsor's "explanation" that a check from vendor to sponsor did not show wrongdoing because it went to out-of-town affiliate of sponsor.

In his further review of B'nai Torah files, Feldman found a check *to* the Pinter subsidiary Special Programs for Americans *from* the vendor Meals & Snacks, dated well before the beginning of the summer program. Assuming it reflected further on the questionably close relationship between Pinter and its vendors, Feldman questioned a B'nai Torah official, who assured Feldman that he had misinterpreted his discovery. "That check was not for the New York Special Programs for Americans," the official explained. "It was for the *Philadelphia* Special Programs for Americans."

Feldman, Lang, and Holtzman had taken on a national criminal conspiracy to divert most of the $180 million that Congress had appropriated for this program that year into the pockets of politically connected crooks. They only had one effective weapon: the press. If they could generate enough bad publicity, they could move government officials, who might well be complicit, into reform. And the press would lose interest after the summer ended. Three people, in essence, had to fight hundreds, including some shrewd operators. This required virtually around-the-clock efforts. Feldman reported that at least one night a week that summer, he had to work through the night, taking a three-mile jog in the morning to restart his brain sufficiently for it to operate through the next day. The nights he did sleep, he rarely got more than five hours. He did not get weekends off.

Step 9. Discovering the nation-wide scope of criminal conspiracy to defraud the SFSP.

After Feldman learned that B'nai Torah reached beyond New York, he quickly surveyed other states, and discovered its operations in St. Louis, Chicago, and New Jersey, as well as Philadelphia. Of all the vendors in the United States who supply food, Pinter had managed to determine that the same principal vendors he used in New York City, George Ribowsky's Meals & Snacks and Hi-Score, and Barry Goldstein's Food Service Dynamics and JABCO, supplied the best food at the lowest price in each of those locations as well. As Holtzman said in her September 7 press release, "the statistical likelihood that this was the result of free market forces and competitive bidding is virtually zero."

Step 10. Determining that the check reflected a bribe: an "interest-free loan with no date of repayment specified."

Meals & Snacks had written a check to Special Programs for Americans because B'nai Torah had required, as a condition of being permitted to bid, that each aspiring vendor give the B'nai Torah subsidiary an interest-free loan, with no date of repayment specified. This arrangement would ordinarily be called a "bribe." Only the New Jersey administrator of the SFSP refused to permit such an arrangement.

The director of the Illinois program responded to this revelation with an interesting revelation of his own, reported by the *Chicago Daily News*: "That's why I wanted to reject the contract. But we have a written statement from the U.S. Department of Agriculture that this does not violate the terms and conditions of the program."

Step 11. Alerting the public via press releases to further evidence of collusion (poor quality of vendors, terms of contract unacceptable to legitimate vendors) and to a nation-wide scope of conspiracy.

The B'nai Torah group was not alone in its abuse of the program. Holtzman's office found problems in more than half of the SFSP contracts in New York. HCUC, as noted earlier, also engaged in collusive bidding, and also operated nationally. Road Chef International, Four Star School Feeding Corporation, and other vendors associated with the Macaluso family, served many of the programs run by local community corporations with close ties to corrupt City Council members and state legislators, and earned the distinction of providing the most repulsive meals prepared under the least sanitary conditions. Road Chef's president, Salvatore Fariello, pled guilty to larceny in 1969 in connection with his efforts to terrorize a rival soft ice cream company. Road Chef made about $1 million in profit in sales to the SFSP in about two months, with a profit margin of about 25 percent, when food companies in similar businesses ordinarily attempt to achieve 5 percent profit margins. Every one of the eleven sponsors who chose Road Chef as their vendor failed to comply with competitive bidding requirements. One of those sponsors was Accion Civica Evangelica—one of the two groups that had sent the picketers to Holtzman's office on August 12.

Step 12. Reviewing health inspection reports on vendors: determining that city, state, and federal health inspectors had cited major vendors in SFSP for serious health and sanitary deficiencies.

Step 13. Revealing inspection reports: alerting the public via press releases highlighting the contrast between glowing sponsor justifications for their choice of vendors and actual nauseating records of vendor practices.

Accion Civica also used another vendor, Latin Belly Limited. A federal inspection report of Latin Belly listed an infestation of flies, the absence of hot running water, and a filthy food processing area, and concluded that its operation "should be terminated immediately because of the filthy conditions found in this plant." But it was not terminated. Accion Civica explained its selection of Latin Belly over a lower bidder because it "specializes in Latin food and food is of good quality." Road Chef's violations in 1976 included dirty food production areas, failure to observe sanitary waste disposal procedures, and unpalatable and nutritionally unacceptable food. Four Star's violations in 1975 included possible rodent harborage, garbage and debris; and in 1976 unrefrigerated trucks, garbage on the floor, and nutritionally inadequate food. Typical sponsor explanations for selecting Road Chef over a lower bidder included Rockaway Community Corporation, which said Road Chef's menu was "superior in content and quality"; and Tremont Community Corporation, which said "Road Chef provided us with excellent references and high quality products." Typical sponsor explanations for selecting Four Star over a lower bidder included Colony-South Brooklyn Houses, which said "the previous experience of this company is especially appealing"; and Fort Greene-Crown Heights Youth Services Council, which said "We did not concern ourselves with the lowest bid [but] with . . . identifying the best lunches we could get. . . ."

Step 14. Triggering criminal prosecution: raising questions about underlying relationships facilitating, enabling, and protecting fraud by dirty sponsors among sponsors, key member of Congress, and Department of Agriculture—supplying US attorney with evidence—resulting in criminal prosecution and conviction of B'nai Torah officials and US Rep. Daniel Flood.

As each of Holtzman's charges in turn proved accurate, her credibility on the matter grew. On December 5, she called for New York State to remove the SED officials responsible for the program, Thomas Calvin and Stanley Campbell. On January 18, Campbell acknowledged his reassignment. The US Attorney for the Eastern District of New York thanked Feldman for supplying SFSP information that "indicates possible provable criminal violations by vendors." On December 9, 1977, three B'nai Torah officials were convicted of looting the SFSP.

But Holtzman's office had dug deeper. They had sought an explanation for the way the Agriculture Department had looked the other way, or worse. B'nai Torah had bestowed its Humanitarian Award on Secretary of Agriculture Earl Butz and on then-Vice President Gerald Ford, it was true, but that seemed an inadequate explanation. Much more to the point, by August 1976 Feldman was asking, "Who is Pinter's man in Flood's office?" Congressman Daniel Flood chaired the Subcommittee on Labor, Health,

Education and Welfare of the House Appropriations Committee. He controlled the appropriations from Congress to the Department of Agriculture for the Food and Nutrition Service, and thus for the SFSP. If the department wanted to continue to get its programs funded—and agencies ordinarily like to keep or expand their "turf"—it would do well to keep Flood happy.

Rabbi Lieb Pinter was sentenced to two years in prison in 1978, the year after his associates were convicted, for bribing Flood. On January 31, 1980, Flood resigned from the congressional seat he had held for thirty-one years, and the next month pled guilty to violating the campaign finance laws by taking bribes. By that time suffering some degree of dementia, he was permitted a sentence of probation instead of prison. "Pinter's man in Flood's office" was Steven B. Elko, a member of Flood's staff who served as his "bagman," and who ultimately testified against Flood in return for more lenient sentencing for himself. In May 1980, Barry Goldstein, one of Pinter's main vendors, pleaded guilty to defrauding the federal government by accepting payment for lunches he had never supplied, and using the money for kickbacks to B'nai Torah. (In a stunning example of oversight failure, the Federal National Mortgage Association, commonly known as Fannie Mae, some years later assigned more than $40 million worth of mortgage servicing rights to Pinter and Goldstein, who attempted to walk off with the money. In 2009, both pled guilty to their new scam, and were again sent to prison.)

In March 1979, the pastor of Red Hook Methodist Episcopal Church, the organization that did not actually exist, pled guilty to fraudulent claims for close to 1 million lunches, and admitted getting at least $10,000 in kickbacks from Four Star School Feeding, part of the Macaluso group. Joseph Macaluso, who headed that group, was also indicted. The pastor had won eligibility for his "church" as a nonprofit organization by claiming that it was part of the Christian Methodist Episcopal Church, which "denied any connection" with him.

Step 15. Reforming the SFSP: pressing Congress and the Department of Agriculture for reform—enacting amendments to the National School Lunch Act and promulgating regulations pursuant thereto.

But Holtzman had more important things to do than assure the convictions of Pinter and Flood. With the credibility she had earned, she succeeded in forcing Congress to restructure the operation of the SFSP under legislation she had gotten introduced by Carl Perkins (D-Ky.), the long-time chair of the House Committee on Education and Labor. No longer would tax-exempt status with the IRS suffice to enable a nonprofit organization to participate. None would qualify without careful vetting of officers, directors, and histories. States would no longer have an incentive to allow the numbers to be inflated: The federal government would not reward them with an automatic percentage of total outlays for their administrative expenses. Lunches would no longer be distributed by random organizations that had acquired not-for-profit status by doing little more than applying for it, but only by established schools and children's camps. All meals would have to be consumed on-site, and only by children. And criminal penalties would be imposed for violations.

Step 16. Following up: maintaining vigilance over the program. Forcing Agriculture to follow the law by excluding dirty vendors; forcing the state and federal administrations to hire an honest administrator.

In 1978, administration of the program in New York reverted to the Department of Agriculture because the state claimed that the federal government was not providing enough money to run it. Apparently, the B'nai Torah gang still had some of its hooks into the Department of Agriculture, because Agriculture's administrator approved Food Service Dynamics as a bidder. This time, however, when Agriculture learned that Holtzman was still watching, it backed down literally hours after Holtzman warned that she was about to publicize the approved list. Not only did Agriculture take Food Service Dynamics off the approved list, it demoted its coordinator for the program in New York City, putting the city program under the direction of Carol Steinberger. Steinberger had been the New Jersey administrator who in 1976 refused to allow B'nai Torah to insert its "bribe" requirement into its vendor contracts, despite the Agriculture Department's approval. Under pressure from Holtzman, for the 1977 program the New York SED had hired Steinberger to replace its former administrator. Now, rather than face a new barrage of criticism from Holtzman, the Agriculture Department acquiesced as well.

Jealous of the headlines Holtzman had accumulated during her investigation, other politicians tried to repeat her feat in later years. None succeeded. For many years thereafter, the program has run clean.

Oversight of Abuse of Power by a "Lame Duck":
The Firing of the US Attorneys

As noted in the introductory chapters about the various areas of focus for oversight, abuse may be the most difficult to define. Fraud, waste, and corruption—such as the examples discussed in the SFSP case study—all speak to various levels of misappropriation. Abuse, however, may have little to do with the misuse of funding—it often is about the misuse of the law.

In later chapters, we discuss the nexus between abuse and law enforcement. Suffice it to say that the notion of nondiscriminatory application of the law—especially the criminal law—is a core value and its abuse frequently demands oversight attention.

A key to the protection of rights and liberties is the independence of law enforcement and the criminal justice system. It is why federal judges—and some state judges—are appointed to life terms, why some law enforcement officials are appointed to set terms and are only removable for cause. On the other hand, some judges and some law enforcement officials are elected at the local and state level. And even appointees to law enforcement positions within the federal government are selected for political reasons. A purely merit-based selection process would not have likely resulted in the appointment of Robert F. Kennedy as US attorney general: It probably helped that he was the president's brother.

Still, one of the most shocking and disturbing episodes in recent American history was when President Nixon demanded that his attorney general fire the special prosecutor who had been appointed to investigate Watergate. When Attorney General Richardson refused, Nixon fired him. When Deputy Attorney General William Ruckelshaus similarly refused, the president fired him as well. Then, Solicitor General Bork—acting as attorney general—fired the special prosecutor, Archibald Cox. The episode quickly came to be known as the Saturday Night Massacre.

The full story of the firing of seven US attorneys after the 2006 elections will probably never be known. The Bush administration effectively ran out the clock—with its term in office ending before Congress could force the issue. Still, in many ways, the issues that faced Congress were similar to those of the Saturday Night Massacre and both the House and the Senate recognized that the alleged abuse of power had triggered a serious constitutional confrontation.

US attorneys are the local prosecution arm of the federal government: There are ninety-four in districts across the nation. In many ways, they are political appointees—with the president making the appointment and appointments subject to Senate confirmation.

Beginning in January 2007, both the House and Senate Judiciary committees began investigations of the firing of US attorneys, specifically the role that politics may have played in the decisions to demand certain resignations. Although politics in the appointment of US attorneys was somewhat the norm, the concern was that certain US attorneys were being dismissed for their failure to adhere to a political agenda. If US attorneys believed that their jobs were on the line if they made decisions that were politically unpopular, it would compromise their independence.

Between January and August 2007, the Senate Judiciary Committee held ten hearings on the issue. The House Judiciary Committee also held six hearings. Senate Committee staff conducted an additional fourteen interviews with witnesses outside of the hearings.

A former Justice official testified before House Judiciary Committee under grant of immunity to "improperly screening career employees for political loyalty and wielding undue political influence over key law enforcement decisions and policies." Both the Senate and House committees heard from the fired former prosecutors as well.

In the course of its investigation, the Senate Judiciary Committee "uncovered grave threats to the independence of law enforcement from political manipulation . . . with participation from the highest political ranks in the White House, including former White House Deputy Chief of Staff Karl Rove. The evidence shows that senior officials were focused on the political impact of Federal prosecutions and whether Federal prosecutors were doing enough to bring partisan voter fraud and corruption cases."

Specifically, David Iglesias was asked to resign as US attorney for New Mexico due to complaints about his handling of voter fraud and political corruption cases: he was seen as not aggressive enough in cases involving potential criminal activity by state Democrats.

Although the Committee could not determine the conclusive reason for the firing of John McKay, former US attorney for Washington's Western District, media reports suggested that it was his failure to investigate charges by Republican political leaders of voter fraud following the 2004 state governor's race.

Justice Department officials stated that Carol Lam, US attorney for California's Southern District, was fired because of her prosecution of firearm and immigration cases. Subsequent investigation suggested that it was more likely that she was fired due to her successful prosecution of Republican Congressman Randy "Duke" Cunningham.

Todd Graves, the former US attorney for the Western District of Missouri (and the brother of Rep. Sam Graves), was asked to resign due to "complaints to the White House Counsel's Office by Senator Bond's staff regarding his decision not to respond to a demand from Sen. Bond's staff member to get involved in a personnel decision in Rep. Sam Graves congressional office."

According to the Senate Judiciary Committee's final report, "The evidence we have found supports a conclusion that officials from the highest political ranks at the White House, including Mr. Rove, manipulated the Justice Department, turning the Department into a political arm of the White House to pursue a partisan political agenda . . . the list for firings was compiled based on input from the highest political ranks in the White House."

As significant as the firings were, however, the investigation quickly came to focus on the administration's efforts to cover up and stonewall. Ultimately, the committee concluded that "the reasons given for these firings were contrived as part of a cover up and that the stonewalling by the White House is part and parcel of that same effort." The Justice Department and the White House refused to turn over documents and sought to prevent testimony by current and former officials. The Senate Judiciary Committee noted that "This stonewalling is a dramatic break from the practices of every administration since World War II in responding to congressional oversight. In that time, presidential advisors have testified before congressional committees 74 times, either voluntarily or compelled by subpoenas. . . . The veil of secrecy this Administration has insisted upon is unprecedented and damaging to the tradition of open government that has been a hallmark of this Republic."

Bush White House officials invoked a broad claim of Executive Privilege to support their lack of cooperation.

What is Executive Privilege? Consistent with the principle of separation of powers, the president is allowed to receive confidential advice from his or her key aides. To the extent that the legislature seeks to breach this confidentiality, it can impede honest and candid advice and the functioning of the executive. As a result, certain communications between the executive—in this case, the president—and key aides are privileged, much as communications between an attorney and his or her client.

Just as there is no explicit statutory or constitutional language defining Congress' power to investigate, executive privilege is also not well defined in law. But the courts have rejected the notion that it is absolute—especially where the privilege would limit Congress' ability to hear testimony or receive testimony or obtain information that is not otherwise available. Finally, in 1974 in *United States v. Nixon*, the Supreme Court held that "when the privilege depends solely on the broad, undifferentiated claim of public interest in the confidentiality of such conversations, a confrontation with other values arises." In other words, there must be a balancing of constitutional and public interests.

Both the Senate and the House sought remedies for the lack of White House cooperation, with the Senate recommending a resolution of contempt and the House seeking judicial remedies. The US District Court for the District of Columbia found that failure to turn over documents in response to congressional subpoena was unlawful: "The Executive's current claim of absolute immunity from compelled Congressional process for senior presidential aides is without any support in the case law."

Yet, before Congress could act on the contempt issues, the administration came to an end with the 2008 election of Barack Obama.

Still, even in the face of stonewalling, congressional oversight of the firing of the US attorneys had a real impact. In August 2007, Attorney General Alberto Gonzales resigned under pressure and the new attorney general, Michael Mukasey, sought an investigation by the Justice Department Office of Inspector General and the Office of Professional Legal Responsibility. That report, released in 2008 and compiled without White House cooperation found that the "firings were unprecedented and that partisan political considerations played a role." The Senate Judiciary Committee reported that it concluded that "Attorney General Gonzales and Deputy Attorney General McNulty bore primary responsibility for the deeply flawed process that led to the firings."

In reaction to the investigation, Congress passed new legislation rescinding the power of the attorney general to make interim US attorney appointments and allowing those appointees to serve indefinitely.

Finally, Mukasey appointed an independent prosecutor to determine whether there was criminal conduct. That investigation concluded that although the firings violated department policy, they were not violations of criminal law and that misleading statements by the attorney general and others did not rise to the level of a crime.

Conclusion

Congressional investigations may be one of the most important checks available on executive abuse at the federal level. Yet, the history of congressional investigation is spotty at best. As we discuss in this chapter, there are different types of congressional oversight—some dependent on individual members and some more dependent on the institution. The "lone-wolf" member of Congress or the Senate who has no special institutional relationship with the federal agency he or she may be investigating will be less inclined toward a "protective" stance, and will more likely engage in a thorough, hard-hitting effort. Special or select committees, appointed in response to newly perceived matters of great public concern, likewise should be less vulnerable to cooptation, as should committees devoted primarily to investigation or reform.

On the other hand, committees with responsibilities in the same policy area as the agencies they oversee—banking, transportation, defense, or anything else—are more likely to sympathize with what should be the targets of their oversight work, even in the unlikely event their members have not received substantial campaign contributions from private sector players enjoying benefits from those government agencies. Lobbyists so assiduously cultivate members of committees with budgetary and appropriations responsibilities that they rarely delve deeply into the depredations committed on their behalf by government agencies.

Liz Holtzman's "lone-wolf" investigation, Truman's work on defense contracting—first as a lone and then as the head of a special committee, Kefauver's special committee, the Senate Select Committee that investigated the Watergate affair in 1973, and the House and Senate Select committees on intelligence in 1975 all acted consistently with the principles of effective oversight that we have articulated earlier in the book. All were either lone wolf or special or select committees.

In contrast, the Armed Services committees of the House and Senate failed miserably to conduct any meaningful oversight of the vast waste and scandalous abuse attached to the war in Iraq.

But the guidelines for analysis just presented do not account for the fact that the Senate Banking Committee—a standing committee that presumably had pre-existing relationships with the industry in question—conducted a scathing investigation of the financial collapse of 1929, whereas the Senate Committee on Investigations hearings on the financial collapse of 2007 were pathetically ineffective. The House Judiciary Committee conducted an effective investigation of Watergate, while the special joint committee of the House and Senate investigated the Iran-contra affair incompetently if not dishonestly

The institutional failure even of special committees in these instances reflect at least two other factors: "protective partisanship," as was noted in the chapter; and the increase in corporate influence over Congress. Illinois Sen. Richard Durbin said in 2009 about Congress that the banks "own the place." With the decline in power of unions and political organizations, the financial industry may indeed have preeminence among the corporate powers, but few would deny that the chief executives of the defense industry, oil companies, pharmaceuticals, insurance, and other sectors have some share of that "ownership" as well. Although the present era may not have given us the absolute nadir of congressional oversight responsibility (after all, it was not recently that Mark Twain called Congress "the only native American criminal class"), it is bad enough to justify public outrage.

Congress' failure to defend its institutional oversight role has played an important role in the growing public perception of Congress as a "broken branch" of government. Too often, partisanship seems to get in the way of Congress doing its job. Absent legal limits on the oversight process and with media providing incentives for the partisan investigative process, the only check on the quality and substance of legislative oversight must come from the public. Yet the partisanship that appears to drive much of the oversight process feeds and plays to real and existing divisions within the public. And, for less partisan Americans, it breeds a cynicism about government that deters their participation.

The quality of congressional oversight will thus only improve when the public demands so, when it recognizes that the exercise of the oversight authority is, as Woodrow Wilson stated, as important a role for Congress as the exercise of its legislative authority. The failure of congressional oversight may be one reason that by the end of 2010, the Gallup Poll found that just 13 percent of Americans approved of the performance of Congress compared with 83 percent who disapproved. It is worth noting that in August 1974, immediately after President Nixon's resignation, 47 percent of Americans approved of Congress' performance compared with 34 percent who disapproved.

As Kriner noted, "Until voters begin to value effective oversight as much as academics, partisan electoral incentives may continue to trump institutional incentives" to engage in oversight.

Chapter 6

Government Accountability Office

What's in a name? That which we call a rose, by any other name would smell as sweet . . .

—William Shakespeare, *Romeo and Juliet*

There's a joke about a high school football team—the Eagles—that goes four whole seasons without a single victory. Finally, the team's coach huddles with his team in the locker room and he says, "Boys, if we don't win today the school administration has decided that we have to change our name to the Possums." At which point, the starting quarterback turns to the coach and asks, "the Possums, why the Possums?" The coach replies, "because we play dead at home and get killed on the road."

For its first eighty-three years, the GAO was the General Accounting Office. Yet, in 2004, Congress kept the initials but changed the GAO's name to the Government Accountability Office. This was not simply a bureaucratic shuffling of the deck, although one wonders just how much the name may have cost federal taxpayers in new letterhead alone. Still, David Walker, then comptroller general of the GAO explained the name change in the following way:

> [O]ur old name, as familiar and reassuring as it was, had not kept pace with GAO's evolving role in government. The truth is that "accounting" has never been our chief mission. Stereotypes, however, can be hard to shake. Some college students we were trying to recruit mistakenly assumed that you needed an accounting degree to work at GAO. . . . In fact, a recent crossword puzzle in The Washington Post asked for a three-letter term describing a GAO employee; the answer was "CPA."

This chapter outlines the evolution of the GAO from accounting to accountability and discusses how this evolving role fits into the overall framework of government oversight at the federal level. With oversight provided by Congress, IGs, and the GAO, just who does what and when presents something of a blurred picture at the federal level.

From Accounting to Accountability

The GAO was born as the federal government—and federal spending—was beginning to grow. The 1921 Budget and Accounting Act established the Government Accounting Office as "an independent auditor of government agencies and activities." In the 1921 act, the GAO was given the power to "investigate, at the seat of government or elsewhere, all matters related to the receipt, disbursement and application of public funds."

Just eight years earlier, the 16th Amendment was ratified providing Congress with the power to impose an income tax. With World War I, federal debt tripled to more than one third of annual gross domestic product (GDP). Growth in federal spending demanded the creation of a single, centralized accounting entity.

During its first twenty years, the GAO went through a "green eye-shade" period where auditors and accountants would literally review federal spending on a transaction-by-transaction basis. GAO functioned more as the nation's bookkeeper than its auditor. Change began following World War II—with the continued expansion of the federal government—and the GAO moved away from transactional audits. Operationally, the GAO replaced its Accounting and Bookkeeping Division with an Audits Division. As Jonathan Walters and Charles Thompson note, "voucher clerks were replaced with accountants capable of a much more sophisticated big picture look at agency fiscal practices."

This shift coincided with a real reduction in the size of the GAO workforce—going from 15,000 employees in the 1940s to approximately 7,000 in the 1950s. Undoubtedly, over time, changes in technology also aided the shift to a less labor-intensive focus on accounting.

With fewer resources and a growing federal government, it was simply impossible for the GAO to function as it had been. Instead, it began to set standards for accounting with the expectation that the operating arms of the federal government would comply with those standards: Regular audits would assess levels of compliance. Under the Budget and Accounting Principles Act of 1950, the GAO was required to prescribe principles and standards for accounting in federal agencies.

The GAO's role continued to evolve through the 1960s. Just as World War I, World War II and the federal response to the Great Depression had changed the federal government, so did the Vietnam War and the Great Society programs enacted during the presidency of Lyndon Johnson. Between 1948 and 1968, total annual federal spending went from 11.6% of GDP to 20.5% of GDP: Between 1962 and 1968, federal domestic spending went from 6.7 to 7.7% of GDP.

It was during this period of federal growth that the GAO began to build on its focus on audits and accounting standards and moved increasingly into program evaluation and analysis. In 1972, the GAO issued the first version of what came to be known as the Yellow Book—the Government Auditing Standards, the widely accepted standard for government audits.

By the 1970s, as Walters and Thompson note, the GAO "which had primarily employed accountants, began to hire physical scientists, social scientists, and computer professionals, along with experts in healthcare, public policy tax law and information management."

With growing federal deficits, debate in Washington during the late 1970s shifted from determining whether programs were working to how to reduce federal spending. Ronald Reagan was elected president in 1980 with a pledge to bring federal spending under control. Although there had been efforts to pass a constitutional amendment requiring that the federal budget be balanced since the 1930s, the House of Representatives actually passed a balanced budget amendment for the first time in 1982.

Increasingly, Congress turned to the GAO for ways to cut spending. In 1985, Congress passed the Balanced Budget and Emergency Deficit Control Act—known for its Senate sponsors Phil Gramm, Warren Rudman, and Ernest Hollings. Under the law, Congress authorized automatic cuts in federal spending in the event that deficit spending exceeded certain targets. Gramm-Rudman-Hollings required the heads of the president's Office of Management and Budget (OMB) and the Congressional Budget Office to report on deficit estimates and program-by-program budget reductions. The head of the GAO—the comptroller general—was required to make final recommendations to the president for specific cuts—through sequestration of funds—to achieve spending targets. The president was then required to make these cuts unless Congress achieved alternatives in a specified period of time.

In *Bowsher v. Synar*, the Supreme Court in 1986 held that this extraordinary grant of power to the comptroller general was unconstitutional. The Court noted that the Gramm-Rudman-Hollings law placed decision making and executive authority with the GAO. In effect, the law gave the comptroller general the power to direct the president to make specific budget cuts. The Court found that the GAO was part of the Legislative Branch and that, therefore, vesting this executive authority in the GAO constituted a violation of the separation of powers doctrine.

Although the GAO's direct role in deficit reduction was limited by *Bowsher*, it was clear that Congress was increasingly relying on the agency for more than just oversight: The GAO was seen as an independent source of information on how to address broad budgetary issues. Shortly after the enactment of Gramm-Rudman-Hollings, in 1990, the GAO began to issue a regular report on high-risk federal programs and agencies where the risk for fraud, waste and mismanagement was the greatest. The series, which is ongoing, had a clear focus: "GAO's recommendations to address these high-risk areas and major challenges could lead to billions of dollars in savings for the federal government."

In 1993, Congress also passed the Government Performance Results Act (GPRA), which required federal departments and agencies to engage in strategic planning, set specific and measureable performance goals, and report annually on their performance. Congress turned to the GAO to play a major role in performance management as it had in the budget process. GPRA requires the GAO to regularly report on agency progress in implementing reforms and improvements and to work with the OMB and the Office of Personnel Management in training federal staff to achieve such implementation.

The GAO Today

The GAO's current role began to take shape in the mid-1990s and was the result, in part, of a change in leadership in Congress. Republicans gained control of the House of Representatives for the first time in more than forty years: Thus, in 1994, both the Senate and the House were under Republican leadership. After years of Democratic control of Congress, the GAO had come to be seen as a tool for Democrats to attack Republican administrations.

The comptroller general post was left vacant for two years after the term of Charles Bowsher expired in 1996. And the GAO sustained a 25 percent cut in staff in federal FY 1996 and 1997. The GAO began its turnaround in 1998, with the appointment of David Walker as the new comptroller general.

In many ways, Walker sought to continue the evolution that had occurred under his predecessors. The GAO, however, became far more attuned and more responsive to Congress—as opposed to functioning as an entity that was somewhat independent of both the Executive and Legislative Branches, with GAO staff and the comptroller general identifying areas for review and audit. Congress was the primary "client" and consumer of GAO work. By the early 2000s, GAO reported that 80 percent of its work was driven by congressional requests. This included GAO reports, as well as specific support for congressional committees and—by 2010—nearly daily appearances at congressional hearings.

In 2003, Walker reported, "GAO's mission of assuring accountability has been and will remain closely linked to supporting congressional oversight and improving government efficiency and effectiveness."

Congress has also continued to rely on the GAO for recommendations on the budget. Financial benefits—how much GAO's work actually achieved in cost savings—became a key measure of GAO success. The comptroller general began to regularly testify about GAO's return on investment: In FY 2003, for example, GAO reported $26.4 billion in financial benefits and 906 needed improvements in effectiveness and efficiency (eg, reductions in improper payments). In FY 2010, GAO reported financial benefits of $49.9 billion—or $87 for every dollar invested in the GAO.

At the same time, Congress has continued to rely on the GAO to conduct broader oversight. For example, the landmark Dodd-Frank financial regulation law specifically directs the GAO to conduct a half dozen major studies of financial regulation.

As the GAO continued to evolve, it also reorganized, placing greater emphasis on planning, personnel and performance. Again, Comptroller General Walker argued that "GAO should be the federal government's model for best practices in every major operational area."

In 2011, the GAO celebrated its ninetieth anniversary under the banner of "Accountability, Integrity and Reliability." It still provided many of the services that it had long provided:

- Auditing and evaluating federal programs and operations
- Special investigations of criminal laws related to conflict of interest, procurement, and contract fraud
- Legal services to Congress
- Resolving bid protests
- Prescribing accounting principles and standards for the executive branch (Yellow Book)
- Detailing GAO staff to congressional committees

But those roles have come to be more strategically framed in the context of evaluation, audit, analysis, and investigation. The GAO now functions less as a pure investigative and audit agency. Instead, the GAO focuses on both insight—such as determining what programs work—and foresight—such as understanding large operational and fiscal trends within the federal government. And, unlike inspectors general that are assigned to specific departments, the GAO has the ability to look at issues across the federal government—whether it is particular multidepartmental functions, such as procurement, or policy areas, such as financial regulation.

According to Walker, "[B]y making recommendations to improve the practices and operations of government agencies, we contribute not only to the increased effectiveness of federal spending, but also to the enhancement of the taxpayers' trust and confidence in their federal government."

Ensuring Independence, Resources, and Power

Both the Supreme Court decision in *Bowsher* and the subsequent reductions in the GAO budget in the mid-1990s demonstrate the limits to GAO's independence.

In many respects, GAO's independence is guaranteed by the appointment process and term for the comptroller general. The comptroller general is appointed by the president on the recommendation of a bicameral commission, and subject to the advice and consent of the Senate: The commission must recommend three individuals but the president can ask for additional names or nominate someone else. Comptrollers general hold their position for a fifteen-year term, but are limited by law to a single term.

From 1921 to 2008, there were just seven comptrollers general. During the same period, there were fifteen presidents, sixteen different individuals who served as Speaker of the House of Representatives, fifteen individuals who served as Senate Majority Leader. In tenure, the comptroller general is most comparable to a chief justice of the Supreme Court.

Although the independence of the GAO from the Executive Branch is fairly well established, its independence from the leadership of Congress is more limited. First, as demonstrated by the budget reductions of the mid-1990s, the degree to which the GAO is responsive to the Congress can and will affect its resources. Second, Congress does have the power to remove a comptroller general mid-term. As noted by the Court in *Bowsher*, the intent of the Congress in creating the GAO was that the agency should be responsive to the demands of Congress. Congress "felt that [the comptroller general] should be brought under the sole control of Congress, so that Congress, at any moment when it found he was inefficient and was not carrying on the duties of his office as he should and as the Congress expected, could remove him without the long tedious process of a trial by impeachment." During debate on the 1921 Budget and Accounting Act, Rep. Hawley commented:"[H]e is our officer, in a measure, getting information for us. . . . If he does not do his work properly, we, as practically his employers, ought to be able to discharge him from his office." Thus, the comptroller general and the GAO are ultimately accountable to the Congress and their priorities and focus is driven by their "client."

To perform its evolving role, the GAO needs resources—staff and funding. The GAO today is one fifth its former size in the 1940s when it essentially filled the role of bookkeeper for the federal government.

As of 2008, the GAO had more than 3,100 staff and an annual budget of $507 million. It is the largest of the agencies designed to support Congress—such as the Congressional Budget Office—but it is no longer the largest of federal oversight agencies. The federal IG program, discussed in detail in Chapter 7, now employs four times the staff of the GAO with a FY 2010 budget of $2.2 billion.

Thus, the GAO's historic investigative role has in many ways been transferred to the IGs. The "GAO looks horizontally at programs and functions across government, whereas the IGs have been the "local cop" on the beat focusing on combating fraud, waste, abuse and mismanagement within their respective agencies." The GAO has only a very small unit dedicated to criminal investigations and there is no clear protocol has to how and when GAO analysts are to refer specific allegations of fraud to law enforcement.

The effectiveness of the GAO—and all oversight agencies—depends on access to information. Historically, the GAO has had the power to require the production of documents as a part of its investigative and audit authority. More recently, the GAO has received statutory authority to compel interviews with certain government contractors. But the GAO does not have broad subpoena power—nor does it even have the power to subpoena documents.

Instead, the GAO has relied upon its broad investigative authority under the 1921 Budget and Accountability Act to require records—especially records in possession of federal agencies. There was, however, no specific means of enforcing such requests until 1980 when Congress authorized the GAO to enforce its investigatory powers by bringing a civil claim in federal court.

The 1980 statute, however, sets forth a specific process that the GAO must follow prior to resorting to a civil claim. First, the comptroller general must make a written request to the agency head stating the reason and authority for requesting the right to review records. Second, if twenty days pass without receiving access to such records, the comptroller general may file a report with the president, the director of OMB, the attorney general, the agency head and Congress. If, after another twenty days, the agency continues to deny access to the records, then the comptroller general can file a claim requiring access to the records.

Three types of records are specifically exempt from this process:

1. records designated by the president as foreign intelligence or counterintelligence activities;

2. where a statute exempts records from disclosure; or

3. where after filing the twenty-day report, the president or OMB director certifies that disclosure of the records "could be expected to impair substantially the operations of the Government."

The first test of the 1980 statute came with a 2001 action brought by the comptroller general against Vice President Cheney. The vice president had been designated by President Bush to lead an administration initiative on energy policy and chaired the National Energy Policy Development Group. On the request of members of Congress, the GAO initiated an investigation of the group. Specifically, members of Congress—minority members of the House of Representatives—raised concerns about how the development group was proceeding and who was involved in the process.

The vice president's office refused to provide all of the information requested by the GAO. Instead, the vice president raised a series of legal issues that challenged the scope and authority of the GAO investigation and suggested that the GAO's ability to require such information was limited by executive privilege.

Ultimately, the comptroller general brought a claim in federal court demanding access to the undisclosed documents. As the court noted, the lawsuit raised clear, contrasting views of the separation of powers. The court, however, ruled on far narrower grounds—finding that the comptroller general lacked standing to bring the action. The court—and the GAO did not appeal the case beyond the district court level—sought to stay out of what it interpreted as a dispute between an official of the Congress and the Executive Branch. Instead of relying on the judiciary to resolve this dispute, the court noted that the GAO had other alternatives. If the agency had the support of the Congress, it could have asked a congressional committee to subpoena the documents in question. But, in this case, the Congressional Republican majority in the House of Representatives was not in support of the investigation.

Therefore, to a certain extent, the court's ruling suggests that absent the clear support of Congress in its investigative work, the GAO's ability to compel the Executive Branch to provide information is extremely limited. The ruling in *Walker v. Cheney* (2002) thus further limited the GAO's independence from the Congress and its ability to fully investigate an uncooperative Executive Branch—at least where there could be issues of executive privilege.

Overseeing the Overseers

If the GAO is ultimately accountable to the Congress, who effectively monitors its performance and activities to ensure that the 3,100-person bureaucracy that today is the GAO is free of fraud, waste, and abuse. In other words, who is left to oversee the overseer?

One of the federal IGs described in Chapter 7 is the IG for the GAO. Since 1996, the GAO has had an IG and the position was provided for by statute under the Government Accountability Office Act of 2008.

What Does the GAO IG Do?

Despite the GAO's description of the federal IGs as "cops on the beat," the IG both monitors internal controls and seeks to provide oversight of the overall effectiveness of the GAO. In 2009 and 2010, the GAO IG issued a total of four reports and provided testimony once to a congressional committee. While a December 2010 report called for additional controls on the use of travel cards and a 2009 report focused on information security, the IG also monitored the GAO's use and reporting of performance measures on its own operations.

The existence of an IG for the GAO highlights yet another function that the agency has taken on—after all, if an IG monitors the GAO, who monitors the federal inspectors general program? Although the Council of Inspectors General on Integrity and Efficiency—discussed in Chapter 7—is something of a self-regulatory body of IGs, the GAO monitors IG performance.

Conclusion

The GAO's change in name reflects the more important change in the role of the agency over time. Once the nation's bookkeeper, the GAO has evolved into an organization focused on accountability.

The distinction between accounting and accountability is one, with a real difference. In earlier chapters, we distinguished between financial and performance audits and between audits and investigations. The evolving role of the GAO suggests yet another difference—between audits and investigations and program and policy evaluation. More than other audit agencies at the state and local level, the GAO has emerged as more of a program evaluator than a financial auditor. Increasingly, its work has been to provide not just oversight support but policy support to its client, the Congress.

The result is that the GAO of today is clearly not the GAO of its origins or even the GAO of the 1990s. Although the GAO remains focused on the dollars and cents of federal spending, it more frequently looks at the operations of the federal government through a lens focused on policy prescriptions rather than just a green eyeshade. In some respects, the desired outcome remains the same—efficiency and effectiveness in the spending of federal dollars. In fact, the new path of the GAO calls on the agency to reach beyond accounting and performance review to making clear judgments about underlying policy as well.

Yet, a large portion of the work of the GAO remains the same "meat and potatoes" brand of oversight common to auditors and watchdogs engaged in oversight at all levels of government—financial audits, calls for better planning and assessment, improved documentation, and tighter internal controls.

The relationship between the GAO and its client, Congress, has also evolved. To the extent that the GAO now more clearly reflects the will of Congress, it is less likely to pursue an independent agenda and more likely to engage in oversight affected—if not guided—by political aims and motivation. The congressional history discussed above suggests that Congress has always seen the GAO as an extension of itself, but there clearly were periods of greater GAO independence that caused Congress to effectively rein in the organization over the past two decades.

These changes in the work and mission of the GAO coincide with limits on its resources. It may not be clear what the exact relationship is between changes in political environment, access to information, and resources and the GAO's role and mission. But clearly a relationship exists.

The GAO's evolution is also a reflection of the changes in congressional oversight—discussed in the prior chapter—and the growth of yet another arm of the federal government charged with similar same responsibilities—the development of the federal IG system that is the subject of the next chapter.

Chapter 7

The Federal Inspector General System at Thirty-Five

It's really true, when the gods want to punish they first make mad. In what did that nincompoop resemble an inspector general? In nothing, not even half the little finger of an inspector general.

—Nikolai Gogol, *The Inspector General* (1836)

The question is are you there as a policeman or are you there as a cheerleader?

—Sen. Claire McCaskill (2008)

Even the Egyptian pharaohs hired accountants to assure that the books were kept honestly, as did the ancient Chinese, Greeks, and Romans.

Governments have used the title "inspector general" for a long time. In English, the term appears to have originated as a military office, responsible for military performance, not especially for preventing or exposing waste or corruption. The 1913 edition of *Webster's Dictionary* defines the term as "a staff officer of an army, whose duties are inspection, and embrace everything relative to organization, recruiting, discharge, administration, accountability for money and property, instruction, police, and discipline."

George Washington appointed Baron Frederick Wilhelm von Steuben as IG of the US Army, with the rank of major general, in 1778. The job, as in the British military tradition, required him to assure that soldiers were adequately prepared for combat and had mastered standard protocols for drills and maneuvers, and had little or nothing to do with fraud, waste, abuse, or corruption. Washington could, of course, have used his own generals to assess the combat readiness of his troops, instead of recruiting a foreigner. But his generals might well have been embarrassed to admit that

97

they had failed to prepare the troops adequately. This points to the need for independence in a position entrusted with oversight. Note also that Washington refused the request of the Continental Congress to have the IG report to them as well as to him. Washington was not willing to grant the IG that much independence from him, but the oversight function is intimately entwined with the concept of checks and balances.

In 1836, Nikolai Gogol wrote a play (in Russian) about corrupt officials in a small town in Russia fearing a visit from the IG from the national government in St. Petersburg. Apparently, in Russia the term had already become understood to transcend the military role. The title became better known in the United States in 1949 when Danny Kaye made a very funny movie, using that title, out of the Gogol story.

To provide a clearer sense of the nature of the federal IG system, this chapter discusses the system of federal IGs at the thirty-fifth anniversary of the 1978 Inspector General Act. We also discuss the origins and history of the IG system and the precise role of IGs in the federal government.

Federal IGs Today

There are now seventy-three statutory IGs monitoring federal departments and agencies with a collective budget of approximately $2.2 billion and a total of approximately 13,600 employees. Federal IGs are charged with investigating, auditing, and evaluating a federal budget of $3 trillion and a civilian staff of 2.1 million full-time employees.

Thirty departments and agencies—including cabinet departments (eg, Defense and Health and Human Services); agencies (eg, General Services Administration) and specific parts of federal departments (eg, Tax Administration)—are covered under the 1978 Inspector General Act. These departments and agencies each have an inspector general appointed by the president subject to Senate confirmation.

There are another thirty-three IGs for certain agencies and commissions—from the Corporation for Public Broadcasting to the Securities and Exchange Commission—where the IG is appointed by the agency head.

Finally, there were ten IG offices created pursuant to separate statutory authority and with different terms of appointment. These include IGs for the following:

- the Central Intelligence Agency (appointed by the president, subject to Senate confirmation)

- Afghanistan Reconstruction (appointed by the president)

- Iraq Reconstruction (appointed by the secretary of defense, in consultation with the secretary of state)

- Troubled Asset Relief Program (appointed by the president, subject to Senate confirmation)

- US Capitol Police (appointed by the agency head)

In addition to differences in the appointment process (which are discussed in detail later), it is worth noting two overarching issues related to the federal IGs.

First, unlike some state and local IG and investigative offices and unlike the GAO, there is no single federal IG to whom the individual department and agency IGs report. We discuss the role of the Council of the Inspectors General on Integrity and Efficiency (CIGIE), but the fact remains that most IGs have a very specific department or agency focus, with no formal means of working across departments.

Second, the budget and staffing of the IG offices varies greatly but has little relationship to department or agency budget staffing or area of responsibility. As of FY 2006, the two largest federal departments in the government—Health and Human Services and Defense—had the largest IG budgets and the most IG staff. Yet, although these two departments combined for approximately 45 percent of federal outlays, their IGs had just over 20 percent of IG staff. By comparison, the HUD IG had approximately half the staff of the Defense Department IG and agency outlays of less than 10 percent of the Department of Defense.

In reporting the accomplishments of federal IGs, CIGIE highlights eight key metrics achieved through a combination of audits, investigations, inspections, and evaluations. In FY 2010, federal IGs were responsible for:

- Better use of federal funds: IGs identified $42 billion in potential unnecessary spending and department and agency management agreed to recommendations related to $23.7 billion

- Questioning costs: IGs identified $62.2 billion in questionable costs and management agreed to recommendations related $56.6 billion

- Investigating receivables and recoveries: IGs, through criminal and civil cases, recovered $7 billion for the federal government

- Prosecutions: IG investigations led to 5,610 indictments and information and 5,593 convictions or successful conclusions of prosecutions

- Civil actions: IG investigations led to 973 civil judgments, settlements, or other successful civil cases

- Suspensions and debarments: IG investigations led to 5,114 suspensions and debarments of federal contractors or individuals or entities with business dealings with the federal government

- Personnel actions: IG investigations led to reprimands, suspensions, demotions, or terminations in 4,249 cases of government employees, grantees, or contractors

In thinking about the resources devoted to the IGs and the benefits of their collective efforts, it is important to remember that virtually none of this was in place a generation ago. To understand the current role of federal IGs, it is important to understand not just where we are today but also how we got there.

Origins of the Federal IG System

Paul C. Light wrote the classic history of the federal IG program, published in 1993, and much of what follows is based on his work, although of course not the discussion of events subsequent to 1993.

The modern federal IG system was built on several decades of appointments of individual statutory and nonstatutory inspectors general for different federal agencies and departments.

In 1959, an act of Congress created the job of "inspector general and comptroller" for the State Department. In 1961, Congress made the State Department IG (by then, just "inspector general") a presidential appointment with the advice and consent of the Senate; charged that office with promoting economy and efficiency, in addition to its existing audit and inspection duties; gave it statutory access to State Department records concerning foreign aid that could only be countermanded by a presidential assertion of executive privilege; and authorized up to $2 million annually for its operation, thereby protecting it from budget retaliation from the secretary of state. Unlike subsequent grants of power to IGs, this one included the ability to halt agency activities under its review. The State Department IG no longer has that power, nor such a high level of access to foreign assistance records, with national security implications such as military and security support to various regimes. And indeed, a few years before the enactment of the 1978 Inspector General Act, when the Agency for International Development unilaterally created its own IG, the State Department IG was abolished.

Although the State Department IG was in reality a vital precursor to the modern federal IG, commentators usually credit as seminal the 1962 nonstatutory establishment of the Department of Agriculture IG. Billie Sol Estes, a friend of then Vice President Lyndon Johnson, had become wealthy based on schemes involving defrauding the Department of Agriculture. When the frauds were revealed, in a colloquy between the House Subcommittee chair and Orville Freeman, then secretary of agriculture, the former noted that the Agriculture Department had enough bits of information about Estes to have halted his frauds much earlier, had the information "been in one central office," as opposed to being scattered. Freeman responded that his order would establish an Inspector General to bring all such information—"all audit and investigation work that is taking place anywhere within the Department"—to one place.

But the Agriculture IG was completely subordinate to the Agriculture secretary, to whom the IG reported, and who hired and could fire the IG. Worse, in 1974 Earl Butz, Nixon's choice as agriculture secretary, abolished the entire position, restoring separate offices for investigations and for audits. The IG, although subordinate to the secretary, had been prominent enough to present some challenge to the secretary, by way of public embarrassment if dismissed. By dividing the power and thereby facing far less prominent oversight, Butz would face no significant challenge. His own worst enemy, Butz was forced to resign after his racist and anti-Catholic jokes became public knowledge, and was later convicted of tax evasion. Robert Bergland, secretary under Jimmy Carter, restored the post of Agriculture IG in 1977. This history helped build political support for the understanding that IGs needed a measure of independence from their agency heads.

On December 22, 1974, Seymour Hersh broke the story in *The New York Times* of illegal CIA activities including domestic surveillance, illegal wiretapping, and assassination plots. The 1975 *Report to the President by the Commission on CIA Activities Within the United States* signed by Nelson Rockefeller, Ronald Reagan, and six other prominent commission members, included among its recommendations an increase in the powers and independence of the CIA's nonstatutory IG. This highly credible recommendation, in the freighted context of the clandestine services, also served to build support for the importance of IG independence in less sensitive agencies. However, resistance to a statutory IG at the CIA was not overcome until 1989 and it wasn't until 1996 that the CIA IG, instead of the director of Central Intelligence, was given the power to report illegalities in CIA operations to the attorney general.

A few other federal agencies designated inspectors general over the years. Then a Senate investigation revealed close to $2 billion of Medicaid funds lost to fraud and a House investigation revealed that what was then the Department of Health, Education and Welfare (HEW) had hardly any capacity to combat such fraud (in 1979, Congress split HEW into the Department of Health and Human Services and the Department of Education). As at Agriculture, Congress noted that "Units responsible for combating fraud and abuse were scattered throughout HEW in a haphazard, fragmented, and confusing pattern, with no single unit having the overall responsibility and authority necessary to provide effective leadership." As a result, neither HEW nor Congress could get the information needed to combat fraud and abuse. But Congress had learned a lesson from Butz's abolition of the Agriculture IG. In 1976, Congress legislated the establishment of an IG at HEW (and while it was at it, at the Department of Energy as well, successor to the Atomic Energy Commission).

There was clearly a growing distrust of the federal government. In the 1970s, between Watergate, labor racketeering, and corruption in programs such as the Comprehensive Employment Training Act, drug abuse treatment, and the Summer Food Program for Children, Congress found sufficient political incentive and support to enact major legislation to combat fraud, waste, abuse and corruption. The Senate committee report accompanying the Inspector General Act announced that fraud, waste, and abuse in federal government were "reaching epidemic proportions."

Some members of Congress backed expansion of the IG concept as a means of performing their own oversight role. Individual members have in fact used IG testimony and reports for more personal publicity, either basing serious substantive policy proposals on information so provided, or trumpeting some scandalous findings by an IG. Some observers find that revealing misfeasance wins more points for members of Congress with the press and the public than enacting legislation. In any event, budget deficits make it more difficult and rare to create new or improved policy programs, so by default, members of Congress may focus on investigations. If they have to share attention with IGs who actually uncovered the problems, some attention is better than none.

Thus, the pre-1978 State Department and Agriculture IGs offered two competing models. At State, the IG was envisioned as an independent watchdog and a counterforce to the secretary, and in fact had the power, for a while, of halting State Department operations the IG thought questionable. At Agriculture, the IG was supposed to strengthen the secretary's power to protect the agency against inimical forces, and was expected to give advice and counsel to the secretary: in Light's words, "to dig up the dirt but not spread it."

Congress Makes a Law

Debates within the House Government Operations Committee, between the House and Senate, and between Congress and the executive branch over the best form of the IG Act reflected ongoing issues about the role of the IG that continue to this day.

Ben Rosenthal, a liberal New York Democrat, first fought for his vision of the IG—"junkyard dog"—in trying to shape the bill for the HEW IG. Remembering how Butz abolished the entire IG office in his department, he wanted to make sure that no department head or secretary could fire the IG at will. He wanted an IG that would not be subservient to the secretary, but would focus solely on abuses and weaknesses within the department, without spreading its efforts also over private sector clients of HEW, even if some of those clients were parasites preying on recipients of Social Security or Medicare. Rosenthal's IG would be an investigator with full subpoena powers, not an auditor, with a ten-year term, removable only if impeached, designed to torment an uncooperative HEW secretary to the maximum possible extent.

L.H. Fountain, a conservative North Carolina Democrat, wanted the IG to have audit responsibilities as well as investigative responsibilities, and saw the role at least in large part as working to strengthen the agency by identifying structural weaknesses it could correct, as well as by exposing malfeasance. Thus, the IG would have more opportunity and responsibility for performance monitoring and capacity building, instead of mere compliance monitoring. Fountain's version—"strong right arm" of management—prevailed in the HEW IG bill that Congress enacted in 1976.

But as Congress began to move toward the omnibus IG bill, the Carter administration expressed strong discomfort even with the Fountain model. Because it still included dual reporting, to Congress as well as to the Secretary or agency head, it seemed to place a mole of Congress in each agency. As a result, "all twelve departments covered under the [original] act testified in opposition." Even Congress's own GAO initially disapproved of the legislation, claiming that the fight against waste and fraud "was everyone's responsibility." Perhaps the GAO feared competition on some of its own turf. But the GAO issued three reports that underscored weaknesses the IGs would help to correct: the federal government had far too few auditors for the size of its staff and budget; used inadequate audit tools and techniques; and entirely failed to perform annual financial audits on many of its programs.

By the time it issued the third report, the GAO had moved toward a compromise position, where it would support legislation to establish the office if it included "auditor" in the title, such as "auditor and inspector general." Although ultimately the title remained simply "inspector general," of course the audit function remained at the core of the legislation, along with the investigation function.

The administration's opposition was overcome as well. Joseph Califano, the HEW secretary, was satisfied with the performance of its IG, so his testimony before Fountain's subcommittee essentially told the Carter administration not to worry. Meanwhile, the House made further compromises. It passed a version by Jack Brooks, chair of the entire Government Operations Committee, which was even milder than the Fountain version. Among other things, it removed the IG's power to issue a letter to Congress only seven days after offering it to the department head, and it moved the IGs from some of the smaller agencies into a lower status and less pay, somewhat undercutting their credibility and legitimacy. However, it added a requirement that IGs issue semiannual reports, including a full list of their activities, thereby alerting Congress to everything even possibly suspicious in the agency.

The Carter administration was happy, but the Senate was not. Sen. Thomas Eagleton (D-Miss.) and Abe Ribicoff (D-Conn.) made sure the Senate bill included both the semiannual report and the seven-day letter, put back the original House removal clause (the president could only remove an IG for cause, which had to be explained to both houses of Congress), provided for publication of all IG reports after two months, gave IGs new powers to review proposed bills and regulations, and prohibited agency heads or their deputies from interfering with IG audits, investigations, or subpoenas. This was stronger than Fountain's version, if not as strong as Rosenthal's. The final conference committee bill enacted by both Houses had all these elements, rejecting only Senate efforts to add a Defense Department IG and to adopt the GAO recommendation of calling the job "inspector and auditor general." The Defense Department IG was not established until 1983.

The 1978 bill established twelve new IG offices. The Council of the Inspectors General on Integrity and Efficiency website summarizes the mission of an IG to:

- conduct independent, objective audits, investigations, and inspections;

- prevent and detect waste, fraud, and abuse;

- promote economy, effectiveness, and efficiency;

- review pending legislation and regulations; and

- keep agency heads and Congress fully and currently informed.

In passing the 1978 IG Act, Congress in effect decided that it could combine the pursuit of three kinds of accountability under one officer:

1. compliance accountability: the enforcement of rules and regulations, usually in the context of exposing and punishing fraud, waste, abuse, and corruption by deterring further problems and exposing underlying structural problems;

2. performance accountability: using promotions, bonuses, and other incentives to inspire efficiency and economy; and

3. capacity-based accountability: using careful recruitment, optimal technology, and smart organizational structure to maximize performance success.

The 1978 act also sought to bring together two different approaches to oversight: audits and investigations. According to IG James Richards, "Audits are done of programs and operations, and are general in nature, while investigations are done of allegations of waste, fraud, and abuse, and are specific in nature." Auditors are "introspective, technically oriented," investigators are "gung-ho, go-for-broke." Investigators frequently see the media as the primary audience for investigative reports, whereas auditors primarily see Congress, agency heads. or managers as their primary audience.

By combining the audit and investigation professions under one officer (the IG), Congress reinforced its gamble that very different approaches could be hitched to each other with good results. Auditors determine whether generally accepted accounting principles, standards, and techniques have been correctly used. Investigators catch crooks. By attempting to enforce adherence to proper forms, the former try to assure that organizations operate within a framework that tends to prevent dysfunction of various kinds, criminal as well as merely counterproductive. By catching and exposing dishonesty, the latter try to dissuade potential wrongdoers and reassure the public that their tax dollars are being protected.

The 1978 act, "by establishing the two assistant IGs, one for audit and one for investigation," officially separating the two, may have made it more difficult to merge their talents. In contrast, the US Postal Inspection Service calls both sets of professionals "inspectors." Rivalry isn't the problem; competition can inspire more effort. The bigger concern, according to Light, was that the investigators' ethos seems to dominate, even swallow up, the auditors'. As the GAO testified in 1978, this result favors short-term results at the expense of "the benefits of auditors' suggestions for improving governmental efficiency and economy, recovery of overpayments to contractors and grantees, and identification of ineffective activities and programs."

However, it was the shortage of investigators that provided much of the motivation for the 1978 bill. Eventually IG investigators helped the Civil Division of the Department of Justice by increasingly taking on responsibility for *qui tam* cases under the Federal False Claims Act Amendments of 1986, which strengthened the role of citizens in pursuing those who defraud the federal government; and these have been very worthwhile cases. The FBI also sought and obtained IG assistance in 90 percent of their fraud cases, and would have been hard pressed to meet its responsibilities there otherwise.

The 1978 bill bravely attempted to do a number of additional difficult things.

By making the IGs report to both Congress and the president (and, through the president, implicitly to his or her appointees as heads of their respective agencies), it made them both defenders and attackers of their agencies, a very difficult balance.

It required IGs to be selected "without regard to political affiliation and solely on the basis of integrity and demonstrated ability." Although some appointments reflected this requirement, the fealty of various presidents to the requirement, in other cases, has been much more open to question.

The president can remove any IG, but must notify Congress first—enabling Congress to create a political problem for the president if Congress can show that the removal was unjustified.

IGs are supposed to be somewhat autonomous within their agencies, working with but not controlled by their respective agency heads. Agency heads do not have the authority to interfere with their audits or investigations. IGs can issue warning letters that the agency heads can hold up for seven days, but that go to Congress after that. They, not their agency head, appoint their own top deputy for audit and top deputy for investigations, and can hire and fire their staff. Their power to obtain whatever information they needed for their audits and investigations was supposed to be untrammeled. Any "information, documents, reports, answers, records, accounts, papers, and other data and documentary evidence" they need for this purpose must be supplied to them, and they have subpoena power for such documents, although not for witness testimony.

Carter and Reagan IGs

The selection process for IGs reflected some of the same conflicts that arose during legislative debate. An existing non-IG employee of an agency may understand the agency better than others, and have a gentler learning curve as IG, but poses the risk for over-identification with and overprotectiveness toward the agency. An existing IG staff employee of an agency in some way poses a worse risk: Selection by the agency head may suggest that the agency head is too comfortable with the IG, and sends a message that junior IG staff, if they please the agency head, may someday be appointed IG. Both IG and non-IG agency staff also would come to the IG role with years of friendship and perhaps enmity with various other employees of the agency, either being unfortunate baggage for that role.

The Carter administration, hiring the first IGs under the new statute, wisely did not ask the agencies for recommendations, but recruited on its own, and then offered each agency two or three names over which they had no veto, but could express their opinions. Light quotes a Carter White House staff member as pointing out that if the agency heads had been allowed to pick their own IGs, they would have picked weak ones, as less challenging and threatening to their control. But the Carter administration probably made a mistake in having the agency heads, by and large, notify the IGs of their appointment, thus signaling that the IGs were part of the "team." The Reagan administration, more astutely, tended to have the OMB welcome them to their new posts. Nonetheless, unfortunately, "most IGs believed the department or agency had a prominent role in their selection."

Still, most IGs were not welcomed warmly by their agencies. Even with the best of intentions, high-level administrators resented losing audit and investigation powers to outsiders, saw the IGs as adversarial, and concluded therefore that they would fragment and undermine agency responsibility and morale. The Carter IGs came in as the Civil Service Reform Act was being implemented, with assistant secretary appointments taken out of the Civil Service and made political, along with personnel ceilings, so IGs, who took many of those slots, were especially unpopular. The Reagan IGs came in with extra baggage too, since they were generally introduced by OMB, not by the agency heads.

The Carter IGs quickly faced a hiring freeze, which left many of them very short-staffed. After a while, "Congress and the president took [staff] from government offices that worked on the front-end of the policy process to supply the search for fraud, waste, and abuse at the back end." Slightly more of the Carter IGs thought of offering their audit work to Congress than to their agency head or agency program managers. But twice as many Reagan IGs thought in terms of offering their audit work to agency heads or managers than to Congress. As to investigations, a plurality of each group saw US attorneys as their primary audience, but the plurality among the Carter group was much greater (50 percent as opposed to 32 percent), with most of the difference accounted for by the much larger percentage of the Reagan group who would present to agency personnel first.

The Reagan group, despite their initially chilly welcome from the agencies, saw congressional pressure as their main problem, while the Carter group mostly had trouble organizing their own IG offices, presumably because of interference by their agencies. However, the Reagan group reported almost as much resistance to change from their agencies as did the Carter group.

Light quotes a Carter IG as saying "Everybody wants a strong IG operation until it starts investigating them." The Reagan administration wanted to cut spending, did not want to hear reports that called for more investment in agency capacity, and clearly signaled its preference for compliance monitoring. Reagan fired all the Carter IGs, ultimately rehiring two at existing agencies and three at new agencies. The signal to the new IGs was to rack up "dollars saved and cheaters caught" to score points with this administration.

One justification for the mass firing was that targeted firings could have resulted in lawsuits alleging one or another form of discrimination, perhaps on the basis of political views, which would have violated the provisions of the 1978 statute prohibiting political considerations in filling the posts. Another was that it was more humane to fire them all, so that no one would take it personally. But the firings created considerable insecurity among IGs, and infuriated key members of Congress and the press.

Although he probably did it to counteract the bad press from the firings, Reagan's creation of a new organization composed of the IGs, the President's Council on Integrity and Efficiency (PCIE), would ultimately serve as a useful lobby for the IGs, even though it was headed by an OMB deputy director. That director, Ed Harper, and his successor, Joe Wright, would become strong allies of and proponents for the IGs. Under their leadership, the IGs themselves became the primary recruiters of new IGs, throughout the Reagan administration. Not surprisingly, this resulted in the vast majority of new IGs having previously served on the staff of other IGs, which is how the IGs got to know the new candidates. The agency head could still register disapproval, which the Reagan administration might honor, but the alternative names on the list were not likely to be very different. OMB had the final say (although of course nominally Reagan himself had the final say).

OMB also did much to alleviate the staff shortages that IGs had faced under Carter, by supporting IG budget requests much more fully—indeed, for the duration of the Reagan hiring freeze, allowing the IGs to bypass it. Congress supported and encouraged the IG up-staffing as well. Light was not fully enthusiastic about this. He quoted, sympathetically, a common sentiment of federal managers: "I wish I had as many people doing as I have reviewing."

OMB, charged with fulfilling the funding requirements for the president's agenda, benefited from the identification of mismanagement or high risk for fraud in an agency's programs and operations identified by the IGs. As a result, OMB won increased bragging rights for the Reagan Administration to claim victories against fraud, waste, abuse, and corruption, and the IGs won more independence from their agencies. Now, however, instead of, or in addition to, distrusting their relationship with Congress, the agencies distrusted the IGs' relationship with OMB.

By 1985, the IGs' relationships with Congress had weakened considerably, but their relationships with their own agencies seemed to have strengthened. Agency resistance to change only bothered about 20 percent of them, compared with 50 percent of the 1979 group and 61 percent of the 1981 group. Only 20 percent would first bring their audit findings to Congress, as compared with 42 percent of the 1979 group. Seventy percent would first bring them to agency heads or managers. Only 10 percent would first bring their investigative findings to Congress compared with 25 percent of the 1979 group. Fifty percent would first bring them to agency heads or managers (and 30 percent to the US attorney, as compared with 50 percent of the 1979 group).

In 1988, just a decade after the initial IG Act was passed, Congress passed a series of amendments.

IGs won an important measure of security when the Inspector General Act Amendments of 1988 provided that if they were fired as IGs, they would remain members of the senior executive service and therefore would continue to serve in relatively high levels of the federal government. Thus, noted one IG, the IGs became members of the " 'Go-to-Hell' club"—an IG could now do the right thing at considerable political risk, because if he or she would still have a good job if fired as IG, and "become a 'hero' " to boot.

Congress also created IGs for Treasury and the Justice Department, although Justice's Office of Professional Responsibility would continue to monitor alleged misbehavior by the US attorneys. IGs would get their own separate appropriations independent of their agencies' budgets. Congress created IGs in thirty-three additional agencies, mostly small ones but including the US Postal Service, who would be selected by agency heads. These IGs would not get appropriations separate and independent from those of their agencies. However, the agency head would be prohibited from interfering with their work, and would have to report reasons to Congress if he or she were to fire the IG.

IGs Under Bush I

With the inauguration of the first President Bush in 1989, the "glory years" of the IGs ended. First, Congress had to intervene when the head of the 5,000-employee Government Printing Office fired and replaced his IG with a compliant one, who agreed to lose about half of his forty-two staff members and downgrade the titles of others. Then, the Bush administration failed to appoint Justice and Treasury IGs for over a year and for nine months, respectively, and left at least five other presidentially appointed IG positions open for a year as well. The IGs already in place were not officially reappointed, and did not know whether they would be. OMB no longer let the IGs recruit replacements; recruitment reverted to the White House, and the White House gave the agencies much more influence on the selection of IGs. The White House itself politicized the process somewhat: a few of the small agencies got former Bush Secret Service agents as IGs, and Mary Sterling, a former Bush campaign worker who served for three years as an assistant US attorney, with brief experiences in other high-level federal posts, was appointed Transportation IG in 1990.

In 1989, the solicitor of the Labor Department, instead of resolving the internal question of whether the Labor IG could take over some criminal investigation responsibilities that Labor's Pension Welfare Benefits Administration actually wanted to get rid of, or at worst asking the Office of Legal Counsel of the Justice Department to answer that narrow question, insisted on an answer from Justice to the broader question of whether the Labor IG could investigate any statutory violations under the Labor Department's jurisdiction, and therefore by extension whether any IG could investigate any statutory violations under its agency's jurisdiction. Douglas Kmiec, for Justice, responded that the IG "may investigate the Department's conduct of regulatory investigations but may not conduct such [regulatory] investigations himself." That is, says Light, "If the statute did not involve a federal employee or a federal dollar, and was therefore regulatory in nature, the IG was not to be concerned." The Kmiec memo was based on a likely misreading of the legislative history of the 1978 statute.

Although IGs could probably find ways to circumvent the Kmiec memo, it appeared to reflect a general lack of sympathy for IGs in the new administration. The HHS IG, Richard Kusserow, had been investigating FDA generic drug approvals, initially when manufacturers were thought to have bribed FDA officials to get those approvals, but then, also by means of defrauding the FDA officials. On the basis of the Kmiec memo, the former would have been a legitimate focus of an IG investigation, because federal employees would have been involved in the misbehavior under scrutiny, but not the latter. So, in 1990 the HHS Secretary stopped the Kusserow investigation and turned it over the regular FDA inspectors. The House Energy and Commerce Subcommittee on Oversight and Investigation accused FDA of leaving consumers vulnerable to fraudulent generic drugs on this basis. OMB did not or could not resolve the matter. Sen. John Glenn, however, held up the nomination of William Barr as deputy attorney general pending resolution of the dispute. Barr himself worked out the "compromise," after which the IGs went back to business as usual.

In light of the Kmiec memo, in 1992 the Education Department IG fought to retain his own counsel and not use department counsel. The IG and the education secretary might become adversarial. The department counsel had offered to assign one attorney permanently and solely to IG issues, but under the condition that her signed written legal advice must be cleared by department counsel, she couldn't represent the IG when the IG was in conflict with the secretary or in any way when she hadn't gotten clearance, and the IG had to try to resolve any issue with counsel before taking a contrary position. Again, Glenn intervened and got the IG his own independent counsel.

IGs Under Clinton, Bush II, and Obama

The 1992 Executive Order that established the PCIE, the body that in theory promotes inter-IG cooperation and advancement, also provided for it to be chaired by the deputy director for management of OMB. Clay Johnson III, who served in that role under Bush II, undermined the independence of the IGs with messages stressing their role in working "cooperatively" and "more closely with agency management." Alice Rivlin, when she was deputy director of OMB under Clinton, communicated a very similar message. More than 60 percent of George W. Bush's IGs had prior political experience, as contrasted with less than 25 percent of Bill Clinton's IGs.

During the past decade, Congress has turned increasingly to the IG concept to address concerns over fraud, waste, abuse, and corruption—almost to the exclusion of exercising its own investigative and oversight powers.

For example, Congress established the Special Inspector General for Iraq Reconstruction (SIGIR) in 2004, in the same legislation that authorized the expenditure of $18 billion for such reconstruction, and in order to promote economy and efficiency and detect and prevent fraud, waste, and corruption in the context of that expenditure. The SIGIR reports to both the Departments of State and Defense, as well as to Congress. Like the chair of the Recovery Accountability and Transparency Board, created to monitor administration of the 2009 stimulus package (see later), the SIGIR emphasizes proactive measures, like more careful assessment of the actual needs of Iraqis before committing US dollars to investments. Unlike the Recovery Board, the SIGIR has identified a very substantial amount of waste in the Iraq Reconstruction program: between $5 billion and $6 billion, or about 10 percent of the total spending of about $53 billion on the program since 2003. The SIGIR has effectively identified significant fraud, waste, and abuse. However, the elected branches of government do not seem to have the will to take meaningful measures against the most powerful of the companies, like Halliburton, that continue these practices.

In 2008, Congress adopted the Inspector General Reform Act of 2008. That act abolished bonus and merit awards for IGs, and raised their pay; it also established the Council of Inspectors General on Integrity and Efficiency, to be chaired by the deputy director of OMB. The latter provision created an organization that could play the same role that the PCIE played in the Reagan years, when the PCIE essentially became not only the trade union and lobby for the IGs, but the body that in practice selected many of the successor IGs. However, nothing guarantees that the president will allow the new CIGIE to play quite as strong a role. The role of OMB is substantially different: At the PCIE, the OMB sets the agenda, tilting IG allegiances toward the president; at the CIGIE, the OMB is more like the secretary, with less influence over the IG agenda. The 2008 legislation reflected Democratic Congressional reaction to the infiltration of the White House/OMB into the IG's independence. Under the 2008 IG Reform Act, the IG Council now has the authority and the resources to investigate allegations of IG misconduct, and if necessary to expose established wrongdoing.

Another provision of the law now clearly established the right of each IG to have his or her own counsel, independent of counsel to the agency. An agency counsel, in an agency in which the IG did not have independent counsel, insisted on major redactions in an IG report before he would allow it to be posted publicly. The IG disagreed, but had no choice. Nonstatutory IGs were members of the Executive Council on Integrity and Efficiency (ECIE), while statutory IGs were members of the PCIE. The three legislative IGs—for the Library of Congress, the Government Printing Office, and the Capitol Police—were statutory (under other, individual statutes) but were also members of the ECIE, to avoid placing them even under a limited degree of executive control via the PCIE. However, the 2008 Reform Act merged the two councils into the CIGIE or IG Council, provided it with some funding for IG training and the advancement of the profession, and gave it staff counsel whose services would be made available "on a reimbursable basis" to the designated federal entities (DFE) IGs, who did not have their own independent counsel and could not borrow counsel from another IG.

The 2008 Reform Act also took an important step toward alleviating the politicization of IG appointments by authorizing the new IG Council to recommend IG candidates to the president and, for non-presidential appointments, to agency heads. Another problem was that while the 1978 IG Act required that statutory IGs be appointed on the basis of objective qualifications, the requirement did not apply to nonstatutory (now, more accurately, "non-presidentially appointed") IGs. The IG Reform Act of 2008, P.L. 110-409, remedied this deficiency as well, imposing that requirement on all IGs.

The American Recovery and Reinvestment Act of 2009, famously providing $787 billion in an attempt to stimulate economic recovery after the fiscal crisis of 2008, included provisions for the creation of the Recovery Accountability and Transparency Board to prevent, combat, and expose fraud, waste, and corruption in the use of those monies. The thirteen members of the board are all sitting federal IGs, and the chair is a former IG. The board acts as a sort of super IG, empowered by the legislation to audit and investigate expenditures of the stimulus funding.

If the viewpoint of the chair represents the prevailing attitude, this new generation of IGs has moved beyond the "gotcha" notion of oversight. In his testimony to the House Oversight and Government Reform Committee on June 14, 2011, the chair proudly reported open investigations on "less than half a percent of all reported Recovery contracts, grants, and loans," criminal convictions reflecting less than $2 million out of the roughly $630 billion of the stimulus money spent by that date. The chair recognized that neither he nor anyone else can identify undetected fraud. Still, he relied on the wealth of talent and experience at the disposal of the board to remain reasonably confident that the incidence of fraud, waste, and abuse was in fact minimal, and not by accident. The board had "trained more than 130,000 people in fraud prevention." Early on, testifying before the same committee in March 2009, he had made it quite clear that while fraud detection remained an important goal, the board regards fraud prevention as the higher priority.

Conclusion

Thirty-five years after the creation of the federal IG system, some of the same tensions that were discussed during the debate over its creation remain unresolved.

There is tension inherent in the structural design that requires the IG to report to agency heads, which can subvert the loyalty of IGs to Congress and to the public at large. A well-documented letter of 2007 from the executive director of the Project on Government Oversight (POGO) to OMB accused the NASA and SEC IGs of protecting officials of their agencies against important investigations instead of pursuing those investigations in an appropriately independent manner; and accused the Commerce Department IG of retaliating against employees who were investigating his own abuse of government resources. In 2003, the HHS IG and the Postal Service IG resigned in the face of allegations that they had respectively tried to undermine an investigation and wasted public funds.

Controversy generated by this structure persisted into President Obama's administration when the president removed Gerald Walpin, the IG for the Corporation for National and Community Service (AmeriCorps), after a report from that IG criticizing a strong Obama supporter, Kevin Johnson, a former NBA star and subsequently mayor of Sacramento, California.

Although he left on his own initiative, Neil Barofsky, the Special Inspector General for the Troubled Assets Relief Program from late 2008 through early 2011, revealed far more serious efforts to interfere with his work by both the Bush and the Obama administrations. *Bailout*, his 2012 book, offers the fascinating details of the back-and-forth between an IG and the Treasury Department whose behavior he tried, and occasionally succeeded, in conforming to the public interest.

While in Barofsky's circumstances, every ounce of effort he could bring to the adversarial side of his job was more than warranted, sometimes there is pressure on IGs to stress compliance monitoring at the expense of performance monitoring and capacity-building, and related pressure to stress the investigator side of the office at the expense of the auditor side.

Barofsky, a credible source, denies that most IGs meet their responsibility to act as "fiercely independent watchdogs." Still, under some circumstances, Light can be correct that there is too much reliance on compliance monitoring, "a metaphor for a broad philosophy of government that rests more on fear than inducement." Compliance monitoring generates pressure for the kind of reforms "that are less expensive, more politically palatable, cleaner jurisdictionally, and faster to implement" than the kinds of reform that capacity-based accountability brings forward. Light may have been thinking of H.L. Mencken's line, "For every complex problem, there is an answer that is simple, neat, and wrong."

According to POGO, "there are some who believe IGs should be helping agencies prevent problems rather than merely uncover them (working on the big picture vs. playing 'gotcha')." POGO then says "the real value of an IG is the ability to bring the critical outsider's eye into the agency." But the two are not incompatible. IGs should be "buzzing at management like mad hornets" until officials adopted such recommendations. Some IGs take foolish, wrongheaded pride in not "aiming for headlines." When bureaucratic intransigence blocks reform, "the IG's work must be shouted from the rooftops." Although the comments just quoted reflect POGO's impatience with passive IGs, it also recognized that IGs can go too far in the other direction, by releasing reports to the media without first submitting them to their agencies and to Congress. This kind of behavior hurts their credibility with the agencies and with Congress and may, at least in the long run, reduce their impact.

The quality of IGs' work is measured by their effectiveness, and often, the effect of their semiannual reports. The 1978 act requires IGs to include in their semiannual reports masses of statistical data and lengthy lists, often resulting in extremely boring reports, and possibly, in further consequence, causing their congressional audiences not to read them. As we saw, this may have been an important cause of the failure of Congress to prevent the HUD scandals of the 1980s under Secretary Pierce, despite warnings buried in the relevant IG reports. For example, the act requires IGs to list "matters referred to prosecutive [sic] authorities and the prosecutions and convictions which have resulted." But such referrals could be good cases or bad cases, sloppy referrals or the results of careful investigation, major matters or unimportant; and a focus on the referral of criminal cases could be wise, or reflect a foolish disregard for far more important civil or administrative matters or issues of performance monitoring or capacity-building.

Similarly, the semiannual reports must include "questioned costs" but such listings need not and often do not indicate whether the expenditures were ever recouped. Especially when the items on such lists are trivial and multitudinous, such lists are not only boring but virtually useless. Some of the fault lies with Congress, which for example has since 1906 required the State Department to review each and every one of its diplomatic posts in the world at least every five years, so the State Department IG, inheriting the job, runs down the same check-list of items at each post.

Clearly, reports stressing goals, objectives, and recommendations would be more useful. Among other things, Congress could tell whether an OIG's goals and objectives for its forthcoming audits and investigations target the main vulnerabilities and problems it identified at its agency.

Certainly any IG can be intolerant of injustice and abuse, and many are. Any IG who understands the responsibilities of the office must engage in meaningful oversight. And with documentary subpoena power, the IG has more ability to gather information than many others engaged in oversight; the absence of testimonial subpoena power disadvantages the IG no more than it disadvantages most other "watchdogs."

But some institutional realities constrain the ability of a federal IG to adhere to our guiding principles. When it comes to using "the continued threat of bad publicity" and follow-up, the IG sometimes faces limitations. A purely adversarial approach may be inconsistent with the IG's full mandate, which is to strengthen the agency as well as criticize it. Also, because the IG reports to the agency as well as to Congress, the personal relationships involved may make the adversarial relationship uncomfortable.

Some federal IGs have nonetheless been harshly critical of their agencies. But that attitude can worsen a different serious problem. Often, effective follow-up requires the hiring of more expert professional, better staff training, more sophisticated information technology, or simply more personnel. With modern-day resistance to spending, IGs have a hard enough time persuading Congress to allocate such resources. If the IG also levels harsh criticism at the agency, Congress will be even more loathe to "reward" it with support.

Thus, on the spectrum of oversight roles ranging from protective to adversarial, federal IGs often, of necessity, fall into the middle range. This need not be a bad thing, but it makes adherence to some of our oversight principles more problematic.

Under Dodd-Frank, Congress required the GAO "to report on the relative independence, effectiveness and expertise of inspectors general." In its September 2011 report, the GAO found that the federal IGs reported potential savings of $43.3 billion resulting from FY 2009 audits and investigations. With a budget of $2.3 billion, the IGs identified savings of $18 for every dollar invested. IGs also reported 5,900 criminal actions, 1,100 civil actions, 4,400 suspensions and debarments of federal contractors and 6,100 criminal indictments—thus validating the perception of the inspectors general as the "cops on the beat" on the fraud, waste, abuse, and corruption corner. Estimates of "potential savings" no doubt exceed real savings, and probably by a substantial margin. The various defects of the IG system need remediation. Still, overall it seems rather clear that the federal IGs have proven their worth.

Chapter 8

State Legislative Oversight

A legislative body—be it the British House of Commons, or either house of Congress, or a state legislature—is endowed with the investigative power in order to obtain information, so that its legislative functions may be discharged in an enlightened rather than a benighted basis.

—Telford Taylor, Grand Inquest:
The Story of Congressional Investigations (1955)

Both of us started our careers in government as interns. Feldman worked as an intern in the mayoral administration of John Lindsay where he worked on the creation of a new, administrative process for adjudicating parking tickets in New York—the Parking Violations Bureau (PVB). Little did he realize that he had helped to create a monster—one that a decade later he would help to reform after it was the center of one of the worst corruption scandals in New York City history.

In 1980, when Feldman was running for the State Assembly, he received multiple parking tickets—all on the same day—for having an expired vehicle registration or tag. He paid all of the tickets. Some months later, he went to register his new car. After waiting in line for hours, just as he thought he was about to get his new registration, the clerk at the window said, "Oh no. Sorry. We cannot give you your registration. You owe $200 in parking fines." Having paid that figure quite memorably, Feldman tried to persuade the clerk, to no avail. The clerk told him he could not argue with the computer.

The next day Feldman found his cancelled check, and took it down to the PVB headquarters on Chambers Street in Manhattan. There, clerks found the record of payment, but explained that the computer with *that* information was not compatible with the computer that told the Department of Motor Vehicles about unpaid tickets.

Feldman thought that some publicity might encourage the PVB to invest in a computer that treated citizens better, so he sent out a press release. One of the tabloids picked up the story. The PVB changed nothing, but Feldman began hearing from motorists all over New York City with similar tales of woe, stories about dunning letters threatening liens on their homes for tickets they had already paid, or tickets that they had proven were improperly issued. The effort required to prove that they did not owe the money often involved days off from work, which most could not afford. Essentially, the PVB's message meant "pay us this money you do not owe us, or we will take your car or your house, or you will lose several days of pay fighting us." When someone says "pay money you do not owe, or the alternative will be worse," we call that extortion. This was extortion.

Feldman decided to sue the city on the grounds that it "enforced" the parking laws in an arbitrary and capricious manner. The judge said, "You're a legislator. Change the law!" Feldman took the advice. He wrote a bill enabling a motorist to be paid up to the amount the PVB wrongfully demanded, as long as the motorist could prove that he or she had already sent proof that the demand was unjustified. This would not merely refund a wrongful bill the motorist paid, but it would be money out-of-pocket for the city, with the motorist refusing to pay the new bill altogether. Feldman theorized that such legislation would give the city a financial incentive to make its system fairer.

Oversight demands results, not just complaints. While lobbying against his bill in Albany, the PVB instituted a proceeding to allow motorists to fight wrongfully issued tickets by mail. In 1984, the Assembly passed the bill, but the city lobbyists held the Senate in check, despite an editorial of June 26, 1984 in Albany's *Knickerbocker News* that called on them to pass it, pointing out that "Bureaucracy should pay for its mistakes—not the motorist."

In March 1985, US Attorney Rudolph Giuliani was investigating the way the PVB had awarded a contract to supply handheld devices to identify parking scofflaws by their license plate numbers. That investigation would target Queens Borough President Donald Manes—who committed suicide—and would lead to the imprisonment of the head of the Bronx Democratic party, the former city transportation commissioner, the PVB director, and the deputy PVB director. By 1987, it also resulted in the revelation that the PVB's extortion, as Feldman called it, had been netting the city about $20 million a year, or about one-eighth of the PVB's total revenues at the time, much of which, of course, was landing in the pockets of the various miscreants who were stealing from it. Roughly 80,000 citizens *a year* complained about the wrongful dunning. Under the pressure of what was now a barrage of support for Feldman's legislation, the Senate finally acceded. The PVB's new director announced that it had replaced its old data systems. Ray Kerrison, a columnist for the New York *Post*, wrote under the headline "Feldman writes final chapter to PVB harassment," "With new technology, new management and the Feldman-Goodman bill, the PVB should finally become a reasonably efficient and honest government operation. It's time."

This chapter discusses the role that state legislatures play in the oversight of the state executive branch. Feldman served as the principal investigator for three years for an oversight subcommittee and then an oversight full committee of the New York State legislature, and then for eighteen years as a member and as a committee chair with the responsibility for oversight of the state's jails and prisons in that same legislature. Because that history gives us access to a rich mine of detailed oversight data, this chapter focuses disproportionately, overwhelmingly even, on his work.

Still, the chapter touches on the work of other legislatures and other legislators, like the special joint legislative oversight committee in Texas that oversees a particular water district, or the general joint legislative committee for oversight in Iowa, or various state legislative committees and commissions on administrative rules and regulations.

An Overview of State Legislative Oversight

The underlying theory of legislative oversight at the state level is much the same as it is for Congressional oversight at the federal level. Legislators should oversee the implementation of programs and laws that they have adopted and enacted. Moreover, state legislative oversight can play the same role of "informing" public opinion as congressional oversight does at the national level.

According to the National Conference of State Legislators, state legislatures have increased their capacity to engage in oversight over the past three decades—coinciding with the aftermath of the "heyday" of congressional oversight and the Senate Watergate Committee discussed in Chapter 5.

State legislatures mimic Congress in organization and structure. As a result, state legislative oversight is performed through many of the same vehicles—standing committees on particular areas of government may engage in oversight; some legislatures may have special oversight committees; and legislatures engage in oversight during the budget process as well.

The nature of separation of powers at the state level is, however, somewhat more complicated. State legislatures engage in more direct forms of oversight. For example, administrative review committees can advise their legislatures to override certain regulations issued by the executive. Moreover, legislative members are frequently represented on certain boards and commissions that possess executive authority.

For example, in New York, the Public Authorities Control Board must approve certain financings and construction projects by eleven of the state's public authorities before they can proceed. Although the governor appoints the chair and members of the board, four of the five-member board are appointed on the recommendation of the Speaker of the Assembly and the Senate Majority Leader: all are legislators.

In Tennessee, the State Building Commission is responsible for approving projects and contracts related to improvements, acquisitions, leases, and disposal of state property. The commission's seven members include the governor, the commissioner of finance and administration, the secretary of state (appointed by the legislature), the comptroller (again, appointed by the legislature), the Speaker of the House of Representatives, and the leader of the Senate.

State legislatures generally do not have all of the same tools that Congress has to perform their oversight function. For example, few legislatures have quasi-independent arms like the GAO. California may be the closest with its Legislative Analyst's Office, overseen by a sixteen-member bipartisan committee. Even large states like New York have no comparable support for its legislature, instead relying on staff personnel that work for individual members, legislative leaders, and committees.

Unlike members of Congress, most state legislators are part-time, limiting the amount of time and attention that they can and do devote to their oversight role—as opposed to, for example, constituent services. A 2009 National Conference of State Legislators analysis divided the fifty state legislatures into three categories—red, white, and blue. Members of red legislatures spend approximately 80 percent of their time working as legislators—and earning salaries allowing them to do so. Members of white legislatures annually spend about 66 percent of their time on legislative business and generally must supplement their compensation with other work. Finally, members of blue legislatures spend only about 50 percent their time on legislative work and earn an average of $15,000 a year in compensation. As of 2009, there were just four red legislatures, six "light" red legislatures, twenty-three white legislatures, and seventeen blue legislatures.

The same study also addressed another hindrance on state legislative oversight—the general lack of staff resources. On average, red legislatures had 8.9 staff members—both central staff and staff assigned to individual members—per legislator, compared with 3.1 staff per legislator in white legislatures and just 1.2 staff per member in blue legislatures. California's nationally recognized Legislative Analyst's Office oversees California's $85.9 billion budget with approximately sixty analysts and support staff.

Role of the Standing Committee: New York Assembly Committee on Correction

New York State Assembly Speaker Mel Miller created the Assembly Committee on Correction in 1987. Before his ascension to the speakership that year, he had chaired the Assembly Codes Committee, with jurisdiction over the state's criminal code as well as all other bills involving criminal penalties, and also over the funding and laws governing prisons and jails in the state. When he appointed Feldman as its first chair, he explained to Feldman that with the growth in the state's prison population from 12,500 in 1972 to more than 40,000 by 1987, the Codes chair—dealing with the death penalty, then a hot issue, dozens of controversial criminal procedure questions, and more than 1,000 other bills each session—simply did not have the time to devote to the oversight the state's prisons and jails clearly warranted.

The Committee on Correction would review far fewer bills than Codes—perhaps one-tenth as many, if that—but could oversee the operation of a system costing more than $1 billion a year. If it met its responsibilities, it would determine whether that money was properly spent, where it should spend more and where it should spend less, and what other changes it needed to perform better. In some ways, then, the history of that committee offers an unusually illuminating picture of the oversight function of a standing committee of a state legislature.

Oversight of Budget and Operations

The chair took his responsibilities seriously. In 1987, his first year, he would stay in his office till 1 am or so at least one night a week studying all he could find that might illuminate his new responsibilities. At the same time, with David Hopkins, his diligent committee counsel, and Terry Crowley, his hard-charging program assistant, he went on the road, visiting most of the state's 53 prisons, or "correctional facilities," generally located in far-flung, rural, lonely communities. Correction officers regularly and persuasively complained that staffing had not kept up with the population increases, so in the fall, Feldman convened and chaired hearings on staffing levels in Albany, Buffalo, New York City, and Plattsburgh.

He found that many inmates had fallen victim to the AIDS epidemic. Many more inmates than in the past, therefore, needed to visit outside medical facilities. Someone other than the inmate had to drive, and someone else had to guard the inmate. Management did not factor this need into staffing calculations. Management, attempting to put a more acceptable face on reality, also designated many correction officer posts as "contingency" posts, posts that did not always or necessarily have to be staffed, so they did not have to count them as unfilled, even if leaving them unfilled in reality would endanger other officers and inmates. And management did not properly factor into their staff-need calculations legitimate Workers Compensation and sick leave absences. All told, the committee found that the system needed 757 more officers.

The committee did not limit its inquiries to staffing needs. It learned that developmentally disabled inmates, more than physically weak inmates, suffered disproportionate bullying and abuse by other inmates. After a joint hearing with the Assembly Committee on Mental Health, Mental Retardation and Developmental Disabilities, the committees recommended the construction of three fifty-bed Special Needs Units for inmates with developmental disabilities, mental retardation, learning disabilities, and similar vulnerabilities.

The committee did not shout its recommendations into a vacuum. The chair used his authority to insist on inserting into the state budget for FY 1988–89 funding for "three 50-bed Special Residential Units for inmates with developmental disabilities," and at the substantial initiative of Terry Crowley at the staff level, "two mental health units . . . for up to 60 mentally ill patients" each, in response to the growing awareness of the migration of the mentally ill from the old state "warehouse" facilities for them, which had been closed, to the streets, to the prisons.

Feldman saw increasingly that the massive incarceration of low-level nonviolent drug offenders under the Rockefeller drug laws was driving the increase in the prison population, at enormous cost to taxpayers and at the expense of more productive uses of tax dollars. The politics of New York State was still far too conservative for Feldman to win outright repeal of the Rockefeller drug laws, but he could use the Correction Law to shape *how* sentences would be served, and with that "back-door" approach cut losses.

In the 1987 budget negotiations, as the Assembly's representative for prison issues, he negotiated with Republican Sen. Christopher Mega, chair of the Crime and Correction Committee in that House, and with Larry Kurlander, the governor's criminal justice coordinator, radical changes in incarceration policy known as "shock incarceration" and "earned eligibility." The former allowed certain qualifying inmates who would otherwise serve much longer sentences to go through a type of "boot camp" training for six months, followed by parole. The latter, for longer-term inmates who qualified by successfully completing in-prison drug abuse treatment programs or educational programs, would automatically qualify for parole upon their first eligible parole release date, when most inmates are not paroled until their second or third such parole hearing.

Also at Feldman's initiative, in view of his new awareness that the overwhelming majority of inmates had substance abuse problems, that 1987 budget included language requiring every state prison to have a drug abuse treatment program. By the end of 1988, he was able to report that although only eighteen facilities had such programs in 1987, almost all of the now fifty-four facilities had them. Only 2,594 inmates had undergone such treatment in the first five months of 1987; 4,678 inmates had done so in the first five months of 1988.

The committee also learned that AIDS transmission within prison from some sexual encounters and even some drug use in prison via smuggled-in needles could be deterred by educating many inmates with so little education or sophistication that they actually did not know any better. However, inmates so distrusted prison officials that the internal AIDS education program had little effect. But because prison administrators tend toward xenophobia, they had refused to allow outside educators to come in.

At Feldman's insistence, the 1987 budget also included more than $1 million for the AIDS Institute, a private, not-for-profit outside expert organization, to provide that training. But xenophobia won out: The prison system dragged its feet, the state did not transmit the money to the AIDS Institute, and the inmates never got the training.

With the Rockefeller drug laws still driving low-level addicts into prison, Feldman could not resist the pressure to build more cells. He acceded to demands from correction officers and politicians to fund thirteen new prison facilities, with 5,900 new beds, in the 1989 budget. But he got 2,150 of the beds to be designated for drug abuse treatment, two more special needs units for developmentally disabled inmates, $6.7 million for 481 additional officers, and a new appropriation of $1.4 million for the AIDS Institute—this time, with a firm commitment to use it.

By 1990, Feldman's frustration with the Rockefeller drug laws had increased. His annual report for that year called for "outright repeal of that part of the second felony offender law which forces us to incarcerate non-violent, low-level, infinitely replaceable addicted sellers of drugs. . . . There is no rational argument to support our present policy, which is the incarceration of [those] whose removal from the street makes no difference to the drug trade and whose prosecution and incarceration wastes scarce resources we so desperately need for violent criminals." In February 1991 he argued against the Rockefeller drug laws again, on the Op Ed page of *The New York Times*, noting that "Arrest and incarceration of low-level addicted peddlers directs scarce resources away from where they would best hamper the drug trade. . . . Our streets are more dangerous, not safer. We can hardly do worse. We can easily do better." But he still couldn't get the legislature to go along.

However, Feldman's oversight efforts, his recognition of the inefficient and counterproductive nature of the state government's approach toward the illegal drug problem, helped build the foundation of public and editorial opinion on which repeal of the Rockefeller drug laws would finally rest in 2009.

Oversight of Abuse and Localized Management Deficiencies

While Feldman continued his efforts to force more rational allocations of budgetary resources for the prison system as a whole, he began to investigate specific complaints at individual prisons as well. Of course he regularly received dozens of letters a month from inmates with complaints, but for the most part they either reflected unrealistic perceptions and hopes or they could be resolved fairly readily with a telephone call to Correction Commissioner Thomas Coughlin or his staff, who had become increasingly responsive. However, when seven inmates and ten prison staff suffered serious injuries in a riot at Wende Correctional Facility outside Buffalo in May 1990, Feldman and Hopkins personally interviewed inmates and staff at the facility. They found it apparent that overcrowding created a "tinder box," but once again were forced to agree to new construction in face of their inability to repeal the Rockefeller drug laws causing the overcrowding.

On May 7, 1991, at the request of deeply concerned correction officers and George Winner, the Republican Assembly colleague representing the area, Feldman visited the Southport Correctional Facility near Elmira, New York. Southport had opened in 1986 as a maximum-security facility, but starting in January of 1991 it had become a much more dangerous place. The Department of Corrections was now using it to house inmates who had been administratively sentenced to "segregated housing units" and solitary confinement—inmates whose behavior in prison was out of control, who had killed other inmates or assaulted guards or committed other serious violations. Southport was now a "maxi-max": entirely populated by inmates in solitary confinement. The other prisons no longer had enough room for all the inmates they so assigned. Traditionally, the worst inmates and the worst officers were assigned to the worst prisons, known for brutality. Feldman had agreed that the Southport approach promised to be more civilized.

However, Feldman saw that the officers' concerns had a very serious basis. He and Winner suited up in head-to-toe plastic coveralls to protect themselves against "throwers": inmates who would throw their own feces at officers. As they toured the facility, they saw flimsy fences in the exercise pens, poor security in the visiting rooms, lockers with thin metal frames suitable for conversion into "shivs" or homemade knives, and, as usual, insufficient staffing levels. While they were there, one inmate stabbed another. Immediately after the tour, Feldman sent an urgent message to Coughlin calling on him to remedy these vulnerabilities, predicting that otherwise inmates could stage a takeover in the recreation area.

Three weeks later that is exactly what happened, when about fifty inmates took three guards as hostages. Three other guards were injured. Coughlin and other Department of Correction officials negotiated with the inmates, who ultimately released the hostages and returned to their cells. In November, Feldman returned to the facility, reported that substantial improvements had been made, but some additional staff positions still needed to be filled.

In 1993, Feldman and committee staff traveled to the Onondaga County Public Safety Building, that county's jail, to investigate allegations of brutality against and inadequate medical care for inmates there. In March 1994, the committee turned over its findings to the US Department of Justice, which reported the following October that the facility violated inmates' 8th Amendment rights against cruel and unusual punishment, including its failure to provide decent medical treatment. The following year, the county closed the old jail, replacing it with a new Onondaga County Justice Center, providing "a safe and secure environment for those detained or sentenced at the jail facility."

In 1993, the committee received a letter from an inmate, Maurice Mathie, in the Suffolk County Jail alleging that he had been the victim of sexual assaults by jail sergeant Roy Fries, who was the jail's chief of security. Because the inmate had himself killed someone some years earlier, the letter did not immediately stand out as especially worthy of attention. However, on closer perusal, it seemed to include some persuasive details and logic. Although an internal investigation rejected Mathie's charges against Fries, it noted that Fries had Mathie in his office sevenfold as much as any other inmate. Also, Fries had Mathie in his office at night, and somehow, Mathie had Fries' home telephone number, although it was unlisted.

When Feldman visited the facility with a Suffolk County legislator, the legislator pointed out the new paint over an area of pipe in Fries' office to which Mathie had claimed Fries had handcuffed him before sodomizing him. This evidence was enough to convince Feldman that Suffolk County had no business retaining Fries as chief of security, whether or not he had actually attacked Mathie. In 1995, he sent letters to Gov. George Pataki and Suffolk County Executive Robert Gaffney to this effect, and urging that the management of the jail be changed. Fries took his pension and retired.

But Mathie sued Suffolk County. Feldman turned over his findings to Mathie's lawyer. In August 1996, Mathie was awarded $750,000 in federal court. The Second Circuit Court of Appeals reduced the judgment to $450,000, but otherwise upheld the ruling.

Role of Special Oversight Committees: Iowa, Texas, and New York

Iowa Joint Oversight Committee

The Iowa Legislature created a Joint Oversight Committee as a permanent, standing committee. It actively investigates the waste and abuse of taxpayer dollars. For example, on several occasions during 2010 it heard testimony in response to its concerns about the possible waste and abuse of taxpayer dollars by the Iowa Association of School Boards (IASB). The committee investigated allegations that the organization bypassed the list of candidates for executive director that came from public announcements of the position to hire someone with direct connections to board members. That executive director, who resigned after the inquiry began, took more than $350,000 in annual compensation from the group when her contract called for $210,000, and a consultant used the IASB credit card for a personal trip to Bora Bora. Taxpayer dollars provide the only support for the IASB. The IASB's new executive director started his job in July 2011, more than a year after the investigation began.

Facing withdrawals of membership by some of the school boards, the new director pledged "a new course of action" of "transparency and fiscal responsibility." Both houses of the Iowa Legislature, with Democratic majorities in 2010, passed a law specifically requiring the IASB to open its books to scrutiny, but the Republican governor vetoed it.

Texas Bexar Water District

In 1946, the Texas Legislature created a special body, the Bexar Metropolitan Water District, with a mandate to impose rational planning and governance on water usage in western Texas near San Antonio, where some counties had faced serious droughts because upstream jurisdictions had used up too much water to allow for sufficient irrigation for others. After several decades, however, evidence emerged that the district had begun to create as many problems as it solved, with corruption and mismanagement on the rise. Facing costs it could not meet, in September 2010 the district suspended its fluoridation program.

In view of the critical importance of the water supply to parts of Texas that are usually parched even in the best of times, the Texas Legislature in 2007 established a special joint committee of its two houses, the Bexar Metropolitan Water District Oversight Committee. The bill required the district to report to the Committee and to the Texas Commission on Environmental Quality; and required the district to be audited by the State Auditor's Office. The auditor, commission, and committee found poor management and financial practices, and hostile relationships among the district board members and the management staff they employed. The board decided to suspend fluoridation, for example, against the advice of the staff, in violation of a San Antonio ordinance, and without inviting or allowing any public input. After its general manager was indicted in 2008, the board waited fifteen months before hiring a replacement. It dallied even longer when faced with the need to locate new water storage capacity, flouting its responsibility to assure an adequate water supply for the areas within its mandate.

The committee found that since the board members are elected by district, each member tends to take an adversarial and competitive stance toward the others. Given the district's history, the committee recommended a binding referendum among the district's customers in which they could choose to have the San Antonio Water System—the existing competitor—take over its responsibilities, ending the district. Temporarily, pending a takeover or else reform and rehabilitation, the committee urged empowering a water utility expert as conservator for the district, whether an individual or a new board of some kind.

As of mid-summer 2011, Wells Fargo cancelled the district's credit line and demanded immediate repayment of a $10 million loan. The district's manager blamed Sen, Carlos Uresti, sponsor of legislation enacted providing for the election the committee recommended, for the district's troubles.

New York State Assembly Subcommittee on City Management and Committee on Oversight and Investigation

Subcommittees ordinarily mean very little in the New York State legislature. They have no independent authority and very small budgets. When the Assembly leadership created the Subcommittee on City Management for Charles Schumer out of the Assembly Cities Committee, he intended to use it as a "watchdog" against waste, corruption, and mismanagement in New York City's government, but he could not issue subpoenas without the approval of the Assembly speaker, and he was allocated $15,000 as the initial budget for the subcommittee—not much with which to hire a staff even in 1977. He used it to hire Feldman as counsel to the subcommittee, responsible for conducting its investigations.

Awarding Schumer the subcommittee chair title might have constituted some sort of nominal designation of institutional support for his oversight efforts, but practically speaking he acted as a "lone wolf," at least at the beginning. As time went on, he persuaded the Assembly speaker to increase his funding for the subcommittee so that he could hire a few more staffers, but the chairmanship of a subcommittee, in the New York State legislature, remained a post with little institutional stature.

The subcommittee conducted a series of investigations, including

1. mismanagement at the city's Health and Hospitals Corporation responsible for as much as half of its deficit for 1978;

2. a cover-up of five patient deaths at one of its institutions, the Queens Hospital Center;

3. understated fire fatalities in an apparent attempt to hide the serious effects of budget cuts to the fire department;

4. profound flaws in the city's much-ballyhooed "computer match" system for detecting welfare fraud; and

5. vast overcharges by bus companies for transporting handicapped children to summer school.

The subcommittee undertook perhaps its most dramatic effort, however, in attacking the control of the city's supply of asphalt by a mob-connected cartel.

New York City employees, not the subcommittee, took the first two steps in breaking the cartel. Anonymous staff of a small city agency then called the Corruption Analysis and Prevention Bureau first discovered that the companies dominating the supply of asphalt were charging the city much more than they were charging private sector purchasers or even other public entities. Their report compared prices charged and quantities purchased from 1973 through 1976. New York City, which was buying about a half a million tons a year, paid $11.90 ton in 1973, increasing to $23.75 a ton in 1976. The investigators did not get comparative figures for every other purchaser for each year, but Nassau County, which only bought about

2,700 tons a year, paid $9.54 a ton in 1973 and $14.09 a ton in 1975, whereas the Port Authority, which bought about 5,500 tons a year, paid $14.15 a ton in 1975 and 1976. Given that the city's huge quantities should have won it considerably *lower* prices than those charged to the other purchasers, these findings had even more significance.

But the city did nothing with the findings. A brave whistleblower, outraged by the city's acquiescence in being robbed, walked into the subcommittee office with the report, altered so as not to reveal the identity of its authors. The whistleblower took a chance: the subcommittee staff could identify him, but he trusted the staff to protect his anonymity.

Schumer, excited by the report, could not simply release it. The subcommittee had to verify its findings, and make sure that the situation had not changed in the year and a half since its preparation. The subcommittee staff had established a relationship with the Port Authority in the course of a different project, so with relatively little difficulty it was able to verify the Port Authority purchase figures, and update them to 1977. A confidential source at Con Edison, which also purchased asphalt but which had not been included in the earlier study, supplied the subcommittee with the prices it had paid in 1975 and 1977 for about 800 tons in the former year and about 2,200 in the latter. On the basis of those figures, the subcommittee calculated that the city would have saved between $5 million and $6 million had it bought its asphalt at the prices the Port Authority or Con Edison had paid.

With the help of the city employee whistleblower, the subcommittee went further. The asphalt contracts, under law, had to be won through a competitive bidding process. The whistleblower made copies of the bidding records available to the subcommittee. Of course, the subcommittee, like any citizen, had a right to such records. But the staff feared that an official request would be met at best by foot-dragging, and at worst by destruction of the documents.

Only seven company names, all located in Queens, appeared to be connected with bids for the city's contracts: Jet Asphalt Corporation, Asphalt Road Products, Metropolitan Asphalt Paving Company, Willets Point, Mascali, Road Materials, and Interboro. Jet, Willets Point, and Mascali all had addresses within 4,000 feet of each other. The subcommittee noticed that although Mascali charged the Port Authority $14.15 a ton for asphalt, it bid $19.15 a ton for one of the city contracts that year, losing out to Jet, who bid about $18 ton. If Mascali wanted the contract, why didn't it bid lower? If it didn't want the contract, why did it bid? Most likely, its bid merely served the purpose of creating the appearance of competition, when in reality the various members of the cartel had predetermined whose turn it was to win that contract.

Almost all the bids stayed within 10 percent of each other, and usually within 1 percent. Furthermore, the city required companies to list a back-up company on their bid offer, to supply any shortfall in the primary company's ability to supply the product. Mascali, Willets Point, and Asphalt Road Products all selected Jet. Jet selected Mascali. Willets Point and F. Mascali at one point had a joint telephone number, and won a city contract in a joint venture, with both as the primary supplier.

Under the headline "Legislator Reveals: City Pays $ Millions Too Much for Asphalt," the subcommittee's press release of February 14, 1978 set out the foregoing information. New York City's three major daily newspapers carried the story.

Ed Koch had taken office as mayor only a few weeks earlier. The subcommittee's prior work had exposed waste, mismanagement, and corruption in the administration of his predecessor as mayor, Abe Beame, while Koch was running against Beame in the Democratic primary, so Koch was well disposed to the subcommittee's work. Additionally, he seemed to have a personal commitment to combating such deficiencies. Less than two weeks after the subcommittee's press release, Koch directed his new general services commissioner, Peter Smith, to change the bidding conditions that had limited eligibility to the Queens cartel, such as the requirement of heated silos. All the cartel members had such silos, but well-qualified potential competitors did not, and the silos were no longer necessary to assure delivery of the asphalt at the requisite temperatures, due to technical advances. The new bids would be opened on March 14, and the winning bid selected shortly thereafter. The request for bids for the new contract would also allow delivery from as far as twenty-five miles outside the city, instead of the previous six-mile limit, so more companies in Nassau and Westchester counties and in New Jersey could bid; and it would require the bidder to swear under oath that the city was getting as low a price as was available to any other customer.

On March 6, John Cody, the head of Teamsters Local 282, the union that represented the workers at the asphalt plants, sent a telegram to Schumer asking for a meeting regarding the next asphalt contract, and complaining that Smith's reforms would "prevent New York City contractors from competing with non New York City contractors." But when Jay Henneberry, a new young staff assistant with the Subcommittee, attempted to set up such a meeting with Cody, Cody said, "you tell that Schumer f----er that he's really gonna get his!" Henneberry asked "Is that a bodily threat?" There was a random audible click on the phone, which Cody interpreted differently, and asked "Oh—did you turn on your bug?" Henneberry responded, "No, we don't have any taping devices here." Cody concluded, "Well, my threat is political. I control a lot of votes in this town."

When the bids for the new contract were opened on March 14, 1978, Jet and Mascali jointly offered the lowest bid: more than $1.5 million less than the City had paid for the same amount of asphalt the previous year. But notwithstanding Smith's efforts, no company outside the cartel had bid. Some New Jersey asphalt companies had attempted to bid in previous years, and may even have met the contract specifications, but had been rejected likely on specious grounds. So even when Smith opened up the bid specifications, the New Jersey companies may have remained skeptical that the city was serious in soliciting their business.

In a furious effort to break the cartel, Smith decided to reject the bids and offer the contract again. Cody's friends did not fight the battle with "bodily threats" or with "votes": They fought it with lawyers and investigators. They brought suit to force Smith to honor the March 14 bids, and they won. Then they took the next step: They did their own investigation of Smith, and learned that he had engaged in stealing from a client at a law firm many years earlier. They leaked the information to the press, and Smith was forced to resign.

Although Schumer, through the subcommittee, had forced the cartel to lower its prices as a public relations move, he would have won but a temporary victory if the cartel kept its monopoly over the asphalt supply. With outside companies apparently still reluctant to bid, despite Smith's effort to loosen the bid specifications, an attractive alternative beckoned—an alternative that would appear radical, were it not for the fact that the city had used it before.

In fact, until 1973 the city had produced about 20 percent of the amount of asphalt it usually needed in its own asphalt plant in Queens. At that time, Mayor Lindsay, persuaded by some credible evidence of its obsolescence, together with similarly credible evidence of featherbedding and other inefficiencies, decided to close it. Anthony Ameruso, then an employee of the city's Highway Planning Department, had warned against leaving the city entirely vulnerable to the private asphalt producers, but the general superintendent of the city's asphalt plant in Queens in those days, a higher-ranking official, had collected $10,000 in political contributions from officers of Jet and Mascali to help pay the debts of Mayor Lindsay's by then defunct presidential campaign. The city closed the plant.

The subcommittee recommended that the city get back into the asphalt business. That way, the city could also threaten to provide most or all it needed if the cartel got too greedy again. In September 1978 Mayor Koch announced his plans to do just that, with construction planned for 1979 and operational capacity for 1980 or 1981.

Shortly thereafter, the subcommittee went out of existence—or rather, it transformed into a full committee.

Assembly Speaker Stanley Steingut had established a unit of the Assembly reporting directly to him called the Office of Legislative Oversight and Analysis, headed by veteran New York *Post* and *Herald Tribune* reporter Bill Haddad, assisted by investigative counsel David Langdon. Among other accomplishments, using the subpoena powers of the Speaker's Office, Haddad and Langdon had exposed the way that the big pharmaceutical companies had kept cheaper generic substitutes out of the hands of most consumers.

But in the Democratic primaries of 1978, Steingut lost his party's nomination for the Assembly from his own Brooklyn district, and therefore lost his Assembly seat and the speakership. Stanley Fink, from a different Brooklyn district, who succeeded him as speaker, terminated the Office of Legislative Oversight and Analysis, replacing it with the Assembly Committee on Oversight and Investigation, promoting Schumer from his post as City Management Subcommittee Chair to chair of the new committee, matching Schumer's new title to what he had actually been doing anyway as subcommittee chair. This, however, gave Schumer the proper institutional authority for oversight and ended his "lone-wolf" status. It also gave him more funding to for what had been the rather underpaid members of the subcommittee staff, such as Feldman, who now became Committee Counsel, and Josh Howard, the ace public relations expert who later won a number of Emmy awards as a producer of *60 Minutes*.

In his new role, Schumer exposed profligate federal spending enriching the investors of housing projects under the Section 8 program in the Diego-Beekman project in the Mott Haven section of the South Bronx, run by the HUD. He charged that although the investors profited, the tenants lived with non-working intercoms, promised washing machines never delivered, leaking pipes, broken elevators, unreliable heat, "security" that failed to protect them against drug dealers, muggers, and rapists. He exposed waste and mismanagement in the planning and preparation of Battery Park City. He criticized the inefficiency and time-wasting procedures of the jury selection process in New York, and proposed a call-in system. He showed that more than half of city buses ran significantly behind schedule.

And he persisted in his efforts to protect New York City taxpayers against the asphalt scam.

Meanwhile, Jack Newfield, a great investigative reporter, had published some interesting additional information about John Cody, under the *Village Voice* front page headline, "This Felon Controls the Most Corrupt Union in New York." Cody had been arrested, but not convicted, for attempted rape, assault, and robbery. Carlo Gambino, the Mafia chief, was an official greeter at his son's wedding. His chauffeur, Bruce Kay, had been charged with murdering a loan-shark, whose body was found in Kay's car trunk. His business agent was Harry Gross, formerly a contract killer for Murder Incorporated, the Jewish syndicate of the 1920s. Cody had business relationships with the owners of some of the companies for which his union members worked. Under Cody's leadership, some of those companies were permitted to shortchange, or entirely forget about, the money they were supposed to pay into pension funds for the workers. To finance business deals of his own various interests, Cody had cost his union members hundreds of thousands of dollars. Seven months after the Newfield piece appeared, Kay, the chauffeur, was himself found dead in a car trunk, shot in the back of the head.

So Schumer and Feldman now had a better idea of what they were dealing with.

Jim Capalino, Peter Smith's replacement as general services commissioner, now made another push for new bidders for the asphalt contracts. A New Jersey company, Bossert Asphalt, had decided to test the city's seriousness, and offered the low bid. Bossert, sixteen miles from Manhattan, would not have been permitted to bid under the old six-mile limit. But Bossert did not have a "lock" on the contract. It was less than 5 percent below the bid of the Metropolitan Asphalt Paving Company. Under a city ordinance adopted to keep as much business in the city as possible, companies located with the city could win city contracts so long as their bids were no more than 5 percent higher than the bid of an outside company. The Board of Estimate, a body comprised of the five borough presidents, the mayor, the comptroller, and the city council president, had the power to decide in such cases. (Both the Board of Estimate and the position of city council president have been abolished since then.)

On April 5, 1979, Feldman, representing Schumer, testified to the Board of Estimate that "outside suppliers have been so discouraged from bidding that the present New Jersey firm is the *only* bidder this year from outside the Metropolitan Asphalt Paving Association [the cartel]. Basically, the other competitors have given up hope that New York City would ever make an award to an outside firm. . . . If this outside firm loses, it is unlikely that we will see much further competition from outside in the future." But the representative of the Queens borough president asked to table the motion for two weeks to make the award, and his colleagues accommodated him.

That night, Feldman prepared to engage in his usual 7:30 pm Thursday ritual beer at Armstrong's, a bar near John Jay College where he taught administrative law to MPA students each week. About to cross the street, he saw a Metropolitan Asphalt Paving Company truck pull into a no-parking space in front of Armstrong's. On an intellectual level, he understood the tremendous odds against his imminent demise. Still, he tried to use a street lamp pole to shield as much of his body as possible on the small chance that it would be needed to deflect the machine-gun bullets.

There were no machine gun bullets. Workers emerged from the truck to fix a pothole in the street. But one day before the Board of Estimate was to make its final decision, Bossert's back-up plant, Little Ferry, withdrew. Schumer called on the city's Department of Investigations to determine whether Little Ferry had been threatened: "It is unlikely that in the ordinary course of business a close friend would leave another suddenly 'in the lurch' just in time for that friend to lose an important contract." Little Ferry refused to explain to a *Village Voice* reporter why they had pulled out.

Although Mayor Koch had included funding for a city asphalt plant in his proposed budget for 1979, Queens Borough President Donald Manes had managed to exclude it. Throughout June 1979, Schumer and Feldman assured the Highways commissioner that if the plant did not make it into the 1980 budget, the committee would bring the matter back into the headlines. In 1981, Feldman, by then a newly elected member of the Assembly, visited the city's new functioning asphalt plant off the Gowanus Highway in Brooklyn.

Administrative Rules and Regulations Review Committees and Commissions

Most state legislatures have committees or commissions that perform a special oversight function, in that they review rules and regulations proposed or issued by state agencies in an effort to block those that citizens or businesses might regard as overly intrusive or burdensome. These committees and commissions emerged with the backlash against "big government" in the 1970s and 1980s. A few examples follow.

The New York State Legislature established its Administrative Regulations Review Commission pursuant to Section 1 of Chapter 689 of the Laws of 1978, with a statement of legislative purpose explaining "continuous legislative review of administrative regulations is necessary to monitor the implementation of the ever increasing exercise of rulemaking by executive agencies. . . . [Such] regulations affect the economic, environmental and social wellbeing [*sic*] of this state and should therefore be subject to legislative oversight." The commission is ordinarily co-chaired by one member of the Assembly and one member of the Senate. As Charles Lavine, the then newly appointed Assembly chair wrote in 2011, it tries to "ensure that new regulations are well designed and old, outmoded ones are eliminated, and that the burdens on local governments and businesses are no greater than what is necessary to protect the public." Under the state's Administrative Procedure Act, a local government may escape the burden of a state agency regulation if it can show the agency that an alternative approach would achieve the same goals without damage to the public's health, safety, or general welfare. Erie County had submitted the only such known request as of mid-March, 2011, for a waiver of compliance with rules regulating the provision of services to victims of domestic violence. As with such legislative units in other states, the commission has no independent power, but can only advise the legislature, which may impose such legislative restrictions on agencies as it sees fit; or suggest appropriate courses of action to agencies.

Wisconsin's Joint Committee for Review of Administrative Rules determines whether agency regulations meet its standards. In the 2011 legislative session, it reviewed such measures as fishing and hunting regulations offered by the state's Department of Natural Resources, restrictions on payday lenders from the Department of Financial Institutions, and rules governing income and franchise taxes and deductions by businesses moving to the state, from the Department of Revenue. Every rule proposed by a Wisconsin state government agency must go to the legislature for review. If a substantive committee of either house of the Wisconsin legislature objects, the chief clerk of that house must refer the proposed regulation and the objection to the joint committee. If the joint committee objects, it must devise a plan for the introduction of legislation supporting the objection.

The Administrative Rules Review Committee (ARRC) of the Utah Legislature, like most such committees and commissions, cannot itself prevent the adoption of a rule or regulation, but reports its finding to the legislature as a whole. If the ARRC finds that the rule or regulation has a net negative effect on the economy, the operations of government, or on the people it affects, or doesn't carry out the intent of the legislature, it must report its findings to the legislative leadership and may report them to each legislator. The legislature, in turn, may enact limits on the authority of the agency that promulgated the rule.

As of 2011, California does not have a specific legislative unit dedicated to the review of agency regulations, but more than one legislator has proposed to require the California Legislature's standing committees to hold hearings to review such regulations proposed by agencies with estimated costs of more than $10 million to effectuate.

Conclusion

Although more popular than Congress, state legislatures also have relatively low levels of approval. July 2011 polls by Survey USA found approval ratings ranging from 12%—in California—to 29%—in Kansas. A December 2011 Quinnipiac poll showed a 26% approval rating for New York's state legislature, compared to a 68% approval rating for Gov. Cuomo.

Although this chapter offered a number of examples of highly effective oversight by members or committees of state legislatures, they are the exception, not the norm. Indeed, our principal examples of effective oversight come from the New York State Legislature in the 1980s and 1990s, whereas in the past decade that legislature has far more often been the subject of scathing oversight by academics, prosecutors, and journalists than the source of such oversight. As with Congress, today's poor performance probably does not break new ground. Henry Demarest Lloyd wrote in an 1881 issue of the *Atlantic Monthly* that "The Standard [Oil Company] has done everything to the Pennsylvania legislature except refine it."

As for their measure of adherence to our principles of effective oversight, today's state legislators' intolerance for injustice and abuse probably varies inversely with political contributors they receive from the American Legislative Exchange Council, whose "mission is to bring together corporations and state legislators to draft profit-driven, anti-public interest legislation, and then help those elected officials pass those bills in statehouses from coast to coast," according to the president of Common Cause. In addition to its own annual $7 million budget, those legislators curry favor with, and support from, its many corporate sponsors, such as Exxon Mobil, Shell Oil, Chevron, Texaco, Philip Morris, Lorillard Tobacco, Bank of America, Pfizer, GlaxoSmithKline, Koch Industries, and hundreds of other corporations.

Even if some recognize their responsibility to engage in meaningful oversight, they may lack both the skill and inclination to take on major reviews. Congressional "watchdogs" may at least have a reasonable expectation of attracting national media to their efforts. Congress also has ample staff and other resources. So state legislators, who are often part-time, not only have fewer tools to do the job, making information gathering and follow-up more difficult, they have less incentive and less ability to expose malfeasance, in that is harder for them to generate press attention.

Still, our examples prove the possibility and value of effective oversight by state legislators. More of them need to make the effort—both because it is a legislative responsibility and because they can thereby lift public opinion and confidence in their performance.

As states grapple with tough budgets, the need for effective oversight to curb waste could not be clearer. Too few legislators seem to see oversight as an important role to be performed. We hope some of the examples in this chapter—all of which produced real results—can serve as models.

Chapter 9

State Inspectors General

[The Inspector General's] operation would have to generate a perception and a reality that wrongdoing would be detected and would result in significant punishment.

—Thomas D. Thacher II, former inspector general,
New York City School Construction Authority (1995)

Why do some people lie on their résumés? Sometimes people exaggerate their qualifications to get a job that they otherwise would not be qualified for. But sometimes people seem to lie just for the sake of lying . . . and that raises clear questions about their integrity.

When you lie on a job application to work in the private sector, the worst thing that can happen is that you may get discovered and either not get hired or get fired if your lies are discovered after the fact.

When you lie on a job application with a government agency, it can rise to the level of a crime. But it only does so if the lie is discovered.

State auditors and IG are who you have to worry about if you lie when applying for state jobs or seeking the award of state contract dollars. They are the ones most likely to discover the lie.

A number of years ago, David Eichenthal was working for an IG for a state public authority. To combat corruption, the IG reviewed every firm even before it could bid on an authority contract. In conducting the review to prequalify one firm for bidding, someone noticed that the resumé of the principal owner of the firm indicated that he had graduated from McGill University. McGill is a fine university in Montreal, Canada. But nothing in the owner's resumé had indicated that he had otherwise ever spent time in Canada. It seemed odd.

In fact, the owner had never attended—or graduated—from McGill. In an interview, when he was asked to "sing the McGill fight song" he admitted that he had lied, but offered no explanation. His firm was denied the potential of millions of dollars in public contracts.

Another day in the life of an IG.

This chapter focuses on the work of IGs at the state level. Unlike the somewhat ubiquitous federal IG system, state IGs are less common. Some states have investigation commissions instead of IGs and some—including, not surprisingly, New York—have both. In addition to statewide IGs, there are also specialized IGs at the state level and, as in the case just described, there are some IGs responsible for state public authorities.

At the end of this chapter, we look in detail at the work of the New York City School Construction Authority (SCA) IG in the early 1990s and its investigation of what came to be known as the "school lease fleece."

State Inspectors General: An Overview

As of 2011, just over half of all states had an IG system in place. Most of the states that have IGs have them for specific agencies or programs. For example, both New Mexico and North Carolina have IGs for their departments of transportation. A half dozen states—Arizona, California, Colorado, Oregon, Missouri, and Texas—have IG programs for their correction departments, typically one of the largest state agencies and over the past several decades one of the fastest growing.

As of August 2011, ten states had IG offices responsible for rooting out fraud, waste, abuse, and corruption across state government. New Jersey previously had a state IG, but the office was recently abolished and moved into the state comptroller's office. Three states—Connecticut, Delaware, and Nevada—are actively considering proposals to create IG offices.

Two states—Pennsylvania and Massachusetts—both lay claim to being first in the creation of statewide IG programs. Both states moved to create IG offices within just a few years of the enactment of the 1978 federal IG Act.

In 1979, the Pennsylvania IG's office was created by a gubernatorial executive order for the Department of Transportation; in 1987, the Pennsylvania IG's office was moved within the executive office of the governor and given authority to conduct investigations of all state agencies.

In 1981, Massachusetts created its Office of Inspector General by statute. Creation of the office came on the recommendation of a legislative commission investigating corruption in the construction of public buildings in the state. The commission concluded that "[C]orruption is a way of life in the Commonwealth of Massachusetts" and recommended creation of an IG to provide "a mechanism for self-criticism and self-correction."

The division between statutory and nonstatutory IGs seen at the federal level exists at the state level as well. In addition to Pennsylvania, Georgia and—most recently—South Carolina have IGs created by executive order rather than statute.

In Florida, there is a state chief IG, but there also are individual department and agency IGs, including IGs for state universities. In 2011, the Virginia General Assembly passed a new law creating a new statewide IG by consolidating the offices of IG of the Departments of Behavioral Health and Developmental Services, Corrections, Juvenile Justice, and Transportation, and the Department of State Internal Auditor.

In Illinois, the State Officials and Employees Ethics Act provides for five independent offices of executive IG—one each for the governor, the attorney general, the secretary of state, the comptroller, and the treasurer.

Generally, state IGs focus on allegations of employee misconduct and ethics violations. For example, in FY 2010, the Louisiana IG reports that its investigations led to:

- the arrest of a Division of Administration employee for bank fraud and forgery for a scheme involving the theft of just over $4,000;

- the arrest of a fertilizer supplier charged with defrauding State Prison Industries of $177,225 through overbilling by providing lower quality fertilizer than ordered by the state; and

- the arrest of a state worker with two full-time salaries for public payroll fraud.

Other offices have both greater jurisdiction and roles that go well beyond investigation and referral for prosecution.

The Massachusetts IG has jurisdiction to conduct investigations of municipal government as well as state government. In Massachusetts, the IG conducts audits and investigations. The office also reviews state legislation and provides training and technical assistance to local governments on government procurement.

In Indiana, the IG provided ethics training to more than 30,000 state employees in 2010. Attorneys in the IG's office also provide informal advisory opinions on ethics issues for state employees.

Concerns over independence that continue to drive debate over the appointment and accountability of federal IGs have led to a variety of models at the state level.

In Florida, individual department heads are responsible for appointing department-level inspectors general: the governor appoints the chief IG. The IGs serve at the pleasure of the appointing authority.

In nonstatutory IG states like Georgia and Pennsylvania, the IGs are appointed by and serve at the pleasure of the governor. Even in statutory states like New York, Ohio, and Indiana, the IG is appointed by the governor and serves for the term of the governor: The IG may only be removed for cause.

Perhaps it isn't a surprise that some states with more fabled stories of corruption have slightly more complicated appointment and removal provisions in an attempt to shield IGs from political pressures.

- In Louisiana, the governor may only remove the IG with the approval of both houses of the legislature.

- In Illinois, IGs are appointed to a five-year term and are subject to a three-fifth vote confirmation by the state senate.

- Finally, in Massachusetts, the IG is appointed to a five-year term by a majority of a three-member panel consisting of the governor, the state auditor and the attorney general.

Those states that have statewide IGs have staffs and budgets of varying size. Georgia's IG only has a staff of four. Illinois and New York have IG offices with budgets in the range of $6 million to $7 million annually and approximately sixty staff members.

Independence, budget, and staff are critical to state IGs. In South Carolina, where a new governor appointed the state's first IG in 2011, he resigned after just six weeks on the job. The IG attributed his resignation to issues related to staffing and budget authority and recommended that the position be independent of both the legislature and the governor.

In addition to statewide and departmental IGs, there are also IGs for independent authorities and boards created under state law. For example, in California, the 1993 state law creating the Los Angeles County Metropolitan Transportation Authority mandated creation of an IG office, although California does not have a statewide IG. In Florida, the 1994 IG Act mandated IGs for state water management districts. And, in New York, public authorities like the Metropolitan Transportation Authority and the SCA have their own IGs as well.

Federal and State Partnership: Medicaid and Welfare

Eleven states that don't have statewide IGs do have IGs specifically for Medicaid, health and human services. The reason is a unique federal–state partnership that allows states to combat certain kinds of corruption on the dime of the federal government.

Every state, as a condition of participating in the Medicaid program, is required to have a Medicaid Fraud Control Unit (MFCU) to "investigate and prosecute Medicaid fraud as well as patient abuse and neglect in health care facilities." Although state employees staff these units, their operations are largely driven and funded by the federal government. The federal Department of Health and Human Services Office of Inspector General certifies and recertifies state MFCUs on an annual basis. MFCUs are largely funded by the federal government: The federal government provides 90 percent of an MFCU's cost in its first three years and 75 percent thereafter.

The level of resources and staffing applied to Medicaid fraud is far greater than any state's effort to curb other forms of public fraud or abuse. In FY 2010, the federal government provided $205.5 million to state governments and the District of Columbia for MFCUs—some in IG offices and some elsewhere within state government. Nationally, state MFCUs employed more than 1,800 staff members.

The returns, in criminal convictions and recoveries, were equally extraordinary. MFCUs conducted 13,210 investigations in FY 2010 resulting in 1,603 indictments and 1,329 convictions. Additionally, MFCUs recovered more than $1.8 billion in civil and criminal cases.

In addition to Medicaid, other states have created specialized IGs for welfare fraud. In Pennsylvania, the state IG is responsible for Medicaid fraud, welfare fraud, and fraud involving the federal food stamp or Supplemental Nutrition and Assistance Program program and state long-term care programs.

MFCU staffing and activity generally dwarfs the efforts of statewide IG offices. For example, in Georgia where the IG has four staff members for investigations of abuse in the other parts of state government, there are forty-two staff dedicated to the MFCU. Even in New York, with a staff of 59 and a $5.6 million budget for the state IG, the MFCU has a staff of 306.

On average, as of 2010, Medicaid accounted for 22 percent of state spending. The effect of federal funding for MFCUs is to skew investigative and oversight resources for Medicaid—leaving other areas of state government, the other 75 percent to 80 percent of government spending and activity, without similar levels of oversight and accountability.

School Lease Fleece: The School Construction IG

New York City has the largest school system in the United States, with about 1 million students. (Los Angeles, with about 700,000 in 2010, was second.) After years of declining enrollment and a period when school buildings in the city were closing, demographic change in the late 1980s and early 1990s resulted in a growing demand for classroom capacity.

At the same time, years of underfunding and inefficient management had left many of the school system's existing stock in disrepair. It was clear that to meet increases in enrollment and to assure safe space for its student population, there would need to be significant new investment in building and repairing schools. It was equally clear that the city's school system—the Board of Education—was ill prepared to carry out this mission.

In 1988, then New York Gov. Mario Cuomo and the State Legislature created the New York City SCA, an independent public authority led by a board consisting of appointees of the New York City mayor and the governor, along with the chancellor of the New York City Board of Education. The SCA was charged with the responsibility for overseeing a five-year, $4.3 billion construction program—the most ambitious investment in school construction ever.

To meet its mandate, the SCA was given extraordinary powers to cut red tape that had previously limited the efficiency of the school system in building and repairing schools. SCA projects were no longer subject to the same land-use regulations that other public projects were required to meet. Laws guiding the process for bidding out contracts—specifically laws requiring multiple subcontractors—were waived for a five-year period. And, perhaps most importantly, the SCA was permitted to prequalify bidders for its projects. In other words, it could prevent contractors with a history of poor performance or worse from even submitting a bid.

Shortly after the creation of the SCA, another arm of state government issued a report that called the integrity of all public construction programs into question. In New York, the governor and the state attorney general jointly appoint a special prosecutor for organized crime who leads an Organized Crime Task Force (OCTF). During the 1980s, the OCTF joined with others—most notably the US attorney for the Southern District—for a series of prosecutions of the leaders of New York's organized crime families. Frequently, those prosecutions—and their underlying investigations—revealed the influence of organized crime on New York's construction industry.

In 1990, OCTF issued a comprehensive report on corruption and racketeering in the New York City construction industry. The report concluded that corruption in construction was endemic. Moreover, it concluded, "public construction projects are more vulnerable to fraud, waste and abuse than private construction projects."

The leadership of the new SCA recognized that—with billions of dollars in play—it had to develop a program to protect against being victimized by corruption in general and organized crime in particular. The SCA IG was born.

The SCA turned to the author of the OCTF report—Thomas D. Thacher II—to develop a solution. Thacher called for an IG's office that had broad investigative power as well as the ability to play a critical role in the day-to-day operations of the authority. For example, whereas the SCA contracting unit would administer the prequalification process, the IG would screen potential bidders on the basis of integrity and performance issues.

Thacher's model called for a significant investment of staff and resources. Initially, he proposed a 100-person staff—more than the current staffing level for any state IG. The SCA IG's office wound up with an initial staff of fifty and a 1990 budget of $3 million. In addition to the IG and the chief of operations, the staff also included a counsel—who led cooperative efforts with state and local prosecutors. There was an investigations staff—with attorneys, investigators, engineering auditors, and forensic accountants—and, somewhat uniquely, a research and analysis unit that oversaw intelligence collection that aided in the prequalification process and investigations. The research and analysis unit sought to provide a steady stream of policy recommendations to the SCA designed to prevent waste, fraud, and abuse.

The role of the IG within the SCA was also unique. Thacher sought to be both an insider and an outsider. As an insider, the IG could provide regular input on the operations of the SCA with an eye to minimizing corruption risk. Yet, the IG needed sufficient independence to proceed without fear of being limited in its investigations for political reasons. The result was that the IG reported to the president of the SCA and was a member of the leadership team, holding the title of vice president. At the same time, the IG also had a direct report to the board—guaranteeing independence from the president of the authority even as he was a member of his leadership team.

The combination of powers, staffing, and resources and independence provided the SCA IG with unique authority and capacity to tackle the issue of corruption in the construction process.

Between January 1990 and December 1995, the office reviewed 3,844 applications for prequalification. In the cases of nearly eighty firms, prequalification was conditioned on specific steps that contractors were forced to take to reduce risk for fraud or other misconduct. Another six firms were required to hire independent monitors. More than 200 firms were barred from doing work for the SCA due to past misconduct.

SCA investigations—and close cooperation with law enforcement—led to dozens of prosecutions and the recovery of millions of dollars.

Despite all of these indicators of success, the work of the SCA IG was at risk in 1995. The chair of the SCA Board from inception and a strong backer of the IG model, Meyer "Sandy" Frucher, was an appointee of Gov. Mario Cuomo. In 1994, George Pataki defeated Cuomo and it was likely that Frucher would be replaced. The election of Rudolph Giuliani as mayor in 1993 and the appointment of Chancellor Rudy Crew in 1995 meant that the entire SCA Board—the board that had overseen the adoption of the SCA IG model—would turn over in just one year.

Concerns about the future of the SCA IG model were heightened when, in 1995, Gov. Pataki appointed Paul Atanasio to the SCA Board, replacing Frucher. By any standard, Atanasio was a political appointee—with little to no experience in construction: By contrast, Frucher had led the redevelopment of Battery Park City and Giuliani's new appointee, Donald Zucker, was a prominent developer. Atanasio was an investment banker who had run for Congress as the candidate of the Conservative Party, a prominent backer of Pataki's successful campaign for governor. Atanasio soon appointed Frances Vella-Marrone as his assistant at the SCA: Marrone was a member of the State Conservative Party executive committee.

Concerns over the politicization of the SCA leadership were compounded by connections between Marrone, Atanasio's key aide at the SCA, and Hercules Construction. Frances Vella-Marrone's husband, Gary, had been a project manager for Hercules and both Marrones had owned a firm that had been a Hercules subcontractor.

In January 1995, the SCA IG had participated in the execution of a search warrant at the headquarters of Hercules Construction: The firm, which had $40 million in outstanding work with the SCA, was required to take on a monitor as a condition of being permitted to continue on the projects. Eventually, in August 1996, Hercules' president pled guilty to federal charges that he bribed a Board of Education official to win a school renovation contract and to inflating costs on school, city Housing Authority, and US Army contracts. The monitor appointed by the SCA IG also found that Hercules' president had illegally laundered thousands of dollars in campaign contributions to politicians through third parties.

As concerns mounted over Atanasio, the SCA IG had identified a series of new programs that were in development or being implemented that effectively short-circuited the IG review of contractors. Under a Mentor program, certain women- and minority-owned businesses were identified for work by private construction management firms without IG review. An even larger gap in the review process, however, came with the Board of Education's lease build-out program.

The SCA was not building new school capacity fast enough to keep up with growing enrollment demands. As a result, the Board of Education decided to invest $170 million in a lease build-out program whereby the board would enter into long-term lease arrangements with commercial landlords and provide funds for build-out of the existing space into a school. The lease-build-out program was to create 15,000 new classroom seats and would account for one-third of all capital dollars dedicated to creation of new classroom space.

Unlike new construction or repair of existing schools, the SCA had only a limited role in the lease and build-out process. Under the state law creating the SCA, the authority had special powers that exempted it from certain land use regulations allowing for an expedited lease process. As a result, all of the actual leases were done through the SCA. But the Board of Education was responsible for identifying the locations, negotiating the leases, and winning approval. And because the landlord selected the contractor for the build-out, there was no contract or prospective contractor to review. The SCA IG's process of screening contractors was absent in the lease and build-out process.

New York City agencies—including the Board of Education—had a long history of scandal and corruption in leasing. After all, if Pittsburgh had steel and Detroit had cars, New York was all about real estate. Investigative journalists Jack Newfield and Paul DuBrul had previously highlighted corruption in leasing of private facilities for day-care facilities. More recently, the SCA IG had helped investigate and prosecute cases of corruption in leasing by the Board of Education. In 1994, Operation Tightrope, the SCA IG's investigation of kickbacks and bribery in the award of Board of Education leases, led to indictments of two Board of Education senior staff, an attorney, and seventeen others.

By early 1995, the SCA IG's office needed a fairly public "win" to demonstrate the unique value of the office and to insulate it against the changing political winds. Although it would have been ideal to have a criminal investigation ready to break, there was none. Moreover, the IG's office always would need to coordinate any investigative or prosecutorial efforts with outside law enforcement—limiting the IG's ability to control the timing of any criminal investigation. A more limited review, with a focus on reform rather than a criminal case, had more potential to meet the strategic needs of the office. And the school leasing program offered a target that was rich in vulnerability and opportunity for change.

At the time, David Eichenthal was the assistant IG for policy at the SCA. Every day, Eichenthal would drive from his home in Brooklyn to the SCA IG's offices in Riverdale. And every day, he would pass three lease-build-out sites. One of those was at 350 Gerard Avenue, just off the Bruckner Expressway in the South Bronx.

After some very basic investigation, it turned out that 350 Gerard Avenue was a ripe target for review and had an interesting—and certainly newsworthy—history. In the 1980s, the building was the home of the Wedtech Corporation. Wedtech had become a major defense contractor, winning millions of dollars in contracts through a set-aside program for minority contractors. At the time, Wedtech was in fact not minority-owned.

Moreover, the firm engaged in other fraudulent activity to win more and more contracts—this included the award of shares to former Bronx congressman Mario Biaggi. Reagan administration Attorney General Edwin Meese was, before becoming attorney general, a lobbyist for Wedtech. An independent counsel report cleared Meese of criminal wrongdoing.

According to testimony at the criminal trial of former Bronx Borough President Stanley Simon, Simon had demanded a job for his brother-in-law at Wedtech in return for his support of the 1982 sale of 350 Gerard Avenue by the City of New York to Wedtech. Eventually, twenty federal, state, and local officials were convicted of crimes related to Wedtech. Some of those convictions were eventually overturned.

In 1986, Wedtech went bankrupt as a result of the scandal. As a result, the 350 Gerard Avenue site went to the mortgage holder, Yorkville Federal Savings and Loan. In the early 1990s, Yorkville S&L was one of nearly half of all savings and loans in the United States to go bankrupt. Federal bailout legislation turned over the property holdings of the failed S&Ls to a new federal agency, the Resolution Trust Corporation (RTC). By 1993, RTC was the owner of 350 Gerard Avenue.

Through a review of property records, Board of Education records, and newspaper articles, the foundation of the investigation was in place. On top of that foundation, IG staff conducted a series of interviews with former and current board and SCA staff as well.

The SCA IG investigation of the Board of Education lease for 350 Gerard Avenue found that the property's history of corruption continued, with the Board of Education as the latest target.

- In July 1994, the new owners of 350 Gerard Avenue acquired it after foreclosing on the mortgage for the property that they had obtained at auction the month before for $400,000.

- Even before the new owners had acquired the property, the Board of Education approved a fifteen-year, $12 million lease, with provision for a $12.1 million build-out, for 350 Gerard Avenue. In other words, the board agreed to a $12 million lease on a property that it could have acquired for $400,000.

- Initially, a Board of Education staff member had rejected the idea of leasing 350 Gerard Avenue for a school: He believed that the cost of the build-out would be "prohibitive" and the school would be located in the middle of a manufacturing district.

- The decision to go forward with the lease was recommended by a Board of Education staff member who subsequently resigned from his $46,000-a-year position with the board to accept a $400,000 consultant contract with the board's landlord at 350 Gerard Avenue. In fact, the same staff member obtained consultant work on two other lease-build-out projects for another $350,000 in contract fees.

- The firm selected to do the build-out of 350 Gerard Avenue—the cost of which had ballooned to $13.4 million, the most expensive build-out project for the Board of Education at the time—was also selected as the contractor on a $6 million lease-build-out project. Its only prior experience was a $1.75 million lease-build-out project for the Board of Education. Moreover, the firm's key principal was a convicted felon who was indicted on multiple counts of conspiracy, bank fraud, making false statements, illegal loan participation, money laundering, and bribery: He was on federal probation at the time of the project.

And thus, the school lease fleece was born. The report was sent to the president of the SCA and the SCA Board of Trustees—and almost immediately found its way into the hands of reporters. It had the desired effect.

The Board of Education terminated the head of the program and brought in a seasoned bureaucrat to oversee all school facilities. After putting a moratorium on new leases, the Board of Education announced a reform plan in November 1996. The plan called for background checks of landlords, more market research to ensure that lease terms were favorable to the board, and a heightened level of environmental review for all proposed leases.

Both investigative journalists and law enforcement turned to the school lease program to apply additional oversight.

After running an editorial in response to the 350 Gerard Avenue story—"Rich Times at Wedtech High" (a play on the title of the epic 1980s coming of age comedy, *Fast Times at Ridgemont High*)—demanding reform, the *Daily News* ran a week-long investigative series on the school leasing program, identifying a series of failures in the leasing process and other landlords with apparent sweetheart deals.

In 1996, the Manhattan district attorney indicted the landlords of a
school lease-build-out site for fraud. A sixty-four-count indictment charged
that the landlords had submitted phony invoices in support of the build-out
costs. The landlords were convicted of grand larceny, criminal possession of
a forged instrument, and filing a false instrument.

The former board official who went to work for the owners of 350
Gerard Avenue was barred from further work on school lease sites and
never received payments on his consulting contracts. A 2006 court decision
affirmed the Board of Education's decision to bar him from further payments. The court found that "the fact that the circumstances surrounding
the conversion of the subject property into a school facility was permeated
with such fraud and deceit compels a finding that the plaintiffs should not
be allowed to benefit from such conduct."

The problems of the school leasing scandal, however, continued to
manifest over the years. In 1997, the Board of Education opened P.S. 141
in a leased facility in Manhattan that formerly housed a laundry. In October 1995, just two months before the SCA IG report, the board leased
the building for $5.2 million for fifteen years: It had an assessed value of
$130,000. The landlord had initially hired the same former Board of Edu-
cation official hired by the owners of 350 Gerard Avenue to oversee the
build-out: The board forced the landlord of the P.S. 141 site to cancel the
$1 million agreement with the former board official.

Just a week after the school was opened, it was closed due to high
levels of perchloroethylene, a cancer-causing fluid used in the dry cleaning
process. P.S. 141 has never reopened at that site.

And the SCA IG's concerns about Atanasio were borne out over time.
Vella-Marrone pressured SCA officials to hire her husband as a project
officer. After initially refusing, the SCA president was forced out and the
interim president hired Gary Marrone. In 1998, Marrone was the project
officer on a Brooklyn school construction site, P.S. 131. The contractor's
failure to construct a sidewalk shed directly led to the accidental death of
a student on the site when building material fell during construction.

A 1998 report by the SCA IG highlighted Marrone's role in the
death—and the circumstances that had led to Marrone's hiring by the SCA.
On release of the report, Atanasio resigned as an SCA board member.

The work and structure of the SCA IG continued until 2002, when
state legislative changes to the Board of Education altered the membership
of the SCA Board as well. The schools chancellor, previously appointed by
the Board of Education—comprised of appointees of the Mayor and other
officially—was now a mayoral appointee: as a result, the mayor would have
practical control over two of the three SCA Board members. Thus, although
the SCA continues, all three of its board members are now mayoral appoin-

tees. Structurally, the SCA now functions within the Board of Education and the head of the SCA is directly accountable to the mayor and the chancellor. As a result, the SCA IG is now much more closely tied to the Department of Investigation.

Conclusion

The IG system that is now ubiquitous at the federal level exists in only about half of all states. And in those states, not all state departments or agencies are under the oversight of the state IG.

Different states have adopted different models to address the issue of independence through multiyear terms and limits on removal. Still, in some cases the IG is appointed by and can be removed by the governor whose administration they are charged with overseeing.

More states have IGs narrowly focused on abuse in Medicaid and welfare. These efforts, well funded compared with some statewide IG offices, are the result of a rather unique partnership between states and the federal government.

Ultimately, the success or failure of IG offices at the state level is the result of structural issues related to independence and resources. At its core, the school lease fleece case study is about both of these issues.

The New York City SCA IG was specifically designed to both play an inside and an outside oversight role. In part, this allowed the SCA IG to have a far greater say in preventing wrongdoing and corruption than it would have been able to have if it acted purely as an external watchdog. It also, undoubtedly, made it easier to win the resources necessary to play the role of internal watchdog in a way that truly protected the agency.

To the extent that IGs attempt to block opportunities for corruption, they must always be looking for vulnerabilities and holes in the dam. The type of corruption that occurred in the school lease fleece would have been easily detected through the normal review of contracts and contractors by the SCA—both in prequalification and contract review. Creating an exception to that normal process allowed for abuse. Few systems of prevention are perfect and efforts to achieve perfection are often unreasonably costly in resources and bureaucracy. For example, if you determined that it was acceptable to never actually build a school, it would be possible to create an impenetrable wall to block out corrupt forces from ever competing. Thus, one of the most important tests of effective oversight is the ability to defend the structure of the program. But it requires resources to be able to build preventive systems—resources that were invested at the SCA but not in the Board of Education leasing program.

Changes in political environment required the SCA IG to act to maintain its independence. The case study shows that even nonpolitical oversight actors need to be strategic in their application of investigative resources and cognizant of the political environment that they operate in. Most people assume that to the degree that independent, appointed overseers become "political" that is a bad thing. Although partisanship compromises independence, understanding the political context of investigative work is essential—whether a legislator, an elected auditor, or an appointed IG conducts it.

In a sense, the school lease fleece case study demonstrates how even independent IGs are accountable: The SCA IG's office needed to demonstrate its value to new leadership and it did. But independence is hard to achieve and failure comes at a price. Remember, the SCA IG had concerns about Vella-Marrone and about her husband. When Gary Marrone was hired by the SCA, the SCA IG raised questions—because of nepotism issues, because of his past association with Hercules Construction, and because of his own minor criminal record. Yet these concerns did not prevent the hiring of Marrone or his failure of performance that may have played a role in the death of a sixteen-year-old girl.

Chapter 10

Other Elected and Appointed State Officials

Comptrollers, Auditors, and Attorneys General

Put not thy trust in princes . . .

—Psalm 146:3

State governments in the United States do not follow the structure of the federal government. That is, although the ballot in November allows citizens only one choice of a national executive officer team (president and vice president), most every ballot for statewide executive officers allows citizens choices for several different offices. These always include governor, and usually attorney general and comptroller. However, the many variations sometimes include, for example, commissioners or auditors and sometimes exclude attorneys general and comptrollers.

The reason for the distinction goes back deep into American history. The Framers relied on Congress as a check against executive power, but the authors of the state constitutions, even more suspicious of executives, wanted additional safeguards. Therefore, they set up other independently elected state officials to divide that power among competing forces. Because governors remain the strongest of them, those other statewide executive officials exercise important oversight responsibilities. Of course, those state constitutions that provide for the appointment, instead of the election, of the additional statewide officials, assure a lesser degree of independence, so those officials may tend to be less effective "watchdogs" over the governor's power structure, if indeed their roles involve such monitoring at all.

Naturally, the standard agency heads appointed by the governor— commissioners of health, taxation, insurance, and so forth—are not expected to monitor others. Attorneys general, comptrollers, and auditors, in varying degrees, whether elected or appointed, do have that responsibility. They do not only monitor those parts of state government under the control of the governor, but the legislative and judicial branches and each other, as well.

This chapter explores the role that comptrollers, auditors, and attorneys general play as government watchdogs. We discuss the different duties of these different auditors and how they provide oversight over other state agencies—and, occasionally, government activity at the federal and local levels as well.

Comptrollers, Treasurers, and Auditors

Audits are the heart of the oversight function of state comptrollers and state auditors. The New York State Constitution, for example, requires the comptroller "to audit all vouchers before payment and all official accounts." As noted in Chapter 3, audits by nature tend to be less dramatic than investigations, so the work of those officials often seems less dramatic as well. But every state agency knows that its books are subject to audit. That knowledge helps to "keep them honest," and when it doesn't, sometimes the audit itself will do so. What the role of comptrollers and auditors makes them sacrifice in drama, it makes up in comprehensiveness: They audit across the board, across the entire range of state government operations.

Of course, with an annual budget in a state like New York of $134 billion for FY 2012, or indeed in any state, auditors cannot possibly review more than a small fraction of individual expenditures. But normal random audits, and the occasional targeted audit, have considerable effect.

New York, like most states, elects its chief auditor, whether the post is called "auditor" or "comptroller." California elects both its controller, responsible for audits of local government as well as state government agencies, and its treasurer, responsible for investment and finance, but its governor chooses its state auditor from among three candidates nominated by a Joint Legislative Audit Committee of both houses of the Legislature on the basis of merit, not party affiliation. This selection process seems to make no difference in the nature and quality of the audits the office produces. By substituting "New York" for "California" in the titles, a representative sample of audits from the California State auditor from July 2011 could just as easily have come from the New York State comptroller, or any other state's chief auditor: "University of California: Although the University Maintains Extensive Financial Records, It Should Provide Additional Information to Improve Public Understanding of Its Operations," "California

Energy Resources Conservation and Development Commission: Status of Funds Provided Under the American Recovery and Reinvestment Act of 2009 for the State Energy Program," "Sex Offender Commitment Program: Streamlining the Process for Identifying Potentially Sexually Violent Predators Would Reduce Unnecessary or Duplicative Work," "Department of Community Services and Development: Status of Funds Provided Under the American Recovery and Reinvestment Act of 2009 for the Weatherization Assistance for Low-Income Persons Program."

Press coverage for the appointed California State auditor's audits, similarly, does not seem any less vigorous than for an elected comptroller or auditor: "California taxpayers' money wasted, misused, State auditor finds," "Audit finds years-long backlog of investigations into accused teachers," "California employers could be hit with big tax bill for jobless benefits, auditor warns."

Indeed, the audits of California's own elected controller seem, if anything, less newsworthy than those of the appointed state auditor: "California Department of Health Audit Report: Administrative and Internal Accounting Controls Over the Office Revolving Fund," 2009; California Department of Corrections and Rehabilitation: California Prison Health Care Services, Report of Review, Administrative and Internal Accounting Controls Over the Service Contract Process," 2008–9; California Department of Water Resources Audit Report: Central Valley Water Project Construction Fund," 2000–2008.

In 2011, at least, the controller seemed to get more press attention for announcing audits than for releasing them: "California to audit 17 redevelopment agencies" and "California orders audit of Montebello finances"; although he was also featured in "Redevelopment agencies shortchanged California schools $40 million, controller's review finds."

The Tennessee comptroller of the Treasury is not elected by the public, but by the two houses of that state's Legislature, voting jointly. Unlike the situation in California, only the comptroller has significant audit responsibility. Some 2011 audits include Office of Legislative Administration, May 2011, Tennessee Local Development Authority, June 2011; Tennessee Board of Regents: Tennessee Technological University, June 2011. Some press coverage of the comptroller's audits included "Audit Sacks Riverdale QB Club"; "Audit: Health Company Misused $1.2 M"; "Audit finds fault with state's drug task forces." The typical audits by a state comptroller, auditor, or treasurer concerns a small amount of money relative to the size of a state budget. In August 2011, the Tennessee comptroller released an audit charging that a high school cheerleading coach stole $12,000 or so from funds that were supposed to support the team over a two-and-a-half year period starting in January 2008. This audit was slightly unusual only in that it was released to the public without seeking prior comment from the subject or the subject school system. Some of the other audits released by the Tennessee comptroller during the same month did and some did not include prior comments from the subjects.

Maryland's Office of Legislative Audits audited the state treasurer's office, which audits other state agencies, and found weaknesses in its monitoring of those agencies' bank accounts. It is not so unusual to have one state auditor decide to audit another, and then find fault. More notably, the state treasurer of South Carolina announced that he would have his own office audited, although he would engage an outside, independent auditor for the job.

The similarity in styles of audits, whether issued by elected or appointed officials called treasurers, comptrollers, controllers, or auditors, has a logical basis. With resistance to tax increases growing among the public in recent decades, the pressure for more efficient use of taxpayer dollars has created a demand for aggressive performance auditing. Every variety of state auditor prefers to please the public. That is why we continue to see relatively hard-hitting audits: as the author of a 1991 *Public Administration Review* article on the subject wrote, the current breed of auditors is likely "to see the public (and its representatives) as their ultimate clients, rather than the auditee, or management, as in traditional financial auditing."

Attorneys General

The two primary responsibilities of a state attorney general are to represent the public interest and the officials of the state government. When a state attorney general, engaging in oversight, encounters a state official involved in what he perceives as wrongdoing, these goals may clash. Such clashes generate controversy, and courts sometimes stop an attorney general from proceeding when they rule that the attorney general's duty to a client extends to the state official in a manner that would conflict with suing that official. But most of the time, courts hold that the attorney general's duty to the general public prevails over his or her responsibility to the official "client."

A few states, such as Alaska, Delaware, and Rhode Island, have no state or local prosecutors other than the offices of their attorneys general. In those jurisdictions, then, of necessity oversight must extend to the criminal prosecution of those public officials whose malfeasance involves criminality. In other states, like Maine, the state constitution confers on the attorney general the power to prosecute official corruption cases, even though

Maine does have other local prosecutors. The Pennsylvania attorney general charged top legislators and key legislative staffers with official corruption in that state's "Bonusgate" scandal in 2009. The New Mexico attorney general prosecuted that state's investment officer and deputy state treasurer for extortion. The U.S. Court of Appeals for the 10th Circuit ruled that although the New Mexico attorney general represented those state officials in their official capacity, no conflict or privilege barred him from prosecuting them for actions, like extortion, taken outside their official capacity. The New Jersey attorney general, who under that state's constitution is appointed by the governor, in her capacity of exercising oversight over the operation of New Jersey government agencies, in the course of two months announced the indictment of an official of the State Department of Transportation and guilty pleas from two former New Jersey Turnpike toll collectors.

In 2010, former New York State Comptroller Alan Hevesi's guilty plea to bribery charges brought by New York State Attorney General Andrew Cuomo highlighted the attorney general's three-year investigation corruption in the comptroller's office, an investigation that also brought about felony convictions of several other participants, including the state's former chief investment officer. Cuomo could prosecute Hevesi and the others because they violated their duties as fiduciary investors for the state's pension funds on behalf of retired public employees. New York's unusual Martin Act gives its attorney general the powers to seek civil and criminal penalties for misrepresentations or omissions in the sale or purchase of securities. Because Hevesi did not reveal that he had received personal gifts as an inducement to make certain investments of the retirees' pension funds, he could be prosecuted under that statute.

Historically, however, it has rarely been possible for New York state attorneys general to prosecute corrupt state officials, because under most circumstances they could only do so upon referral from other state officials or upon an existing indictment when the related prosecutor wishes to transfer the matter, which has not happened. But an agreement between Comptroller Thomas P. DiNapoli and Attorney General Eric Schneiderman in 2011 could overcome that barrier. The comptroller's audit responsibilities and powers extend to all state agencies and branches of the state government, even including public authorities. If those audits uncover evidence of fraud or corruption, the comptroller agreed to refer the matter to the attorney general for prosecution. Furthermore, when the attorney general launches an investigation of a government entity, he agreed to have the comptroller conduct a simultaneous audit, when appropriate. At the initiation of their agreement, the attorney general served a subpoena on a questionable local development corporation while the comptroller hit it with a notice of impending audit.

Although attorneys general rarely launch criminal prosecutions of other state officials, their authority for civil litigation is less controversial, up to and including suing their governors. Of course, what constitutes oversight varies with the individual attorney general. In 2005 the Kansas attorney general thought that his responsibility to protect the public interest against abuse required him to sue his governor to stop Kansas from subsidizing abortions for poor women.

A State Comptroller Audit: Abilities!

In 2009, the parent of an autistic child approached an acquaintance of his in the comptroller's office with allegations that the State Education Department paid the Henry Viscardi School on Long Island hundreds of thousands of dollars for excessive and exorbitant emoluments to Edmund L. Cortez, the president of "Abilities!," a closely affiliated organization, enriching himself at the expense of taxpayers and the school's disabled students. The friend set up a meeting between the parent and auditors for the Comptroller's Division of State Government Accountability. Two years later, the office issued its audit publicly, but addressed to the commissioner of the SED and the new director of the Henry Viscardi School. Cortez retired once the audit started.

The auditors, as auditors typically do, reviewed the financial records of the school, interviewed employees and the school's certified public accountants, and focused on the details of certain suspicious cost items.

Beyond the $156,000 annual salary of the school's executive director, at Cortez's direction, the school claimed state reimbursement for an additional $280,000 a year for himself and the secretary of Abilities! for "additional leadership expenses." The auditors could not identify any such "additional leadership" services, and so disallowed the reimbursement for the two years covered by the audit, FY 2008 and 2009. Abilities! also gave $165,000 in bonuses to Cortez and the secretary in 2008, charging $88,275 of that to the school and thus to the state. They found another $186,392 in expenses illegally charged to the state or unsupported by proper documentation. One such charge was the new Lexus automobile leased for Cortez's use each year, with no records indicating that he used it for the school's business. Others were for his personal utilities bills and for payments into his supplemental retirement plan. The auditors disallowed these charges as well, for total disallowed charges of $835,074 of the roughly $27.8 million the school had claimed for the two-year period.

They found almost $500,000 in questionable charges based on extra payments to employees of Abilities! for work they had supposedly done for the school, but one such employee told the auditors she had done no work for the school, and others did not seem to have done nearly enough to justify the additional amounts for which the state was charged. The auditors did not disallow these charges immediately, but asked the SED to perform its own detailed review of the questioned payments.

News coverage of the audit noted that Cortez received compensation worth more than $1 million for the two-year period audited, with his residence on-site paid for by the school.

The SED agreed with the comptroller's recommendations in their entirety. The school disagreed with the disallowances, but had little choice in the matter. The state would recover the money out of future disbursement to the school.

Federal Oversight by a State Attorney General

A state attorney general can put the varied powers of that office to use in the service of oversight in sometimes surprising ways. State attorneys general have the power to supervise charities, to make sure their purported beneficiaries actually benefit. This power and responsibility has come down from the medieval English ancestors of the modern attorney general. In New York, if a charity cheats its intended beneficiaries, the attorney general can sue the charity's officers and directors for damages and even dissolution, among other remedies. In 2000, Attorney General Eliot Spitzer used those powers to exercise oversight and combat waste and corruption in a *federal* program under the auspices of the HUD.

In June 1999, Feldman, then head of Spitzer's Legal Policy and Program Development Unit, sort of an internal "think-tank" within the attorney general's office, received a telephone call from his old friend Jerry O'Shea, head of the Brooklyn Tenants Council. Tenants normally complained to the Council, but O'Shea had not expected complaints from tenants in buildings blessed with mortgage loan guarantees from the HUD. HUD's 203(k) mortgage loan guarantees required the not-for-profit organizations that won them to improve their buildings in order to generate increased occupancy and/or rent levels so that they could repay the loans. Not only were the buildings not being improved, complained the tenants, the landlords failed to provide even such basic amenities as heat, hot water, ordinary repairs, or pest control.

O'Shea gave Feldman a number of addresses in marginal neighborhoods in northern Brooklyn, all for buildings owned by the Helpline Soul Rescue Ministry. Feldman began investigating Helpline. A real religious organization would be exempt from registering as a not-for-profit organization with the attorney general's Charities Bureau under New York State law, but Feldman suspected that Helpline was not exempt. In that case, its status as a not-for-profit organization would give the attorney general's office jurisdiction to sue Helpline's officers and directors for restitution, damages, or dissolution, if in fact they diverted to themselves money intended for the beneficiaries of the charity.

He visited some of the addresses O'Shea had supplied, and verified the tenants' complaints. He learned that Helpline had no housing experience whatsoever before its participation in the 203(k) program. He found that Helpline had purchased hundreds of buildings in the past few years, with the help of almost $14 million in federal mortgage loan guarantees. When he reported his findings to the attorney general, Spitzer brought in personnel from the Charities Bureau and the Investor Protection Bureau to assist in the investigation.

Soon, the attorney general's staff determined that the two key officers of Helpline were a married couple, Gennie and Nelson Phillips. Michael Fox, a vice president of Mortgage Lending Company of America, had made the loans to Helpline. Beatrice Sukhdeo, the proprietor of Tri-Metro Realty Corporation managed the properties for Helpline. The attorney general's office began sending subpoenas to others who could testify about the nature of the transactions among those key players. One subpoena subject refused to testify unless the attorney general's office could give him immunity not only from its own eventual prosecution, but from prosecution by the US attorney for the Eastern District of New York. Of course the New York State attorney general's office had no such power, but it now learned that another prosecutor was investigating as well.

In their meeting with the attorneys in charge of the Eastern District investigation, the state attorney general's representatives learned that yet another prosecutor's office, the Manhattan district attorney, was involved, working with the Eastern District. Feldman and his state colleagues agreed to pursue civil remedies while leaving criminal charges to the federal prosecutors and the district attorney.

As the investigation proceeded, the nature of the scheme unfolded. Sukhdeo would locate a likely building. It had to be located in a neighborhood bad enough but promising enough to plausibly meet the 203(k) program objective of housing improvement; and it could house no more than four families in order to meet the eligibility requirements. Before Sukhdeo bought the property, Fox and Sukhdeo would hand pick the appraiser. Sukhdeo would pay the market price for the property, but record the sale at a false price, usually double the actual price, supported by the appraisal. Fox, the mortgage lender, would then "lend" Helpline the full amount of the false price, in theory to allow it to buy and renovate the building. Because Fox could tell HUD that the owner was a not-for-profit organization, HUD would give Fox a loan guarantee, so if Helpline "failed" in its rehabilitation role, defaulted and could not repay the loan, HUD would reimburse Fox's mortgage lending institution, or whichever institution held the mortgage. And Fox did not, in fact, hold the mortgage, but could and did easily sell the mortgage on the secondary market to another financial institution, since HUD, not the buyer, would bear the risk.

Congress had created the program to encourage banks and other mortgage lenders to make such mortgage loans, understanding that housing renewal in marginal neighborhoods involved some degree of risk, and that lenders might well need encouragement. Gennie and Nelson Phillips, Fox, and Sukhdeo, however, did not intend default as a risk—they intended it as a certainty. Sukhdeo would spend less than the bare minimum necessary for repairs and maintenance. She, the Helpline officials, Fox, and perhaps the appraisers would skim off a generous chunk of the cash, once they had it, among themselves. The buildings, and the lives of the tenants in them, would only get worse.

On November 29, 2000, Spitzer announced that he was suing Helpline, Fox, Sukhdeo, and Nelson Phillips personally for stealing $2.3 million from the loan proceeds from HUD, and would ask the New York State Supreme Court to dissolve Helpline. Gennie Phillips had died of cancer the previous month. A few weeks later, the US attorney arrested seven other people in connection with 203(k) fraud. Two more officials of Mortgage Lending of America were included among them. Mortgage Lending had deals with other phony not-for-profit groups, such as the St. Stephen's Bible College Realty Management Corporation (that also failed to engage in religious activities), issuing more than 250 bad loans under the program. The Manhattan district attorney arrested another nine defendants two days later.

Ultimately, Spitzer's lawsuit would recover only several hundred thousand dollars from the Helpline group, which the attorney general's office would distribute among those few tenants who had not moved out, and it could therefore still locate, as well as some legitimate organizations assisting tenants. Those tenants, of course, should have been the beneficiaries of the mortgage loan proceeds the defendants skimmed out for their own use. In response to a proposal from New York City's housing commissioner, in 2002 HUD and the New York City Department of Housing Preservation and Development undertook to buy and rehabilitate hundreds of the foreclosed-upon buildings that had suffered as a result of the 203(k) abuses, in order to protect the tenants still in residence and to achieve the initial goals of the program.

But the HUD 203(k) scandal had a back story that says much more about how the oversight role of a state attorney general can interface with the roles of other officials with institutional responsibilities for oversight.

The staff of Susan Gaffney, HUD's own IG, had warned about weaknesses in the program in 1997, calling it "highly vulnerable to waste, fraud, and abuse by investors and non-profit borrowers." In a review of 442 loans made with federal guarantees under the 203(k) program in various states not including New York, auditors found that 406 of the loans involved "[l]and schemes intended to turn quick profits between identity-of-interest parties. . . . Rehabilitation work not completed or improperly performed." Properties were "overvalued" and/or suffered "[h]igher loan defaults and unsupported fees," among other problems. The audit included a restatement of recommendations by the IG that HUD had not implemented, including "[l]imit the amount of reimbursement for overhead and profit for loans to non-profit borrowers," "[e]stablish criteria for approving the borrower to act as the general contractor," "require the contractor to maintain complete records for the rehabilitation cost," "[l]imit the number of loans to an investor or non-profit borrower to 15 at any one time," "[i]ssue a Mortgagee Letter warning lenders of the program abuses that have been found, the penalties which may be imposed for such abuses, and HUD's intention to impose sanctions and refer abusers for criminal prosecution."

The following year, another audit of the program showed better results, with most of the corpus of the loans reviewed having been used to "acquire and substantially improve" the properties. Nonetheless, eighty percent of the loans included at least one of the following problems: they were issued for ineligible projects, the rehabilitation work was incomplete or shoddy, or the loans were not based on verification of borrowers' actual costs.

Apparently, HUD's then secretary, Andrew Cuomo, was not happy with the work of his IG. Gaffney had been HUD's IG since 1993, with twenty-three years of previous honorable government service in responsible positions in housing and investigations. Four months after releasing the second audit, testifying before the Senate Government Affairs Committee on the twentieth anniversary of the 1978 Inspector General Act, Gaffney provided considerable detail about how the HUD secretary, unhappy with the role of an independent IG, interfered with her work, personally berated her, and had his aides smear her publicly and privately. Apparently some of Gaffney's other criticisms of HUD programs and projects annoyed Cuomo; she gave no indication that her office's reports on the 203(k) program played any particular part in the conflict; but Cuomo's general dislike of the IG's role may help to explain his failure to respond appropriately to the IG's warnings about that program as well.

After Spitzer announced his lawsuit, Gaffney noted that much of the fraud could have been prevented had not the agency reduced staffing for the program to the point where it could not monitor it effectively.

In June 1999, just as Feldman began his investigation for Spitzer, the GAO complained to a House Subcommittee that "HUD has done little to address the problems identified by its Inspector General and others," allowing "risky property deals and overstated property appraisals," although "many of the homes had not been properly rehabilitated." The report went on to note that HUD did not effectively monitor the program because it did not have enough staff and failed to train properly the staff it had. The GAO noted that although HUD endorsed about 4,000 loans under the program in 1994, by 1997 that number had mushroomed to more than 18,000, implying that it had grown beyond HUD's ability to supervise it. The GAO tried to find out whether a nonprofit organization that "defaulted on all the mortgages it had taken out" had met HUD's eligibility criteria in the first place, but the HUD field office in charge did not know because it had lost its records. GAO did determine, however, that "nonprofit organizations' 203(k) loans are so risky and problematic that one of the largest lenders of funds for the program decided to no longer make or purchase 203(k) loans. According to a senior official at this lender, most of the nonprofit loans the bank acquired have eventually gone into default."

In its follow-up report in 2001, the GAO more explicitly credited the HUD IG for having noted the program's risks in 1997 and in 1998. It noted that in May 2000, at long last, HUD finally set forth procedures "for identifying high-risk 203(k) lenders and targeting them for annual monitoring." It also noted that in fiscal year 2000, it endorsed only about 10,000 loans.

With oversight provided by congressional committees, the HUD IG, and the GAO, it was apparently the lawsuit initiated by Spitzer in 1999 with the follow-up indictments by the US attorney and the Manhattan district attorney generating headlines blasting the program publicly, that provided HUD with sufficient incentive to clamp down. Oversight by a state attorney general, more commonly exercised with respect to state or local government behavior, may when necessary, at its furthest reach, even result in reform of a federal program.

Conclusion

Oversight by audit is the central responsibility of state auditors, comptrollers and—where their statutory mandate includes it—treasurers. We may presume that every holder of such office accepts that responsibility. But politics and chance determines whether any particular state auditor, comptroller or treasurer feels a deep-seated intolerance for waste, abuse, and injustice. The "low boiling point" valuable in an investigator may be less important in the audit version of oversight. After all, in theory the ideal audit begins without prejudice: auditors should determine whether systems and procedures in fact serve well to safeguard public assets, and should be equally satisfied if they find that that do or if they find that they don't.

The offices of state auditors, comptrollers and treasurer usually appear to have the institutional resources to meet their responsibilities, with some caveats. On one hand, they are equipped with staffs of trained auditors who enjoy statutory and/or constitutional powers to gather the information they need from the agencies they review. Notwithstanding their theoretical neutrality, their desire for reelection, reappointment, or political advancement should provide sufficient incentive for them to seek public exposure of the deficiencies they find. As to another of our guiding principles, the need for follow-up, Generally Accepted Government Auditing Standards require their performance audit reports to "facilitate follow-up to determine whether corrective actions have been taken."

On the other hand, while federal government has grown enormously, the reach of state government has also grown, to the point at which no auditor, comptroller or treasurer could possibly review more than a tiny fraction of the work of the agencies of their respective states at any given time. The "spot checks" they can perform may serve as a deterrent to tolerance for sloppy systems by management and for abuse of weak internal controls by miscreants, but inevitably much misbehavior will go undetected. We cannot fault them for this, however: No degree of adherence to the guiding principles of oversight can magically create the almost unlimited resources that comprehensive reviews of state government would require.

State attorneys general play a very different role, although that role also varies from state to state. To the extent that attorneys general act solely as prosecutorial officers, their work falls outside of the scope of oversight that we defined early in this book. But some occasionally pursue and prosecute misbehavior among government agency personnel with an eye toward systemic change. The 2011 agreement between New York State's comptroller and attorney general for symbiosis among their investigative, auditing, and prosecutorial efforts may provide a model for other states that would expand the oversight role of state attorneys general in this regard. The case of the New York attorney general's investigation of issues related to the federal 203(k) housing program demonstrates how these offices can use their civil authority to bring cases that lead to the systemic types of reform that we look for from watchdogs. In that case, the New York attorney general's efforts extended to a federal program—and produced more results than previous work of either federal IGs or the GAO.

However, because state attorneys general often are required to defend other state officials and more often required to advise them, they face psychological and legal barriers to an adversarial stance. As intolerant of fraud, waste, abuse. and injustice as they may be in other respects, when it comes to litigation against their state officer clients, their hands may be tied. Furthermore, most of them lack jurisdiction to pursue criminal action against such officers. In all other respects, they are institutionally equipped to exemplify our principles of sound oversight, but most of the time, the barriers they do face make it difficult if not impossible.

Chapter 11

Local Legislative Oversight

All politics is local.

—Former House Speaker Thomas P. O'Neill

On the third season of the HBO series, *The Wire*, viewers are introduced to Tommy Carcetti, a Baltimore City councilman who chairs the Subcommittee on Public Safety. Carcetti reaches out to the police department deputy commissioner and asks for the inside scoop on the department— offering to help the department on budget and staffing issues in return. When the deputy commissioner refuses, Carcetti's next subcommittee hearing focuses on overtime spending in the department and spending on travel for department heads to a conference in Florida.

Carcetti eventually gets his way . . . and gets elected mayor.

On paper, the New York City Council may have the strongest mandate for oversight of any local elected legislative body. The New York City Charter requires that the mayor twice annually report on the operations of the city and—following the release of the Mayor's Management Report—the council is required to hold hearings on the findings.

Several years ago, one of us was attending the council hearing on the Mayor's Management Report findings on the city Youth Services Department. There recently had been a series of budget cuts and not surprisingly, the mayor's report suggested that there had been a significant reduction in the number of young people served by the city's programs.

Inexplicably, no one on the council committee holding the hearing had drawn the connection between the spending cuts and the reduction in services. Moreover, no one on the council had asked how the department had adapted to its smaller budget through efforts to increase efficiency or productivity.

167

Finally, a note made its way to a member of the committee suggesting this line of questioning. The councilmember read the note, nodded, and when called on proceeded to ask the department commissioner a series of tough questions. Until the committee chair interrupted: "Councilman, this is an oversight hearing. Why are you asking questions about the budget?"

No matter how strong the mandate, you can lead a council committee to oversight but you can't make the chairman think.

This chapter explains why effective local legislative oversight is relatively unusual, and gives two examples—not necessarily salutary ones—of local legislative oversight in action.

Oversight at the Local Level

Legislative oversight, common at the federal level and practiced at the state level, is far more limited at the local level. There are a number of reasons that explain the limited application of legislative oversight in cities and towns.

First, the separation of powers that exists at the federal and for the most part, at the state government level is far more complicated at the local level. Nationally, the majority of local governments lack a strong executive. In most counties, cities, and towns, executive functions are carried out by city or county managers hired by city councils or county commissions rather than by elected mayors or county executives. According to the International City County Management Association, 58 percent of US cities with more than 100,000 residents in 2007 had council-manager governments.

Even in those cities with a mayor, their powers are largely ceremonial. In these "weak mayor" cities, much of the day-to-day operations remain under the control of the legislature. Naturally, when the local legislature controls government operations, it is less likely to engage in the skeptical scrutiny that effective oversight requires. In other cases, the mayor is not necessarily elected citywide: Members of city councils can be appointed mayor for a term by their colleagues.

In most cities and counties, executive authority may be divided among several elected officials. For example, sheriffs are frequently independently elected officials who have substantial authority, budgets, and power independent of a county or city mayor.

In the case of commission-style government, individual members of the council may have authority over specific departments of government. Take the small city of Chester, Pennsylvania, just outside of Philadelphia. Chester has an elected city council of five members. The mayor sits as a member of the Chester City Council and also serves as the director of public affairs—with responsibility for the Chester Police Department. The other members of the council serve as the directors of parks, recreation, and public property; accounts and finance; streets and public improvements; and public safety.

Even where there is a relatively strong and independent executive, the legislature at the local level frequently plays a far greater role in what would—at the federal level and in most states—be considered an executive role. Individual contracts and personnel decisions sometimes require approval by the city council or county commission. These are not policy or legislative decisions—whether to outsource certain functions or increase staffing in departments: Legislative officials sign off on specific contract awards and hiring decisions.

The lack of separation between executive and legislative power makes traditional legislative oversight far more complicated. In effect, council or commission members have the equivalent of "pre-audit" authority. In other words, executive decisions or actions are as much their own actions as that of a single executive.

In local governments with clearer division between the executive and legislative functions, there are other obstacles to oversight. Because they are smaller in size, city councils and county commissions are more likely to adopt collegial approaches to governance with a strong mayor.

Although Congress—the House and Senate—has 535 members and the number of state legislators ranges from forty-nine (the unicameral in Nebraska) to a half dozen states with two hundred or more members, city councils are much smaller. Among the nation's ten largest cities, Chicago (fifty) and New York (fifty-one) have the largest local legislatures. But for most cities of 1 million residents or more, the city council ranges in size from eight—in San Diego and Phoenix—to seventeen—in Philadelphia. Smaller legislatures render all politics not just local, but personal as well. It is hard to imagine a president having a personal relationship and rapport with all members of Congress: That's less true for a mayor who sits with eight colleagues on a city council.

Local legislatures are also more likely to be nonpartisan. As a result, the normal oversight from the party out of power is less of an issue. Even where there are partisan elections, minority parties may be so small as to be ineffective: Of New York's fifty-one councilmembers, less than a handful have been elected as Republicans at any given point in the past twenty years.

In those cities with strong mayors, councilmembers who are aggressive in pursuing oversight investigations risk retribution that can exact real political costs. Mayors have the ability to steer capital projects and other funding. In Chicago, it used to be said that streets in the one reform stronghold in the city—Hyde Park—would go unpaved for decades as payback to reformers who took on the Democratic machine. Mayors also have the ability to tap citywide political and fundraising resources to quiet councilmembers who take on their administrations.

The uniquely local nature of government at the city or county level also means that legislators are even more dependent on their ability to deliver funding for local projects than members of Congress or state legislators. Little political credit accrues to a member of a city council or county commission among his or her own constituents for rooting out waste. At the local level, constituents expect service delivery and new parks and schools—not necessarily headline-making investigations.

Finally, local legislative oversight is impeded by a lack of capacity in most cities and counties. The majority of councilmembers and commissioners are part-time: They have other full-time employment and earn relatively low salaries for the amount of time that they spend attending meetings and addressing the basic needs and demands of their constituents. They simply don't have the time—or in many cases, the experience—to pursue the same types of investigations that their colleagues at the federal or state levels can.

Usually, local legislative staff are primarily administrative, or work with the elected officials to address constituent demands. With some rare exceptions, legislative oversight staffing capacity is extremely limited at the local level.

For all of these reasons, legislative oversight at the local level is really the exception rather than the rule.

There are, however, exceptions. Although politics more often than not is a reason not to pursue an investigation, there are cases of open warfare between some executives and the city council. In the early 1980s, the clashes between the city council and Mayor Harold Washington in Chicago were regularly referred to as Council Wars—and led to a parody of *Star Wars* with Washington as Luke Skywalker and then council leader Ed Vrdolyak as Darth Vader.

More recently, a series of council investigations in the nation's capital produced different results—and it was all about politics.

The Rise and Fall of Adrian Fenty

In 1999, Adrian Fenty was elected to the District of Columbia City Council at the age of twenty-nine as a reformer and independent. He won an upset victory over a council incumbent who had served her district for twenty years. On the council, Fenty was an outsider who pursued his own agenda—with what the *Washington Post* called an "independent, contrarian style."

In 2006, Fenty ran for mayor of Washington. His principal opponent was the then chair of the Washington City Council. Not a single member of the council endorsed Fenty's campaign for mayor; one accused him of grandstanding on the council, saying "he is not a serious person."

Fenty won the primary in 2006 with 57 percent of the vote, winning every one of the city's 142 precincts. In the general election, Fenty won with 89 percent of the vote.

Early in his term, Fenty sought and won control over the District of Columbia public schools and the power to appoint a new schools chancellor, Michelle Rhee. Rhee moved forward with a series of controversial reforms to the system's contract with teacher unions, winning national acclaim from education reformers and earning the enmity of organized labor.

As Fenty was being elected mayor, Vincent Gray was elected as the new chair of the District of Columbia City Council. Gray had served for just two years in one of the council's district seats before becoming chairman.

By 2009, the council and Mayor Fenty were battling on a series of issues. The conflict came to a head, however, with the revelation that the Fenty administration had awarded a series of contracts for the construction and renovation of recreation centers, ball fields and parks through the District of Columbia Housing Authority (DCHA). In going through DCHA, the Fenty administration had avoided the requirement that city contracts of at least $1 million be reviewed and approved by the city council.

Beyond the issue of process, public attention quickly turned to the beneficiaries of the contracts—a small group of close allies and friends of Mayor Fenty. The mayor's college friends and some of his political supporters led two of the firms. Simply put, to the public and the press, it appeared that the Fenty administration had violated city procurement rules in order to award contracts to friends. If ever there was an issue of fraud, waste and abuse ripe for oversight investigation, this was it.

Under Gray's leadership, the District of Columbia City Council pounced on the opportunity. Under council rules, committees are permitted to conduct "roundtables" as a prelude to formal hearings. In October 2009, the chairs of four council committees convened a joint oversight roundtable to review the projects and the procurement process. The city administrator and other administration officials, as well as community members, testified.

Just days later, one of the committees passed a formal resolution directing an investigation and authorizing the use of subpoenas "to compel the attendance of witnesses, to obtain testimony, and to require the production of documents." Between the beginning of November 2009 and the end of January 2010, the committee held no fewer than six roundtables and heard testimony from city officials and from one of the contractors involved in the project. When one of the contractors refused to appear to testify the council moved to enforce the subpoena and a judge ordered testimony before the committee.

In response to the refusal of one of the contractors to testify, a council committee passed a resolution authorizing the hiring of a special counsel to assist the committee in its investigation. Over the next year, the special counsel issued fourteen document requests that covered both public records and bank and other records of a series of firms linked to the two principal contractors at the center of the allegations. The special counsel deposed fourteen witnesses, interviewed another thirty individuals and obtained written answers to a series of interrogatories from Mayor Fenty.

The council committee voted to retain special counsel in early March 2010. By the end of the month, Mayor Fenty had a new opponent in the September 2010 primary—City Council Chairman Vincent Gray.

The council investigation created an issue for Gray and for other opponents of the mayor.

A *Washington Post* poll released two weeks before primary day found Gray leading Fenty 53 percent to 36 percent among likely voters. The poll results highlighted the effect of the ethical questions raised by the council investigation. Among all voters, 67 percent agreed that Fenty had brought necessary change to the district, 64 percent agreed that he had accomplished a great deal, 59 percent believed that the district was "moving in the right direction" and by a 44 to 17 margin, voters agreed that the quality of life was improving rather than getting worse—all poll numbers that would otherwise lead to re-election.

Why was Fenty losing? Clearly, Rhee's tenure as school chancellor was having an effect—55 percent of voters indicated that it would be important to their decision on who to vote for. But, by a 41 to 40 margin, most voters indicated that it would be a reason to vote for Fenty's re-election.

Fenty, however, faced a trust gap—one that was likely exacerbated by, if not the result of, the pending council investigation. When asked whether Fenty was "honest and trustworthy," 46 percent of voters disagreed and only 39 percent agreed. By comparison, when asked the same question about Gray, voters agreed by a 61 to 13 margin.

Gray defeated Mayor Fenty, 54 percent to 44 percent, in the September 2010 primary and won the general election, taking office in 2011.

A year after being appointed, the special counsel released its report on the investigation of the Fenty administration's contracts for parks and recreation facilities. The findings of the report raised serious questions related to the relationship between the lead contractor on the projects and subcontractors. Specifically, the investigation found the following:

- The lead contractor selected an inexperienced subcontractor to perform initial work on the project on a sole source basis.

- The subcontractor was selected to provide all engineering work on the project on the basis of a response to a request for qualifications. The investigation found that the response contained material falsehoods—including falsely identifying individuals as employees of the subcontractor.

- The principal reason for the subcontractor's selection was that it met requirements for being a certified small business contractor (CBE); yet the investigation found that the subcontractor did little of the work and instead subcontracted the work to other non-CBEs at significant markups.

- The investigation found a series of financial relationships between the lead contractor and the subcontractor through affiliate firms, including $1 million in payments from a firm connected with the contractor to another firm owned by the principal of the subcontractor.

- Noting the lack of cooperation of the principals of the contractor and subcontractor in providing documents and testimony, the special counsel concluded that their "claimed failure of recollection was so extensive and so complete that it was unworthy of belief . . . their performance left us with the clear impression that they believed they had something to hide."

On the basis of these findings, the special counsel recommended that the council refer the matter to the US attorney for additional investigation and consideration for criminal prosecution.

But what about Mayor Fenty's role? Was this entire scheme designed for his benefit?

The special counsel found that "our investigation uncovered no wrongdoing on the part of the Mayor, and we found that the DPR [Department of Parks and Recreation] capital funds were not transferred for the purpose of avoiding Council oversight."

In other words, the core of the allegation—that the Fenty administration had manipulated the contracting process to benefit political allies—was disproven. Instead, Fenty's allies had taken advantage of an effort by the administration to expedite worthy projects. The special counsel concluded, "District officials gave priority to the need for speed while ignoring the preference for price competition that is embodied in both District and DCHA procedures and would have better served the District's interests."

At the conclusion of the special counsel's 258-page final report, there are four recommendations for legislative action, in addition to the referral to US attorney. The special counsel calls for:

- A detailed council analysis of District construction procurement and project management practices

- Council consideration of whether there should be additional monitoring and reporting when District agencies enter into memoranda of understanding with other public entities to conduct construction activities on their behalf

- Council clarification of existing rules related to when agencies are required to seek council approval for contracts

- Council review of the application of CBE requirements to subcontractors

Although the council's investigation may produce criminal indictments and certainly highlighted failures in the city's contracting process, its greatest impact to date has been the election of Gray as mayor of Washington, D.C.

The Council Investigation of Gray

Gray faced his own allegations of corruption, stemming from his 2010 campaign for mayor. A minor candidate in the 2010 election, Sulaimon Brown, made allegations that Gray's campaign offered him funds and a position with the new administration if he remained in the race and campaigned against Fenty. In fact, Brown was appointed to a $110,000 post with the city's Department of Health Finance despite an arrest record.

A July 2011 *Washington Post* investigation also found that Gray's campaign accepted cash contributions in violation of the city's campaign finance laws and recorded contributions in the names of individuals who claim not to have made contributions.

As these allegations were raised, the District of Columbia Council again stepped into the oversight role. Beginning in March 2011—just two months after Gray was sworn into office—the council conducted a series of five public hearings to examine allegations related to the mayor's political appointments. In June, the council created a Special Committee on Investigation of Executive Personnel Practices.

The committee's August 2011 draft report discusses the scope of the investigation—examining nineteen witnesses and reviewing 20,000 pages of documents. The committee concluded the following:

> children of senior officials were illegally hired, that the Gray administration engaged in cronyism, that senior officials in the Gray administration received salaries that exceeded the legal salary cap, and that standard personnel practices were not followed. There is also strong evidence that Howard Brooks, a senior member of the Gray campaign, provided funds to Mr. Brown during the Mayoral campaign and that senior officials in the Gray campaign promised Mr. Brown a job in the Gray administration.

Yet, as in the case of the Fenty investigation, the council investigation cleared Gray of wrongdoing, noting that "there is little evidence in the record to suggest that he was aware of nepotism and cronyism, or that standard personnel practices were being violated." Instead, the report places blame on the mayor's top aides—including his chief of staff, who hired her son to a $55,000 position with the Department of Parks and Recreation. Specifically, the report finds Brown's testimony that he received funds from the Gray campaign with Gray's knowledge and approval as "unreliable, unsubstantiated and exaggerated."

Several facts, however, distinguish the Gray investigation from the Fenty investigation. First, Gray asked the council to conduct its investigation—despite the fact that there were already pending investigations that had been publicly disclosed by both the US attorney and Congress. Second, the council did not seek outside counsel to assist it in its investigation as it did in the Fenty investigation. Finally, although the mayor sought the council investigation, there is no indication that the council sought his testimony in the matter, either through appearance before the committee or, as was the case in the Fenty investigation, through written interrogatories.

When it comes to local legislative oversight, the case of the District of Columbia Council and mayors Fenty and Gray points to the overwhelming importance of local politics. In both the Fenty and Gray investigations, council investigations found serious issues of misconduct—in government procurement in one case and personnel in the other. In both cases, initial allegations pointed to potential involvement at the highest levels of District of Columbia local government.

In the Fenty matter, the timing of the council oversight investigation coincided with a primary challenge by the chair of the council to the principal target of the investigation—Mayor Fenty. The very existence of the investigation and the allegations of cronyism helped to defeat Fenty and elect Gray. The eventual clearing of Fenty—though certainly not his allies—provided little solace coming six months after his political defeat.

In the Gray matter, the council—in its timing and approach—appears to have played a very different role. In effect, the council investigation sought to pre-empt the outcome of the criminal investigation by the US attorney. If nothing else, its findings regarding the credibility of the principal witness in what would be a potential criminal case against the mayor, Sulaimon Brown, appear to have damaged that case before it was ever brought. The council went so far as to refer Brown to the US attorney for potential prosecution for perjury. The council's decision to absolve Gray early in the investigation and focus all blame on his aides, without even seeking Gray's testimony, raises real questions as to the focus of the council's inquiry.

Conclusion

Councilman Tommy Carcetti is the exception, not the rule. There is not a lot of truly effective legislative oversight that occurs at the local level. The combination of blurred separation of powers, part-time legislators, limited staff and the very local nature of local politics creates serious hurdles to local legislative bodies going beyond constituency service, their role in the local budget and basic legislative activity.

Given the important role that local government plays in the lives of most people—from the delivery of essential services like fire and police to funding and running the nation's school systems—the lack of effective local legislative oversight should be an area of great concern.

The case study on the role of the District of Columbia City Council in its investigations of two successive mayors certainly offers a cautionary tale of how local legislative oversight can be even more political—even more of an example of "politics by other means"—than anything we discussed at the federal level.

And that's a problem. We have already noted that real cases of corruption at the local level can have a crippling effect on the overall operations of local government and make a city or a county less competitive economically. To the extent that limited resources devoted to oversight are focused on partisan investigations, it means that less attention is or can be devoted to the real issues related to local governance.

In a subsequent chapter, we'll discuss how the lack of oversight at the local level—and apparent complicity on the part of some legislators—led to a massive scandal in the small city of Bell, California. In the case of Bell, the press ultimately played the oversight function that the city council was unable or unwilling to perform.

As in the case of Congress, it is unlikely that local legislative bodies will do more or better unless there is an expectation of more on the part of voters.

Chapter 12

Local Auditors and Inspectors General

In the main, of course, the Commissioner [of Investigation] must do what the Mayor permits.

> —Wallace Sayre and Herbert Kaufman
> (*Governing New York City*, 1965)

Why are our public pension systems and plans in such precarious financial condition? Of course there are some examples of excessive pensions, of double-dipping and of "gaming" the system to "goose" the pension amount. But these are few in number. . . . The inappropriate investments that caused these massive pension fund losses were not an accident. The pension fund field caught the Wall Street contagion—financial corruption.

> —William Lerach (Blame Wall Street, Not Hard
> Working Americans, for the Pension Funds Fiasco, 2011)

Recently, a group of federal officials visited a struggling, mid-sized midwestern city. The city had lost half of its population over a forty-year period, along with many of the jobs that its residents used to hold.

The group of federal officials was there to identify the city's capacity needs—with a goal of offering assistance. They asked about the city's process for hiring and firing employees. "Well, we really don't have very many resources to focus on that," they were told. Next, they asked about the city's contracting policies. "Well, there is really just one person who works on that and we try as best as we can to follow the law." Finally, they asked about the city's internal auditor. "That's easy, we don't have one."

To quote Claude Rains as Captain Renault in *Casablanca*, the federal officials were "shocked, shocked" to learn of the absence of these basic controls.

As noted in the previous chapter, mostly part-time local legislators with limited staff resources are usually unable to play the same type of oversight role that the legislative branch plays at the federal—or even at the state—level.

This chapter focuses on two of the most common local watchdogs—auditors and IGs. As discussed in previous chapters, these watchdog roles are very different and their independence, focus, and resources often determine their scope and effectiveness. This is particularly true for smaller local governments, where there may be no IG and at most a one- or two-person internal audit unit.

At the conclusion of this chapter, we look in detail at how a mid-size city government with limited staff and resources undertook an oversight effort on an unlikely and powerful target—two of Wall Street's largest financial houses.

The Local Audit Function: An Overview

The role of auditors at the local government level is well established. Virtually every local government is subject to an annual financial audit. Most local governments are required to publish annual financial statements, sometimes prepared by state officials, local audit departments, or outside accounting firms. Larger local governments publish a comprehensive annual financial report (CAFR) that may be prepared by their own audit staff members, outside auditors, or a combination thereof.

The prevalence of the local audit function is, in part, explained by the desire of local governments to enter the municipal bond market. CAFRs are frequently critical components of the presentation of bond offerings by local governments and state law frequently prescribes the content of the annual financial statements. Underwriters and purchasers of municipal bonds would be unwilling to sell or purchase debt in the absence of financial statements prepared in a manner consistent with generally accepted accounting principles (GAAP). These statements go directly to the question of whether or not the issuer has the capacity to take on debt—and whether bondholders will be paid.

Although there has been considerable discussion recently about the fiscal stability of many cities and states, municipal bond default remains extremely rare. In part, this is because of the relatively intense process of financial review carried out as this most basic part of the audit function.

Additionally, under the federal Single Audit Act of 1984, local governments—and in fact, any federal grant recipients—that receive and spend more than $500,000 in federal funds annually are required to account for those funds as part of their annual financial reporting.

Thus, there are federal and often state and market-based requirements that cause local governments to invest in the most basic type of financial auditing on a regular basis.

Many local governments also have their own internal auditors who perform financial audits and sometimes performance audits as well. As at the federal and state levels, financial audits focus on accounting—can the department or program account for the expenditure of all the dollars allocated to it and revenues collected by it? Financial audits can identify missing funds, and the presence or lack of internal controls to ensure appropriate collection and expenditure of resources; and can sometimes address fraud and abuse issues—were funds misdirected?

Performance audits can look both to the appropriate expenditure of funds (ie, did the spending comply with applicable rules?) and to whether those funds were wisely used (ie, did the expenditure result in the desired outcomes?) They can assess whether the overall program or a department spent funds efficiently and make recommendations for improvement. Performance audits also can examine questions around effectiveness—did the program or department achieve the results that it was designed to achieve?

Local financial audits can disclose fraud and abuse—dollars that went to line the pockets of a local alderman rather than to provide food or clothing for the poor—but they do not always speak to the quality of service provided or to the wisdom of the underlying policy. Performance audits, on the other hand, can look at policy and service quality questions but can miss fraud and abuse issues—the well-run program by the mayor's brother-in-law who kicks back part of his salary to the mayor.

An effective local audit function requires a combination of both financial and performance audits.

Some local auditors have gone beyond day-to-day oversight and are directly involved in programmatic evaluation, performance measurement, and performance management. This leads to a very different type of oversight.

For example, in San Francisco, the city controller is the chief accounting officer and auditor for the city and county. Additionally, the controller publishes a bimonthly government barometer report that tracks forty different performance indicators—from average monthly water use to on-time performance of the city's MUNI system to the number of calls answered by the city's 311 system in sixty seconds or less. But the San Francisco controller's role in performance measurement is limited. Although the controller reports the data, the office does not audit the data to ensure validity.

What Gets Audited and What Audits Say

The choice of what to audit (what program, what department) and what the focus of the audit should be (financial or performance) is an area of enormous discretion and great importance. Given limited resources, the decision of what gets audited and how is often the most important decision that an auditor can make. This form of "shot selection" frequently determines whether audit resources are maximized or not.

Financial audits are the norm. They don't require extraordinary policy or programmatic expertise and largely rely on basic accounting. Performance audits require a greater level of understanding and, in some ways, are more subjective.

Other than the preparation of annual financial statements, auditors usually determine their own audit priorities. In some cases, their discretion is limited by local charter requirements. For example, in New York, the city's auditor, the *comptroller*, is required by city charter to audit at least one aspect of every city department, large or small, at least once every four years. The difference in spelling from the last *controller* is intentional, not a typographical error, but the meaning is the same.

Local government auditors may respond to specific audit requests from a mayor, county executive, city manager, or chief administrative officer. Their responsiveness to those requests may depend, to some extent, on the reporting structure of the auditor and the role of the requesting party in determining the auditor's budget. Some local governments also have independent audit committees that may advise, if not oversee, the audit function. Auditors frequently establish annual audit plans that outline the areas that will be examined in any given year.

Like federal and state auditors, local government auditors may perform audits in a manner consistent with Generally Accepted Government Auditing Standards. The Yellow Book prescribes the audit process and the basic contents of an audit. Audits are not designed to be policy analyses. Still, especially in the case of performance audits, they contain both factual analysis and recommendations. Recommendations are based on interpretations of facts and an understanding of best practices.

Finally, financial or performance audits can all identify signs of fraud or abuse—sometimes requiring high specialized forensic audits.

The Relationship between Structure and Auditor Independence

The independence of the audit function is essential to the credibility of audit findings and audit independence is at the core of requirements for government auditing. Local governments have taken a number of steps designed to ensure auditor independence, but independence is often complicated by the size and structure of local government.

The overall structure of local government in the United States varies greatly. Some cities are governed by strong mayors and city councils, but a majority of cities are governed by a council–manager structure, with either no mayor or a weak mayor and a city manager appointed by the council. At the county level, there is similar variation—with most counties governed by a commission or board of supervisors and an appointed county manager or chief administrative officer, although some large counties have an elected county executive.

The appointment and role of auditors at the local government level varies, in part, based on the overall structure of the local government. These variations affect the independence of the audit function and the willingness of auditors to take on a chief executive or key appointees. A 2011 analysis of the twenty largest US cities and counties found the following:

- In the nation's largest cities, seven of twenty auditors are appointed by the city council. Another two auditors are appointed by the city manager, who is an appointee of the city council.

- Six of the auditors in the nation's twenty largest cities are appointed by and report to the mayor. In both Boston and Chicago, the audit role is within another mayoral appointee's office, the Department of Auditing in Boston and the Office of Compliance in Chicago.

- In five cities (New York, Los Angeles, Houston, Philadelphia, and Columbus, Ohio), the chief auditor is an elected official.

- In the nation's largest counties, most auditors are appointees of a county commission, board of supervisors, or judicial board. In several cases, county auditors report to the county's chief financial officer.

- Five county auditors—actually auditor-controllers—are elected, all from California counties.

- Only one county auditor (in Cook County, Illinois) is an appointee of the county chief executive, in that case, the president of the Board of Supervisors.

In some cases, the result of local events can create more support, if not a greater need, for a robust audit function. Orange County, California presents an interesting and unique case. In 1994, Orange County became the largest US municipality to go into bankruptcy. The bankruptcy resulted from $1.7 billion in investment losses due to a highly risky investment strategy. The county treasurer eventually pleaded guilty to six felony counts.

Perhaps not surprisingly, Orange County now has three auditors. In addition to an elected auditor-controller, the Board of Supervisors has also appointed an internal auditor and created a separate Office of Performance Audit. The Santa Clara County Board of Supervisors also has its own Management Audit Unit, in addition to the primary audit function for the county performed within the office of the county finance officer.

In addition to the appointment structure, local governments also take additional steps to ensure auditor independence. County and city charter provisions often include detailed specific grounds for potential removal of an auditor, as opposed to at-will termination, and definite terms of appointment. For example, San Diego, Detroit, and San Francisco all have ten-year appointments for their auditors. In Broward County, Florida, the County Commission appoints the auditor on the basis of a recommendation from an independent selection committee.

Just as at the federal and state levels, there is a tradeoff between the independence of the audit function and the ability of audits to result in change. Internal auditors may be less independent, but should, in theory, be able to more directly influence decisions by the executive and legislative officials who appoint them. It is far more difficult for executive and legislative elected officials to dismiss or disregard the findings of their own appointees. Moreover, in many cases, internal auditors may be conducting reviews at the specific request of these officials.

Independently elected auditors or appointed auditors with a fixed term may be more independent, but more frequently may have to rely on the media and the bully pulpit to attract attention to their findings and recommendations. Often, the subjects of critical audits from independent auditors will, in the case of elected auditors, dismiss audit findings as political or politicized.

As in the case with other offices designed to maximize independence, it can come at the sake of accountability. An independent auditor appointed to a ten-year term is accountable to no one for the performance of his or her office.

Auditors may have multiple roles beyond just the audit function. For example, the New York City comptroller has responsibility for a variety of administrative functions related to city investments, contract registration and the settlement of claims. In Columbus, the city auditor is largely responsible for tax collection, playing a role closer to that traditionally associated with a local government finance department or treasurer's office. In Dallas, the Office of Internal Audit is also responsible for grant compliance.

The mixing of multiple roles is a double-edged sword. On the one hand, the auditor's administrative and management powers could be used to help move toward implementation of certain audit recommendations. For example, in New York, comptroller audits on procurement carry greater weight because of the office's direct role in and direct ability to address problems in the procurement process.

On the other hand, these other functions could drain an office's resources or create questions as to the independence of auditors. Even with a growing national process of peer review, the question remains, who audits the auditor? This is even more relevant where auditors are examining functions that other parts of their offices are directly involved in.

Ultimately, what gets audited and what the focus of audits are depends significantly on the availability of resources for the audit function. Again, this varies greatly from jurisdiction to jurisdiction.

With a total budget of $70 million and more than 700 staff members in 2011, the New York City comptroller's office was the largest local government office with audit functions. Of its staff, 155 were assigned to the Bureau of Audit. In smaller cities and counties, although still among the largest in the nation, there are dramatically fewer auditors, less resources to conduct audits, and less specialization. Indianapolis, Charlotte, and Memphis and large counties such as Sacramento, all had fewer than ten staff in their audit units as of 2011.

There may be political and cultural reasons for the emphasis, or lack thereof, on the audit function. As of 2011, Chicago reported having just four internal auditors in its twenty-eight–person Office of Compliance. And the Cook County, Illinois auditor has a staff of ten and a budget of under $1 million annually. By comparison, Maricopa County, Arizona, with a population equal to just three-fourths of that in Cook County, had an internal auditor with a staff of seventeen and a $1.6 million budget.

Local Inspectors General

As discussed in the sections on the federal and state governments, IGs play a somewhat different role than auditors. Both types of office seek to identify and prevent fraud, waste, and abuse. But IGs also often are tasked with identifying, seeking to prevent, and bringing cases to prosecutors punishing criminal activity within the local government. Although auditors are almost always accountants and can refer a case to a prosecutor for action or to police for investigation, IGs frequently have background in law enforcement.

It is easy, however, to see how the lines can be blurred or competitive, especially at the local level. The largest local IG agency in the nation is New York's DOI. The DOI was born out of a municipal audit function. In 1873, in the aftermath of the Boss Tweed and Tammany Hall scandals, the state legislature created the commissioner of accounts. In 1920, a change in the New York City Charter created the Department of Investigations and Accounts. And although attorneys and investigators predominantly staff the DOI, it still also employs auditors and accountants to assist in the financial aspects of its investigations.

In other local governments, the two functions are joined. The Los Angeles County auditor-controller also oversees the Office of County Investigations.

Although virtually every local government has some audit function and most large local governments have their own auditor or internal audit staff, relatively few local governments have a separate IG.

By far, New York City's DOI is the largest local government internal investigations agency in the nation with a 2011 staff of 219 and a budget of $19.3 million. As in the case of the federal government, each department of city government has its own IG, but in New York City each also reports to the DOI commissioner.

The DOI is directly involved in the day-to-day functions of city departments. It administers aspects of a detailed system of background checks for employees and contractors. As of 2011, the DOI conducts more than 2,000 background reviews of city employees annually and makes approximately 150 policy and procedure recommendations to city departments on an annual basis.

The DOI frequently works in concert with state and local law enforcement agencies in criminal investigations. When the DOI learns of potential criminal activity in a city department, it may conduct initial steps in an investigation but will frequently then call in appropriate law enforcement agencies. Similarly, law enforcement agencies that initiate investigations of criminal activity involving city government will frequently request support from the DOI.

Among the twenty largest cities, in addition to New York, only three others have a similar agency and none compare in size or resources.

As of 2011, Chicago had a larger IG function than its internal audit function, with a staff of thirty-two and a budget of $2.6 million. The role of Philadelphia's IG was recently reshaped by Mayor Michael Nutter. The office, with a direct report to the mayor, had a 2011 budget of $1.3 million and a staff of nineteen. In 2009, the office received 688 complaints of misconduct—up from 478 just the year before. Philadelphia Office of Inspector General (OIG) cases resulted in twenty-four arrests and indictments and four convictions, as well as the termination of thirty-four employees. In 2010, the City of Houston created an OIG within the Office of the City Attorney with a staff of eight and a $1 million annual budget.

Among the nation's largest counties, only Miami-Dade County has a separate IG function. Its OIG was created in 1997 and includes investigations, audit, administrative, and legal units. In its 2008 annual report, the Miami-Dade County IG reported having identified $123.9 million in questionable costs and lost revenue and realized $68.7 million in savings, prevented losses and restitution since inception, with $15.2 million in the last year alone.

Montgomery County, Maryland, Sacramento County, California and Palm Beach County, Florida also have IGs. as do many county or regional public authorities or government agencies (eg, board of education, water management districts, transit authorities).

Other cities and counties have functions similar to IGs. In Detroit, complaints about misconduct are referred to a city ombudsperson. And several cities and counties have IG functions specific to individual departments—such as school districts, sheriffs, and police departments.

The IG/investigations role is also often intertwined with related functions—ethics commissions, conflict-of-interest boards, and whistleblower hotlines.

Although still relatively small in number, the concept of a local government investigations or IG function is growing. Often in response to local scandals, mayors and city councils have reacted by creating OIGs.

Government executives or legislators need not create local IGs. Palm Beach County, Florida and Jefferson Parish, Louisiana are interesting in that the residents created IGs through referenda.

One of the newest local government IG offices is in Cuyahoga County, Ohio. Its creation presents an interesting case study of why local governments frequently turn to an IG approach.

For years, Cuyahoga County and its largest city, Cleveland, had been the butt of national humor as the city's population and surrounding industry declined. In 1969, the Cuyahoga River caught fire, a fact subsequently immortalized in Randy Newman's song "Burn On." For years, the Cleveland Indians were last in the American League, going forty years between World Series appearances and becoming the subject of the movie comedy *Major League*.

Cleveland and Cuyahoga County, have been on something of a come-back—with a revitalized downtown and waterfront. The city and county still face a myriad of problems familiar to historically industrial cities.

In more recent years, Cleveland and Cuyahoga County attracted new unwanted attention for a massive corruption scandal in county government. Six former or current countywide elected officials were named in one of the widest ranging corruption scandals in the history of Ohio. They include county judges, one member of the county's three member-commission, the county auditor, and the county sheriff. In response, a citizen–business coalition supported a referendum to create a county charter replacing the three-member commission with a county executive and county council. A citizens' transition committee also recommended appointment of an IG, in addition to the newly created position of county director of internal audit. The county's first elected county executive, a former FBI agent and prosecutor, campaigned on the promise to create an IG and did so within his first days in office.

As was the case for auditors, the question of funding and resources has an obvious effect on the breadth and scope of the type of investiga-tions that inspectors general are able to undertake. In Miami-Dade County, the law creating the OIG established a funding mechanism. A significant portion of the costs related to the operation of the Miami-Dade County OIG is derived from a fee imposed on certain County procurement and construction contracts, whereby one-fourth of 1 percent of the cost of the contract is appropriated to the IG.

The same issues of independence and authority raised in the context of the audit function are important for the IG or investigative function as well. In New York, the commissioner of investigation is an appointee of the mayor. Although the DOI's IGs are largely independent of the depart-ments that they oversee, there is a history of criticism related to the DOI commissioner's independence.

Under Mayor Rudolph Giuliani, the first DOI commissioner was Howard Wilson, a long-time friend, colleague, and political supporter of the mayor. The relationship between Wilson and Giuliani raised serious questions regarding the independence of the DOI when it came to allega-tions that touched on City Hall, rather than operating departments of city government.

Serious wrongdoing by Giuliani's key allies and political supporters first came to light through investigative reporting, not investigations by the DOI. For example, Bernard Kerik had been Giuliani's driver during his 1993 campaign for mayor before later being appointed as commissioner of correc-tion and then police commissioner. It was only the vetting process for his appointment as head of the federal Department of Homeland Security, on Giuliani's recommendation to then-President Bush, that revealed that Kerik had failed to pay taxes on an illegal immigrant hired as a nanny: This led to his withdrawal from the Homeland Security nomination. At the time, reporting by multiple newspapers disclosed that Kerik had, while working for the city, sought to intervene on behalf of a firm that had been barred from working with the city due to links to organized crime. In fact, the DOI had questioned Kerik about his actions but took no further investigative steps. Subsequent reporting and follow-up investigations found evidence that in return for Kerik's support, the firm had provided him with $250,000 renovation of his home. Kerik was indicted, subsequently pleaded guilty to tax fraud, obstruction, and making false statements and was sentenced to a four-year prison term.

In New Orleans, the OIG was created through a 1996 referendum. The ordinance implementing the law, however, was not enacted until 2006. Under the ordinance, the IG is appointed by the City Ethics Board, not the mayor or City Council. Former city employees and elected officials are barred from being appointed as the IG for four years. IGs serve a four-year term and may only be removed from office by a two-thirds vote of the Ethics Board. The OIG can only be abolished by a two-third vote of the City Council.

At the same time, the need for independence is often at conflict with the need for accountability. Unlike auditors, there is no standard process for an IG review—although the New Orleans IG and others conform to the so-called "Green Book" standards promulgated by the Association of Inspectors General.

Chattanooga vs Wall Street

For the majority of city and county governments, however, there is no IG or equivalent position. In most of these cities and counties, mayors, county executives, and city managers can only react "after the fact" when it comes to allegations of waste, fraud, and abuse. In other words, they learn about the allegations from prosecutors and then are left to scramble to respond.

There are examples of smaller local governments that have undertaken efforts to attack waste, fraud, and corruption even in the absence of an IG. The case of Chattanooga, Tennessee's efforts to expose fraud related to the city's general pension fund is an example of just that.

Chattanooga is a city of approximately 170,000 residents located in the southeast corner of the state. Chattanooga is one of the nation's great urban turnaround success stories. After losing more than 10 percent of its population in the 1980s, Chattanooga became the only US city with more than 100,000 residents to have sustained that level of decline in the 1980s and to then gain population in the 1990s: Its population increased by nearly 10 percent in the most recent decade.

In 2001, Chattanoogans elected a local business executive, Bob Corker, as mayor. Shortly after taking office, the budget became priority one for Corker. In response to a large budget gap, Corker called for enactment of a property tax increase that was approved by the City Council on September 11, 2001.

One of the major causes of Chattanooga's budget woes was the growing cost of providing for pensions for the city's workers. Like most local governments, Chattanooga had what is known as a defined benefit plan. In other words, city employees join a pension plan and are guaranteed certain benefits on retirement. The pension plan for most city workers—all but its firefighters and police officers—is known as the General Pension Plan (GPP). The GPP was funded by a Charter-mandated contribution of 2 percent of wages of city workers and an annual contribution by the city based on recommendations by the GPP's actuary.

Like other local government pension funds, Chattanooga's GPP assets were invested to increase their value. Generally speaking, the amount that the city was required to contribute to its pension fund annually was based on past contributions, investment returns, and projected future expenditures.

During the late 1990s, Chattanooga's pension fund had enjoyed significant success on Wall Street. Between 1997 and 2001, the amount that the city needed to contribute to the plan to fund the actuary's recommendations had dropped from 9 percent of employee salaries to zero. In other words, the combination of investment returns and employee contributions had been sufficient to keep the plan adequately funded.

With the downturn on Wall Street between 2000 and 2002, that equation changed dramatically. After contributing nothing to the GPP in FY 2002, the city's pension contribution was $2.1 million in FY 2004—making the contribution to the GPP one of the fastest growing expenditures in the city's $150 million general fund budget.

In 2002, Corker hired David Eichenthal—one of the authors—as the city's first director of performance review. Eichenthal came to Chattanooga after spending twelve years in New York City government, including stints as both an assistant deputy comptroller and an assistant IG.

The Office of Performance Review (OPR) had a small staff—eventually totaling five other positions—and wide responsibilities. OPR included the city's two-person internal audit unit, oversaw grant management, and took on a series of special projects, including implementation of the city's new "one call" or 311 center. In establishing OPR, Corker's goal was to create an internal oversight mechanism, primarily designed to measure and manage performance of local government. Eichenthal sought to replicate the Compstat approach adopted by the New York Police Department—and subsequently dozens of other local government agencies—that used timely and accurate data to help drive performance.

Less than a year after appointing Eichenthal as director of the OPR, in February 2003, Corker named him to serve as the city finance officer (CFO), with responsibility for the city budget. In what was the last "worst fiscal period for cities since the Great Depression," Eichenthal faced immediate shortfalls in the city budget as well as long-term challenges related to employee compensation.

With his dual role as director of OPR and CFO, Eichenthal sought to focus the city's internal audit resources on the identification of possible savings in those areas where costs were growing the fastest or where opportunities for new revenue were being ignored. The result was a series of performance reviews focused on overtime, city golf courses and municipal facilities, the performance of the city court, and the capital construction bidding processes.

When Eichenthal became CFO, Corker asked him specifically to focus on the GPP, in part because of the rapid growth in the city's contributions. Eichenthal's predecessor as CFO served as a member of the GPP board and Eichenthal was appointed to replace him in that position as well.

In reality, the public pension fund crisis much discussed in 2010 and 2011 started years earlier. Decisions to increase benefits and overreliance on the investment returns of the 1990s bull market had created many of the issues that have come to dominate discussion of pension liability in this decade. In 2004, a front page story in *The New York Times* reported "Some Cities Struggling to Keep Pension Promises." A 2005 report proclaimed a "public pension crisis" and noted, "Mounting public sector retirement costs pose a serious threat to state and local governments."

The 2006 report by the global accounting and consulting firm Deloitte identified a series of factors driving the pension fund crisis: increased benefits, growth of supplemental benefits, lucrative early retirement packages, and relatively small employee contributions. One area that it did not point to, however, was the role of the money managers and investment advisors charged with meeting pension plan investment targets. Yet, a subsequent June 2007 GAO report pointed out that conflicts of interest involving investment advisors could result in lower returns for pension funds.

How? Most public pension funds have their assets actively invested. In other words, they make investments in a portfolio of domestic and international equities and, in some cases, more risky investments that offer higher rates of return, such as real estate, private equity, and hedge funds.

Few public pension funds, other than the very largest, have the internal staff or expertise to make these decisions on their own. Instead, they rely on investment advisors or consultants.

As pension funds were benefitting from Wall Street returns, so were the money managers and investment consultants working for them. Through a combination of fees, serving the investment needs of public pension funds was an extremely lucrative business.

In 2003, when Eichenthal joined the board, the Chattanooga GPP was a relatively small public pension fund, with approximately $180 million in assets. The seven members of the pension board of trustees were all mayoral appointees, and the mayor also sat as an ex officio member of the board. With the exception of the CFO, however, none of the other board members were public officials and few had significant experience in money management.

The board chair, a former banker, had served for fourteen years. The board counsel had been its attorney since 1995 and had previously served as a trust officer with the fund's custodian. But the board was largely dependent on its investment advisor.

Although the fund board met monthly, there were never agendas distributed before the meetings. The board, a part of city government, did not meet at City Hall. Instead, it met in the boardroom of a local bank. The board did not have its own bylaws and there was no scheduled annual election of officers. There was no budget for the pension plan that addressed administrative and other costs and there was no process of trustee education. Board members had, however, voted to pay themselves $100 for every meeting that they attended.

In other words, there was very little accountability for a public body responsible for one of the fastest growing areas of Chattanooga's city budget, let alone the economic security of hundreds of its employees. All of these factors led Eichenthal and Corker to be concerned that there was an environment that might have left the pension system vulnerable.

In December 1995, shortly after the election of the board chair and the selection of the board counsel, the GPP selected William Keith Phillips to act as its investment advisor. Initially, Phillips was part of PaineWebber Inc. and then, in 2000, joined Morgan Stanley Dean Witter.

Phillips was paid, at the recommendation of board counsel, through an arrangement known as soft dollar compensation. As a result, there was no set fee but instead compensation was based on commissions off the trades of the fund's assets.

At the same time that Phillips was working for Chattanooga, he also was the investment advisor for the Metro Nashville government's pension fund. In March 2000, Metro Nashville released a review of the performance and operation of its pension fund that it had commissioned from the accounting firm, KPMG, which focused on the role of Phillips as its investment consultant. The KPMG report disclosed a series of conflicts of interest related to Phillips and his relationships with outside managers. As a result, Metro Nashville terminated its relationship with Phillips. Shortly after the KPMG report, Phillips moved his business to Morgan Stanley Dean Witter.

When the Chattanooga GPP board was informed of these developments in Nashville in 2000, it entered into a new consulting agreement, with Phillips in his new role at Morgan Stanley.

In 2002, Metro Nashville, UBS PaineWebber, and Phillips entered into a settlement agreement based on the KPMG audit of two years before. UBS PaineWebber and Phillips agreed to pay $10.3 million to Metro Nashville. Later that year, the Chattanooga GPP board rebid its contract for consultant services and in early 2003, a new consultant was selected. Phillips conducted his last meeting with the Chattanooga board in May 2003, shortly after Eichenthal was named to that board.

Although Phillips was no longer advising the Chattanooga GPP, no action had been taken to determine whether Chattanooga had been victim of the same conflicts of interest that led to the settlement with Metro Nashville. And the leadership of the board showed little or no interest in pursuing the matter. In fact, the board counsel suggested that the allegations against Phillips in Nashville had been politically motivated.

Since joining the board in February of that year, Eichenthal had been gradually pushing for basic reforms in the GPP to increase accountability and transparency. And, given Corker's mandate and concerns related to accountability, he was taking a hard look at the potential review of Phillips' performance. The board chair and counsel—as well as other long-time board members—resisted change.

A number of the board members had been serving past their appointment date. Eichenthal persuaded Corker that the only way to change the approach of the GPP would be to change some of its board membership. Matters came to a boiling point when Corker, on the recommendation of

Eichenthal and with the approval of the City Council, appointed a young African-American woman, an attorney at the city's largest law firm with a practice focused on employment law, to the GPP board.

Shortly after her appointment, the board chair and counsel informed Eichenthal and Corker that they intended to refuse to seat her as a member of the board, arguing that she lacked the requisite qualifications. At the October 2003 board meeting, Corker made an unusual appearance. He argued to board members—backed by the city attorney and members of the City Council—that there was no basis for their refusal to seat his appointee. The city attorney also noted that, under the city charter, he was responsible for the appointment of any counsel to the board.

The new board member was seated. The city attorney fired the board's counsel, and took over the legal support of GPP. A month later, the board chair resigned and Eichenthal was elected as the new chair of the GPP board. At the same meeting, a series of reforms, from adoption of bylaws to an end to the per diem payment to board members, were enacted. And the board voted to hold future meetings at City Hall, not inside a bank building.

But Eichenthal, with his performance review hat on, still had significant questions regarding the past actions of the pension fund's former investment consultant. With just two auditors on staff, and neither with a background in the intricacies of money management, he had to find new resources to get answers.

Just one month after his election as board chair, Eichenthal sought and won board approval to retain an outside investigator to examine whether Phillips had engaged in wrongdoing against the Chattanooga pension fund as well. The board engaged Edward Siedle, a former enforcement attorney with the Securities and Exchange Commission, to conduct the review. Siedle had also conducted a follow-up review of Phillips for MetroNashville following the KPMG audit and had negotiated the Nashville settlement.

By March 2004, Siedle had concluded his initial investigation and produced a forty-seven–page investigative analysis. The review involved interviews with pension fund money managers and city officials, detailed examinations of correspondence between the pension fund and Phillips and its managers, and careful analysis of records of trades involving Chattanooga pension fund assets over a seven-year period. The review focused on some of the same conflict issues raised in Nashville. Additionally, it identified a series of cases where—on the advice of Phillips—the GPP board had violated some of its own policies, including the criteria for selecting money managers and how investments were allocated.

The Siedle investigation concluded that Phillips, both with UBS Paine Webber and Morgan Stanley, had breached his fiduciary duty and placed its own monetary interests ahead of the Chattanooga pension fund. Phillips, focused on revenue from the soft dollar arrangement that allowed fees to be paid through trade commissions, had become the gatekeeper for money managers to the pension fund's assets. Conflicts of interest drove recommendations to the Chattanooga fund on critical issues such as management selection, fees, and how the fund's assets should be allocated. Money managers were coaxed to run their trading through PaineWebber and then Morgan Stanley in return for their selection to manage fund assets. The result was that money managers were selected on their willingness to pay commissions, rather than their abilities or qualifications.

The GPP was paying more in fees, and underperforming managers selected through conflict of interest were increasing the need for the city to make contributions to its pension fund.

Siedle's investigation concluded that Chattanooga might have a potential multimillion dollar claim against Phillips, UBS Paine Webber, and Morgan Stanley. Based on Siedle's investigation, the GPP retained outside counsel and in October 2004 filed a complaint against UBS Paine Webber and Morgan Stanley with the National Association of Securities Dealers citing a "fraudulent and deceptive scheme" that cost the pension plan more than $20 million.

In February 2006, the UBS PaineWebber and Morgan Stanley settled the pension fund's claims for $5.7 million—the largest civil recovery on behalf of the City of Chattanooga ever.

In addition to the recovery, the investigation of Phillips led to a series of reforms at the pension fund. The board adopted a new asset allocation policy, reducing reliance on equity investments that had been recommended by Phillips to drive trade commissions. Between 2003 and 2005, the fund replaced or reduced allocations to seven of the eleven mangers who had been recommended by Phillips and were managing pension fund assets at the time that Phillips' contract was not renewed. By the close of 2004, the pension fund had allocated almost 15 percent of its assets to less risky passive investments.

In addition to the accountability and transparency initiatives immediately undertaken in 2003, the board contracted for a 2005 independent review of its investment consultant.

The story of William Keith Phillips did not end with the 2006 settlement with Chattanooga. In July 2009, the Securities and Exchange Commission (SEC) announced that Morgan Stanley had agreed to pay a $500,000 penalty to settle charges that it had misled customers of William Keith Phillips about the money management firms that it recommended and from which it received commissions. According to the initial SEC complaint, Phillips steered clients to unapproved firms that had not been subject to Morgan Stanley standard internal reviews, despite assurances to clients that they had. Those firms paid at least $3.3 million in commissions and fees to Morgan Stanley and to Phillips.

In January 2010, the SEC settled its case against Phillips as well. Phillips paid an $80,000 civil penalty and was suspended from association with an investment adviser, broker, or dealer for four months.

Despite limited resources for internal audit or investigation, the City of Chattanooga was able to identify a high potential target of opportunity for review and bring in the necessary investigative and financial resources to conduct an oversight review of its pension plan. The result was a significant savings in taxpayer dollars, a series of internal reforms, and the predicate for further enforcement activities by federal regulators.

Conclusion

There are a lot of local auditors, but most are focused more on the day-to-day finances of the local government and less on rooting out systematic waste, fraud, abuse, or corruption. At the local level, auditors may be elected independently, appointed by the local legislative body or appointed by the executive. Different cities and counties have addressed issues related to auditor independence in different ways.

On the other hand, IGs—with broader oversight powers—are few and far between at the local level even in the nation's largest cities and counties. The number of IGs or DOIs is, however, growing. Often, the creation of an IG position is a direct response to scandal.

As is true for all watchdogs, effectiveness often depends on a combination of independence and the availability of resources—both of which vary greatly across cities and counties and between auditors and IGs.

The Chattanooga case study points to how the role of investigation and audit can be fulfilled even in the absence of a clear structure or significant resources—the norm for most smaller and mid-size local governments in the United States. It also takes us back to some of the principles that we outlined in describing an effective watchdog in Chapter 1.

Chattanooga's zeal in going after wrongdoing related to its pension fund was clearly a reflection of then-Mayor Corker's demand for reform. Intolerance of abuse—and willingness to take on entrenched interests on the City Pension Board—opened the door for the investigation that subsequently led to the findings related to the city's pension fund consultants and, ultimately, to the successful civil recovery.

The Chattanooga case study also demonstrates the effective use of the press in pursuit of an investigation. Local press coverage helped to build political capital for the mayor and a national story in *The New York Times* on the issue clearly helped to propel the eventual settlement. An internal investigator or auditor can use the same tools as an outside watchdog, especially when the target of the investigation is external to the actual city organization—such as an outside consultant.

Chapter 13

Other Elected and Appointed Local Officials

With the Knapp Commission on police corruption as a precedent, the most fundamental challenge for the Independent Commission is to recommend reforms that will help insure that such an incident is not repeated in Los Angeles or elsewhere in the nation.

—Report of the Independent Commission on the Los Angeles Police Department (1991)

We're still responding to things that were put in place by the Christopher Commission, their recommendations, the Inspector General, the role of the Police Commission. . . . All that traces its way back to Rodney King.

—Los Angeles Police Chief Charlie Beck (2011)

There are many versions of the "three envelopes" story. Perhaps not surprisingly, the one we know best is about a new mayor.

So, the story goes, a new mayor is elected and sworn in and when she goes to her office for the first time, she finds a note from her predecessor along with three envelopes. The note reads:

There will be times on this job when you will face great crisis. When you do and find that you can't figure out what to do next, open one of these three envelopes in numbered order. Good luck.

The new mayor looks at the three envelopes, laughs, and sticks them in a desk drawer and forgets about them. The beginning of the new mayor's term goes very well—on-time budgets, new initiatives to improve the school system—until the middle of the third year. Then, one day, a front-page news story reports a massive corruption investigation of a multimillion-dollar city contract. The new mayor is worried and uncertain of what to do. She remembers the three envelopes, finds them in her desk drawer and opens the first envelope. Inside, there is a single sheet of paper with the words: "Blame your predecessor."

That day, the mayor holds a press conference decrying the corruption of the past administration and vows change. Her boldness is lauded and her approval ratings soar. She is re-elected.

In the first year of her second term, she receives a call late one night from the local US attorney informing her that the FBI has just arrested her chief of staff on bribery charges. She races to the office, opens her desk drawer and opens the second envelope. Inside, she finds a single sheet of paper with the words: "Appoint a blue ribbon commission."

The next morning, the mayor announces an eleven-member blue ribbon commission to reform local government from top to bottom. Editorials praise her ability to get in front of the issue and her promise of change. Her chief of staff's indictment has little to no effect on her approval ratings and talk begins of a possible race for governor.

Two years later—and two weeks before she is to announce her re-election campaign—she receives a letter from HUD. It turns out that the earlier contracting investigations were just the tip of the iceberg. HUD informs her that it discovered fraud in the letting of a federally funded contract between the city and a nonprofit agency . . . run by her brother-in-law.

Desperate, the mayor turns to the last of the three envelopes, opens it and reads the final piece of advice from her predecessor: "Prepare three envelopes."

As we've discussed, not every local government in the United States has a significant internal watchdog staff. Most large local governments have internal audit units—although they are frequently limited to pure financial audits focused more on compliance than corruption and have limited staff resources. And very few local governments have IGs.

So, when there is a corruption crisis or some other crisis demanding a public response, local government heads will frequently turn to the advice of the second envelope—the appointment of a group of citizens charged with conducting some form of oversight investigation or review and publicly reporting their findings. Local officials—other than local legislators, auditors, or IGs—also may have and exercise limited power to conduct oversight.

This chapter focuses on the role of these other elected and appointed officials who conduct oversight at the local level, with a particular focus on oversight of local government's role in law enforcement and public safety. At the conclusion of this chapter, we look in detail at how one other elected official, with limited staff and resources, played a role in reforming the New York City Police Department.

Blue Ribbon and Permanent Oversight Commissions

Local governments appoint "blue ribbon commissions" to investigate a wide variety of allegations of waste, fraud, and abuse and to review other issues. The mayor, the council, or a combination of the two, usually appoints commission members, who frequently are business leaders or civic leaders and may sometimes include government officials.

Depending on the nature of the allegations and the charge of the appointing official or body, these commissions may have substantial investigative authority equal to or even surpassing that of IGs or auditors. For example, some commissions may be granted subpoena power, may have significant staffing, and in some cases may have law enforcement personnel assigned to their staff. In other cases, the scope of the commission may be far narrower, limited to fact-finding and research with a goal of producing recommendations rather than arrests.

Local governments also now have a surfeit of permanent citizen commissions charged with addressing conflict-of-interest or ethics issues. As local governments have imposed limitations on elected and appointed officials, lobbyists, and government contractors, they have frequently established independent boards or commissions designed to both provide advice in the interpretation of these laws and to rule on specific allegations of conflict of interest that do not necessarily rise to the level of criminality.

In New York City, for example, conflict of interest issues are not addressed by either the comptroller or the DOI, the two other local oversight offices discussed earlier in this book, but instead by a separate Conflicts of Interest Board (COIB). COIB staff members render advisory opinions and offer training, whereas the board itself acts on allegations of violations of the Conflict of Interest law. Other departments of city government regulate lobbying (city clerk) and campaign finances (the New York City Campaign Finance Board).

Local Oversight and Law Enforcement

Perhaps the one area of local government where there is the greatest attention to oversight, both through blue ribbon and permanent commissions, is law enforcement. This makes sense for at least two reasons.

In most local governments, especially those without direct authority over schools, a majority of spending and staffing is dedicated to public safety. In many city governments, the police department is the largest in staff and budget, whereas in county governments, the jail system is usually among the largest in staff and dollars spent. But, perhaps more importantly, the police and correction functions are the two areas of local government where the potential for serious abuse, in the use of force and deprivation of liberty, may be the greatest.

The appointment of a blue ribbon commission is a frequent response to issues of abuse within the criminal justice system.

In Los Angeles, the 1991 police beating of Rodney King, captured on video, spurred then-Mayor Tom Bradley to appoint a commission to review the Los Angeles Police Department. The commission, led by Warren Christopher (who eventually served as US secretary of state), produced a damning review of the persistence of abuse of authority within the department that eventually led to changes in department leadership and a series of specific reforms.

In New York, oversight investigations to review allegations of police misconduct and corruption have occurred on a regular basis for the last century. In the 1890s, a state senate investigation, the Lexow Committee, found systematic corruption within the New York Police Department (NYPD). Less than twenty years later, a City Council oversight committee, the Curran Committee, called for the removal of the police commissioner. Yet another state probe, the Seabury Commission, highlighted corruption in the court system and NYPD linked to New York's political machine, Tammany Hall: The Seabury Commission investigation led to the resignation of then-Mayor Jimmy Walker in 1932.

Perhaps the most famous investigation of the NYPD was the 1970s Knapp Commission. The Knapp Commission revealed that extortion and bribery had become almost the norm within the ranks of the NYPD, including everything from small payments to massive schemes to pay off police officers to look the other way when it came to gambling and drug operations in the city. In 1970, New York Mayor John Lindsay had initially appointed a small, five-member group to review allegations of police corruption. But a subsequent front-page *New York Times* story detailing allegations of corruption pushed the mayor into naming a larger panel chaired by Whitman Knapp, a former prosecutor who eventually served as a federal court judge.

The star witness before the Knapp Commission, and the source of *The New York Times* front-page story that fueled the inquiry, was NYPD Detective Frank Serpico. Serpico testified about the pressures within the department to participate in payoffs and the failure of department officials to respond to his allegations of corruption, allegations that almost cost him his life.

The Knapp Commission produced a series of departmental reforms designed to curb corruption—including the reorganization of the department's Internal Affairs Division, charged with investigating corrupt officers. Yet, twenty years after the final Knapp Commission report, the NYPD was embroiled in yet another corruption crisis involving allegations related to the drug trade. In 1992, Mayor David Dinkins created the Mollen Commission to investigate both allegations of corruption in the NYPD and the department's response to corruption. In its 1994 report, the commission found that although corruption was nowhere near as pervasive as it was in the 1970s it still remained a stain on the department.

In addition to these blue ribbon commission investigations, a series of permanent entities have also been created to address corruption and abuse within the NYPD. In 1995, Mayor Rudolph Giuliani created a permanent Commission to Combat Police Corruption following the recommendation of the Mollen Commission. New York also has a Civilian Complaint Review Board (CCRB) that, much like the COIB, investigates and makes recommendations on complaints related to police misconduct that do not rise to the level of criminality.

New York is not unique in its application of civilian oversight of policing. A 2005 report by the Police Assessment Resource Center identified eleven different models of police oversight. In some cases, police departments actually report to independent police commissions rather than a mayor, in other cases oversight bodies have broad responsibility to monitor police performance, and in still other cases, oversight bodies are designed to make recommendations or adjudicate specific allegations of police misconduct.

The level of oversight applied to the policing function within the criminal justice system is not entirely unique. Given the potential for abuse, it is not surprising that there are similar mechanisms for the oversight of local correctional systems. The City of New York created an independent Board of Correction in 1957: For years before riots led to federal litigation, the board warned of the effect of overcrowding on conditions of confinement. In Pennsylvania, California, and Florida, there are similar local oversight bodies that monitor and inspect jails.

An Ombudsman's Approach to Police Oversight

There is yet one other office in New York that has authority to review and monitor the NYPD: the Office of the Public Advocate.

Before 1990, New York City had a quasi-bicameral legislature. Although the City Council had exclusive legislative authority, a Board of Estimate was the more powerful check on mayoral power. The board had authority to approve certain contracts, land use decisions and, along with the council, the city's budget. The membership of the Board of Estimate consisted of the mayor, a citywide elected city council president, a citywide elected comptroller, and five borough presidents representing each of the city's five boroughs or counties. Each of the citywide officials had two votes, whereas each of the borough officials had one vote.

In 1989, the Supreme Court held that the voting structure of the Board of Estimate was unconstitutional in that it violated the principle of one person, one vote. For some reason, the Court could not see the logic of the people of Staten Island, with roughly 350,000 residents, having the same voting power as the people of Brooklyn, with more than 2 million residents.

Instead of reforming the voting structure of the Board of Estimate, the voters of New York City adopted a new charter that abolished it. Without the power of a vote on the Board of Estimate, the position of city council president was redefined. Although the council president did, like a vice president, preside over the council, he or she did not have much other power within that body. And, unlike a vice president, the council president was not elected as part of a ticket with the mayor. So, the same charter commission that recommended the abolition of the Board of Estimate vested the council president, who was renamed "public advocate," with the power to act as a citywide ombudsman while also keeping the office first in line of succession to the mayor.

In theory, residents unsatisfied with the response of a city department or agency to a complaint could turn to the public advocate for assistance and relief. Many cities have a similar ombudsman function. New York's charter, however, was unique. First, the ombudsman was independently elected. Second, the new charter also gave the public advocate the power to go beyond assisting individual residents. The office would be able to detect patterns in complaints—that no individual member of the council would be able to do without a citywide perspective—and conduct oversight investigations related to how departments were handling those complaints.

Specifically, the charter empowered the public advocate "to review complaints of a recurring and multi-borough or city-wide nature relating to services and programs, and make proposals to improve the city's response to such complaints." And, as important, the charter granted the public advocate near-subpoena power to obtain documents for these reviews from city departments, declaring that "the public advocate shall have timely access to those records and documents of city agencies which the public advocate deems necessary to complete the investigations, inquiries and reviews required by this section."

Elected in 1993, Mark Green took office in 1994 as the city's first public advocate under the new provisions of the charter. Green came to the job with a lifetime of experience as an advocate. Fresh out of Harvard Law School in 1970, Green went to work as one of the original "Nader's Raiders" working with Ralph Nader to conduct public interest investigations of Congress and federal regulatory agencies. More recently, Green had served as the city's commissioner of consumer affairs—the lead local regulator of the business community. In his consumer affairs role, Green had been a strong advocate in efforts to curb abuses by the tobacco and private carting industries.

Green was elected in the same year and at the same time that Giuliani was elected as mayor. With the public advocate first in line of succession to the mayor, Green quickly emerged as the leading Democratic voice in opposition to Republican Giuliani.

The two did not like each other, personally or professionally. Both were sworn in at the same ceremony and both delivered inaugural addresses. The day after, Giuliani's top deputy mayor called Green to complain that his remarks had been "too mayoral." Just months later, on the day Giuliani delivered his first city budget address, Green responded with a detailed alternative. Over time, Green and Giuliani would battle on almost a daily basis. Twice, Giuliani created charter revision commissions with the stated intent of abolishing the Office of Public Advocate. Both efforts failed.

Although the two could not agree on much, they could agree on the city's number one problem as they both took office in 1994—crime. After reaching record numbers in 1990, the crime rate had started to decline under Giuliani's predecessor, Mayor David Dinkins. But there were still nearly 2,000 homicides in New York in 1993. A tough economy and racial conflict didn't help, but it was clear that Giuliani's election was due in large part to a sense that, as a former US attorney, he could do a better job bringing crime under control in the city.

And Giuliani was extremely successful in his efforts to do just that. Under the leadership of Giuliani's first police commissioner, William Bratton, crime rates in New York dropped dramatically. Aided by a surge in the number of officers that had been funded under the city's Safe Streets, Safe City program launched by Dinkins, homicides declined by almost 20 percent and robberies were down by more than 15 percent in Giuliani's first year in office

By 1997, the year that both Giuliani and Green were up for re-election, homicides had been cut in half since 1993, going from 1,946 to 983 in 1996; New York was leading a historic nationwide reduction in crime. But there was an underside to the reduction in crime in New York City. As crime rates declined, complaints to the CCRB about officer misconduct increased. Between 1993 and 1995, CCRB complaints were up by 57 percent. New York City also continued to pay out millions of dollars annually in civil settlements arising from allegations of excessive use of force by police officers.

Although all New Yorkers were happy to see record reductions in crime, black and Latino residents, who often lived in those neighborhoods where crime had declined the most, had rising concerns about police abuse and misconduct.

Increasingly, the complaint process for officer misconduct, the CCRB, was seen as ineffective. A very small percentage of complaints to the CCRB were ever "substantiated." In other words, complaints would go to the CCRB and essentially get dismissed for a lack of evidence.

Complaints about misconduct—and the CCRB—began to come to the public advocate in a variety of ways. In one meeting, the public advocate met with a group of black parents whose children had allegedly been the subjects of taunting and abuse by officers while they were on their way to school. Black members of the public advocate's own staff told of their experiences, including being stopped by police officers for the "crime" of "driving while black."

At the time, the public advocate's chief of policy was David Eichenthal, one of the authors. Eichenthal also was the lead in the office on criminal justice issues. He was a lawyer, had worked on criminal justice issues in the New York City comptroller's office and had worked with a national organization of prosecutors.

The issues of police misconduct were not new to him. As a teenager, Eichenthal had become friendly with the Arnold Kriss, the NYPD's deputy commissioner of trials, who became a mentor. Kriss presided over departmental trials of officers for allegations of misconduct and Eichenthal frequently came to watch.

In his first job out of law school, Eichenthal worked for Dan Johnston, a former ACLU attorney who had gone on to become the chief prosecutor in Des Moines, Iowa. When Johnston moved back to New York, he served on the CCRB.

How could the public advocate, with limited powers and staff and a crowded field of oversight agencies already in place, play an effective oversight role in the area of police misconduct? As important, how could the office address the issue without the elected public advocate appearing to be "anti-police" or unsupportive of the successful effort to curb crime?

Most of the focus on the issue of police misconduct had been on the CCRB and its failure to substantiate all but a small percentage of cases. Ultimately, however, the CCRB only had the power to recommend sanctions against police officers. The ultimate authority for disciplining police officers continued to reside within the police department and with the police commissioner.

Green and Eichenthal detected a trend, largely unnoticed, when it came to those complaints that had been substantiated. Even where the CCRB was substantiating complaints against abusive officers, the NYPD rarely took action against the officer. In 1995, the last full year under Commissioner Bratton, the department disciplined 48.8 percent of officers with substantiated complaints. A year later, under a new police commissioner, that rate declined to just 21.1 percent. In other words, although there were problems with the CCRB process, there were clear signs that the police department itself was not taking even the most serious cases of misconduct seriously.

Green, Eichenthal, and Laurel Eisner, the public advocate's general counsel, devised a strategy that would both allow the office to play a meaningful oversight role in the area of police misconduct and test the office's more general oversight powers. Departments and agencies that reported to Mayor Giuliani routinely were ignoring requests for information from the public advocate, despite the office's powers under the city charter.

The public advocate decided to conduct an investigation on how the NYPD was responding to allegations of police misconduct by obtaining and reviewing department case files describing disciplinary actions against officers with substantiated CCRB complaints. Presumably, the files would describe in detail how and why individual substantiated cases were either pursued or not. These files were otherwise not available to the press or public because of a specific exemption from the state freedom of information law for police personnel files. Green, however, sought the records under his city charter power.

Green sought the records in January 1997 and, as Green expected, the NYPD declined his request. The next step was to take the matter to court. Under the charter, the city's corporation counsel was charged with responsibility for providing legal representation to all departments of city government, including both the public advocate and the police department. In the event of a conflict, outside counsel could be retained. The public advocate sought representation from Richard Emery, a well-known attorney formerly on staff at the ACLU who had also represented the plaintiffs in the successful challenge to the structure of the Board of Estimate.

In April 1997, in the midst of his re-election campaign and as the NYPD was celebrating a record reduction in crime, the public advocate sued the NYPD to gain access to the files. By any standard, it was a politically risky move. Green was on his way to easy re-election, with strong support in the black and Latino communities. The lawsuit could only lead to opposition from pro-Giuliani voters who had also voted for Green four years earlier.

In August 1997, while the lawsuit was still pending, public opinion about police misconduct began to shift and shift dramatically. Abner Louima, a Haitian immigrant, was arrested outside of a Brooklyn nightclub and brought into police custody. While in custody, police officers brutalized and assaulted him. As part of the assault, he was sodomized with the handle of a plunger. Initial press reports indicated that, while committing their assault, the officers yelled, "It's Giuliani time." Subsequently these reports proved to be false, but the impact on public opinion was lasting. Giuliani failed to reach out in any way to the black community. Suddenly, the issue of police misconduct was front-page news. The Louima case sparked public protests, including a march on City Hall.

Two months after the Louima incident, the court ruled for the public advocate in his lawsuit against the police department. State Supreme Court Justice Edward Lehner wrote:

> [I]t is evident that the intent of the [Charter] Commission was to make the Public Advocate a 'watchdog' over City government and a counterweight to the powers of the Mayor. . . . The vision of the office was an independent public official to monitor the operations of City agencies with the view to publicizing any inadequacies, inefficiencies, mismanagement and misfeasance found, with the end goal of pointing the way to right the wrongs of government. Misconduct by those invested with police power is now, and always has been, an area of concern to government.

Subsequent appeals by the NYPD were denied. The Court of Appeals, New York's highest court, denied the final appeal on April 1, 1999. Less than two months earlier, a second high-profile case of alleged police misconduct gripped the city. On February 4, a 23-year-old Guinean immigrant, Amadou Diallo, was shot and killed by four plain-clothed police officers. A total of forty-one shots were fired at Diallo, who was unarmed.

Thus, by the time Green had access to the disciplinary records, the political and policy environment had dramatically changed. Although the public was still supportive of the successful effort to reduce crime, there was growing concern that public safety was coming at the cost of civil liberties. A 1999 poll by *The New York Times* found that nearly nine of ten blacks believed that the police often engaged in brutality against blacks. In June 1999, a Quinnipiac College poll found that 97 percent of blacks, 91 percent of Latinos, and 76 percent of white New Yorkers believed police misconduct was a serious problem.

Green now had access to the records, but the hard work of the investigation was only beginning. The public advocate lacked city budget resources or staff to lead the investigation. To supplement city resources, Green sought funding from several local and national foundations. Eichenthal realized that there was a need to bring in a professional with law enforcement experience to lead the investigation on a day-to-day basis. He retained Richard Aborn, a former assistant district attorney in Manhattan who had led the national effort to win enactment of the Brady Law in the early 1990s, to do so. Aborn brought on a small group of junior researchers to support the effort. Additionally, Green convened a panel of law enforcement experts—including both Kriss and Johnston—to provide advice on the project.

Between April 1999 and July 2000, the public advocate's office reviewed 760 cases involving substantiated complaints against 1,084 New York police officers. Each of the substantiated complaints was coded for more than three hundred different variables. Variables included extensive information on the victim, the complainant to CCRB, the CCRB investigation and review, the background of the police officers who were allegedly involved, various steps in the police department's own process, and the final outcome of the case. Case files were kept at the police department: Every day, researchers from the public advocate's office would cross Police Plaza from the Municipal Building to review the files.

In addition to the review of files and consultations with members of the panel of experts, Green also conducted a daylong hearing on the issue of police misconduct. Staff also sought input from community leaders and participated in local police precinct community council meetings.

The investigation led to two reports, a September 1999 interim report and a July 2000 final report. The 1999 report, which was the subject of front-page coverage in *The New York Times*, found that hundreds of officers who were subjects of substantiated CCRB complaints had those complaints dismissed without investigation when those cases reached the department for possible disciplinary action. In fact, in 90 percent of cases reviewed the department rejected the CCRB recommendation without further investigation.

In one of the cases discussed in the 1999 report, no action was taken against officers who were accused of hitting two high school students even though the students' allegations were supported by medical evidence and eyewitnesses. The public advocate's final report detailed more than two-dozen cases where the department had failed to act.

Among the findings in the final report, the public advocate reported the following:

- Police officers with substantiated CCRB complaints were more likely to be promoted than fired.

- The NYPD was less likely to bring charges against superior officers even though complaints against superior officers were more likely to involve serious misconduct.

- The NYPD regularly failed to bring charges against police officers who lied to the CCRB.

- Even when the NYPD initially filed charges against police officers, 60 percent of those cases resulted in dismissals.

- Among officers with substantiated complaints, 83.2 percent had at least one prior complaint, with an average of five past complaints.

- Nearly one in four cases involved alleged misconduct that took place in a police precinct and nearly one in five involved victims who were under age twenty.

In addition to the detailed findings, the final report of the public advocate included twenty-two detailed recommendations for action.

Most important, however, was the effect that the investigation itself had on the NYPD's conduct. In 1996, the year before Green brought his lawsuit, just 21 percent of substantiated CCRB complaints resulted in disciplinary action against police officers. That rate started to rise in 1997 to 32.2 percent. By the second half of 1998, the disciplinary rate was 58.4 percent and in 1999, it reached 61 percent.

Green's investigation had proven the application of the Hawthorne Effect to oversight: Experiments that study human behavior are subject to bias that is the result of the observation because of how the subjects react to being observed.

In 2001, Green conducted another, narrower study of police misconduct. The four officers involved in the shooting of Amadou Diallo were criminally tried and acquitted. Acquittal in a criminal matter, however, does not necessarily mean that they cannot be subject to administrative disciplinary action. The public advocate sought and obtained the NYPD files documenting the department's consideration of disciplinary action against the Diallo officers. Despite Mayor Giuliani's public statement that none of the officers involved had violated department rules, the public advocate review found that department investigators had revealed that the officers had made tactical errors.

Conclusion

The public advocate's police misconduct investigation points to a series of practical lessons for watchdogs, especially at the local level.

It is important to understand and maximize the impact of the investigation itself. Before Green's staff had examined a single case file, the NYPD's response to substantiated CCRB cases had started to change. Sometimes, just the launch of an investigation can lead to reform.

The public advocate investigation is also a clear example of the benefits of a more adversarial oversight investigation. The issue addressed by the public advocate could clearly have been the focus of reviews by the mayor's Commission to Combat Police Corruption, the city comptroller (through a performance audit), the City Council, or the CCRB itself. In the case of the commission and CCRB, the mayor, who also appointed the police commissioner, controlled both bodies. In the case of the council and the comptroller, elected officials who were unwilling to invest political capital to take on a popular mayor and NYPD, controlled both.

The public advocate's investigation went forward precisely because Green was willing to take on Giuliani. Green understood that the role of the public advocate, irrespective of who the mayor was, required that he act as a watchdog, not just an ombudsman. And he had the political capital to invest in that effort, even when it might not always be popular.

Press, in its role of oversight in informing and driving public opinion, was extremely important. In part, Green's political capital included his ability to command and hold press attention. Green was considered masterful at getting press coverage, regularly holding Sunday press conferences and talking with reporters. His tenure at Consumer Affairs had built his popularity citywide largely through positive earned media attention. So, when the time came to generate attention, first for the lawsuit and then for the investigation and its findings, the public advocate's office was extremely well positioned to focus light on the issue.

The investigation also benefitted from a clear strategy. Based on the initial data, the public advocate and his staff knew that it was likely that the investigation would uncover problems at the NYPD and that the department would decline to provide the requested information. The result was a multiyear initiative that produced multiple stories, and allowed the public advocate to become a voice in the larger discussion around police misconduct issues when the issue exploded.

The public advocate's office also anticipated that the department would look defensive, and it did, when it declined to provide the documents prior to the lawsuit. And they also realized that no matter what, the police commissioner and the mayor would attack the process and the findings—and they did. The public clash between Green, Giuliani, and the police commissioner only served to gain more attention for the investigation.

Green and his staff also clearly recognized that this investigation was perhaps the strongest case to set a precedent on the larger watchdog role of the public advocate's office. Thus, the investigation became bigger than any single issue.

Staff understanding and expertise mattered . . . a lot. Eichenthal knew and understood the CCRB and police disciplinary system in a way that few others outside of the NYPD did. He also understood the importance and value of bringing in a law enforcement expert like Aborn to run the investigation on a day-to-day basis. Both Green and Eichenthal understood the importance of bringing in experts to both assist in the development of the final report and to validate its findings.

Finally, the police misconduct investigation demonstrates the importance of persistence. It was clear from the beginning that it could take years and considerable resources to obtain the data even to begin the investigation. The success of oversight depends on both the willingness and ability to invest time and resources over the long haul.

Chapter 14

The Role of the Press

Were it left to me to decide whether we should have a government without newspapers or newspapers without a government, I should not hesitate a moment to prefer the latter.

—Thomas Jefferson (1787)

No reporter from the Washington Post is ever to be in the White House again. . . . None ever is to be in. Now that is a total order. And, if necessary, I'll fire you. Do you understand?

—President Richard Nixon to Press Secretary Ronald Ziegler,
Nixon Tapes Transcript, December 11, 1972

In the 1939 movie, *Mr. Smith Goes to Washington*, Jefferson Smith, the leader of the Boy Rangers, is appointed to fill a vacant US Senate seat. Smith wins the appointment in large part because the corrupt political bosses of his state believe that he will do no harm. Unsophisticated, Smith is the perfect sap but his good government, pro-kid credentials make him a popular and uncontroversial appointee.

All of that changes when Smith proposes a law that would create a boys camp, funded by contributions from boys, on real estate that the corrupt political machine was seeking for use as the site for a lucrative new dam project. When Smith refuses to back down, the Taylor machine goes after him, charging that he is corrupt. Rather than defending Smith, the home state newspapers put out phony allegations against Smith at the prodding of the Taylor machine.

To defend himself and to publicize the Taylor machine's corruption, Smith puts out his own newspaper through his network of Boy Rangers. Realizing the risk of being exposed, the Taylor machine works to literally knock the Boy Ranger newspaper off the streets.

Frank Capra probably didn't realize it, but in his plot line, he had invented the use of social media to expose corruption about eighty years before Facebook.

Throughout this book, we have discussed the important role that the press plays as a partner to other oversight actors. To the extent that an important part of oversight is, as Wilson suggested in relationship to Congress' investigative role, the power to inform, the press is the means by which information has been most frequently conveyed to the public. A large part of the notion of checks on executive power depends on a free press to inform public opinion and the executive's sensitivity to public opinion and scrutiny.

The focus of this chapter, however, is on the role that the press plays in oversight through investigative journalism. Although the press can play an important role in publicizing the oversight work of others, it also plays a critical role in performing its own investigations. In many instances, as illustrated in case studies set forth in earlier chapters, government oversight actors and the press can work together. But at other times, the press, through investigative journalism, really takes the lead.

In this chapter, we discuss some of the history of investigative journalism, highlight some of the current challenges and opportunities for investigative journalists, and detail two cases studies where investigative journalism at the local level led to reform and results.

Investigative Journalism: From Nelly Bly to Jon Stewart

By 2010, the most regularly relied on source of news was local television news: A Pew research survey found that 50 percent of respondents regularly watched local TV news, 39 percent of the public regularly watched cable news channels, and 28 percent regularly watched network television news.

The same Pew survey found that 40 percent of respondents regularly read a daily newspaper, whereas 30 percent regularly read a weekly newspaper. A smaller share of the public, 5 percent or less, read a national newspaper like *The New York Times, Wall Street Journal,* or *USA Today.* By comparison, respondents were twice as likely, at 11 percent, to report regularly listening to National Public Radio (NPR) for news.

The Pew survey highlighted the growing importance of newer sources of news. Sixteen percent of respondents regularly receive news from social networks; 11 percent from blogs; and as many as one in ten respondents indicated watching shows such as the *O'Reilly Factor* or *The Daily Show.*

The history of investigative journalism closely tracks the history of where Americans obtain their news. For most of the nation's history, newspapers were the primary source of news. Technology has driven changes over the past century, with the advent of radio, moving pictures, television, and more recently the Internet. Multiple media now offer multiple outlets for investigative journalism. The nature of those outlets, however, greatly affects the amount and manner in which investigative journalism can be offered.

Turn-of-the-Century "Muckrakers" (1880s–1920s)

While working as a reporter for the *New York World*, Nelly Bly pretended she was insane in order to be admitted to the Women's Lunatic Asylum on Blackwell's Island. The exposé she wrote of the horrible conditions there, published in her 1887 book *Ten Days in a Madhouse*, instigated a grand jury investigation of the asylum, resulting in major reforms along lines she proposed, and a substantial budget increase for care of the mentally ill.

Although Jacob Riis was for years a police reporter for the *New York Tribune*, his photographs even more than his writing captured the horrors of urban poverty in New York City at end of the nineteenth century. He collected his stories and photographs in several books, including *How the Other Half Lives*, published in 1890. His work was extremely influential in inspiring settlement houses and other programs of assistance to the poor. After inspecting the upstate streams supplying New York City's drinking water, he wrote for the *New York Evening Sun* that "Populous towns sewered directly into our drinking water. I went to the doctors and asked how many days a vigorous cholera bacillus may live and multiply in running water. About seven, they said." The Croton Reservoir, which has supplied much of New York City's drinking water since, was purchased largely in response.

Lincoln Steffens exposed urban political corruption at the turn of the twentieth century in articles for *McClure's Magazine*, many of which appear in his 1904 book *The Shame of the Cities*. Intending to expose abusive and exploitative labor conditions, Upton Sinclair wrote his 1906 novel, *The Jungle*, about the meatpacking industry. Its revelations about the nauseating practices at the plants, however, motivated the Bureau of Chemistry (which in 1930 became the Food and Drug Administration) to inspect and monitor meat quality, First, however, American meatpackers lost half of their overseas sales.

I.F. Stone and The Nation

As an editor of the alternative news magazine *The Nation* in the early 1940s, I.F. Stone exposed the stupidity of FBI Director J. Edgar Hoover's methods of identifying subversives in the government. He listed some of the questions Hoover would ask his agents about the targets: "Does he mix with

Negroes? Does he . . . have too many Jewish friends? Does he think the colored races are as good as the white? Why do you suppose he has hired so many Jews?" and, although any informed person at the time knew that France's Vichy government took its orders from the Nazis, "Is he always criticizing Vichy France?"

Stone said, "I made no claims to inside stuff. I tried to give information which could be documented, so the reader could check it for himself. . . . Reporters tend to be absorbed by the bureaucracies they cover; they take on the habits, attitudes, and even accents of the military or the diplomatic corps. Should a reporter resist the pressure, there are many ways to get rid of him. . . . But a reporter covering the whole capital on his own—particularly if he is his own employer—is immune from these pressures." Unlike virtually any other reporter, he scoured the Congressional Record, rather than relying on press releases issued by appointed or elected government officials, or leaks, often self-serving, from such officials.

In 1953, he created *I.F. Stone's Weekly*, which he wrote, edited, and published. Lyndon Johnson got Congress to pass the Gulf of Tonkin resolution, authorizing him to send combat troops to Vietnam, based on his incorrect version of North Vietnamese attacks on an American warship there (our warship was engaged in provocative intelligence operations, was not in international waters, and a claimed second attack never happened). In that year, 1964, the *Weekly* may have been the first and only news medium to report that Johnson's claim was a distortion, and in any event was among the very few who questioned it at all.

Print Investigations: Clark Mollenhoff and Seymour Hersh

Between 1950 and 1978, except for a nine-month stint as counsel to President Nixon in 1969 and 1970, Clark Mollenhoff worked as an investigative reporter based in Washington for Cowles Publications, including the *Des Moines Register and Tribune* and *Look Magazine*. His articles in the late 1950s exposed labor union corruption and racketeering, including revelation of corrupt dealings by Teamsters president Jimmy Hoffa Sr. almost a decade before Hoffa finally went to prison in 1967. Along with investigative reporter Jack Anderson, his even-handed investigations helped expose the Sherman Adams—then chief of staff to the president—scandal in 1958, forcing President Eisenhower's "right-hand man" to resign in the face of revelations that he accepted an expensive coat from a textile manufacturer then under investigation by the Federal Trade Commission.

Mollenhoff set forth seven basic rules for investigative reporting, which endure. Professional journalism associations highlight them on their websites to this day. In brief paraphrase, they are: (1) no political partisanship; (2) be equally aggressive with public officials you like and public officials you distrust; (3) know your subject; (4) don't exaggerate or distort facts or law; (5) be honest with sources and with targets; (6) obey the law or prepare to take the consequences; and (7) use direct evidence when accusing.

Seymour Hersh's best-known exposé revealed the massacre of dozens of Vietnamese civilians in March 1968 led by US Army Lieutenant William Calley. The news story, which appeared in *The New York Times* on November 12, 1969, galvanized the peace movement and arguably led to the withdrawal of American troops from Vietnam five years later.

In May 2004, the *New Yorker* ran Hersh's story exposing the abuse of US prisoners at Abu Ghraib in Iraq, and that the abuse was part of then-Secretary of Defense Donald Rumsfeld's effort to take control of clandestine operations away from the CIA. In response to his earlier 2003 discussions, also in the *New Yorker*, of Rumsfeld and Cheney's bypassing more reliable CIA information in order to persuade President Bush and the nation to invade Iraq, then-Assistant Secretary of Defense Richard Perle in an interview with Wolf Blitzer on CNN called Hersh "the closest thing American journalism has to a terrorist."

Woodstein

Perhaps the single most famous episode in modern investigative journalism was the coverage of the Watergate conspiracy by *The Washington Post* that prompted President Nixon's outburst at the beginning of this chapter. Chronicled in the book and film, *All the President's Men*, the work of *Post* reporters Robert Woodward and Carl Bernstein both uncovered the depth of the conspiracy and encouraged a generation of investigative journalists.

Five men were caught by the police having broken into the headquarters of the Democratic National Committee, located in the posh Watergate housing complex in Washington, D.C., while in the process of trying to plant eavesdropping devices and copy documents. *The Washington Post* reported this as a minor story on June 18, 1972.

Woodward and Bernstein decided to dig deeper, although the White House called it "a third-rate burglary" and virtually no one else in the country thought it significant. But the two *Post* reporters found and reported links between the burglars and President Nixon's reelection campaign, with the appropriate acronym "CREEP," the Committee to Re-elect the President. Shortly before Nixon's reelection in November 1972, Woodward and Bernstein discovered and reported that top White House aides were involved in directing the burglars' efforts. As a direct result of Woodward and Bernstein's relentless digging, the Senate created its special committee to investigate these events. By May 1, 1973, when White House Press Secretary Ron Ziegler apologized to the two reporters for his previous criticism of their stories, several of Nixon's top aides had resigned because they could no longer deny or hide the extent of their involvement. Fifteen months later, President Nixon himself resigned in disgrace.

Woodward and Bernstein never revealed their confidential sources. Mark Felt, the high-ranking FBI official whom they called "Deep Throat" in their stories and book, himself admitted his role in May 2005, three years before he died.

Television: Is Jon Stewart the New Edward R. Murrow?

A newspaper reporter or a blogger can work alone; a television reporter needs camera crews, technicians, lighting, and so on. Also, the economics of television constrain research: Most television news shows compress many stories into limited time slots. These conditions do not favor serious investigative reporting. Of course, one may cite exceptions.

The greatest giant of television broadcasting, perhaps not coincidentally, graced the airwaves before the years of television's greatest commercial success, near the beginning of the television era. Among his many other contributions to the highest echelon of reporting, Edward R. Murrow's broadcasts in the early 1950s exposed the outrageous lies of Sen. Joseph McCarthy and may have been the single most important factor leading to the downfall of that vicious demagogue whose purported hunt for Communists destroyed the lives of so many people.

Mike Wallace may have been the best-known television reporter for *60 Minutes*, the iconic television news hour. His off-camera producer, Lowell Bergman, did the real investigative work, but no matter: between them, they reported allegations of inhumane treatment in a California prison, CIA involvement in the smuggling of cocaine into the United States, and innumerable other stories. But in 1995, under perceived or actual pressure from ownership and management, who had major economic interests in tobacco companies, Wallace and Bergman did not break the story bravely given to them by a tobacco company insider exposing the lies and deceit of the tobacco industry. Only after the *Wall Street Journal* printed the exposé on February 1, 1996, did *60 Minutes* run it, and then in a watered-down version leaving out many of the damning details. This history illustrates one kind of problem with television's investigative reporting.

In 1972, a young investigative reporter for ABC-TV, Geraldo Rivera, exposed the disgraceful conditions under which the thousands of young developmentally disabled residents of the Willowbrook State School were kept by the State of New York. True, print stories originally breaking the story in local Staten Island newspapers had drawn Rivera's attention, but Rivera put in his own hard hours of serious investigation before airing the broadcast that generated enormous publicity and sparked the lawsuit that forced reforms, before the state ultimately closed Willowbrook.

Two decades later, the *Daily News* called Rivera "tabloid TV's titan of trash," with few to defend him. Rivera's sensationalistic television shows drew good ratings and made money for his sponsors, but his serious investigative work was a thing of the distant past.

What about Jon Stewart? According to the Pew survey, as many as one in twenty Americans regularly receive their news from Stewart's nightly half-hour program, *The Daily Show*. The temptation to dismiss his work as mere entertainment ignores the facts.

First, even Murrow ventured frequently, albeit reluctantly, into entertainment, as did *60 Minutes* even in its heyday. Second, although Stewart has argued that his show is not journalism, a 2008 brief by the Pew Center for Excellence in Journalism noted that "given its comedic core, its blurring of truth and fiction, and its ignoring of many major events, that is true in a traditional sense. But it's also true that, at times, *The Daily Show* aims at more than comedy. In its choice of topics, its use of news footage to deconstruct the manipulations by public figures and its tendency toward pointed satire over playing just for laughs, *The Daily Show* performs a function that is close to journalistic in nature—getting people to think critically about the public square."

But even if *The Daily Show* ventures into a journalism of the kind of humorous columnists or editorial cartoonists, is it even close to investigative journalism? The clearest example of Stewart as investigative journalist would be the show's coverage of congressional efforts to provide funding for health benefits for 9/11 responders. The bill had been stymied in Congress and had generally not received a great deal of press attention.

Stewart devoted night after night of coverage to the proposal—functioning as an advocate, but also exposing underlying issues—that Congress ultimately passed. Reminiscent of Murrow's famous stand against McCarthyism, Stewart devoted an entire show to the legislation. New York Mayor Michael Bloomberg noted that "Jon shining such a big, bright spotlight on Washington's potentially tragic failure to put aside differences and get this done for America was, without a doubt, one of the biggest factors that led to the final agreement."

We can expect television news to feature important investigative reports from time to time. However, although no medium can be relied on to generate consistent and meaningful investigative reporting, television seems an especially unlikely source.

Threats and Opportunities: Investigative Journalism in the Twenty-First Century

In its 2011 report on the state of media, *The Information Needs of Communities*, the Federal Communications Commission (FCC) chronicled the decline of traditional news media:

- Between 2006 and 2009, daily newspapers cut their annual editorial spending $1.6 billion per year by more than 25 percent.

- Staff at daily newspapers has shrunk by more than 25 percent as well, and some newspapers have reduced their staff by 50 percent or more.

- Television network news staff has declined by 50 percent from the late 1980s.

- The number of all-news radio stations has declined from 50 in the mid-1980s to 30.

Perhaps the greatest threat to the future of investigative journalism is the decline of the newspaper. As the FCC report notes, at the state and local level, "with larger staffs, newspapers carried the heavier burden of reporting—especially of investigative, enterprise and beat reporting."

There were approximately 1,400 daily newspapers in the United States in 2011—down from nearly 1,800 in 1950. Many cities that once had multiple newspapers, creating competition that would drive entrepreneurial journalism to command readership, now have just one.

Both national newspapers, such as *The New York Times* and *The Washington Post*, and local newspapers have faced a decline in circulation and advertising. Based on estimates from data in *Editor and Publisher Yearbook*, daily circulation declined by 30 percent between 1990 and 2010. Between 2006 and 2010, according to the Newspaper Association of America, newspaper ad revenue dropped by 46 percent.

In response, newspapers have reduced staff and investigative journalism has borne a significant share of cuts. In part, this is because investigative work, unlike feature reporting or regular beats, tends to be very labor intensive. Investigative reporters may devote months at a time to focus on a single investigative story. For national newspapers, investigative work also frequently entails travel and other costs.

As just one example, according to the FCC report, a 2008 three-part series by the *Raleigh News and Observer* about probation in North Carolina took up the time of multiple staff over a six-month period and cost roughly $200,000 to produce.

A 2006 Arizona State University study found that although newspapers and editors were still interested in investigative reporting, they did not provide necessary resources: 37% of newspapers had no full-time investigative reporters and 61% did not have an investigative team. "Reporters indicated that there is little travel money, research assistance or training to do investigative work. While most said they get some time away from daily assignments and a bit of money to purchase documents or data, it often isn't enough."

Bob Greene, the one-time head of *Newsday's* award-winning investigative team commented that investigative stories "take up a lot of space, and the trend of sound bites doesn't lend itself to investigative stories. . . . More and more people want their news digested for them and that will hurt investigative reporting."

According to the FCC report, membership in the Investigative Reporters and Editors Association declined by just over 25 percent between 2003 and 2010. Between 1984 and 2010, the number of submissions to the Pulitzer Prize "public service" category dropped by more than 40 percent.

Television, despite the proliferation of cable news at the national level, has not filled the gap created by the reduction in print investigative journalism. From the FCC report: "Investigative [stories], in the eyes of some of the people who looked at the bottom line . . . were not as productive as the reporters turning a story a day."

On the other hand, some of the same factors that have led to the decline in newspapers, circulation and investigative newspaper journalism have also created new opportunities and new outlets for investigative work.

The Internet and email have resulted in dramatic increases in the availability of information for investigative reporting. Government documents that would have at one time taken months of freedom of information requests or hours to track down hard copies are now a click or two away on the Internet. More conversations now take place via email or texting—meaning that somewhere, somehow there is a record of those conversations that would not exist if they were conducted in person or by phone. If those emails or texts were sent to or from a government official, they are generally subject to freedom of information requests. Even if they are not, they can easily and quickly be shared electronically with reporters.

The increased availability of information and access has also fostered "citizen journalists" who both mine and review public information and share their ideas and findings with investigative journalists. Also, anyone with a camera on their phone can now become a photo or video reporter.

As the FCC report notes, "citizens can now play a much greater role in holding institutions accountable. Whether it's snapping photos of potholes that the city hasn't fixed and posting it to a website, or scouring documents to help a news website uncover a scandal, a broad range of Americans can now more easily scrutinize government, companies and other powerful organizations."

In a way, there may be less need for a middle man: anyone can create a website, post investigative findings, and watch as Google and other search engines lead members of the public to their findings.

And, in fact, entire web-based enterprises are now devoted to investigative journalism. One of the best is www.ProPublica.org. ProPublica "is an independent, non-profit newsroom that produces investigative journalism in the public interest." Its mission is "To expose abuses of power and betrayals of the public trust by government, business and other institutions using the moral force of investigative journalism to spur reform through the sustained spotlighting of wrongdoing."

ProPublica started "publishing" online in 2008. It works with partners, such as the *Chicago Tribune, The New York Times,* and NPR that frequently publish or produce stories based on its work. By 2011, ProPublica had 51,000 daily email subscribers, 63,000 followers on Twitter, and more than 20,000 fans on Facebook. ProPublica is led by a nonprofit board and funded by foundations and private donations.

ProPublica's work has already won two Pulitzer prizes. In 2010, Pro-Publica's investigation of what happened at Memorial Medical Center during Hurricane Katrina won the prize for investigative reporting. The story was the result of interviews of 140 people who allowed the ProPublica reporter to recreate the events that led to patient deaths. In 2011, ProPublica won the Pulitzer for national reporting for a series of stories on the financial crisis.

There have been similar efforts at the local level—MinnPost and voiceofsandiego.org, to name just two. But efforts at the national and certainly at the local level remain relatively few in number. And although, through the Internet in general and social media specifically, there are more outlets for investigative reporting, "an abundance of media outlets does not translate into an abundance of reporting."

As we discuss in the next chapter, other nonprofit organizations remain active oversight actors who report on fraud, waste, abuse, and corruption and are reliable sources for both new and old media investigative journalists. Other nongovernmental organizations have produced on-line data sources that inform and ease investigative reporting. For example, The Sunlight Foundation "is a non-profit, nonpartisan organization that uses the power of the Internet to catalyze greater government openness and transparency, and provides new tools and resources for media and citizens, alike."

Sunlight Foundation online tools, available to the public and to the press, include searchable databases on campaign spending, lobbying activity, federal contracts, federal grants, and earmarks—just to name a few. In some cases, Sunlight has taken information that was already on the Internet but made it far more accessible. For example, many states now have online, searchable campaign contribution databases. Sunlight's TransparencyData site, however, allows one to research all contributions in all states over a twenty-year period.

Press Oversight and Local Corruption: Two Case Studies

As the FCC report notes, investigative journalism at the national level remains robust. There are enough traditional media outlets like NPR, *The New York Times,* and even PBS programs such as *Frontline,* and nontraditional ones, like ProPublica, still willing and able to invest in investigations. The greater threat to the future of investigative journalism is at the state and local levels. Some local stories, such as the award winning ProPublica report on Memorial Medical Center in New Orleans, can rise to national attention and reporting.

There are, however, thousands of cities and counties throughout the United States which, as we have noted, are among the least likely to have legislative or other effective local oversight, where investigative journalism has stood as the primary guard against local government fraud, waste, abuse, and corruption. The FCC report notes that it is in the area of local accountability reporting that the decline in newspapers and the decline in investigative resources have had the greatest effect.

> [I]n many communities, we now face a shortage of local, profes-
> sional accountability reporting. This is likely to lead to the kinds
> of problems that are, not surprisingly, associated with a lack of
> accountability—more government waste, more local corruption,
> less effective schools. . . . The independent watchdog function
> that the Founding Fathers envisioned for journalism . . . is in
> some cases at risk at the local level.

Although some cities now have many new local, web-based outlets for news, few cities have the equivalents of a local ProPublica that would produce the type of investigative work that we describe here.

Russell Harding's "Vanity Fair"

One of the great recent losses in investigative journalism has been the decline of *The Village Voice*. Published weekly, for more than five decades, the *Voice* was the source of some of the most detailed and thoughtful investigative reporting in New York City.

Jack Newfield co-authored two of the most comprehensive works on modern New York City government, *The Permanent Government* and *City for Sale*. Newfield started writing for the *Voice* in 1964, nine years after the paper's birth, and stayed until 1988, when he moved to a daily newspaper. Although his annual listing of New York City's "Ten Worst Landlords" struck fear into the hearts of the lower depths of the real estate industry, and his scope was broad, his most important work exposed corrupt political officials.

Wayne Barrett arrived in 1978, beginning as Newfield's protégé. Unlike Newfield, whom Mayor Ed Koch with some justice once called "a politician with a press pass," Barrett's ethics remained pure. Barrett wrote intricately detailed and researched articles exposing corruption at all levels of government, but especially in New York City government, whether the target was the Democratic administrations of Ed Koch and David Dinkins or the Republican administrations of Rudy Giuliani and Michael Bloomberg.

Barrett probably broke more stories on municipal government corruption than any other reporter in the United States over the past thirty years. He was unceremoniously fired from the *Voice* in 2011—a great loss for the *Voice*, for the city, and for investigative journalism. Both of us have been the subject of Barrett's reporting, not always favorably, but he was one of a kind. Although he continues to write online for *The Nation*, the absence of his regular reporting has created a vacuum in local journalism.

One of Barrett's colleagues at the *Village Voice* was Tom Robbins. Robbins was a reporter for the *Voice* and for mainstream New York newspapers, such as the *Daily News*. At the end of the Giuliani administration, Robbins began to look into the activities of Russell Harding, the president of the city's Housing Development Corporation (HDC). As Robbins noted, HDC was "the perfect municipal hideaway": Its budget was generated from fees from developers seeking low-cost financing for housing and "no one, neither the city or state comptrollers, nor the City Council has direct oversight or regulatory authority."

Harding was no mere mid-level bureaucrat. His brother Robert had served as both the city budget director and deputy mayor. More significantly, his father, Ray Harding, had led the state Liberal Party. Giuliani, a Republican, won the Liberal Party line in his race for mayor in 1993, giving Democrats, who in New York were often loathe to pull the Republican lever for any candidate, a way to vote for Giuliani. In 1993, Giuliani's votes on the Liberal Party line were greater than his overall margin of victory.

Ray Harding benefited greatly. His lobbying business soared during the Giuliani administration. He subsequently pleaded guilty to charges related to his role in a "pay-to-play" scheme under New York State Comptroller Alan Hevesi. Hevesi, who had served as city comptroller during the Giuliani administration, also went to prison.

In 2000, after hearing from sources in HDC that Harding might be spending inappropriately, Robbins filed a freedom of information law request to obtain expense records. Harding stonewalled the request, initially providing some documents and then having staff falsely claim that they had turned over all documents when, in fact, they had not. When Giuliani—and Harding—left office, the new administration provided the records to Robbins

Additionally, Robbins developed another source. Harding had established an online relationship with an individual in Indianapolis. As part of the relationship, they had exchanged a series of text messages and Harding had sent his online friend a series of gifts. Robbins reported that "When a friend he [Harding] met in an AOL chat room for movie bugs told him he was watching TV on an old 13-inch Emerson, Harding ordered a new Sony 20-inch combination TV-VCR for him. A couple of months later he had a new DVD player sent as well."

A point in the relationship came when the friend, whom Harding had never met in person, suggested that he would come to visit Harding in New York. When Harding reacted both negatively and harshly, his former friend quickly became Tom Robbins' source.

Beginning in April 2002, less than three months after obtaining the initial records from the city, Robbins began writing a series of stories on how Harding had taken the city for more than $250,000 in travel, dining, and entertainment expenses. The expense records revealed trips to Hong Kong, Vancouver, and Las Vegas and high-priced restaurants at home, as well as books and other personal items.

Harding's online friend turned over text messages. As to the gifts, Harding had texted: "Don't worry about the price . . . I can put them both on an expense report at work. I do it all the time with shit like that . . . just one of the perks of being president:) besides that is how I paid for the tv I got you."

In addition to responding to Robbins' freedom of information law request, city officials also turned records over to the DOI, which launched its own probe.

After the initial stories, Harding repaid $52,000 to HDC. But it was way too little too late. Less than a year after his first story, Harding was indicted on six counts of financial crimes and charges of child pornography. At the time of the indictment, US Attorney James Comey said that Harding had turned "his presidency of HDC into a virtual Roman holiday." In March 2005, Harding pleaded guilty and was sentenced to sixty-three months in prison.

The Harding investigation also led to a series of internal reviews at HDC—resulting in reforms. And Robbins' investigative reporting also prompted the City Council to pass a new law extending new protections to city whistleblowers.

Is a City Manager Worth $800,000?

That was the question posed by the headline of the *Los Angeles Times* on July 15, 2010. Like Robbins, two *Times* reporters, Jeff Gottlieb and Ruben Vives, had heard from sources that the small city of Bell, California was paying big dollars to its city leadership. They were covering another story related to Bell—which had agreed to take over the operations of another city's police department. Bell, a city of 37,000, is one of the poorest in California and approximately 90 percent of its residents are Latinos.

According to Gottlieb, they were sitting with the city manager, Robert Rizzo, when he asked him how much money he made and "he coughed out, '$700,000.' And I wasn't sure I heard him right, and I said, 'How much?' And he said, '$700,000' And Ruben goes 'Jesus Christ'!"

Like Robbins, Gottlieb and Vives sought city records under the state freedom of information law and found that Rizzo's salary was just the beginning. In their initial story they reported that the city's police chief earned $457,000 a year and the deputy city manager had a salary of $376,288. All of these salaries were far higher than counterparts in larger cities, even in California where city managers earn among some of the highest professional local government salaries in the nation. City Council members also were earning close to $100,000 a year for a part-time position. Their earnings were the result of receiving multiple per-diem amounts for service on different city boards.

A week after the initial *Times* story, all three officials whose salaries were highlighted by the investigative report were forced to resign at a closed-door City Council meeting. Then State Attorney General Jerry Brown opened an investigation.

Subsequent stories revealed that the city had illegally increased property taxes, in part, to support the cost of providing high salaries to council and senior city officials.

Criminal investigations resulted in multiple criminal charges. The initial charges, against Rizzo, his assistant, and six former and current members of the City Council, were based on the inflated salaries reported initially by the *Times* and led to indictments in October 2010. In March 2011, Rizzo and his assistant, Angela Spaccia, were indicted on separate charges based on a seven-year scheme to increase their pensions when they left city government. Under the pension plan, Rizzo would earn approximately $1 million a year. The plan also called for the creation of a series of false contracts for the purpose of making Rizzo's salary appear to be smaller. Rizzo was also charged in yet another indictment with conflict of interest for failing to disclose that he and another city employee jointly owned a racehorse business.

California passed legislation requiring greater disclosure related to stipends for attending meetings, the means by which council members were able to inflate their compensation. The mayor, deputy mayor, and one of Bell's councilmembers were recalled.

As part of its coverage of Bell, the *Los Angeles Times* also worked to make data and public information more accessible to Bell residents. The newspaper created an online public records request form and an online site where city documents were posted.

Conclusion

Access to information and disclosure remain the key elements of oversight, whether for citizen journalists, investigative reporters or even probing councilmembers being stonewalled by an executive. More disclosure, in and of itself, also has an ameliorative effect. An Écoles des hautes études commerciales du nord Business School study, cited in the FCC report, found that "greater public access to financial disclosure [internationally] correlated to lower levels of corruption."

Historically, Americans have owed a great debt to investigative journalism. The best investigative reporters have always exemplified the best principles of oversight. Their investigations reflected their fury at abuse and injustice; they accepted their power and responsibility to engage in serious oversight; they pursued every scrap of relevant information; and they would not let go until their reporting had inflamed sufficient outrage to force a public response.

But those are the best investigative reporters, and the best have almost always been print journalists. With the sharp decline of print journalism in recent years, fewer news outlets hire investigative reporters at all, and some of the very best, like Wayne Barrett and Tom Robbins, have been let go by their newspaper employers at the peak of their careers. David Simon, a former newspaper reporter and creator of the hard-hitting although fictional television show about the illegal drug trade and the government of Baltimore, *The Wire*, summarized the impact of these developments on government: "It's going to be a great time to be a corrupt politician."

On the other hand, citizens armed with cell phone cameras fed videos of police abuse of Occupy Wall Street protesters to YouTube and to news reporters and Facebook and other social networks on the Internet reporting brutal incidents of repression played a central role in the Arab Spring toppling of Middle East dictatorships.

We might see a kind of "team" oversight to evolve from this kind of citizen journalism. An individual can fan his or her own fury at injustice and abuse into public flame. Traditional journalists or public watchdogs themselves can assume responsibility for enforcing accountability through oversight. If a story goes "viral" on the Web, more individuals may add to the store of public knowledge. That kind of fact-gathering will work at least for some kinds of oversight, although perhaps not for those that demand more sophisticated and professional inquiry. And public anger can fuel persistent follow-up. Although maybe no one actor will adhere to every one of our principles of effective oversight, the collaborative effect may be just as successful.

The FCC report concludes that the need for accountability journalism requires both more nonprofit journalism, like ProPublica, and a collaboration between old media and new media: "Professional reporters can go where volunteers do not have the time or access to go—for instance, prisons, war zones, the restricted corridors of city hall—and citizen reporters can, through their numbers, be in more places than reporters possibly can." If every citizen accepts the responsibility to become at least a potential source, if not a whistleblower, we may yet prove Simon wrong.

Chapter 15

The Role of Public Interest and Other Nongovernmental Oversight Organizations

The reasonable man adapts himself to the world; the unreasonable one persists in trying to adapt the world to himself. Therefore, all progress depends on the unreasonable man.

—George Bernard Shaw (Man and Superman, 1903)

The only way to keep government upright is to lean on it from all sides.

—Former FCC Commissioner Nicholas Johnson, attributed, 1960s

In the movie *The Pelican Brief*, based on the John Grisham novel of the same name, Tulane Law student Darby Shaw conducts research on the records of two recently assassinated Supreme Court justices. She finds that although they had opposite positions on most issues, both had strongly supported environmental positions in their opinions.

Shaw theorizes that they may have been killed so that they would not be on the bench to hear an appeal of a case involving the ability to drill for oil on wetlands that are a habitat for an endangered species of pelican. She writes a brief that suggests that an oil tycoon with close ties to the president arranged for the assassinations knowing that the president would likely appoint judges to the bench more inclined to rule in his favor.

She initially shows the brief to her professor who then shows it to an attorney for the FBI: Both are killed. The White House attempts to cover up its connections to the oil tycoon. Shaw eventually contacts a reporter who works to verify Shaw's theory.

Reporters are not the only nongovernment players who perform oversight. Most individuals do not go to the extremes of Darby Shaw to uncover corruption. Yet, government investigators and investigative journalists rely on individual whistleblowers to step forward as sources for investigations of fraud, waste, abuse, and corruption.

In addition to courageous individuals, there are a number of nonprofit organizations that are dedicated to government oversight. "Good government" groups, mocked by professional politicians as "goo-goos," preeminent among the nonprofits, continue to enlist idealistic students, earnest young professionals, outraged and fed-up citizens, and others who feel connected enough to the society in which they live to contribute personally to its improvement through cleaner, better government.

There are for-profit watchdogs as well, including certain lawyers, who profit from the exposure of fraud against the government or malfeasance by government. The nonprofit category enjoys a longer and more illustrious history.

A multitude of nonprofit organizations with narrower agendas engage in oversight of government action as well. The Chamber of Commerce, no doubt, fancies itself a watchdog alerting the citizenry to oppose government behavior that undermines business interests. The ACLU mobilizes its constituency to oppose various violations of the Bill of Rights. The National Rifle Association stays on the lookout for government initiatives that, in its view, violate Second Amendment values. The Brady Campaign and various other gun control organizations, with equal commitment although less success, publicize, criticize, and try to defeat government actions that, in its view, threaten public safety. A discussion of each and every such organization would fill not this chapter, but an entire library.

Here, we only provide somewhat extensive illustrations of those not-for-profit watchdog organizations with more broadly defined missions of defending citizen and taxpayer interests; and then some discussion of those major for-profit professionals who also serve a "watchdog" function. For the student of government oversight, a review of some of the highlights of their work may serve (implicitly or inductively) to suggest tactics and guidelines.

The "Goo-Goos"

A number of different organizations at the local, state, and national levels focus on advocacy for government reform. As part of their work, they frequently engage in certain investigative activities as well. These good government groups are usually nonpartisan and often nonideological, taking on all parties in the name of cleaner government.

Citizens Union and the Bureau of Municipal Research

The breathtaking level of corruption in New York City during the Tweed Ring era of the late 1860s, unprecedented and possibly still unequaled, inspired a good government reaction that grew with the turn of the century. In 1895, reformers created a "nonpartisan party," the Citizens Union (CU), in an unsuccessful effort to replace Tammany Hall, the corrupt Democratic organization, in holding the reins of New York City government. Municipal governments throughout the United States, according to a contemporary late nineteenth-century scholar, Andrew D. White, were "the worst in Christendom—the most expensive, the most inefficient, and the most corrupt."

But perhaps the most outstanding early flower of the counterreaction arose where the corruption was greatest. The idealistic young men of the Bureau of Municipal Research, a creation of the CU, literally stood and counted bags of cement at city government construction sites in 1907. They proved that the city was paying tremendous amounts of taxpayer dollars for supplies that it never received. Exposure of the graft and corruption underlying these transactions resulted in the removal of the elected presidents of several New York City boroughs and, more important, the adoption of the first formal budget used by any city agency in the United States. Other cities would follow suit.

Although the Bureau of Municipal Research no longer exists, it gave rise to the Institute of Public Administration in New York City, and the American Society for Public Administration nationally. No longer significant as adversarial government watchdogs, they remain important sources of institutional research in public administration.

The Bureau's parent organization, the CU, continues well into the second century of its existence, although focusing less on investigations and more on advocacy. It has decried the New York State Legislature's control of its own reapportionment, drawing district lines to maximize incumbent protection. In 2011, CU joined with former New York City Mayor Ed Koch and former New York State Attorney General Robert Abrams (who was also president of the CU Foundation) to call for "an impartial process undertaken by an independent body guided by clearly-defined criteria." To aid journalists and the public, CU launched a web tool allowing viewers to see who contributed to the campaigns of members of the New York City Council, what industry employed those contributors, and to which organizations the council member directed public funds—allowing members of the public to determine what kind of relationships, if any, linked those revelations. It joined with its "good government" allies, the League of Women Voters, Common Cause, and the New York Public Interest Research Group

(NYPIRG), in an analysis of contributions to the statewide candidates in New York's 2010 election, concluding the following:

> one quarter of all campaign dollars [in those campaigns] donated by individuals originate from a total of 169 persons. Their donations, on average, exceed $63,200, and these contributors wrote checks from addresses in the Greater New York metropolitan area. In addition to these individuals who gave big bucks, businesses, trade associations and unions provided the lion's share of campaign donations.

On a regular basis, CU interviews candidates for office within New York City and issues reports in advance of primary day and Election Day summarizing its findings about each candidate, but in this regard, exercises a kind of oversight function beyond the scope of this volume.

Common Cause

One of the largest and most influential good government watchdog groups, with more than 400,000 members throughout the United States, Common Cause was created in 1970 by John Gardner to make government more accessible, accountable, and responsive. Independent and nonpartisan, its leadership sees its mission as combating the malign influences on government of money and secrecy. Accordingly, it has helped lead battles for campaign finance reform, lobbying disclosure, open government, the Freedom of Information Act, sunshine laws, the 18-year-old vote, the Clean Air Act, opening the Highway Trust Fund to mass transit, more open congressional budget process, and airline and trucking deregulation.

With a paid staff of about fifty researchers, lawyers, lobbyists, and office workers, it relies heavily on a huge group of part-time volunteers and college summer interns. Membership dues largely fund its roughly $10 million annual budget. By mailed balloting, its membership elects a twenty-eight–member governing board, with staggered three-year terms. The governing board meets quarterly, but generally is guided by the professional staff. Its thirty-five state chapters follow similar decision-making processes. Grassroots support supplements its lobbyists: Local units will have telephone chair coordinators, issue developers, recruiters, publicity personnel, and speakers' bureaus, all volunteers.

In three months of 2011 alone, among many other initiatives, Common Cause revealed that Supreme Court Justice Clarence Thomas failed to report his wife's sources of income for at least five years in violation of law, and urged the Judicial Conference to refer the matter to the Justice Department for formal investigation. It revealed unseemly fundraising, which it called an "invitation to corruption," by members of the congressional budgetary Super Committee, both Democrats and Republicans, during the three months when the Super Committee was supposed to do its work. It showed how corporations such as "Walmart, Coca Cola, Koch Industries, AT&T, Altria and ExxonMobil" contributed more than $370 million in the previous ten years to state legislative campaigns pushing an agenda of opposition to environmental regulation, minimum wage laws, and other labor protections, and open reporting of corporate campaign contributions; and support for measures that increase corporate profits, often at public expense.

League of Women Voters

The League of Women Voters (LWV) was founded in 1920 at the end of the suffragette movement by members who had just won the battle for votes for women (the constitutional amendment was ratified six months later). By 2010, it had 150,000 members (in more than 900 communities in all fifty states). Its goals are to foster education about issues and to promote citizen participation. Historically, the LWV was best known for issuing educational publications like its guides to local, county, and state governments, and to local public school systems—how they work, how to influence them, how to change them; and, in many localities throughout the United States, listings of all elected officials representing the area, with contact information, called "They Represent You," formerly in hard copy and now online. It also undertakes educational campaigns on specific issues. In the late 1990s and early 2000s, for example, LWV sponsored community roundtable meetings throughout New York State on the Rockefeller drug laws, known for their excessive harshness. The LWV effort may have contributed to their significant amelioration in 2009. In 1988, LWV joined with Common Cause and other groups in demonstrations and press conferences supporting an unsuccessful, but highly informative, campaign to require shopping malls to permit political petitioning and electioneering subject to reasonable time, place, and manner restrictions.

Although the aforementioned efforts do not constitute the kind of oversight that is the subject of this book, the LWV, in conjunction with other good government groups, has engaged in that kind of oversight as well. Along with Citizen Action (affiliated with New York's Working Families Party) and Common Cause, in 2009 the LWV filed a formal complaint with the State's Legislative Ethics Commission urging an investigation of State Sen. Hiram Monserrate's legal defense fund. Monserrate, who was convicted only of a misdemeanor after facing charges that he had slashed his girlfriend's face with a broken bottle, almost certainly was guilty of the latter. His legal defense fund by 2009 had reached six figures. The civic groups asked the commission to require Monserrate to identify donors and how much each contributed, claiming the fund violated the gift ban in the Public Officers Law.

An Unreasonable Man: Ralph Nader, Public Citizen, and the PIRGs

Ralph Nader stands out as the single most prominent public interest defender and watchdog of the last third of the twentieth century. He published *Unsafe at Any Speed* in 1965, which attacked the auto industry for knowingly sacrificing drivers' lives to increase profits and implicitly criticized the government as well for its failure to enforce safety standards. In 1970, Nader won a lawsuit against General Motors for its campaign to harass and intimidate him. The campaign included surveillance, threatening, and harassing phone calls, wiretaps, and efforts to trap Nader in illicit relationships.

Nader had already recruited a handful of idealistic young lawyers and law students, shortly to be known as "Nader's Raiders," to study the Federal Trade Commission. On the basis of his analysis of their work, his 1968 report showed how its decisions were heavily influenced by businesses it purported to regulate, with secret ex parte contacts with business and few ways for affected citizens to challenge or confront that influence.

In 1971, Nader founded Public Citizen. By 2000, Public Citizen had 150,000 members nationwide.

Nader's immediate successor as president of Public Citizen, Joan Claybrook, had served as administrator of the National Highway Transportation Safety Administration (NHTSA) between 1977 and 1980 under President Jimmy Carter. She returned the organization to the spotlight in connection with Nader's original issue, auto safety, testifying to the Senate Committee on Commerce, Science, and Transportation on September 12, 2000 on the Firestone Tire Defect and Ford Explorer Rollovers.

When Claybrook was NHTSA administrator, the agency recalled about 7 million Firestone tires, documenting forty-one deaths from their use. Firestone had tried to cover up that scandal too; top management was replaced. Now, she said, a "lethal" combination of Ford Explorers and Firestone tires, by the date of her testimony, had taken 135 more lives. Ford Explorers required low inflation pressure (26 pounds per square inch, or psi) to mitigate rollover problems; The Firestone ATX, ATX II, and Wilderness tires then overheated with highway use, causing the tread to separate, resulting in catastrophic crashes of the vehicle. Company engineers had urged changes to prevent rollovers, but the company refused to delay the introduction date by the ten months that would have been necessary, instead removing air from the tires—and never fully tested the tires at that psi level. Firestone recommends 35 psi for maximum load.

Ford and Firestone had covered up these safety problems since 1990, when Ford Explorer first came out—ten years earlier. Claybrook's testimony—like Nader's book thirty-five years earlier—directly criticized the auto industry. When she warned that Ford and Firestone would continue their cover-up until and unless NHTSA intervened, her criticism of the government's inaction to date was obvious. Once again, Public Citizen's scorching revelations targeted private industry malfeasance at the same time its oversight of a federal government agency exposed scandalous inaction. Claybrook urged Congress to authorize NHTSA to force a company to buy replacement parts from a competitor in the face of an imminent danger and to force reimbursement to customers who made their own replacements; and to notify NHTSA if it gets twenty-five complaints about the same alleged defect, or if it gets three or more lawsuits. She also urged that insurers be required to supply NHTSA with relevant data. She noted that NHTSA's budget, adjusted for inflation, in 2000 was 30 percent below what it was in 1981; its enforcement budget, about 50 percent of the 1980 budget. Her implied message to Congress on that score was obvious.

Three months later, in November 2000, Congress enacted laws adopting a version of Claybrook's proposed notification requirements and others provisions ensuring a greater degree of tire safety and rollover prevention. Public Citizen continues its broader efforts as well.

In 2010, the US Supreme Court decided in *Citizens United v. FEC* that corporations could spend unlimited amounts of money to support political candidates so long as they did not coordinate their spending with the candidates' campaigns. Public Citizen, taking an unusual oversight role as public watchdog over what it deems an anti-democratic decision by the judicial branch of government, then launched campaigns for a constitutional amendment to overturn the decision, federal legislation to require disclosure of such corporate contributions, public financing to reduce the impact of such contributions, state legislation that would bar such contributions from government contractors, and state legislation that would give shareholders a right to overrule and limit management's decision to make such contributions.

Ralph Nader also created the Public Interest Research Group (PIRG), initially as a public interest law firm. Early state PIRGs grew on college campuses, with the first members personally recruited by Nader. About one hundred colleges have campus PIRG chapters. In 1971, the first state

PIRG incorporated. Forty-seven states and at least four Canadian provinces have them now, still heavily reliant on college student activism, although most have professional staffs as well. The state PIRGs created US PIRG as their national advocacy arm in 1980 or thereabouts. Among the oldest and most active are MPIRG (Minnesota), OSPIRG (Oregon), MassPIRG, and NYPIRG. These organizations typically focus on consumer and environmental issues, but identify and expose government malfeasance attributable to moneyed special interests generally, often in conjunction with other good government groups.

For example, Illinois PIRG in 2011 fought to get the Chicago City Council to scrutinize privatization deals to make sure they don't sell valuable sources of public revenue for inadequate one-shot cash infusions; discovered and revealed that companies with government contracts to operate traffic light cameras and collect the traffic fines they generate have lobbied for more cameras, ticket quotas, and automated speed-limit enforcement in order to increase their profits; and reported that federal agricultural subsidies are structured so that Chicago taxpayers subsidize junk food, like Twinkies, with about $9.25 million a year, but fresh fruits and vegetables with only about $143,000 a year. The Arizona PIRG warned their fellow citizens that legislation urged by the state's governor and legislative leaders included a $25 million "deal-closing fund" that did not permit the public to know which companies were being subsidized, or how many jobs were promised or created by those companies. The various state PIRGs have compiled an impressive list of environmental and consumer victories. They use door-to-door canvassing, investigative research, and media exposure as their primary tools.

Project on Government Oversight

The Project on Government Oversight (POGO) makes no bones about its role. Its title announces it. The political humorist Lewis Black calls it "the most ass-kicking, name-taking bunch of goody two-shoes good government types in America." POGO began in 1981. The story of Ernest Fitzgerald helps explain its origin. Sen. Charles Grassley called Fitzgerald "the father of all whistleblowers." Fitzgerald served in a middle management position at the Defense Department. Gigantic cost overruns on the Lockheed C-5A cargo plane horrified him, but his superiors ignored his reports. Frustrated, in 1968 he testified about the $2 billion scam to Sen. William Proxmire's Joint Economic Subcommittee. Soon thereafter, in 1969, Richard Nixon assumed the presidency, and on Nixon's orders, Secretary of Defense Melvin Laird fired Fitzgerald. Before the Supreme Court's ruling in *Nixon v. Fitzgerald* that the president enjoyed absolute immunity from such civil suits,

Nixon paid Fitzgerald $142,000 in liquidated damages, but the Supreme Court held that payment of damages did not moot the question of immunity, upon which a further payment by Nixon to Fitzgerald depended, so it heard the case anyway. Despite harassment and ostracism, in 1982 he was rehired to a less prestigious position in the Air Force.

In 1981, however, Fitzgerald and two Pentagon officials with integrity came to the conclusion that future whistleblowers needed a reliable "front" to which they could forward their information in confidence. That "front" would protect their confidentiality, would verify their information through independent research, and would promote the information to the press. Working at the time for the National Taxpayers Union, Dina Rasor became "the Project on Military Procurement," and in that capacity worked with her sources to expose defense contractor fraud on a significant scale. As Rasor's role soon expanded beyond military spending to other areas of government, her work transformed into POGO.

Since then, POGO has exposed the Defense Department's $7,600 coffee brewer and $600 toilet seat; the Wackenhut Corporation's disgraceful waste of the taxpayer dollars the federal government paid it to defend the American embassy in Kabul, Afghanistan—resulting finally in the cancellation of that contract; and the increase in the Defense Department spending on such independent contractors from $200 billion in 2000 to $500 billion in 2010. When it tried to expose the oil companies' underpayments of $500 million in federal taxes, members of Congress who received large campaign contributions from the oil companies succeeded in bringing contempt of Congress charges against POGO and against its executive director personally, hoping to send her to jail. But she did not go to jail, POGO sued the oil companies under the Federal False Claims Act, and the oil companies ultimately had to pay what they owed. The Dodd-Frank Law includes a provision protecting whistleblowers on Wall Street from retaliation, thanks to POGO.

The foregoing only samples POGO's accomplishments. In 2011 alone, POGO showed that private contractors charged the federal government about twice as much as it would have cost taxpayers had the American military done the work themselves. It showed that foreign governments paid large sums to lobby the "Super Committee" of Congress that was charged with restructuring the federal budget.

- In 2010, POGO had warned Congress about the vulnerabilities of the Treasury Department's emergency contracting authority; in 2011 its warnings were vindicated when the special IG for Troubled Asset Relief Program (TARP) funds revealed that one of the law firms TARP hired billed Treasury

$5.8 million for work it did not specify at all; and much of the remaining $27 million it had paid other law firms for work on the bank bail-out was paid with "unacceptable risk" of excessive cost to taxpayers.

- It exposed internal SEC documents showing that a 2001 investigation of Deutsche Bank for fraudulent statements in its earlier effort to buy Bankers Trust ended suspiciously and suddenly when the director of enforcement for the SEC became general counsel for Deutsche Bank.

- It exposed the Chamber of Commerce's campaign to weaken the Foreign Corrupt Practices Act, thereby making it easier for corporate officers to bribe foreign governments. It released documents strongly suggesting that the State Department created a fictitious officer, "Terry Hogan," to facilitate the use of the "extraordinary rendition" program, designed to have foreign governments torture suspects on behalf of the United States.

- It played a significant role in forcing the resignation in October 2011 of the "top personnel official" official at the Department of Defense, Clifford Stanley, its undersecretary for personnel and readiness, having in previous months revealed his responsibility for wasting millions of dollars in unnecessary private consultants and creating an exodus of skilled personnel by his incompetent management.

The foregoing snapshot of POGO's work presents an even more remarkable picture in light of the fact that it produces these results on an annual budget of about $2.3 million.

Politics by Other Means and the Nonprofit Oversight Sector

Part of the partisanship around oversight investigations has been fed by nonprofit groups that frequently do more to call attention to ethical lapses than to conduct real oversight investigations. Much like the good government groups discussed previously, these organizations do sometimes engage in the more traditional oversight function.

Judicial Watch

Larry Klayman founded Judicial Watch in 1994 as a conservative organization advocating ethics and transparency in government and using litigation as its primary weapon. It regularly sued President Bill Clinton and his administration, and received millions of dollars in funding from prominent right-wing donors. Its litigation usually advances causes sympathetic to conservatives, such as suing to halt a Virginia town's "day labor" program on the grounds that it might further the employment of undocumented aliens.

However, in 2003, Judicial Watch did join with the Sierra Club in an ultimately unsuccessful lawsuit demanding that the minutes of Vice President Cheney's Energy Task Force be made public; in 2006, it launched a successful lawsuit for access to the records of Republican lobbyist Jack Abramoff's White House visits; and in 2002, it sued Cheney and Halliburton for fraudulent accounting practices.

Its 2011 list of Washington's ten most corrupt politicians included two conservative Republicans, as well as eight prominent Democrats. Judicial Watch's traditional oversight role is more limited. For example, in October 2011, Judicial Watch sought public records related to the award of a Department of Labor contract for development of a bilingual smart phone application to allow hourly workers to better track their hours. The contract was awarded to a former technology chief at the Labor Department without competition.

Citizens for Responsibility and Ethics in Washington

Norman Eisen and Melanie Sloan, among others, founded Citizens for Responsibility and Ethics in Washington (CREW) in 2003 to provide a more liberal advocacy organization for ethics and transparency in government in counterbalance to groups like Judicial Watch. CREW's 2011 report of the most corrupt members of Congress included ten Republicans and four Democrats. Although closely associated with the Clintons, it called for the resignation of former US Rep. Anthony Weiner after his sex scandal became public in 2011. Weiner's wife was a key staff member for Secretary of State Hillary Clinton. It also called for the resignation of US Rep. Charles Rangel after his colleagues censured him for a number of ethics violations in 2010. Like Judicial Watch, CREW also ventures into a more traditional oversight role. An October 2011 investigation found that the Department of Defense had failed to comply with a 1999 law requiring it to establish a central database on incidents of domestic violence involving members of the US Armed Forces.

Under the federal freedom of information act, CREW sought data on the number of soldiers accused, arrested, prosecuted, and convicted in domestic violence cases. None of the armed services were able to provide the information—all of which should have been available had the central database been created.

"Oversight for Profit"

Various kinds of private attorneys profit by playing special roles in over-seeing the actions of government and enforcing accountability by suing government for its misbehavior. Prominent among them are the personal injury bar and *qui tam* lawyers, although attorneys in a wide variety of specialties also serve as "watchdogs" of a sort whenever they seek judicial review of government agency action they believe is wrong. Monitors and independent private-sector IGs may be, but need not be, attorneys. They too render oversight services for profit. The following discussion illustrates their respective contributions.

Personal Injury Bar

The personal injury bar takes cases strictly on a "contingency-fee" basis: They charge no hourly fee—no fee at all—but if the plaintiff wins, they get a percentage, usually one-third. If the plaintiff loses, personal injury lawyers get nothing. They perform, if you will, oversight for profit.

When negligence by government causes personal injury, they exercise oversight directly. They may represent plaintiffs injured as a result of medical malpractice in public hospitals, defective signage or construction on highways, mistreatment in public custodial institutions such as homes for the developmentally disabled or mentally ill, excessive force by police, or in any other setting where other forms of oversight have failed to prevent or correct dangers to individuals posed by government malfeasance. Their potential to win money damages for their clients serves as an incentive for government to improve its operation.

Plaintiffs can bring these lawsuits against government notwithstanding sovereign immunity under the Federal Tort Claims Act of 1946, and under comparable tort claims laws enacted by the states. But the personal injury bar exercises a form of indirect oversight even when they sue private defen-dants. When government agencies fail in their responsibility to assure safety, lawsuits brought by these attorneys spotlight those deficiencies. Although they may or may not succeed in forcing reform, no other form of oversight enjoys a guarantee of success either.

Personal injury lawyers represent injured plaintiffs who alleged negli-gence by doctors and other health care providers; transportation providers using defective vehicles or negligent drivers or pilots; manufacturers of phar-maceuticals or other products that injure consumers; and, among others, employers who provide working conditions lacking in appropriate safety.

The personal injury trial bar's use of New York's Scaffold Law protecting workers at elevated construction sites, provides a vivid example. The first version of the Scaffold Law was enacted in 1885 to protect construction workers on New York City skyscrapers from death and serious injury resulting from the failure of contractors to provide safety measures important for employees who must work at great heights. It was codified as part of the current Labor Law in 1921. As it developed over the years, it was amended to exclude comparative negligence as a defense. Before that change, co-workers would always testify that the injured worker was negligent, because otherwise the co-workers would lose their jobs. The record of recent cases brought and won by the personal injury bar make it clear that but for the continued exclusion of comparative negligence as a defense, contractors and owners would continue to escape liability.

The federal Occupational Safety and Health Administration (OSHA) was established considerably later, in 1971. In 2005, the New York State Trial Lawyers Association (NYSTLA), the major trade association for the personal injury bar in New York, released a study of more than 2,500 OSHA construction site inspections in New York, including summaries of the 156 accidents OSHA investigated since 2001. It showed the following:

- OSHA had an average of six inspectors available on a given day to inspect the thousands upon thousands of construction sites in the New York and northern New Jersey area.

- Almost one-third of the violations were of scaffolding or fall protection requirements.

- The overwhelming majority of inspections revealed serious violations of OSHA safety standards.

- More than 80 percent of inspections in Brooklyn, Manhattan, and the Bronx found violations (compared with 62 percent statewide and 50 percent upstate).

- Immigrants were the victims in two-thirds of the accidents in New York City in which a worker was killed or in which at least three workers were hospitalized.

- OSHA penalties against contractors and owners at the sites where safety violations resulted in deaths and injuries were so small—generally well under $2,000—that they did not deter the continuation of equally dangerous practices.

Immigrant workers often were not named on workers compensation policies and lacked health insurance, leaving them, if they were injured, or their families, if they were killed, with no compensation for worksite disasters attributable to the absence of safety equipment. Such workers feared employer reprisals if they complained to authorities about safety lapses, and often spoke little English in any case. Regulation by OSHA clearly had minimal effect in assuring the safety of workers at elevated construction sites.

NYSTLA cited various incidents that had occurred only within a few years prior to the release of its report: Jian Quo Shen was crushed by an unbuttressed concrete foundation that collapsed on him in Elmhurst, Queens; a balcony roof being illegally built in Bay Ridge, Brooklyn collapsed on Angel Segovia; Manuel Falcon fell off a roof of a Queens house having been given no protective cord or belt; overloaded scaffolding collapsed on a Mexican day laborer, name unknown, at an Upper East Side brownstone undergoing renovation. Each of these workers was killed.

The only significant financial or legal incentive for contractors and owners to protect such workers—in New York City, mostly immigrant and non-union—is provided by New York Labor Law § 240, the "scaffold law." In this, as in other area in which oversight by government agencies falls short, the personal injury bar steps into the breach and by its highly visible work prods those with government oversight responsibilities to do better.

Qui tam Attorneys

President Lincoln, infuriated by defense contractors cheating the Union, forced Congress to enact the Federal False Claims Act in 1863, providing rewards for citizens who brought suit on behalf of the government to recover such ill-gotten gains. From the Latin phrase, *qui tam pro domino rege quam pro sic ipso in hoc parte sequitur*, or "he who brings suit on behalf of the sovereign as well as on his own behalf," the statute become known as the "*qui tam*" law.

Over the decades, amendments no doubt sought by those who intended to continue to profit by shady means, weakened the statute. In 1986, however, amendments restored the power of the statute by imposing treble damages on perpetrators, and allowing citizen plaintiffs fifteen percent of the awards if the Justice Department joined them in the lawsuit, and 30 percent if it did not. Plaintiffs may bring such lawsuits only if they base them on information that they themselves have provided and not, for example, if the key evidence has already been reported independently by the press. Of course, if the citizen is an employee of a government agency that has facilitated the fraud, his or her employers may fight back. If they can destroy evidence or otherwise successfully impede the lawsuit, the whistleblower will no doubt face harsh retaliation.

In 2011, for example, the United States collected more than $3 billion in *qui tam* cases from perpetrators of fraud against it, bringing total *qui tam* fraud recoveries since 1986 to more than $30 billion. In FY 2008, "relators," the private citizens who initiated the lawsuits, collected $198 million. Medicare and Medicaid fraud, especially by pharmaceutical companies, accounted for most of the money. More than half the states have their own *qui tam* laws. Some local governments have enacted their own *qui tam* laws as well.

Independent Private Sector Inspectors General and Other Monitors

Two writers on the subject of independent private sector inspectors general (IPSIGs) called them "privately funded overseers of the public integrity." Because monitors, including IPSIGs, only oversee private sector actors, they are not government "watchdogs" in the sense we have been using the phrase in this book. They do serve as such in a different sense, however: Government insists that questionable companies employ monitors as a condition of their avoiding indictment or conviction, or of winning a government contract. Then, the monitor serves as government entity's eyes and ears within that company. In this way, monitors have some powers even in excess of government agency regulators.

Courts have long imposed monitors on the recommendation of prosecutors to scrutinize the operations of companies and unions in lieu of other penalties. For example, in 1991 a federal judge in New Jersey appointed a former New Jersey Gaming Enforcement official to monitor to scrutinize the affairs of Hotel Employees and Restaurant Employees International Union Local 54. He served until 1997, when the union appeared to have essentially freed itself of ties to organized crime. Similarly, courts have replaced the corrupt leadership of companies and unions with temporary trustees and receivers, on the premise that the organizations would improve their behavior so that at some future date they could once again be trusted to select their own leadership. For example, as a result of federal prosecution in 1982, a trustee ran New Jersey Teamsters Local 560 for thirteen years.

In 1989, OCTF proposed the creation of IPSIGs for use with construction industry companies. That industry, when engaged in construction on behalf of the public sector, had been so thoroughly corrupted in the New York region that local government did not really have the option of retaining "clean" companies. Only corrupt companies had the expertise to get the job done. Therefore, OCTF suggested that such companies be permitted to go on with their work, but only on condition that they hire organizations of the sort OCTF described, so that the relevant government entities would have sophisticated monitors, with access to all the companies' people and records, making sure nothing illegal or unethical was going on. If the IPSIG reported serious wrongdoing to the government, indictment, conviction, or at least loss of the contract could follow.

The Tully Construction Company provided a vivid example. Based on alleged organized crime connections, VENDEX disclosure failings, environmental violations and tax liabilities, Tully had been found "non-responsible." In 1996, Tully signed an agreement with New York City allowing its reinstatement as a responsible bidder pursuant to its hiring of an IPSIG, adoption of a Code of Business Ethics, and establishment of an ethics training program for its employees. Tully paid the Fairfax Group $300,000 a year for these services. The Code of Business Ethics (1) required the company to dismiss any employee, officer, or director convicted under state or criminal law for business-related activities; or, absent a conviction, to diligently investigate any such relevant charges against such an individual (2) prohibited the involvement in the company of any member of an organized crime group (3) required anyone involved in the company to report illegal, unethical, or inappropriate activities regarding any city contracts to the city and to the IPSIG.

In 2002, then-Mayor Giuliani employed four construction companies to clean up the World Trade Center site, a multibillion dollar project, but required each to hire an IPSIG as a condition of employment. Each company won a $250 million emergency sole source time and materials contract. The companies had little incentive to work quickly, paid, as they were, on the basis of hours worked, but no significant fraud has been reported on that basis. They completed the work with remarkably little excess in cost or evidence of wrongdoing. Subsequently, the Port Authority of New York and New Jersey imposed the same conditions on the contractors responsible for new construction on the site, again, as of 2011, with salutary results.

IPSIGs have become "state of the art" in terms of government monitoring. Although some question this conclusion, claiming better value from less intrusive and expensive monitors, governments in various parts of the United States now use them. By definition, they include lawyers, auditors, and investigators, and other professionals with skill in loss prevention, research, and management. The International Association of IPSIGs now imposes a code of ethics on its members, and sets standards for industry quality.

Judicial Review of Administrative Action

Whenever citizens go to court to challenge government action, attorneys may be helping them to participate in a form of oversight. Under the Administrative Procedure Act of 1946, citizens may challenge regulations issued by government agencies, as well as agency adjudications, after exhausting administrative remedies. Citizens also may sue individual government employees who overreach. Until the last third of the twentieth century or so, sovereign immunity was understood to provide absolute immunity for officials who must exercise discretionary power and authority in performing their functions. (This did not protect those who merely exercised "ministerial" power—in this context meaning only the power to carry out policies set by others. They were liable—although some, like many police officers, carried personal liability insurance policies.)

The Civil Rights Act of 1871 first limited the sovereign immunity of state and local officials who deprived citizens of constitutional rights or privileges. Now, even policy makers may be liable under § 1981 of the Civil Rights Act, under *Bivens v. Six Federal Agents*, granting only qualified immunity for executive officers for acts performed in good faith and with a reasonable basis for the belief upon which they acted, although plaintiffs have to prove lack of probable cause in a retaliatory prosecution case, *Hartman v. Moore*.

Old King Coal

Even the most compelling stories of fraud, waste, abuse, and corruption can fall on deaf ears. When a legislator or an auditor takes on an oversight investigation, there is usually a clear vehicle for moving it forward—hearings, a report, and eventually a demand for action. Investigative journalists can take their work to wider audiences and, with the support of a newspaper, can push for reform: recall the expression, still true despite the decline of old media, "never argue with someone who buys ink by the barrel."

It is harder for nonprofit organizations. Usually, for their investigative work to be effective, they need to command the attention of government oversight actors or at least an investigative journalist. There are now more outlets. For example, many of the investigations discussed above received only cursory coverage by the mainstream press, but were well publicized by the organizations themselves. Still, the returns on those sorts of investigative efforts are limited: if part of the goal of oversight is to inform, then the number of readers that learn from an investigation is an important measure of its success or failure. And there is a difference between reaching readers through a website read by hundreds versus a newspaper article read by millions.

Nonprofit oversight actors are also constrained in the same way as government agencies and the press by the cost of oversight and limitations on resources. If anything, nonprofits can be more constrained than a government that can collect taxes or for-profit news media that can sell advertising.

In addition to our work in government, both of us have led nonprofit organizations. Dan Feldman was the director of the Trial Lawyers Association during the investigation of noncompliance with OSHA laws in New York. From 2005 to 2011, David Eichenthal was president of the Ochs Center for Metropolitan Studies in Chattanooga. The Ochs Center mostly does data analysis and policy research. It is not an advocacy organization and does not normally engage in the type of ongoing government oversight that groups like Public Citizen and POGO perform on a regular basis.

For several years, however, one of the main areas of concentration for the Ochs Center was work related to the economic and fiscal impact of proposed new coal fired power plants, primarily in the southeast. Whether you think that coal does or doesn't make sense, the proposed development of new plants poses a series of policy choices for the cities and counties where their location is planned. Environmentalists and health advocates lay out a compelling case related to the potential negative effects of coal, both locally and globally. Plant proponents, however, argue that those impacts can be mitigated and—most important for host communities—that plants will create jobs and tax revenue.

It turns out, however, though that—shockingly—sometimes claims of economic benefits are overstated. An Ochs Center study of built coal plants found that frequently job claims did not match reality. The reaction of the coal industry: "It is standard for companies to round up on direct and indirect jobs, and underestimate plant construction costs."

In many cases, new coal plants also don't make sense for consumers, or ultimately for the utilities that build or buy power from the plants. That's the main reason that more than one hundred proposed coal-fired power plants were canceled in the past decade.

Why then do some plants go forward? The Ochs Center studied a proposed plant in Washington County, Georgia. The study and other related studies made a fairly compelling case that there were less costly ways of creating the proposed capacity of the plant that would create a greater economic benefit to communities that would be served by the plant. Moreover, it was absolutely unclear how much the power would cost and who, beyond the electric cooperatives participating in the consortium proposing to build it, would actually buy the power.

At the behest of its funder, the Rockefeller Family Fund, and on-the-ground opponents of the plant, the Ochs Center sought to answer the question of "who benefits from Plant Washington?"

Here's what the Ochs Center found:

It appears that the proposed construction of the $2.315 billion coal-burning power plant in Washington County could create significant economic opportunity for some of the most powerful and politically connected entrenched interests in the State of Georgia.

The owners of the proposed site of Plant Washington are members of the Tarbutton family, one of Georgia's most powerful families. According to Washington County tax records, Hugh M. Tarbutton owns the majority of the site of the proposed Plant Washington: Its assessed value is approximately $1.6 million. In July 2009, four nearby properties were acquired by a firm affiliated with the developer of Plant Washington at a rate of just under $15,000 per acre. At that rate, the cost of acquisition of Mr. Tarbutton's property would be $18.7 million.

Tarbutton family members have served as members of the Georgia Ports Authority (Hugh), the State Board of Economic Development (Charles), the State Board of Regents, Georgia Rural Development Council and Board of Education (Ben J.) and the State Board of Technical and Adult Education (Benjamin). According to data from online campaign finance records, members of the Tarbutton family have contributed more than $500,000 to political committees and candidates for state and federal offices between 2006 and 2011.

Financing of the plant construction would be conducted through the local development authority—two Tarbutton family members served on its board. An analysis of public records also found that Hugh Tarbutton had failed to fully disclose his interest in the site of the plant on disclosure filings required as part of his service on a state board.

A consortium of Georgia electric cooperatives, led by Cobb EMC, proposed the plant. In 2011, the Cobb County district attorney announced a thirty-one–count indictment of Dwight Brown—the then-president of Cobb EMC. The indictment alleged that Brown violated the Georgia Racketeer Influenced and Corrupt Organizations Act by engaging in "a pattern of racketeering activity that included but was not limited to the theft of millions of dollars from Cobb EMC, the theft of millions of dollars in patronage capital from Cobb EMC's members, and false statements to conceal these thefts from Cobb EMC's members." The Ochs Center's review of public records also disclosed that Brown had apparently sought to conceal his actions, which had been the subject of earlier civil litigation, from the Federal Energy Regulatory Commission. In 2012, under new board leadership, the Cobb EMC withdrew its support of the project.

Day-to-day project management of Plant Washington appears to have been led by Dean Alford, a former vice president and board member of a Cobb EMC affiliate whose firms diverted millions of dollars in investments from the Cobb EMC. Between 2002 and 2007, Cobb Energy appears to have lost more than $11 million on the operations of three Alford-led subsidiaries, Allied Utility Network, Allied Energy Services, and Cobb Energy Mortgage. Alford has also partnered with Dwight Brown in two real estate ventures. A former state legislator, he served on a state board with one of the Tarbutton family members: In his disclosure filings with the state, he failed to disclose his interests in the Plant Washington consortium and a series of affiliates.

Finally, the state board on which Alford and one of the Tarbutton family members served, the Board of Technical and Adult Education, which oversees the state Technical College System, sought a $1.5 million federal Department of Labor grant to provide job training for workers who would be involved in plant construction and operation at Plant Washington. The Alford-led consortium was identified as the primary employer partner in the grant. The grant was issued in January 2009. By 2011, there were no plant construction jobs to be trained for and it is unclear how the federal funds were used.

The investigative work that led to these findings required months of collecting documents from the federal government, the state and local government entities. Some of it was obtained by freedom of information act requests—for example, the details of the Labor Department grant—whereas much of the rest, from filings with the Federal Energy Regulatory Commission to data on campaign contributions to financial disclosure statements to property records in Washington County, was obtained on line. There were also more than a few visits to county courthouses.

It was precisely the type of investigation that we have described throughout this book.

And you are among the first to read about it.

As of 2012, there had been no hearings, no audits and no investigative news reports on the Plant Washington story, with the exception of some exceptional local reporting on the aspects of the story related to wrongdoing at Cobb EMC.

It hasn't been for a lack of trying. Over the course of a year, these investigative findings were shared in meetings with the Justice Department, the Federal Energy Regulatory Commission, and a ranking member of House Committee on Oversight and Government Reform.

Similar one-on-one meetings were held with reporters from *The New York Times*, the *Wall Street Journal*, *The Washington Post*, and ProPublica.

No one who reviewed the findings suggested that there was no wrong-doing. But a combination of a lack of resources or a lack of jurisdiction led all, to our knowledge, to take a pass on the story or on further investigation.

If an investigation falls in the woods and no one hears it, it really does not make a sound.

Perhaps until now.

Conclusion

The work of nongovernmental oversight organizations continues to justify Toqueville's 1835 praise of voluntary associations in the United States. Citizen action in the form of voluntary associations seems to have increased, perhaps in response to the legislative institutions that have seemed to forget much of their responsibility for honest and effective oversight.

Many of them exemplify adherence to the best principles of effective oversight: evident anger at taxpayer losses attributable to fraud, waste, abuse, and corruption; thorough fact-gathering and analysis; constant exposure of such malfeasance to the sunlight of publicity, and persistent follow-up. Of course, such organizations ordinarily cannot compel their targets to disclose information, unlike some government watchdogs that may have subpoena power or other statutory access to records, other than through freedom of information laws, which have become increasingly porous and in any case are subject to extensive stalling tactics. However much government may frustrate them with its resistance to their information requests, their passion and persistence have more than compensated for their mild weakness in this regard.

The for-profit oversight sector—personal injury and *qui tam* attorneys, and IPSIGs—seems likewise to have expanded in population and energy. There, of course, we have more difficulty in attempting to determine how much their motivation derives from strongly held beliefs about accountability for injustice and abuse, and how much derives from a desire to make money. However, because human nature drives people to find in themselves the highest motives, that sector likely feels itself to be part of the righteous cause. They bring to the battle important financial resources with which to adhere to our other principles of effective oversight: thorough fact-gathering, artful public relations and publicity, and persistent follow-up.

Overall, nongovernmental oversight organizations remain a bright spot in the oversight cosmos. They give us hope.

Chapter 16

Conclusion

Every day, tens of thousands of Americans wake up and go to work at trying to make their government more effective and more efficient. They work in city halls, county courthouses, state capitols, across the federal government and in the halls of Congress. They are lawyers, auditors, investigators, reporters, and others who practice the art of the watchdog.

We have tried to tell the story of their everyday efforts. Over time and collectively, their work—their art—has saved billions of dollars and human lives. Sometimes, their efforts make headlines but more often than not it is done quietly but effectively. In some cases, however, their failures, either for a lack of resources or effort or because politics becomes the purpose, have cost us no less than faith in our democracy.

We have already said that we believe in oversight. We hope that this book contributes to an understanding of just what oversight is and how it is practiced today. But we also hope that it becomes part of a conversation about how we can do more and better at the work of oversight at all levels of government. We think that is an important conversation to have at this time in our nation's history because so much is at stake.

At no time since Watergate and the aftermath of the Vietnam War have confidence and trust in the government been so low. The most recent survey, as we write, found that just one in ten Americans trusts the federal government to do the right thing most or all of the time. Not an option at the federal level, mayoral and gubernatorial recall efforts suggest that public trust in state and local government is not much higher.

And although our nation has begun a slow recovery from the Great Recession and near financial collapse of 2008 and 2009, Americans are worried about their economic future as well. The recovery that has begun has been uneven at best. At the end of 2011, there were still seven states with unemployment higher than 10 percent.

We think that there is both a governance imperative and an economic imperative for more effective oversight. In this final chapter, we outline the

251

governance and economic case for more effective oversight and try to define just what is necessary to achieve that goal.

Governance Imperative

It turns out that the Founding Fathers' views on separation of powers and a free press were right: Without effective oversight, we cannot have effective governance.

One of us recently had lunch with a senior congressional aide and told him that we were working on a book on oversight. He said, "We spend so much time on politics and appropriations, we don't do nearly enough to make sure that what we spend money on is working. Now that we have to cut spending, it is the worst of both worlds. There are programs that don't work that we should cut and there are programs that do work that we shouldn't cut. Without oversight, we have no way of telling the difference."

And without effective oversight, it should be no surprise that Americans have so little confidence in government's ability to take on society's toughest challenges. *New York Times* columnist David Brooks wrote that the problem with American liberalism was that "Americans may agree with liberal diagnoses, but they don't trust the instrument the Democrats use to solve problems. They don't trust the federal government." Brooks went on to argue that "It's not because they dislike individual programs like Medicare. It's more likely because they think the whole system is rigged. Or to put it in the economists' language, they believe the government has been captured by rent-seekers." In the face of this problem, Brooks concludes that if liberals "can't restore Americans' trust in government, it really doesn't matter what problems they identify and what plans they propose. No one will believe in the instrument they rely on for solutions."

Lack of faith in government affects the conservative agenda as well. After all, distrust in government may explain why large numbers of Republicans are looking to a more libertarian approach to government—one that reduces federal spending on all forms of government, including the military.

As we noted at the beginning of this book, the greatest enemies of the watchdog are those who believe that corruption, or fraud or waste or abuse, exists but there is nothing that can be done to limit it. Complacency about our government is at the core of the distrust found in survey results. Ultimately, a government that lacks the trust of those who are governed is destined to fail.

For the reasons we discussed at the onset, the combination of oversight and reform is essential to restoring confidence in government's ability to solve problems. Few would expect a government absolutely free of fraud, waste, abuse or corruption. Public confidence, however, is eroded when "the system seems rigged" and misdeeds go unpunished and uncorrected. Thinking back, the investigations of the Truman Committee certainly found examples of fraud and waste during World War II. The effect of oversight, however, was not a reduction in support of the war effort, but rather an increased confidence in government's ability to ferret out wrongdoing while still pursuing a worthy purpose. In that case, and in many others, oversight that identified and corrected the problem was a predicate for public support.

The benefits of effective oversight extend beyond greater efficiency and trust in the operation of government. As we noted in our section on Congress, inattention to oversight may be a large reason for lack of trust in Congress as an institution. To "mend" the broken legislative branch, Congress needs to look back to its glory days. Again, while the story of Watergate certainly led to great distrust in the executive branch it also proved Congress' ability to do its job in the face of constitutional crisis.

Economic Imperative

To the extent that effective oversight reduces the likelihood of corruption in government, it is also essential to our nation's economic vitality. The economic imperative for oversight, especially at the local level, has been less documented than the governance imperative but may be at least as important.

In the mid-2000s, the Center for Excellence in Government commissioned a series of surveys of city residents across the United States asking questions related to key factors in economic development. One factor was consistently among the most highly rated: effective local government that is free of corruption. Other surveys have produced similar results.

Business leaders agree. More than high taxes or burdensome regulation, what businesses fear most from local government is uncertainty. Is the building permit going to take two days or two years . . . or will it require payment of a $2,000 bribe to obtain?

The relationship between corruption and economic development is frequently written about in the context of the economic revitalization of Third World nations. A World Bank survey in the mid-1990s found "more than 150 high-ranking public officials and top citizens from over 60 developing nations ranked corruption as the biggest impediment to economic development and growth in their countries." In 2003, the UN General Assembly adopted the Convention against Corruption: At the time, Secretary General Kofi Annan wrote "Corruption is a key element in economic underperformance and a major obstacle to poverty alleviation and development."

As a nation, the United States remains one of the world's great economic powers and comparisons to underdeveloped or undeveloped nations border on absurdity. But prosperity in the United States is not uniform. Parts of the nation have declined over the decades, losing both jobs and population.

In particular, deindustrialization has left many of the nation's midsize and large cities reeling. Jobs left, were not replaced and residents fled. The result are entire neighborhoods of vacant land or vacant buildings, blight, reductions in tax revenue, increasing service needs, and an overall downward spiral that is difficult to pull out of.

For many of these cities, corruption has been a part of or accelerated long-term decline. And just as there is an international consensus that corruption prevention and reduction is critical to development, there should be a local and national consensus in the United States that economic turnaround of these declining cities will require a similar focus on "the basics": effective local government without corruption.

For many places, local government corruption unchecked with effective oversight has gone hand in glove with economic distress. New York City, which as we have seen has a history of investment in anti-corruption oversight efforts, has a different history.

In the late 1970s, New York was the symbol of urban decay in the United States. Between 1970 and 1980, New York lost more than 820,000 residents—a greater than 10 percent decline in population and the equivalent of a city of the size of San Antonio, Texas at the time disappearing. New York in the 1960s and 1970s saw dramatic increases in crime and declines in the city's manufacturing base: Between 1969 and 1999, manufacturing employment in New York City declined by 68 percent. New York barely escaped from bankruptcy and one year, 1977, brought the city a blackout, looting, and a serial killer. Depopulation led to housing abandonment, arson and increased cost to city government as it became New York's largest landlord.

As we have discussed throughout this book, New York City responded to corruption crises in the 1970s and 1980s. The city was able to escape bankruptcy through a series of strict limits on City spending and borrowing imposed by both the state and as a condition of federal loan guarantees for the city. Through revisions to the City charter, the city was required to establish multiyear financial planning, regular reporting on the budget and city operations. And contracting power was centralized in the mayor upon the abolition of the city's Board of Estimate. The NYPD, in the early 1990s, invented the Compstat approach to crime fighting, a reform that many cite as a central reason for the historic declines in crime enjoyed by the city over the past twenty years.

By 1990, New York City had the most elaborate, well-staffed, well-funded anti-corruption effort in the nation. Virtually every department and agency of city government had an IG, reporting to a citywide DOI. The city's chief auditor, the elected comptroller, had hundreds of auditors on staff. City contracting was governed by a new and elaborate set of rules promulgated by a Procurement Policy Board. A Conflict of Interest Board was overseeing ethics laws. Limits on lobbying were enforced through the city clerk. In the late 1980s, New York became the largest local government to enact campaign finance reform with strict limits on campaign contributions and provision for public matching funds.

No system of corruption control will ever be perfect. Still, it appears that local government corruption in New York seems to have declined and the local economy has prospered. In the 1980s, the US attorneys for the Eastern and Southern Districts in New York (the two judicial districts covering New York, as well as surrounding suburbs) averaged 81.7 public corruption convictions per year. A decade later, the average declined to 63.9 and, during the past decade, the average was down to 44.6 per year.

This apparent decline in corruption occurred as New York became the one great economic turnaround story among America's older cities. After losing 10 percent of its population in the 1970s, New York saw a population rebound in the 1980s and a near 10 percent gain in population in the 1990s. With nearly 8.2 million residents, more people live in New York today than ever before. As economist Edward Glaeser notes, whereas other cities continued to decline, "New York came back."

The Case for More Oversight

The case for more government oversight is strong.

Consider that between Congress, the GAO, and federal IGs, there are close to 20,000 federal employees devoted to oversight. That sounds like a lot, but compared with the multi-trillion dollar federal budget and a 2 million employee federal workforce, it is really a minimal investment.

The financial success of the federal IG program and the GAO—as measured by return on investment through recoveries and program reform—suggests that oversight would pay for itself. And, to the extent that it can also right some of the rent-seeking referred to by David Brooks, it also may lead to returns in government confidence that are hard to calculate but appear certain to be realized.

At the state level, the success of federally funded investment in oversight of Medicaid programs would seem to suggest a potential financial value for similar efforts, funded by the states, that would look at programs other than just those focused on health care for low income residents. A return on investment focus for state auditors and more inspectors general with government-wide investigative and oversight authority could be part of any solution to the current fiscal challenge facing state governments.

At the local level, the gap between current resources and demand may be the greatest. Most local governments lack an effective internal oversight mechanism—either through legislative oversight, audit, or investigation. The federal model certainly suggests that the investment can produce real savings.

At both the state and local levels, differences in the respective role of the executive and legislative branches, with some executive roles performed by appointees of the legislature, may make it harder to structure appropriate oversight than at the federal level. Some state and local governments have managed to overcome that challenge, suggesting that others can as well.

Finally, more government oversight is needed now because of the decline of the role of the investigative press in the oversight process. Ideally, newspapers and other outlets would restore their investments in investigative journalism. In the near term, that seems unlikely, although we both hope that there are opportunities for more online media investigative activities such as the local equivalents of ProPublica and the like. But for local governments and those at the state level, media has sometimes played the primary—if not the only—watchdog role. Its decline in the absence of more investment in other oversight mechanisms does suggest that David Simon could be right: It might be a great time to be a corrupt politician.

Is More Oversight Enough?

What does more oversight really mean? It starts with investing in more staff and resources. But increased spending and staffing for watchdogs does not necessarily result in better or more effective oversight.

More effective oversight requires much more.

There needs to be a political environment that recognizes oversight as an essential function of democratic government, not as a form of political attack.

Legislative watchdogs need to recommit to a history of meaningful oversight rather than just "politics by other means"—more Truman, Kefauver, and Senate Watergate committees, less Joe McCarthy. Too often in recent history, the game of revelation, investigation, and prosecution has produced gridlock rather than reform in Washington. Congress needs to assert its oversight power, but with a renewed focus on bipartisanship in its approach to oversight.

One way to do so might be to ensure that both houses have stand-ing oversight committees where the committee membership is intentionally split between Democrats and Republicans, no matter the composition of the Congress itself. There could be similar permanent, bipartisan oversight committees at the state level as well. And the need to distinguish between politics and meaningful oversight is especially important at the local level, where the opportunity for personal vendetta to trump the need for policy reform is particularly great. Of course, individual legislators will still be able to set their own investigative agendas.

For appointed watchdogs, independence is essential to assure that watchdogs are willing to exercise their audit and investigative resources without fear of retribution or retaliation. The model of the GAO, with its leader enjoying a single, fixed non-renewable term, may be the best way to ensure independence in a meaningful way. Again, this structure might also benefit from a nonpartisan appointment process.

More resources should help to ensure more staff, but as we have seen, effective oversight requires the right type of staff as well. To be effective, oversight staff must have the right skills as well as an understanding of the problem, policy or program that they are studying. Too often, oversight staff may have the wrong resumé to realize the right results. Decades ago, the GAO recognized that the audit function, to be carried out effectively, requires a combination of skills: qualified accountants are not enough. At the state and local level, there needs to be a more effective combination of investigative, audit and policy skills to produce oversight that addresses both compliance and performance issues.

Elected and appointed watchdogs need to be both strategic and relent-less. Although politics cannot dictate an investigative agenda, watchdogs need to understand the political and policy context that they are operating in. Tireless investigation and thorough audits will have little impact if their findings and results are not framed in a way that plays into current public debate and discussion. As we have repeatedly noted, oversight conducted by legislators, other elected officials or nonprofits can only produce reform if it is communicated in a way that persuades—or embarrasses—responsible parties into action.

Oversight requires a certain amount of patience—but perhaps that is just a kinder way of saying how relentless watchdogs need to be. Watchdogs must be willing to "dig in" when it comes to certain investigations. Although some audits can be completed in months, effective oversight may require auditors to come back and monitor follow-up over the course of years. Investigators, auditors, and journalists frequently have to fight for access to information—sometimes resorting to litigation and almost always dealing with and trying to overcome delay. Investigations and audits—requiring detailed reviews of records and audits—are labor intensive and can require countless hours of labor. Follow-up—pursuing every opportunity to push forward reforms—can easily take years. When it comes to oversight, there are few short-term victories and a constant need to be committed for the long haul.

Where both exist, there is also a need for greater collaboration and coordination between IGs and auditors. Efficient application of limited oversight resources demand that they work together whenever possible to assure the "biggest bang" for the oversight "buck."

Effective oversight will also require more transparency and access to information. Data and documents generated by government are really owned by the public, not by any individual elected or appointed official. Oversight can be made less costly and more effective by government entities more openly disclosing information. As a result of the Internet, this is certainly the direction of all levels of government. Yet legislatures, internal investigators, and journalists still frequently run up against a stone wall when they seek critical information for their oversight work. In the long run, it would cost both the subjects of oversight and watchdogs less if there were a consistent assumption of free access to information backed up by making as much of it as possible available on the Internet, rather than regularly battling over executive privilege and freedom of information requests. In an age of Wikileaks, government can either move in this direction on its own or succumb over time to what seems inevitable.

Finally, it is important to realize that more oversight cannot be a substitute for more effective, efficient, honest, and ethical public servants who work on behalf of the public interest every day in local, state, and federal government. Just as it would never be possible to have enough police to enforce the law against a public determined to break it, no amount of even the most effective oversight can replace the need for competence and quality in policy making and performance.

Holding Overseers Accountable for Results

Ultimately, the true test of effective oversight is whether the work of the watchdog produces positive results—less fraud, waste, abuse, and corruption. Often, however, watchdogs are judged only on their activity but not outcomes. The measure of effective oversight is not the number of audits or investigation, but the effect and impact that those efforts have.

Arrests, prosecutions, and financial recoveries may be useful interim measures of performance, but they don't always lead to less fraud, waste, abuse and corruption over the long term. Sometimes data can be deceptive.

Earlier we discussed how both the GAO and federal IGs report on their "return on investment," suggesting savings per dollar expended on investment. Although this outcome-based approach to accountability is important, it does not always tell the full story. An audit that produces policy changes that prevent future vulnerability to corruption but produces little in actual savings may be at least as valuable as an audit or investigation that leads to a large financial recovery.

Just as watchdogs hold others accountable, they must be held accountable as well. At the highest level, that means voters need a better understanding of the oversight role that their elected officials should play. Getting voters to expect more effective oversight is no easy feat, but it is essential. Similarly, those who appoint and appropriate resources for other watchdogs need to hold them to results-based standards of performance. If they do, the result will likely be a greater focus on prevention than prosecution, reform rather than recovery and careful allocation of resources rather than across-the-board efforts that are more machete than scalpel.

Accountability must extend to ensuring that the watchdogs—as they practice their art—do not themselves engage in abusive, corrupt or wasteful activity. When they do they can disgrace their office or, worse yet, subject innocent public servants and others to abuse.

We close with a cautionary tale of a public servant whom we both know who found herself in the cross-hairs of an oversight agency that was seemingly unaccountable for its actions, and press that seemed more focused on headlines than investigative journalism.

After a lifetime of public service, our friend Mindy Bockstein found herself the subject of allegations that she abused her position as the head of a state agency by requiring her staff to drive her on personal errands. Not only were the allegations untrue, they were especially unfair to Bockstein, who was, as she put it, probably the only New York State commissioner "with a bus pass." She was also one of the hardest-working public servants we've ever known, who regularly put in fourteen- and sixteen-hour work days. The allegations came from former employees who had been disciplined by her for misconduct. In addition to filing a complaint with the Public Integrity Commission, her former staff leaked their story to the *New York Daily News*, which ran it under the headline "Driving Miss Lazy."

We know that disgruntled employees can be valid sources of information in the conduct of an investigation. So, no one would question the need to investigate. The problem was that while the allegations were made public there was seemingly little movement in the investigation. A half year passed as the Public Integrity Commission did nothing to allow our friend to clear her name. In the meantime, her state agency was consolidated with another agency and she was without a job.

Shortly thereafter her mother died. Facing financial hardship, she looked for work. After three months of searching, the recruiter for a job she sought told her that she would have been hired, but for the *Daily News* story. Of course, if the Public Integrity Commission had found the accusations meritless and cleared her name, the problem would not exist. Had they? No.

Then her father died. With no job offer on the horizon, she fell into a deep depression. The Public Integrity Commission still did nothing.

Finally, long after she had requested a meeting, the Public Integrity Commission agreed to have her speak to them. She still did not know with what, if anything, she was being charged. Of course, she had had no opportunity to confront her accuser. Finally, the commission's executive director sent her a grudging letter, admitting that it had found no basis on which to proceed. Actually, the law did not even require the commission to do that much. The ancient and fundamental oversight problem remains: Who guards the guardians?

One reason that oversight is more an art than a science is because the watchdogs have great flexibility in how they pursue their work. Well applied, that discretion can play an important role in achieving important results. But when abused, or when there are no clear expectations for results, it can fail to achieve the goals of restoring trust or meeting the economic imperative that we articulated above. If the oversight deters talented people from public service, it will fail to reduce fraud, waste, abuse or corruption. In fact, the very performance of ineffective oversight can be abusive and is certainly wasteful.

As believers in oversight and practitioners and scholars of the art of the watchdog, we also know the need to heed Nietzsche's warning: If you would fight monsters, take care lest you become one.

Sources

Chapter 1. The Watchdog

Justice Holmes' quote on taxes comes from Compania General de Tabacos de Filipinas v. Collector of Internal Revenue, 275 U.S. 87, 100 (1927), J. Holmes dissent.

For the story of the African and Asian officials, see Thomas Friedman, The Lexus and the Olive Tree, NewYork: Random House Anchor Books 2000, p. 147.

An internal Justice Department history of the Office of Special Investigations—the subject of a front-page New York Times story by Eric Lichtblau, Nazis Were Given 'Safe Haven' in U.S., Report Says, 11/13/10, http://www.nytimes.com/2010/11/14/us/14nazis.html?_r=1&pagewanted=all—is chockfull of the quotes used in our chapter, Judy Feigin, The Office of Special Investigations: Striving for Accountability in the Aftermath of the Holocaust, U.S. Department of Justice, December 2006, pp. 1–13. http://www.scribd.com/doc/42944549/The-Office-of-Special-Invesigations-Striving-for-Accountability-in-the-Aftermath-of-the-Holocaust; http://www.omsj.org/2010/Nazi%20OSI%202006.pdf.

Chapter 2. What is Oversight?

Juvenal's comment is carried in *Bartlett's Familiar Quotations*, sixteenth edition, Justin Kaplan, general editor, New York: Little, Brown and Company 1992, 109a, as *Sed quis custodiet ipsos custodies*, and translated as "But who is to guard the guards themselves," from the Satires, Volume 6, line 347. The list of twenty-four varieties of procurement fraud comes from materials accompanying a presentation by Tom Caulfield, The Anatomy & Illusiveness [*sic*] of Procurement Fraud, at meeting of the NY/NJ Chapter of the Association of IGs, John Jay College, New York City, 9/14/11. Mr.

Caulfield is executive director of the CIGIE Training Institute. A later version of Mr. Caulfield's presentation appears as a PowerPoint at http://www. theiia.org/chapters/index.cfm/view.public_file/cid/27/fileid/25832.

For the average perception of government waste, see the February 2010 answer to question 28 in the ABC News-Washington Post survey results at http://www.washingtonpost.com/wp-srv/politics/polls/postpoll_021010. html. The story of the federal official who appeared to abandon all common sense in thinking the mother–daughter luncheon a violation of the civil rights law comes from Bernard Rosen, *Holding Government Bureaucracies Accountable*, 3d edition, Westport, Connecticut: Prager 1998, 9.

The Tennessee Bureau of Ethics and Campaign Finance Registry of Election Finance publishes its campaign contribution restrictions pursuant to 2011 Legislative Changes under that title at http://www.tn.gov/tref/Contribution%20Limit%20Increase%202011_7.pdf. The New York State Board of Elections publishes that state's limit on campaign contributions to one of its State Senate candidates at the Contribution Limit page of its website, at http://www.elections.ny.gov/CFContributionLimits.html#Limits.

The Frederick Mosher quotation warning of the tension between compliance and creativity comes from his Comment, in Bruce L.R. Smith and James D. Carroll, eds. *Improving the Accountability and Performance of Government*, Washington D.C.: The Brookings Institution 1982, 72. Woodrow Wilson's famous line about "a murderous fellow sharpening his knife cleverly" comes from his article, "The Study of Administration," *Political Science Quarterly*, Vol. 2, No. 2 (Jun., 1887), pp. 197–222. His comment about the importance of the congressional oversight role comes from *Congressional Government*, 13th edition, Boston: Houghton Mifflin and Company 1898 [1885], page 297, http://books.google.com/books?id=cmUqAQAAIAAJ&p rintsec=frontcover&dq=Woodrow+Wilson+Congressional+Government&so urce=bl&ots=An1T_TaP4u&sig=1XhMlxUD5_T2UUHD8VZKao_fklo& hl=en&ei=0iFkTfeSLIyugQfL44D5AQ&sa=X&oi=book_result&ct=result& resnum=5&ved=0CD4Q6AEwBA#v=onepage&q&f=false.

The Congressional Research Service provides a Congressional Oversight Manual (2007) at http://www.fas.org/sgp/crs/misc/RL30240.pdf. Paul Light discusses the evolution of the GAO's mission and name in *Monitoring Government*, Washington, D.C.: The Brookings Institution 1993, 28, In that book, Light offered the classic exposition of the role of the federal IG. Like virtually any discussion of federal IG, the comments here and later in Chapter 7 owe much to Light.

For the comments about trial lawyers, OSHA, and the various not-for-profit groups, see the sources noted for the more detailed discussions of those topics in Chapter 15.

The state audits cited, under the headlines noted in the text, are, respectively, for New Jersey, at http://www.state.nj.us/comptroller/news/docs/nj_turnpike_pr_10_19_2010.pdf, October 19, 2010; for California, at http://www.bsa.ca.gov/pdfs/factsheets/I2007-1158.pdf, December 3, 2009; for Colorado, Department of Correction Transportation of Inmates Performance Audit December 2000, at http://www.leg.state.co.us/OSA/coauditor1.nsf/All/71A3FC0A15A90D6187256E74007B3B5F/$FILE/1324%20corr%20transInmates%20perf%20FY01.pdf; for California (again), at http://www.kpbs.org/news/2011/feb/15/audit-reveals-misappropriation-funds-gambling-trib/, February 15, 2011. The newspaper headlines announcing the next three audits are at http://www.ksl.com/index.php?nid=309&sid=9709890, February 16, 2010, for Utah; http://www.wate.com/Global/story.asp?S=13466320, November 8, 2010, for Tennessee; and http://www.watertowndailytimes.com/article/20101127/NEWS03/311279969, November 27, 2010, for New York.

The tabulation of New York City comptroller audits for 2010 is available at the website of New York City Comptroller John Liu, Bureau of Audit, http://www.comptroller.nyc.gov/bureaus/audit/yearlyview.asp?selaudyear=2010. The January 16, 2007 press release from the Houston, Texas comptroller's office is available at that website, http://www.houstontx.gov/controller/pressrelease/2007/press011607.html.

The Qui Tam Information Center website explains how that law operates, at http://www.quitam.com/id9.html. At footnote 7 of page 2 of New York State Inspector General Joseph Fisch, Investigation Regarding the Selection of Aqueduct Entertainment Group to Operate A Video Lottery Terminal Facility at Aqueduct Racetrack, October 2010, http://www.ig.state.ny.us/pdfs/Investigation%20Regarding%20the%20Selection%20of%20AEG%20to%20Operate%20a%20VLT%20at%20Aqueduct%20Racetrack.pdf, page 2, footnote 7, the report notes that the IG recused himself from the research for the report, and explains why.

The website of POGO gives the history of the "straddling the barbed wire fence" comment at http://pogoblog.typepad.com/pogo/2008/02/straddling-the.html, in an article by that title of February 29, 2008.

Chapter 3. Tools of the Watchdog

The movie version of *All the President's Men* (1976) has "Deep Throat," modeled on Mark Felt, tell Woodward and Bernstein to "Follow the money." IMDb, Memorable quotes from *All the President's Men*, http://www.imdb.com/title/tt0074119/quotes. However, it appears that Felt never actually uttered those words. They do not appear in the 1974 book. W. Joseph Campbell, Media Myth Alert, 6/25/11, http://mediamythalert.wordpress. com/2011/06/25/those-delicious-but-phony-quotes-that-refuse-to-die/.

Robert Heinlein's *Time Enough for Love*, the source of the second introductory quotation, was first published in 1973 in New York by G.P. Putnam's Sons, now a division of Penguin Group U.S.A. The quotation appears mid-book in the "Intermission: Excerpts from the Notebooks of Lazarus Long."

The Office of the Comptroller of New York State describes its audit process in State Government Accountability: Understanding the Audit Process, http://www.osc.state.ny.us/audits/auditprocess.htm. The dental services audit used in the text as an illustrative example was Office of the New York State Comptroller, Department of Health: Inappropriate Medicaid Payments for Dental Services Provided to Patients with Dentures, Report 2008-S-125, 3/25/09, http://osc.state.ny.us/audits/allaudits/093009/08s125.pdf.

The 2011 Revision of Government Auditing Standards (GAO-12-332G), the GAO's "Yellow Book," appears at http://www.gao.gov/ assets/590/587281.pdf. The GAO's 1999 "Green Book," Standards for Internal Control in the Federal Government, can be found at http://www.gao. gov/special.pubs/ai00021p.pdf.

Tallulah Bankhead's comment, almost as well known, can be found at http://www.thisdayinquotes.com/2011/01/there-is-less-in-this-than-meets-eye.html. Bartlett's Familiar Quotations, 16th edition, Justin Kaplan, general editor, New York: Little, Brown and Company 1992 has Tallulah Bankhead's almost equally famous line on page 710b.

The statistics and much of the other information about the state legislative subcommittee chaired by Charles Schumer in the late 1970s can be found in Daniel L. Feldman, Combatting Waste in Government, 6 Policy Analysis 476 (Fall 1980).

Chapter 4. Limitations on Oversight

The opening quotation from former Member of Congress Lee Hamilton comes from his article, "There is No Substitute for Robust Oversight," on the website of the Center for Congress at Indiana University, 6/9/10, at http://congress.indiana.edu/there-no-substitute-robust-oversight. The opening quotation from Newman comes from "The Lip Reader," from the *Seinfeld* episode of 10/28/93, http://www.youtube.com/watch?v=Rg_4z2adv6Q—in which the Newman character, a postal carrier, describes the importance of controlling information.

Samuel Huntington's argument can be found, for example, in a section of his *Political Order in Changing Societies*, called "Modernization and Corruption," New Haven: Yale University Press, 1968, 59–71. Robert Schwartz, in Oversight/ Regulatory Ethics in Theory and Practice, Conference Paper, 6/2–5/05, http://soc.kuleuven.be/io/ethics/paper/Paper%20WS3_pdf/Robert%20Schwartz.pdf, compared Canadian and Israeli responses to corruption. The World Bank survey is cited in United Nations, *The Cost of Corruption*, 2000, https://www.un.org/events/10thcongress/2088b.htm. One of the present authors, David Eichenthal, also wrote the referenced study of four cities in the United States, Doing Well by Doing Good: Can Corruption Prevention and Government Efficiency Strategies Help Turn Around Declining Cities?, 13 *Government, Law and Policy Journal* 78–86 (Winter 2011), published in Albany, New York by the New York State Bar Association. The chapter extensively cites Frank Anechiarico and James Jacobs' *The Pursuit of Absolute Integrity: How Corruption Control Makes Government Ineffective*, Chicago: University of Chicago Press 1996.

The headlines cited at the beginning of the section on Prevention vs Enforcement are from press releases on DOI annual reports, all of which can be found on the department's website at www.nyc.gov/html/doi/html/pr/annual-reports.shtml.

Paul Light, in *Monitoring Government*, Washington, D.C.: The Brookings Institution 1993, 17, notes the influence of W. Edwards Deming, for which he cites Mary Walton, *The Deming Management Method*, New York: Perigee Books 1986. The chapter relies on pages 69–75 of Light's book for the story of the scandals at HUD during the Reagan administration, and takes some direct quotations from Light's account as well.

Kevin McReynolds played for the New York Mets from 1987 to 1991 and then again in 1994. http://en.wikipedia.org/wiki/Kevin_McReynolds. McReynolds, in 1994, said of the New York fans, "If you can't win, they want to see you fail miserably." Marty Noble, " '62 Mets Had Flaws, But Much Character," 2/22/12 at www.mlb.com.

The fall 2011 semiannual report of the IG for the Department of Defense can be found on her website, at http://www.dodig.mil/sar/SAR_OCT_2011.pdf; and for HUD on his website, at http://www.hudoig.gov/pdf/sar/sar-66.pdf. The Illinois Inspector General 2011 Annual Report can be found at www2.illinois.gov/oeig/Documents/OEIGG_FY_2011_Annual_Report.pdf. And the 2011 Annual Report for the Kansas City, Missouri City Auditor can be found at http://www.kcmo.org/idc/groups/cityauditors/documents/cityauditorsoffice/annualreport11.pdf.

Citizens United versus Federal Election Commission can be found at 558 U.S. 50, 130 Sup. Ct. 876 (2010). The Center for Public Integrity discussion of Congressional oversight of Fannie Mae and Freddie Mac can be found on their website at www.publicintegrity.org/investigations/broken_government/articles/entry/938/. Robert A. Caro explained Lyndon Johnson's relationship with Kellogg, Brown & Root, a.k.a. Halliburton, in *The Years of Lyndon Johnson: Master of the Senate*, New York: Alfred A. Knopf, 2002, 403–409. An editorial, The Halliburton Loophole, *The New York Times*, 11/2/09, http://www.nytimes.com/2009/11/03/opinion/03tue3.html, noted Halliburton's relationship with former Vice President Dick Cheney.

For a brief discussion of the role of special interest money in the successful effort to defeat Rep. Michael Synar, see David Binder, Ex-Congressman Mike Synar, Oklahoma Liberal, Dies at 45, *The New York Times*, 1/10/96.

Mireya Navarro, Hevesi, on Attack, Accuses Badillo of Smears and Lying About Giuliani Aid, *The New York Times*, 10/23/93, http://www.nytimes.com/1993/10/23/nyregion/hevesi-on-attack-accuses-badillo-of-smears-and-lying-about-giuliani-aid.html; Elizabeth Holtzman, Letter, Inexperienced Bus Drivers Risk Student Safety, *The New York Times*, 4/15/95, http://www.nytimes.com/1995/04/15/opinion/l-inexperienced-bus-drivers-risk-student-safety-124795.html?src=pm are good sources of information about Alan Hevesi's campaign contributions from targets of Liz Holtzman's investigations. Ken Whitehouse, Power surge: Accusation against Cooper shuts down congressional hearing, *Nashville Post*, 6/26/08, http://nashville-post.com/node/6519/19695; and Governance and Financial Accountability of Rural Electric Cooperatives: The Pedernales Experience, Hearings before the Committee on Government Oversight and Reform, 110th Congress, 2 Session, 6/26/08, http://www.gpo.gov/fdsys/pkg/CHRG-110hhrg46194/html/CHRG-110hhrg46194.htm similarly provide information about successful pressures on Congress from rural electrical coops to abandon inquiries into their management.

The Giuliani administration's role in suppressing findings of its own IGs was reported in Paul Schwartzman, 2d Rotten Food Deal for City?, *The New York Daily News*, 7/2/95, http://articles.nydailynews.com/1995-07-02/news/17977501_1_homeless-shelters-meals-contract; Wayne Barrett, A Bonanza for a Donor, *The Village Voice*, 5/21/96, 14 and 16; Wayne Barrett, Rudy's Rhetoric vs. Results, *The Village Voice*, 2/20/96, 16; Josh Benson, Liberal Boss Ray Harding: Will He Take Rudy Over Hillary?, *The New York Observer*, 11/8/99, http://www.observer.com/1999/liberal-boss-ray-harding-will-he-take-rudy-over-hillary; Sabrina Tavernise, Ex-Housing Chief Gets 63-Month Sentence, *The New York Times*, 7/22/05, http://www.nytimes.com/2005/07/22/nyregion/22harding.html?ref=russellaharding; Tom Rob-

bins, Where Are the Whistle-Blowers?: Why City Workers Don't Speak
Out, *The Village Voice*, 7/2/02, http://www.villagevoice.com/2002-07-02/
news/where-are-the-whistle-blowers/; and David Firestone and Don Van
Natta, Corruption Watchdog Has Become Mayor's Tool, Critics Say, *The
New York Times*, 8/4/96, http://www.nytimes.com/1996/08/04/nyregion/
corruption-watchdog-has-become-mayor-s-tool-critics-say.html?src=pm.

Chapter 5. Congressional Oversight

The opening quotation from Woodrow Wilson's *Congressional Government*, originally published in Boston and New York: Houghton Mifflin Company, 1885, can be found online in The Project Gutenberg
Ebook of Congressional Government, 2011, http://www.gutenberg.org/
files/35861/35861-h/35861-h.htm#Footnote_57_57, at page 297, as can
the second Wilson quotation from the same source, briefly succeeding the
Schlesinger quotation referenced directly below. The opening quotation from
Chief Justice Earl Warren comes from his decision in *Watkins v. United
States*, 354 U.S. 178, 187, 77 S. Ct. 1173 (1957), http://www.law.cor-
nell.edu/supct/html/historics/USSC_CR_0354_0178_ZO.html. Both the
1972 Columbia Pictures movie and the 1969 musical version of *1776* gave
the John Adams character the comment quoted. See IMDb (the Internet
Movie Database) Memorable quotes for *1776*, http://www.imdb.com/title/
tt0068156/quotes; and see http://www.imdb.com/title/tt0068156/.

The quotation from Arthur Schlesinger comes from his Introduction
to *Congress Investigates 1792–1974*, Arthur M. Schlesinger Jr. and Roger
Burns, eds., New York: Chelsea House Publishers 1975, p. 12. Douglas Kriner made the comment quoted from his work in Can Enhanced Oversight
Repair "The Broken Branch"?, 89 *Boston University Law Review* 765–793,
786 (2009). The story of the 1792 exercise in congressional oversight is
told in Patrick Feng, The Battle of the Wabash: The Forgotten Disaster of
the Indian Wars, The Army Historical Foundation, http://www.armyhistory.
org/ahf2.aspx?pgID=877&id=398&exCompID=56.

Mathew D. McCubbins and Thomas Schwartz, in Congressional Oversight Overlooked: Police Patrols versus Fire Alarms, 28 *American Journal of
Political Science* 165–179 (Feb. 1984), http://www.unc.edu/~fbaum/teach-
ing/PLSC541_Fall08/mcubbins_schwartz_1984.pdf, coined the "fire alarm"
versus "police patrol" usage to describe aspects of congressional oversight.
The famous Louis Brandeis quotation about sunlight as the best disinfectant came from his article, What Publicity Can Do, in *Harper's Weekly*,

12/20/1913 (see http://www.bartleby.com/73/1572.html). The second quotation from *Watkins v. United States* comes from the same paragraph as the quotation from Chief Justice Warren introducing this chapter.

Information about the history of the Senate Homeland Security and Government Affairs Committee can be found at its website, About the committee, http://hsgac.senate.gov/public/index.cfm?FuseAction=AboutCommittee. History and at Guide to the Records of the U.S. Senate at the National Archives (Record Group 46) Chapter 11: Records of the Committee on Government Affairs and Related Committees, 1842–1968, the Center for Legislative Archives, The National Archives, http://www.archives.gov/legislative/guide/senate/chapter-11.html.

Matt Gertz, Rep. Cummings Urges Rep. Issa to Renounce Oversight Practices Used During Clinton Witch Hunts, *Political Correction*, Media Matters Action Network, 1/24/11, http://politicalcorrection.org/blog/201101240009, quoted an open letter from Elijah Cummings (D-Md.), the ranking Democratic member of the House Committee on Oversight and Government Reform, noting that chairs of the Committee generally sought committee votes in approval of their decision to issue subpoenas, although they could have issued them unilaterally.

The quotation about agency testimony before the Appropriations subcommittees comes from Bernard Rosen, *Holding Government Bureaucracies Accountable*, *supra*, 66. The examples of recent hearings, cuts, and comments by the Appropriations Committees come from Senate Committee on Appropriations, website, Press Room, Recent Webcasts, http://appropriations.senate.gov/webcasts.cfm; Marc Boucher, House Appropriations Committee Targets NASA for Deep Budget Cut, *NASA Watch*, 7/6/11, http://nasawatch.com/archives/2011/07/appropriations-1.html; and United Nations Association of the United States of America, Senate Appropriations Committee Approves FY 09 UN Funding Bill, Criticizes Administration Under-Funding of Peacekeeping, *Washington Report*, 7/23/08, http://www.unausa.org/Page.aspx?pid=1085.

The oversight responsibilities of standing committees of Congress are set forth in the Legislative Reorganization Act of 1946, with exceptions specified at 60 Stat. 832, Section 136; 2 U.S.C. 190d (a), set forth with more particularity in House Rules at http://www.rules.house.gov/single pages.aspx?NewsID=131&rsbd=165; a Senate Resolution at 2 U.S.C. Section 190d(a), Partial Repeal, http://uscode.house.gov/download/pls/02C6.txt; and Rules of the Senate, Rule XXV, Standing Committees, http://rules.senate.gov/public/index.cfm?p=RuleXXV.

History of the House and Senate Committees on Intelligence may be found in Gerald K. Haines, Looking for a Rogue Elephant: The Pike Committee Investigations and the CIA, Central Intelligence Agency (undated), http://bss.sfsu.edu/fischer/IR%20360/Readings/pike.htm, and Frederick M. Kaiser, Congressional Oversight of Intelligence: Current Structure and Alternatives, Congressional Research Service, 8/25/10, 16, http://assets.opencrs. com/rpts/RL32525_20100825.pdf.

Most of the information on Harry Truman's investigation of defense contractors can be found in David McCullough, *Truman*, New York: Simon & Schuster 1992, 256–282; in the 2003 Google books version, from 301-328, with Claude Pepper's comment quoted at page 332, http://books. google.com/books?id=8fp1A2s6aQwC&printsec=frontcover&source=gbs_ ge_summary_r&cad=0#v=onepage&q&f=false. The quotation from Truman himself can be found at 18.80, Records of Select Committees, 1921–1946, Guide to the Records of the US Senate at the National Archives (Record Group 46), The Center for Legislative Archives, The National Archives, http://www.archives.gov/legislative/guide/senate/chapter-18-1921-1946. html. Additionally, a useful summary of the investigation is Theodore Wilson, The Truman Committee, 1941 in *Congress Investigates: 1792-1974*, pp. 327–348 Arthur M. Schlesinger Jr. and Roger Bruns eds., New York, New York: Chelsea House Publishers 1975.

The work—and impact—of the Kefauver Committee is summarized in Theodore Wilson, The Kefauver Committee, 1950, pp. 353–380 in *Congress Investigates: 1792-1974*, Arthur M. Schlesinger Jr. and Roger Bruns eds., New York, New York: Chelsea House Publishers 1975. Wilson refers to the effort as "one of the most famous congressional investigations of recent times" on p. 353. His discussion of a "minimum of sensationalism" can be found on p. 366, "the committee's task" can be found on p. 368, the fairness of the proceeding are found on p. 369, the "ugly case of political corruption" on p. 372. The results of the investigation—including the outcome of the "221 legislative recommendations" are found on pp. 378–379.

Additional background and quotes for the discussion of the Kefauver Committee are from Joseph Bruce Gorman, *Kefauver: A Political Biography*, New York, New York: Oxford University Press 1971, pp. 74–102. Gorman's effort is perhaps the most complete Kefauver biography.

The well-known Watergate story can be found in numerous places. *The Washington Post*'s multipart version can be found on its website at The Post Investigates, http://www.washingtonpost.com/wp-srv/politics/special/ watergate/part1.html; The Government Acts, http://www.washingtonpost. com/wp-srv/politics/special/watergate/part2.html; Nixon Resigns, http:// www.washingtonpost.com/wp-srv/politics/special/watergate/part3.html; and Deep Throat Revealed, http://www.washingtonpost.com/wp-srv/politics/ special/watergate/part4.html. It carries the famous Howard Baker quotation at Key Players: Howard Baker, http://www.washingtonpost.com/wp-srv/ politics/special/watergate/baker.html. Another useful source—putting Watergate in the context of other congressional investigations—is Phillip B. Kurland, The Watergate Inquiry, 1973, pp. 467–490 in *Congress Investigates: 1792–1974*, Arthur M. Schlesinger Jr. and Roger Bruns eds., New York, New York: Chelsea House Publishers 1975

Schlesinger's reference to "the sharpest legislative weapon" can be found on p. xii of *Congress Investigates*.

The reference to Congress' "faded glory" is from Mark Green with Michael Calabrese, *Who Runs Congress?*, Bantam Books, 1979, New York, pp. 246–247. Kriner's discussion of Congress as the most disparaged branch is from Douglas Kriner, Can Enhanced Oversight Repair "The Broken Branch"?, *Boston Univ. Law Rev.* Vol. 89, 2009, pp. 765–793, with quotes from pp. 766 and 783.

Our analysis of partisan partisanship also relies greatly on Sarah A. Binder, Thomas E. Mann, Norman J. Ornstein and Molly Reynolds, *Assessing the 110th Congress, Anticipating the 111th, Mending the Broken Branch*, Brookings Institution, Vol. 3, January 2009 and Norman J. Ornstein and Thomas E. Mann, When Congress Checks Out, *Foreign Affairs,* November/December 2006, with the latter the focus of our discussion of Congress' limited oversight role of the Iraq war. The discussion of Joel Aberbach's research, Susan Milligan's investigation and Thomas Ricks' work are all from When Congress Checks Out. The summary of the 9/11 Commission critique of Congressional Oversight is from Can Enhanced Oversight Repair "The Broken Branch" at p. 774.

For a discussion of the Pecora hearings, see Donald A. Ritchie, The Pecora Wall Street Expose, 1934, pp. 221–244 in *Congress Investigates: 1792–1974*, Arthur M. Schlesinger Jr. and Roger Bruns eds., New York, New York: Chelsea House Publishers 1975, especially the quote from p. 223. Discussions of the work of the Permanent Subcommittee on Investigations—as well as a link to their final report—can be found on the website of Senator Carl Levin at http://www.levin.senate.gov/newsroom/press/release/us-senate-investigations-subcommittee-releases-levin-coburn-report-on-the-financial-crisis. The work of the Financial Crisis and the Financial Crisis Inquiry Commission can be found at fcic.law.stanford.edu. Critical reviews of the FCIC can be found at www.cbsnews.com/8301-503983_162-6102039-503983.html (Michael Martin's characterization of the hearings as "critical but yawn inducing") and Alan Brinkley, When Washington Took on Wall Street, *Vanity Fair*, June 2010 at www.vanityfair.com/business/features/2010/06/pecora-201006. The fine report of the U.S. Senate Permanent Subcommittee on Investigations of the Committee on Homeland Security and Government Affairs is JP Morgan Chase Whale Trades: A Case History of Derivatives Risks and Abuses, Majority and Minority Staff Report,

3/15/13, http://www.hsgac.senate.gov/subcommittees/investigations/hearings/ chase-whale-trades-a-case-history-of-derivatives-risks-and-abuses (click on "Related Files"). See also Joe Nocera, The Senate's Muckraker, *New York Times*, 3/18/13, http://www.nytimes.com/2013/03/19/opinion/nocera-the-senates-muckraker.html?_r=0. U.S. Reps. Jackie Speier and Mike Coffman announced the Congressional Watchdog Caucus at http://speier.house.gov/ index.php?option=com_content&view=article&id=950&Itemid=96.

For our discussion of "politics by other means," we rely again on the writing of Arthur Schlesinger in *Congress Investigates Report*, pp. xi–xx. Schlesinger's introduction includes both the cited quotes of Walter Lippmann and Robert Luce. That same volume also includes an excellent summary of the McCarthy hearings—H. Lew Wallace, The McCarthy Era, 1954 in *Congress Investigates: 1792–1974*, pp. 430–460, Arthur M. Schlesinger Jr. and Roger Bruns eds., New York, New York: Chelsea House Publishers 1975.

Ornstein and Mann's quote regarding "an assertive Congress" is from their work with Sarah Binder and Molly Reynolds cited above and can be found on p.14. As noted in the text, we also rely extensively upon—and quote at length from—Benjamin Ginsberg and Martin Shefter, *Politics by Other Means: Politicians, Prosecutors, and the Press from Watergate to Whitewater*, 3rd Edition, New York: W.W. Norton and Company, 2002. Quotes in the text come from pp. 25, 36, 39, 120, 142–143, 146, and 167.

Feldman was first made aware of criticism of a Summer Food Program sponsor in a telephone call from Franklin Kent of the federal Food and Nutrition Service, memorialized in Memorandum, Dan Feldman to Elizabeth Holtzman, 6/26/75, in author's files, and corroborated by a letter from Kent to Elizabeth Holtzman, 7/30/75, in author's files. A good deal of the statistical and other information about the Program is covered in Chapter One: Sandwiches in the Streets, in Daniel L. Feldman, *Reforming Government*, New York: William Morrow & Co., Inc. 1981, 21–39. The General Accounting Office (now called the Government Accountability Office) reported on the Program in Elmer B. Staats, Report to the Congress: An Appraisal of the Special Summer Food Service Program for Children, Comptroller General of the United States, GAO Report RED-75-336, 2/14/75.

Food Program Loses $8.5 M, *New York Post*, 8/11/76, and Richard Meislin, Food-Program Contracts Questioned, *The New York Times*, 8/10/76, 32, covered the story of the 16,000 abandoned sandwiches and other irregularities. Richard J. Meislin, Data on Summer Lunches Stolen From Office Files, *The New York Times*, 8/19/96, 39 and Press release, Office of Rep. Elizabeth Holtzman, 10/12/76, in authors' files, reported Program files stolen from the State Education Department. Press release, Office of

Rep. Elizabeth Holtzman, 8/31/76, in authors' files, and Richard J. Meislin, Food Program Sponsors Accused of Bid Violations, *The New York Times*, 8/31/76, 31 reported highly suspicious irregularities in the bidding process run by sponsors.

Press release, Office of Rep. Elizabeth Holtzman, 9/7/76, in authors' files, noted that Carol Steinberger, the New Jersey administrator, refused to approve the "bribe" requirement set by sponsors. Harlan Draeger, Contract for kids' free meals attacked, *Chicago Daily News*, 9/76, day and page unknown, reported the Illinois administrator's comment that the Department of Agriculture told him it did not violate the Program's requirements. Arthur Browne, Summer Lunch Firm Nets $1 Million, *New York Daily News*, 11/4/7, 2, and Arthur Browne, Summer-Lunch Czar Tied to Mister Softee Squeeze, *New York Daily News*, 11/6/76, 5 reported criminal connections and inordinate profits of Road Chef, a major vendor for the Program. Press release, Office of Rep. Elizabeth Holtzman, 10/12/76, in authors' files and Arthur Browne, Holtzman Scorches Food Program Dealings, *New York Daily News*, 10/13/76, KL7 reported the unsanitary and unpalatable food provided by many of the Program sponsors.

Claire Spiegel, Lunch Program Gets a Chewing Out, *New York Daily News*, 12/6/76, 7 reported Holtzman's call for the removal of the responsible State Education Department officials, and Claire Spiegel, State Ousts Summer Lunch Program Chief, *New York Daily News*, 1/19/77, ML7 reported the reassignment of one of them. A letter from U.S. Attorney David G. Trager to Daniel Feldman, 10/27/76, in authors' files, was the first official recognition of possible criminal culpability by Program sponsors. Find Lunch Officials Dined on Greed, *New York Daily News*, 12/10/77, 7 reported the criminal convictions of three officials of sponsor B'nai Torah International. Beame Rules Out Award Dinner Because Host is Under a Cloud, *The New York Times*, 12/2/76, reported Earl Butz and Gerald Ford had accepted awards from B'nai Torah. Feldman's early question about Congress Member Daniel Flood's connection to B'nai Torah appears in Memorandum from Feldman and Lang to Holtzman, 8/3/76, in authors' files. Marjorie Hunter, Ex-Rep. Flood Pleads Guilty to Conspiracy Count in Federal Bribery Case, *The New York Times*, 2/27/80, A12, reported Flood's plea of guilty. Lieb Pinter, the head of B'nai Torah, had been sentenced to prison two years earlier. The City: 2 Admit Evading U.S. Income Taxes, *The New York Times*, 5/3/80, http://query.nytimes.com/mem/archive/pdf?res=F00B14FD385C12728DD DAA0894DD405B8084F1D3, reported the guilty plea of Barry Goldstein, one of B'nai Torah's main vendors. Martha Graybow, NY Man Ordered to Prison for Defrauding Fannie May, *Reuters*, 3/19/09, http://www.reuters.com/article/2009/03/19/mortgage-fraud-sentencing-idUSN1944099020090319, reported guilty pleas to defrauding an entirely different federal program, some twenty-odds years later, by Pinter and Goldstein. Robert Lane, Brooklyn pastor admits taking bite of lunch fund, New York *Daily News*, 3/14/79, 30, reported a guilty plea and an indictment, respectively, for another Program sponsor and the principal of his vendor, Road Chef, Joseph Macaluso.

The House bill to reform the Program, HR 1139 (introduced 1/4/77 by Carl Perkins, D.-Ky, chair of House Committee on Education and Labor), Bill Summary & Status, 95th Congress (1977-78), H.R. 1139, CRS Summary, Library of Congress, Thomas, http://thomas.loc.gov/cgi-bin/bdquery/z?d095:HR01139:@@@D&summ2=m&|TOM:/bss/d095query.html, became P.L. 95-166, major amendments to 42 U.S.C. 1761, Code of Federal Regulations, Government Printing Office, 7 CFR § 227.2, .4, and .30, http://www.gpo.gov/fdsys/pkg/CFR-1999-title7-vol4/pdf/CFR-1999-title7-vol4-part227.pdf. Arnold H. Lubasch, Food Program Vendors Assailed, *The New York Times*, 6/27/78, http://query.nytimes.com/mem/archive/pdf?res=FB061FF93A5513728DDDAE0A94DE405B888BF1D3 reported the surrender of the New York State Education Department and the U.S. Department of Agriculture to Holtzman's demands for reform.

Part II of the *Washington Post* series, "The Watergate Story," The Government Acts, http://www.washingtonpost.com/wp-srv/politics/special/watergate/part2.html, *supra*, includes a review of the "Saturday Night Massacre."

Senate Report 110-522 of the 110th Congress (2007–2008) of the Committee on the Judiciary, Report to Accompany Resolutions Finding Karl Rove and Joshua Bolten in Contempt of Congress, Part VII. The Privileges and Immunity Claims Are Not Legally Valid to Excuse Compliance, Subpart E. Executive Privilege Not Proper to Cover Up Wrongdoing, http://www.gpo.gov/fdsys/pkg/CRPT-110srpt522/pdf/CRPT-110srpt522.pdf, 11/19/08, pages 34–35, includes the quoted admission of Justice Department official Monica Goodling as to improper political screening of and influence over employees. Part I of the Report, Purpose and Background of the Resolutions, includes the quoted comment about "grave threats to the independence of law enforcement," at page 2. Part IX of the Report, Department of Justice's Internal Investigation Confirmed Judiciary Committee's Findings Though Impeded By White House Refusal to Cooperate, Subpart A. Todd Graves, includes the quotation pertaining to that former U.S. Attorney. Part VII, *supra*, Subpart D. Evidence of Involvement of White House Officials in the Findings Demonstrates Committee's Need for the Information, includes the quotation concerning the conclusion that very high level White House officials were involved in the political manipulation of the Justice Department, as well as the quotation about "stonewalling" by the White House, at page 30. The long quotation concerning such "stonewalling" as a "dramatic break" from the practices of previous administrations comes from Part III. Committee's Efforts to Reach Accommodation Were Futile, at page 11.

Pam Fessler, Voter Fraud: A Tough Crime to Prove, *NPR*, 3/15/07, http://www.npr.org/templates/story/story.php?storyId=8922947, is an example of a media report attributing the firing of US Attorney John McKay to his refusal to pursue flimsy voter fraud allegations. Scott Horsley, Timeline: The Firing of U.S. Attorney Carol Law, *NPR*, 3/18/07, suggests that she was fired for prosecuting Republican Member of Congress Randy Cunningham.

The quotation from *United States v. Nixon* appears at 418 U.S. 683, 706 (1974). The federal district court ruling rejecting the Bush administration's claim of executive privilege is quoted from *Committee on Judiciary, U.S. House of Representatives v. Meiers*, 558 F. Supp. 2d 53, 56 (D.C. D.C. 2008). However, the ruling was stayed pending appeal in *Committee on Judiciary, U.S. House of Representatives v. Meiers*, 542 F. 3d 909 (D.C. Cir. 2008). The quotation from the 2008 report of the Justice Department's IG and Office of Professional Responsibility and the Senate Judiciary Committee's inference from it both appear in Part IX of Senate Report 110-522, *supra*, at page 42. The legislation rescinding the power of the attorney general to make interim US attorney appointments, S. 214, was signed into law on June 14, 2007 as P.L. 110-34. Eric Lichtblau, Prosecutor's 2006 Firing Won't Result in Charges, *The New York Times*, 7/21/10, http://www.nytimes.com/2010/07/22/us/politics/22justice.html, reported the decision of the special prosecutor that the firings did not generate criminal culpability.

For a discussion of the Iran-contra committee's short-comings, see Seymour Hersh, The Iran-contra Committees: Did They Protect Reagan?, *The New York Times Magazine*, 4/29/90, http://www.nytimes.com/1990/04/29/magazine/the-iran-contra-committees-did-they-protect-reagan.html?pagewanted=all&src=pm.

Sen. Durbin's quote comes from Ryan Grim, Dick Durbin: Banks "Frankly Own the Place," *Huffington Post*, 5/30/09, http://www.huffingtonpost.com/2009/04/29/dick-durbin-banks-frankly_n_193010.html.

The 2010 Gallup Poll figures cited come from Congress' Job Approval Rating Worst in Gallup History, *GALLUP Politics*, 12/15/10, http://www.gallup.com/poll/145238/congress-job-approval-rating-worst-gallup-history.aspx. The 1974 Gallup Poll figures can be found at Congress and the Public, *GALLUP*, http://www.gallup.com/poll/1600/congress-public.aspx.The concluding quotation comes from Douglas Kriner, Can Enhanced Oversight Repair "The Broken Branch"?, 89 *Boston University Law Review* 765-793, *supra* at 792 (2009).

Chapter 6. Government Accountability Office

The opening quote from Shakespeare's Romeo and Juliet was found at www.phrases.org.uk. Many variations of the possum joke can be found on line. One—about the University of Virginia Cavaliers, also known as the "Wahoos"—is at www.qsl.net/wa4yha/wahoo1.html.

David Walker's explanation of the GAO's then-new name can be found at David Walker, GAO Answers the Question: What's in a Name? *Roll Call*, 7/19/04. The Budget and Accounting Act of 1921 is Public Law 67-13, 42 Stat 20, 6/10/21. The quote is cited in Frederick M. Kaiser, GAO: Government Accountability Office and General Accounting Office, CRS Report for Congress, Congressional Research Service, Updated 9/10/08 at p. 4.

For our discussion of the history of the GAO, we relied on Jonathan Walters and Charles Thompson, The Transformation of the Government Accountability Office: Using Human Capital to Drive Change, IBM Center for the Business of Government, July 2005 including the quoted references related to the shift from the "green eyeshade" period and the replacement of voucher clerks, from p. 7 of their monograph. We later cite Walters and Thompson, p. 8 for the further shift in hiring in the 1970s. Additionally, the history section of the GAO's website, found at www.gao.gov/history/goodgov.htm, provides an extremely useful summary of the office's changes over time.

All discussion and analysis related to federal spending as a percentage of GDP is based on our calculations of data provided on the OMB website at www.whitehouse.gov/omb/budget/historicals.

Our discussion of the GAO's role in the Balanced Budget and Emergency Deficit Control Act is based on the facts in *Bowsher v. Synar*, 478 U.S. 714 (1986)—as is our discussion of the holdings of that case. GAO's high-risk series is described on the GAO website at www.gao.gov/docsearch/featured/highrisk.htm. The Government Performance Reporting Act is Public Law 103-62, 107 Stat. 285, 8/3/93.

The quotes about the GAO straying from its mission and the use of the GAO to "torment Republican administrations" are from Statement of David M. Walker, Comptroller General of the United States, Transformation, Challenges, and Opportunities, Testimony Before the Senate Committee on Government Affairs, GAO-03-1167T, 9/16/03 at p. 13 and Walters and Thompson at p. 11. Walker's 2003 statements on mission and best practices are from the same testimony to the Senate Committee on Government Affairs.

The foresight and insight roles of the GAO are described in detail in David Walker, Focusing on Foresight, Speech before World Future Society Conference, 7/28/06, GAO-06-1041CG. Information on the history of the comptroller general was found on the GAO website section cited above.

Discussion of the legislative history of the GAO and its relationship to Congress, cited in *Bowsher*, can be found at 61 Cong. Rec. 1081 (1921) and 58 Cong. Rec. 7136 (1919).

Discussion of the historic role and resources of the GAO, including 2008 budget and staffing levels, can be found in Frederick M. Kaiser, GAO: Government Accountability Office and General Accounting Office, CRS Report for Congress, Congressional Research Service, Updated 9/10/08. Data on FY 2010 budget—as well as the financial benefits of the GAO—is found in Statement of Gene L. Dodaro, Comptroller General of the United States, Fiscal Year 2012 Budget Request, Testimony Before the Subcommittee on Legislative Branch, Committee on Appropriations, House of Representatives, GAO-11-453T, 3/11/11. Relative budget and staffing data on federal IGs are from U.S. Government Accountability Office, Inspectors General: Reporting on Independence, Effectiveness, and Expertise, GAO-11-770, September 2011.

The discussion of the GAO's investigative power—as well as the court's decision—is from the opinion in *Walker v. Cheney*, 230 F. Supp. 2d 51 (U.S. District Court, District of Columbia, 2002).

For our brief discussion of the GAO IG, we relied on information on the GAO website at www.gao.gov/about/workforce/ig.htm, including Office of the Inspector General, U.S. Government Accountability Office, Semiannual Report, April 1, 2011–September 30, 2011, December 2011.

Chapter 7. The Federal Inspector General System at Thirty-Five

The first introductory quotation comes from Nikolai Gogol, *The Inspector-general*, transl. Thomas Seltzer, A.A. Knopf, 1916, page 117, http://books.google.com/books?id=_-kNAAAAIAAJ&q=translated#v=snippet&q=translated&f=false.) The second was Sen. Claire McCaskill's question about IGs after several were accused of wrongdoing, including hindering instead of leading investigations of the agencies to which they were assigned. Matt Kelly, Bill urges independence for agency watchdogs, *USA Today*, 1/10/08, http://www.usatoday.com/news/washington/2008-01-10-inspectors-general_N.htm.

History of Accounting, Part 4, Accountancy Students: the online accounting community, http://www.accountancystudents.co.uk/resources/read/part_4_accounting_in_ancient_egypt_china_greece_and_rome/ discusses the use of accountants for auditing purposes in ancient civilizations. We found the definition of "inspector general" from the 1913 edition of Webster's Dictionary, reflecting the older American usage of "inspector general" to refer to a military role, in *Hyperdictionary,* http://www.hyperdictionary.com/dictionary/inspector.

Danny Kaye starred in *The Inspector General,* Warner Brothers Pictures, 1949, the movie made out of the Gogol story.

As noted in the text, the chapter heavily relies on Paul C. Light, *Monitoring Government,* Washington, D.C.: The Brookings Institution, 1993. It is generally safe to assume that we based our references to the history of IGs in the United States before 1993 on Light's book, starting with the discussion of Baron von Steuben.

Secretary Freeman's testimony, cited as note 20 to page 34 in Light's book, can be found in *Operations of Billie Sol Estes,* Hearings Before House Committee on Government Operations, 88 Cong. 2 Sess., Government Printing Office, 1964, page 1401. Secretary Butz's history, subsequent to his dealings with the IG for the Agriculture Department, was summarized in Richard Goldstein, Earl Butz, Secretary Felled by Racial Remark, Is Dead at 98, *The New York Times,* 2/4/08, http://www.nytimes.com/2008/02/04/washington/04butz.html.

We cited the Seymour Hersh story, Huge C.I.A. Operation Reported in U.S. Against Anti-War Forces, *The New York Times,* 12/2/74, http://maruta-us.livejournal.com/40692.html. We also referred to a 1975 report calling for a more independent CIA IG, *Report to the President by the Commission on CIA Activities Within the United States,* (http://www.history-matters.com/archive/contents/church/contents_church_reports_rockcomm.htm. L. Britt Snider describes how the CIA finally got a statutory IG in Creating a Statutory Inspector General at CIA, 2007, https://www.cia.gov/library/center-for-the-study-of-intelligence/kent-csi/vol44no5/html/v44i5a02p.htm. The law fully empowering the CIA IG, P.L. 104-93, Title IV, § 403, 50 U.S.C. 403q, took effect in 1996.

Light reports the criticism of HEW's fragmented efforts to combat fraud by a House Subcommittee chair, citing as note 7 to page 40 *Establishment of an Office of Inspector General in the Department of Health, Education, and Welfare,* Hearings Before the Subcommittee on Intergovernmental Relations and Human Resources of the House Government Operations Committee, 94 Cong. 2 Sess., Government Printing Office, 1976, page 1. The Senate Committee report accompanying the 1978 Inspector General Act was *Inspector General Act of 1978,* S. Rept. 95-1071, 95 Cong. 2 Sess., Government Printing Office, 8/8/78.

The direct quotation from Light, "to dig up the dirt but not spread it," appears on page 35 of his book. His comment about the executive department in opposition comes from page 39, and his characterization of GAO's testimony on page 41. The Defense Department IG was established pursuant to Defense Department Directive Number 5106.01, 4/13/06, page 2, http://www.fas.org/irp/doddir/dod/d5106_01.pdf. The summary of the IG's mission can be found at the website of the Council of the IGs on Integrity and Efficiency, http://www.ignet.gov/igs/faq1.html. Light made his contrasting characterizations of auditors and investigators on page 158. His comments contrasting the Postal Service's decision to call both professionals "inspectors," and his quotation of the GAO testimony about the cost of combining the two professions under one roof, all appear on page 161.

The quoted excerpts from the IG Act of 1978 itself, P.L. 95-452, can be found at http://www.nrc.gov/insp-gen/ig-act-excerpts.pdf. That version shows the Act as amended in 1988 by P.L. 100-504, but the amendments did not alter the original language of the two sections quoted, 3(a) and 6(a)(4).

We quoted Light's comments on Carter and Reagan IGs' belief that their agency had a hand in their selection, that the Carter IGs took up job slots that had been occupied by line staff, and that Reagan sent a strong signal to his IGs to catch "cheaters" respectively from pages 89, 94–95, and 103–104. We used Light's quotation of an anonymous senior career executive on page 110, and his quotation of HUD IG Charles Dempsey on the "go-to-hell" club from page 106. The President's Council on Integrity and Efficiency (PCIE) and the Executive Council on Integrity and Efficiency (ECIE) were established by Executive Order 12805, May 11, 1992.

We used Light's quotation from Douglas Kmiec's memo, and we quoted Light's gloss on Kmiec's memo, respectively from pages 138 and 139.

The comments by Clay Johnson and Alice Rivlin are taken from POGO, Inspectors General May Lack Essential Tools for Independence, Washington, D.C., 2/26/08, http://www.pogo.org/pogo-files/reports/government-oversight/inspectors-general-many-lack-essential-tools-for-independence/go-ig-20080226.html ("POGO 1"), page 11. POGO 1 also notes the contrasting degrees of political background in the selection of the Clinton and Bush II IGs.

The Statement of Stuart W. Bowen Jr., IG, Office of the Special Inspector General for Iraq Reconstruction (SIGIR), before the Commission on Wartime Contracting in Iraq and Afghanistan, 4/25/11, http://www.sigir.mil/files/testimony/SIGIR_Testimony_11-002T.pdf#view=fit is the source for our comments on savings identified by SIGIR. The comments of the Chair of the Recovery Accountability and Transparency Board to the House Oversight and Government Reform Committee of 6/14/11 can be found at http://www.recovery.gov/About/board/Documents/Devaney_Testimony_06142011.pdf. Elizabeth Newell, in Stimulus Oversight Panel Continues to Staff Up, *Government*

Executive.com, 3/19/09, http://www.govexec.com/dailyfed/0309/031909e1. htm, reported his prioritization of prevention over detection.

The Inspector General Reform Act of 2008, Public Law 110-409, can be found at http://www.ignet.gov/pande/leg/pl110-409.htm. Section 7 merged the two previous IG Councils and newly empowers the Council of Inspectors General on Integrity and Efficiency. Section 6(a) provide for counsel reporting to IGs, rather than forcing IGs to use counsel subservient to agency heads. POGO 1, at pages 21 and 24, documented the case of the IG who was forced by agency counsel to redact his report for public posting, before the 2008 amendments. Section 2 of the 2008 Act extends the requirement of nonpolitical appointment to the non-presidentially appointed IGs. Fred Palm, the retired former executive director of the Association of IGs, provided the analysis of the difference in the role of OMB with respect to PICIE under President Reagan and with respect to CIGIE under President Obama.

POGO 1, at pages 5–6, reported the charges against the NASA, SEC, and Commerce Department IGs. Project on Government Oversight, IGs: Accountability is a Balancing Act, Washington, D.C., 3/20/09, http://www.pogo.org/pogo-files/reports/government-oversight/inspectors-general-accountability-is-a-balancing-act/go-igi-20090320.html ("POGO 2"), at page 8, reported the charges against and resignations of the Postal Service and HHS IGs.

The controversy over President Obama's removal of IG Gerald Walpin was reported in The White House Fires a Watchdog, Review and Outlook, *The Wall Street Journal*, 6/17/09, http://online.wsj.com/article/SB124511811033017539.html; and John Solomon, Where are the Watchdogs?, Center for Public Integrity, 5/3/10, http://www.publicintegrity.org/articles/entry/2063/. Neil Barofsky's superb book, *Bailout: How Washington Abandoned Main Street While Rescuing Wall Street*, New York: Simon & Schuster [2012], paperback edition, 2013, brilliantly describes the experiences of an IG facing nearly daily crises. He criticizes the majority of IGs especially at pages 51 through 54.

The final quotation from Light is from page 4 of his book. The quotation from Mencken is posted at Watchful Eye: Quotes from H.L. Mencken, http://www.watchfuleye.com/mencken.html. The five final quotations from the Project on Government Oversight are at POGO 1, page 12, and POGO 2, page 26, and POGO's cautions in the opposite direction, against "showboat" IGs, appear at POGO 2, page 25.

It is Section 5 of the 1978 Act, as amended, that requires the various boring components of the semiannual reports. POGO 2, page 21, is the source of the information that Congress has since 1906 required the State Department to review every one of its diplomatic posts around the world every five years.

The Dodd-Frank Act's requirement that the GAO report on the federal IGs, and the results of that report noted in the final paragraph of the chapter, can be found in Inspectors General: Reporting on Independence, Effectiveness, and Expertise, United States Government Accountability Office, GAO-11-770, September 2011, http://www.gao.gov/new.items/d11770.pdf.

Chapter 8. State Legislative Oversight

The opening quotation by Telford Taylor, appears in his book, *Grand Inquest: The Story of Congressional Investigations*, New York: Ballantine Books, 1961 [1955], on page 6, http://books.google.com/books/about/Grand_inquest.html?id=kZwOAAAAMAAJ.

Discussion of the Parking Violations Bureau (PVB) relies primarily on newsletters, "Assemblyman Daniel Feldman reports to the people," issued during the early and mid-1980s, the period in question, and available in the authors' files. The newsletter of December 1982, page 3, quoted a *New York Daily News* editorial of 3/30/82 that advised Feldman to "Pay the faceless monster. You'll never beat him"; and reported the PVB's decision to allow motorists to fight wrongfully issued tickets by mail. The October 1984 newsletter reprinted the quoted *Knickerbocker News* editorial of 6/26/84, page 10A. The December 1987 newsletter reprinted the quoted Ray Kerrison column from the *New York Post* of 8/5/87, page 13. Support for the characterization of the PVB scandal as one of the worst in New York City's history can be found in James Barron, Tangled Strands: Anatomy of the New York City Scandal, 3/23/87, *The New York Times*, http://www.nytimes.com/1987/03/23/nyregion/tangled-strands-anatomy-of-the-new-york-city-scandal.html. Feldman and Benjamin, in *Tales from the Sausage Factory*, Albany: SUNY Press, 2010, 122, assess the quantitative extent of the PVB's extortion during that period.

The National Conference of State Legislatures website includes a discussion of legislative oversight at http://www.ncsl.org/legislatures-elections/legislatures/separation-of-powers-legislative-oversight.aspx.

The website of the New York State comptroller includes a discussion of the Public Authorities Control Board, including explanations of the method of appointment of its members, powers, and duties, at What is the Public Authorities Control Board?, http://www.osc.state.ny.us/pubauth/whatisboard.htm. The website of the Tennessee Department of Finance & Administration includes a discussion of the Tennessee Buildings Commission, at Office of the State Architect, Purpose of the Commission, http://www.tn.gov/finance/OSA/sbcInfo.shtml. The California Legislative Analyst's Office has a website at http://www.lao.ca.gov/laoapp/main.aspx.

The discussion of the New York State Assembly Committee on Correction relies primarily on its annual reports from 1987 to 1995, available in the New York State Library in Albany, New York under call number LEG 549.65-1 88-19880. The 1994 annual report is also available online at http://nysl.nysed.gov/Archimages/7159.PDF and the 1995 report at http://nysl.nysed.gov/Archimages/7160.PDF. For unknown reasons, the reports from 1996 to 1998 are not available. The direct quotations about facilities for inmates with developmental disabilities and mental health issues are from the 1988 annual report, 12/15/88, pages 5–6. Feldman's 1990 comment about the Rockefeller drug laws comes from the introduction to the 1990 annual report, 1/7/91. Institutional xenophobia in corrections is noted for example, in Joycelyn M. Polluck, *Ethical Dilemmas and Decisions in Criminal Justice*, 7th ed., Belmont, California: Wadsworth/Cengage Learning 2012, page 340, http://books.google.com/books?id=RYjpRz9FO JoC&pg=PA340&lpg=PA340&dq=prison+distrust+outsiders&source=bl& ots=VQ7ibUEF9G&sig=feNJhPtCmxuKzMbZTEmD7fPYe4Q&hl=en&ei =zHZNTvjVMcqSgQfuzsmDBw&sa=X&oi=book_result&ct=result&resnu m=4&sqi=2&ved=0CDYQ6AEwAw#v=onepage&q=prison%20distrust%20 outsiders&f=false. The 1991 opinion piece cited was Daniel Feldman, Let the Small-Time Drug Peddlers Go, *The New York Times*, 2/23/91, http:// www.nytimes.com/1991/02/23/opinion/let-the-small-time-drug-peddlers-go.html. Daniel L. Feldman and Gerald Benjamin, in *Tales from the Sausage Factory*, 133-201, *supra*, describe the ultimate repeal of the Rockefeller drug laws in 2009.

Chris Hedges, Convicts Take 3 Guards Hostage At Top-Security New York Prison, *The New York Times*, 5/29/91, http://www.nytimes.com/1991/05/29/nyregion/convicts-take-3-guards-hostage-at-top-security-new-york-prison.html?src=pm, describes the Southport hostage crisis. *Onondaga County NY Sheriffs*, Paducah, Kentucky: Turner Publishing Company 2003, Page 74, http://books.google.com/books?id=zH0NgU 3BlaQC&pg=PA74&lpg=PA74&dq=Onondaga+County+Justice+Cente r+1995&source=bl&ots=EMUh4zOlaG&sig=fak_BKC4XdJeZQbjxTb o435iO3w&hl=en&ei=y5FNTsbAGM3UgAftrv3yBg&sa=X&oi=book_ result&ct=result&resnum=5&sqi=2&ved=0CD0Q6AEwBA#v=onepage &q=Onondaga%20County%20Justice%20Center%201995&f=false describes the new Onondaga Justice Center, replacing the old jail. Donatella Lorch, Judge Rules a Man Was Assaulted by a Suffolk Official, *The New York Times*, 10/9/96, http://www.nytimes.com/1996/10/09/nyregion/judge-rules-a-man-was-assaulted-by-a-suffolk-official.html reports on Maurice Mathie's successful lawsuit. In *Mathie v. Fries*, 121 F. 3d 808 (2d Cir. 1997), http://caselaw.findlaw.com/us-2nd-circuit/1297151.html, the Second Circuit Court of Appeals reduced his award.

Government Oversight Committee, Summary of Inquiry into the Iowa Association of School Boards as of January 1, 2011, http://www.legis.iowa. gov/DOCS/LSA/SC_Fisc/2011/SFRKM001.PDF, includes a record of testimony about abuse of taxpayer funds by the association. Charlotte Eby, School board association scandal may widen, Sioux City *Journal.com*, 2/1/10, http:// www.siouxcityjournal.com/news/local/article_a21f3f1d-4dac-5cf2-b301-6bad9e0221a6.html reported some such abuses. Mike Weiser, School board group: new boss promises 'new course,' *Quad City Times*, 7/16/11, http:// qctimes.com/news/state-and-regional/iowa/article_95ad7bfa-b013-11e0-b8de-001cc4c03286.html, reports the new director's intentions. Editorial–Our view: No Optimism left for School Board Association, *Press-Citizen.com*, 7/19/11, http://www.press-citizen.com/article/20110719/OPINION03/107190304/ Our-View-No-optimism-left-state-school-board-association discusses the unsuccessful legislative effort to impose more transparency.

Report to the 82nd Legislature by the Joint Committee on Oversight of the Bexar Metropolitan Water District, January 2011, http:// www2.mysanantonio.com/PDFs/BexarMetreport.pdf relates the history of the Water District. House Journal, 80th Legislature, Regular Session Proceedings, May 28, 2007, HB [House Bill] 1565, Article 2, http://www. journals.house.state.tx.us/hjrnl/80r/pdf/80RDAY87FINAL.PDF#page=342; signed by Governor, 6/15/07, http://www.capitol.state.tx.us/BillLookup/ History.aspx?LegSess=80R&Bill=HB01565 records the legislation that subjected the Water District to legislative and state auditor scrutiny; and the Joint Committee's recommendation of a conservator pending a referendum on its continued existence. Letters, Senator Carlos Uresti to Tom Gallier, General Manager, Bexar Metropolitan Water District, 7/29/11; Tom Gallier to Senator Uresti, 8/5/11, http://www.bexarmet.org/Portals/0/Documents/ News/2011/Gallier-Uresti_Letters-8-11-11.pdf; and Bexar's credit line frozen over uncertain future, *San Antonio Business Journal*, 7/26/11, http://www. bizjournals.com/sanantonio/news/2011/07/26/bexarmets-credit-line-frozen-over.html?ana=RSS&s=article_search&utm_source=feedburner&utm_ medium=feed&utm_campaign=Feed%3A+industry_2+%28Industry+Banki ng+%26+Financial+Services%29, reflect the continued controversy.

Documentation of the Subcommittee's accomplishments can be found in Record of the New York State Assembly Subcommittee on City Management from Its Inception (March 1977) to the Present (September 1978), available in authors' files; as well as in, for example, Joe Nicholson, Welfare computer shocker: no records on 22% of clients, New York *Post*, 5/12/78; Michael Rosenbaum, Koch urged to ax hospital unit, take over, New York *Post*, 12/19/77, 7; Bob Herbert, Queens Hospital Blamed in Deaths of Five Patients, New York *Daily News*, 2/21/78, 3.

The initial press coverage of price fixing among New York City's asphalt suppliers included John Kifner, City's Asphalt Bill Is Termed Too High, *The New York Times*, 2/14/78, 39; Richard Edmonds, Charges Asphalt Sellers Did a Job on City, New York *Daily News*, 2/14/78, 17, and Michael Rosenbaum, City maps reforms to half 'ripoffs' in asphalt purchases, New York *Post*, 2/14/78, 11. Commissioner Smith's efforts to reform the bidding requirements were reflected in Press release, D.G.S. [Department of General Services] News, 2/25/78, available in authors' files; and New York Revises Rules on Asphalt Bids in Effort to Insure [sic] Lowest Prices, *The New York Times*, 2/26/78, 36. Memorandum, Jay Henneberry to Charles Schumer and Daniel Feldman, Why New Jersey Asphalt Suppliers Did Not Win a City Contract from 1974-1978, 3/16/78, available in authors' files, documented the phone call from mobster John Cody and reported the failure of Smith's initial effort to attract outside bidders. The cartel's successful lawsuit to overturn Smith's decision to throw out their bids was reported in Maurice Carroll, Asphalt Contracts Awarded After Suit, *The New York Times*, 4/4/78, 57. The story of the revelations of Smith's improprieties of many years earlier, and his consequent resignation, can be found in The Complete 1978 New York Quiz, *New York* Magazine, 12/25/78, pages 81 and 112. Nicholas Pileggi, in The Great Asphalt Bungle, *New York* Magazine, 3/20.78, 49–52, told the story of the Lindsay administration's 1973 decision to close the City's own asphalt plant. Arthur Browne reported Koch's decision to restore the city's own asphalt production capacity, in Koch paves way for $1 million savings on asphalt, *The News World*, 9/13/78, 13A.

Reference to the work of the Office of Legislative Oversight and Analysis (OLOA) can be found in Back to the Future, Speech of Bill Haddad at the WTO/WHO Conference on Differential Pricing in Oslo, April 8-10, 2001, http://www.cptech.org/ip/health/who/haddad.html. Various efforts and accomplishments of Committee on Oversight and Investigation, which took over OLOA's work, were reported in press release, Federal Government Spending Millions to House Bronx Families in Rat-Infested Tenements, Schumer Charges, Subcommittee on City Management and Governance, 2/11/79, available in authors' files; Schumer hits firm running Bronx flats, New York *Daily News*, 5/21/79, 13; Calcutta in the So. Bronx?, New York *Daily News*, 2/12/79, 12; Legislator Assails Battery Park City, *The New York Times*, 4/9/79, B3; Charles Kaiser, A Shorter, More-Efficient Term Promised for Manhattan Jurors, *The New York Times*, 3/12/79, B12; Richard Edmonds, city buses trouble in bunches: state, New York *Daily News*, 4/18/79, 18.

Jack Newfield's story, This Felon Controls the Most Corrupt Union in New York, appeared in *The Village Voice*, 11/6/78, 1. Bernard Rabin, Accused in a murder, he's found slain, New York *Daily News*, 6/7/79, 27, reported the murder of Cody's chauffeur. Glenn Fowler, Asphalt Contract May Go to Out-of-Town Concern, *The New York Times*, 4/1/79, 41, reported the failure of the first outside bidder for the asphalt contract. About the City Council, Christine Quinn, Speaker, New York City Council website, http://council. nyc.gov/html/about/history.shtml and Selwyn Raab, 'President' Is Confusing; Council May Alter Title, *The New York Times*, 1/30/93, http://www. nytimes.com/1993/01/30/nyregion/president-is-confusing-council-may-alter-title.html relates some of the history of the old New York City Board of Estimate. Feldman's presentation to the Board of Estimate is memorialized in Testimony of Assemblyman Charles Schumer Before the NYC Board of Estimate on the Award of the Manhattan Asphalt Contract, 4/26/79 [postdated]; available in authors' files; and was reported in Steven Marcus, N.Y.C. is in yet another bidding bind, New York *Post*, 4/11/79, 31. Deborah Orin, Asks probe of pullout on city asphalt bid, New York *Post*, 5/3/79, 17, quoted Schumer on Little Ferry's suspicious withdrawal as Bossert's back-up supplier, which was also reported in Wayne Barrett, Runnin' Scared: Tarred and Fleeced, *Village Voice*, 7/23/79, 3. The committee's continued pressure on the City to restore its own ability to supply asphalt appears on page 136, and other aspects of this history throughout pages 119–137, in Daniel Feldman, *Reforming Government*, New York: William Morrow & Co., Inc. 1981. Assemblyman Daniel Feldman Reports to the People, 5/81, 1 has a photograph of Feldman at the City's new asphalt plant in 1981.

The law establishing New York's Administrative Regulations Review Commission (ARRC) can be found at McKinney's [New York] Legislative Law § 86, http://web2.westlaw.com/result/previewcontroller. aspx?TF=756&TC=4&sr=TC&rp=%2ffind%2fdefault.wl&sv=Split& rs=WLW11.07&db=1000102&cite=N8DF18BC088-C211D882FF8-3A3182D7B4A&findtype=VQ&fn=_top&mt=70&vr=2.0&pbc=DA010 192&RP=/find/default.wl&bLinkViewer=true. Its purpose was set forth as quoted from Charles Lavine, Letter to the editor, Panel will evaluate regulatory mandates, *Syracuse.com*, 2/21/11, http://blog.syracuse.com/opinion/2011/02/todays_letters_center_on_commu.html. The cited provision of the New York State Administrative Procedure Act, Section 204-a, can be found at http://public.leginfo.state.ny.us/LAWSSEAF.cgi?QUERYTYPE=L AWS+&QUERYDATA=$$SAP204-A$$@TXSAP0204-A+&LIST=LAW+& BROWSER=BROWSER+&TOKEN=22120781+&TARGET=VIEW. Erie County's waiver request is reported in Cuomo Administration Contacts Senate Chairman Carlucci and Administrative Regulations Review Commission, Homepage of New York State Senate David Carlucci, posted 3/16/11, http://www.nysenate.gov/press-release/cuomo-administration-contacts-senate-chairman-carlucci-and-administrative-regulations-. New York

State Administrative Procedure Act, Article 2, http://public.leginfo.state.
ny.us/LAWSSEAF.cgi?QUERYTYPE=LAWS+&QUERYDATA=@SLSAP0A
2+&LIST=LAW+&BROWSER=BROWSER+&TOKEN=22120781+&TA
RGET=VIEWl limits the commission's powers.

All Items to Pass Through Committee, Joint Committee for Review
of Administrative Rules, website of the Wisconsin State Legislature, http://
legis.wisconsin.gov/w3asp/commpages/IndividualCommittee.aspx?commi
ttee=Administrative+Rules&house=Joint, explains the jurisdiction of that
committee. It operates pursuant to Wisconsin Administrative Procedure
Act § 227.15, http://legis.wisconsin.gov/statutes/Stat0227.pdf. Utah Code
Title 63G-3-501, http://www.rules.utah.gov/law/uara.htm#S501 sets forth
the role of Utah's ARRC. Its website, Administrative Rules Review Committee, Division of Administrative Rules, Utah Department of Administrative Services website, http://www.rules.utah.gov/arrc.htm, explains how the
Utah Legislature may act on its recommendations. Proposals that California's
legislature review administrative regulations were reported in Around the
Capitol: California Political News & Opinion: California legislation > AB
586, http://www.aroundthecapitol.com/billtrack/analysis.html?aid=232128.

The Survey USA poll results cited can be found at Survey USA Job
Approval Numbers, 7/28/11, Survey USA website, http://www.surveyusa.
com/50statetracking.html. The Quinnipiac poll results cited appear at New
York Voters Confused by Tax Deal, but Love Cuomo, Quinnipiac University
Poll Finds, 12/20/11, Quinnipiac University website, http://www.quinnip-
iac.edu/institutes-and-centers/polling-institute/search-releases/search-results/
release-detail?ReleaseID=1683&What=&strArea=;&strTime=0

For the quote related to the influence of Standard Oil, see Flashbacks:
A Great Monopoly, *The Atlantic Online* website, 11/10/99, http://www.the-
atlantic.com/past/docs/unbound/flashbks/monopoly.htm. For a discussion of
the activities of ALEC, see Mike McIntyre, Conservative Nonprofit Acts as
a Stealth Business Lobbyist, *New York Times*. 4/21/12, http://www.nytimes.
com/2012/04/22/us/alec-a-tax-exempt-group-mixes-legislators-and-lobbyists.
html?pagewanted=all and Right-Wing Watch, ALEC: The Voice of Corporate
Special Interests in State Legislatures, *People for the American Way* website,
http://www.pfaw.org/rww-in-focus/alec-the-voice-of-corporate-special-inter-
ests-state-legislatures#Who.

Chapter 9. State Inspectors General

The introductory quote is from Thomas D. Thacher II, "Institutional
Innovation in Controlling Organized Crime: Reflections on the Recent
Integration of Law Enforcement Personnel with Industry Policy Makers in

New York City School Construction," Presented to the Fifth International Anti-Corruption Conference, Amsterdam, March 11, 1992, reprinted in Cyrille Fijnaut and James Jacobs, eds., *Organized Crime and its Containment: A Transatlantic Initiative.*

Information on individual state IGs—discussed in our overview— comes from the following websites: New Mexico: dot.state.nm.us; North Carolina: www.ncdot.gov/about/regulations/oig; Arizona: www.azcorrec-tions.ogv/Mnh_support_; California: www.oig.ca.gov; Colorado: www.doc.state.co.us/office-inspectorgeneral; Oregon: www.oregon.gov/DOC/INSPEC/index.html; Missouri: doc.mo.gov/director.php; and Texas: www.tdcj.state.tx.us/divisions/oig.

A discussion on the role of the IG in New Jersey is found on the comptroller's website at www.nj.gov/comptroller. For discussions related to proposed IGs in Connecticut and Nevada, see Editorial: Reforming the AG's Office, *Connecticut Law Tribune*, 12/20/10 and Cy Ryan, Sandoval pushes for inspector general office to tackle government waste, *Las Vegas Sun*, 4/4/11.

Information on the current day operations—and histories—of state IGs in Massachusetts and Pennsylvania is from Commonwealth of Massa-chusetts, Office of the Inspector General, 2010 annual report, May 2011, including the quote regarding the creation of the office from p. 1 of the report, and Commonwealth of Pennsylvania, Office of Inspector General, Annual Report, July 2009—June 2010 respectively.

Information on the Georgia IG is available at oig.georgia.gov. And recent efforts in South Carolina are discussed in Jim Davenport, South Caro-lina inspector general resigns, Associated Press, 5/31/11 and Jim Davenport, S.C. Inspector general starts investigations into state agencies, Associated Press, 7/10/11.

Background on the current role of IGs is from the state website at www.floridaoig.com; Office of the Chief Inspector General, State of Florida, Legisla-tive Fact Sheet and Cecil T. Bragg, How Independent are Florida Inspectors General, Florida TaxWatch, March 2010. Virginia's new law on a consolidated IG system is discussed in Abby Rogers, "Consolidated inspector general to provide better state watchdog," Virginia Statehouse News, 2/14/11.

The work of the Indiana and Louisiana IGs is discussed in their annual reports, Office of the Indiana Inspector General, 2010 Annual Report, State of Louisiana, Office of State Inspector General, Annual Report for the 12 Months Ending June 30, 2010, May 4, 2011. Information on California's Los Angeles County Metropolitan Transportation Authority was accessed from the office's website at www.metro-oig.net.

Information on Medicaid Fraud Control Units and the state–federal partnership on Medicaid and welfare fraud prevention is from the website of the Department of Health and Human Services IG website at www.oig. hhs.gov/fraud/medicaid-fraud-control-units-mfcu.

David Eichenthal is the former assistant IG of the New York School Construction Authority (SCA) and much of the discussion of the School Lease Fleece is from his recollections.

Background on the history and development of the SCA—and the Office of IG—is from Mark H. Moore and R. Zachary Tumin, Building Clean: The Control of Crime, Corruption, and Racketeering in the Public Construction Markets of New York City, Final Report to the National Institute of Justice, February 1996.

The quote from the OCTF report, cited in Building Clean, can be found in New York State Organized Crime Task Force, Corruption and Racketeering in the New York City Construction Industry: Final Report to Governor Mario M. Cuomo from the New York State Organized Crime Task Force, New York: New York University Press, 1990 at p. 251.

The relationship between Atanasio and Marrone is discussed in detail in Wayne Barrett, Patronage Outrage: 'Wired' Official neglected Sidewalk Safety Outside School Where Child Died, The Village Voice, 5/5/98. The article also discusses the tragic death of a student at P.S. 131 addressed at the end of the chapter.

The history and findings of the SCA IG investigation of the school lease program are detailed in Memorandum from Thomas D. Thacher II to Donald Zucker, Paul Atanasio, Rudolph F. Crew and Barry Light, Board of Education Leased Facility Program, December 5, 1995. The discussion of day care leases is from Jack Newfield and Paul DuBrul, The Permanent Government: Who Really Runs New York?, New York: Pilgrim Press, 1983, pp. 115–117.

Reforms undertaken in response to the IG report are described in New Chief Named for School-Lease Program, New York Times, 5/29/96. The first of a four part series in the Daily News was Joe Calderone, Kevin Flynn and Tom Robbins, Three R's: Rats, Rubbish & Rip-offs As Landlords Cash In On Dumps, Sweetheart Deals Send Our Children Into Grim Industrial Neighborhoods, New York Daily News, 4/14/96. Daily News editorials included Rich Times at Wedtech High, New York Daily News, 12/6/95 and End School Lease Fleece, New York Daily News, 4/18/96. The indictment of school lease landlords for fraud was reported by Joe Calderone, Tom Robbins, Kevin Flynn, 2 Charged in School Lease Scam, New York Daily News, 11/11/96. And the conviction is reported in the court's opinion in People v. Di Carlo 293 A.D.2d 279 (1st Dept 2002).

The history of the termination of contracts of the former Board of Education employee is discussed in *R.A.C. Group, Inc. v. Board of Education of City of New York*, 21 AD3d 243 (2nd Dept 2005). The discussion of the P.S. 141 lease site is based on one of the author's—David Eichenthal—direct knowledge of the incident and reporting by Jacques Steinberg, Toxic Lease: A Special Report, *New York Times*, 10/11/97.

The current structure and status of the School Construction Authority is described on its official website at www.nycsca.org.

Chapter 10. Other Elected and Appointed State Officials— Comptrollers, Auditors, and Attorneys General

Article V, Section 1 of the New York State Constitution and New York State Finance Law § 8 require the Comptroller to conduct audits.

New York budget figure for FY 2012 can be found at New York State Enacted Budget, Financial Plan for Fiscal Year 2012, page 11, http://publications.budget.ny.gov/budgetFP/2011-12EnactedBudget.pdf. Article V, Section 1 of the New York State constitution requires the state comptroller to conduct audits (as does also New York State Finance Law § 8); and that the winner of a statewide election fills the post. California Government Code, Section 8543.2, https://www.nolo.com/law/CA-GOV8543.2.19952501.html sets forth California's method of choosing its state auditor. The website of the California State Auditor, Bureau of State Audits, website, Most Recent Reports, http://www.bsa.ca.gov/reports/recent, accessed 8/10/11, includes the titles of the audits noted. Headlines of the stories covering the state auditor's audits came, respectively, from Patrick McGreevey, Los Angeles Times, January 19, 2011, http://articles.latimes.com/2011/jan/19/local/la-me-0119-waste-20110119; Jason Song, *Los Angeles Times*, April 8, 2011, http://articles.latimes.com/2011/apr/08/local/la-me-credentials-20110408; and Marc Lifsher, *Los Angeles Times*, March 24, 2011, http://articles.latimes.com/2011/mar/24/business/la-fi-edd-audit-20110325. The website of the California Comptroller's Office includes the titles of those audits noted, respectively at http://www.sco.ca.gov/Files-AUD/11_2010saamentalhealth.pdf; http://www.sco.ca.gov/Files-AUD/06_2010cdcrprisonhealthcare.pdf; and http://www.sco.ca.gov/Files-AUD/08_2009waterresources.pdf. Headlines of the stories covering the California comptroller's announcements of audits came respectively from Catherine Saillant and Jessica Garrison, *Los Angeles Times*, January 25, 2011, http://articles.latimes.com/2011/jan/25/local/la-me-redevelopment-20110125; Hector Becerra and Jessica Garrison, *Los Angeles Times*, April 22, 2011, http://articles.latimes.com/2011/apr/22/

local/la-me-montebello-20110422; and Jessica Garrison, *Los Angeles Times*, March 7, 2011, http://latimesblogs.latimes.com/lanow/2011/03/california-redevelopment-agencies-shortchanged-schools-review-finds.html.

The website of the Tennessee Comptroller of the Treasury, http://www.comptroller1.state.tn.us/shared/about.asp, explains how that state selects its comptroller. The titles of the Tennessee audits cited come from http://www.comptroller1.state.tn.us/repository/SA/pa11029.pdf; http://www.comptroller1.state.tn.us/repository/SA/ag11016.pdf; and http://www.comptroller1.state.tn.us/repository/SA/cu10066.pdf on its comptroller's website. See some audits with and some without prior comments from their subjects at the Division of Municipal Audits subsection of that website. Headlines of the sample stories covering the Tennessee comptroller's audits come from *The Tennessean*, July 14, 2011, http://www.tennessean.com/article/D4/20110714/NEWS07/107140307/Audit-sacks-Riverdale-QB-Club; Duane Marsteller, *The Tennessean*, July 8, 2011, http://www.tennessean.com/article/20110708/BUSINESS05/307080060/Audit-Health-company-misused-1-2M; and by Andy Sher, TimesFreePress.com, July 13, 2011, http://timesfreepress.com/news/2011/jul/13/audit-finds-fault-states-drug-task-forces/, respectively. The audit concerning the high school cheerleading coach can be found at Letter audit report, State of Tennessee Comptroller of the Treasury Division of Municipal Audit to Director of Schools and Member of the Board of Education, Sevier County School System, 8/24/11, http://www.comptroller1.state.tn.us/Repository/MA/Investigative/pigeonforgeschoolscheerleading.pdf. Other examples of Tennessee State Comptroller audits can be found at Investigative Reports Released, August 2011, http://www.comptroller1.state.tn.us/RA_MA_Financial/Report_Investigative.aspx.

Nick Madigan, Audit of state treasurer's office finds failures in banking oversight, *The Baltimore Sun*, 11/5/10, http://articles.baltimoresun.com/2010-11-05/news/bs-md-state-audit-problems-20101105_1_state-agencies-bank-accounts-office-of-legislative-audits, discusses the Maryland Legislative Audit of the Maryland Treasurer's Office. James Gilbert, Loftis Announces Audit of State Treasurer's Office, WLTX.com, 7/28/11, http://www.wltx.com/news/article/145150/2/Loftis-Announces-Audit-of-State-Treasurers-Office, discusses the South Carolina Treasurer's announcement of the audit of his own office.

The quotation concerning the overall trend in modern state auditing comes from Edward M. Wheat, The Activist Auditor: a New Player in State and Local Politics, Public Administration Review, Sept./Oct. 1991, Vol. 51, No. 5, 385-392, 388.

William P. Marshall, in Break Up the Presidency, 115 Yale Law Journal 2442, 2454 (2006), provides scholarly support for the primacy of state attorneys' general duties to the public over their duties to official "clients." Emily Myers and Lynne Ross, eds., State Attorneys General Powers and Responsibilities, 2nd ed., Washington, D.C.: National Association of Attorneys General 2007, at 310, notes those states whose attorneys general have complete criminal jurisdiction and can therefore prosecute official corruption. Office of the Maine Attorney General website, http://www.maine. gov/ag/crime/criminal_justice_system.shtmcl, provides an example of a state whose attorney general does not have complete criminal jurisdiction, but who does have the authority to prosecute official corruption. The Pennsylvania attorney general's prosecutions of official corruption were reported in *Patriot-News* staff and wire reports, Attorney General Tom Corbett Charges 10 in 'Bonusgate,' including former House Speaker John Perzel, Pennlive. com, 11/12/09, http://www.pennlive.com/midstate/index.ssf/2009/11/attorney_general_tom_corbett_c.html. The Tenth Circuit Court of Appeals in U.S. v. Troutman, 814 F.2d 1428 (10th Cir. 1987), paragraph 39, http://law. justia.com/cases/federal/appellate-courts/F2/814/1428/335915/ ruled that the New Mexico attorney general could prosecute a state official whom he formerly represented. Office of the New Jersey Attorney General, 6/30/11, http://www.nj.gov/oag/newsreleases11/pr20110630b.html and press release, Two New Jersey Turnpike Toll Collectors Plead Guilty to Stealing Tolls Funds from the Booths on the Turnpike, website, Office of the New Jersey Attorney General, 7/25/11, http://www.nj.gov/oag/newsreleases11/ pr20110725a.html, reflect prosecutions of state officials by the New Jersey attorney general.

Press release, Cuomo Announces Felony Guilty Plea by Former Comptroller Alan Hevesi in Pay-to-Play Pension Fund Kickback Scheme, Office of the Attorney General website, 10/7/10, http://www.ag.ny.gov/media_center/2010/oct/oct7a_10.html, reports the guilty plea taken by New York's former comptroller after prosecution by its attorney general. New York's Martin Act, New York General Business Law § 352 et seq., and see David J. Kaufmann, Introduction and Commentary Overview, Article 23-A, McKinney's Consolidated Laws of New York, Book 19, General Business Law, West Publishing Company, St. Paul, Minn.,1996, 9, permits such a prosecution for violation of securities laws, but otherwise New York attorneys general rarely have had the opportunity to prosecute a fellow state official under statutory restrictions set forth in New York Executive Law § 63(2), (3), and (4). In 2011 the New York attorney general may have found a way around these restrictions under an agreement with the New York State comptroller, as reported in Nicholas Confessore, Accord with Comptroller Will Help Attorney General Pursue Corruption Cases, *The New York Times*, 5/22/11, http://www.nytimes.com/2011/05/23/nyregion/ny-attorney-general-granted-power-in-corruption-cases.html?pagewanted=all, which also reports their first collaboration under the agreement.

Myers and Ross, supra, 56-7, explain that attorneys' general power to institute civil suits against their governors and other state officials is less controversial than their power to prosecute criminally. Scott Rothschild, Kline Sues Sibelius to End State-Funded Abortion, LJWorld.com, 8/19/05, http://www2.ljworld.com/news/2005/aug/19/kline_sues_sebelius_end_statefunded_abortion/ reported an example of such a lawsuit.

The audit of the Henry Viscardi school in New York can be found at Office of the State Comptroller, Division of State Government Accountability, Henry Viscardi School: Compliance with the Reimbursable Cost Manual, Report 2009-S-70, 4/6/11, 9, http://osc.state.ny.us/audits/allaudits/093011/09s70.pdf. Sarah Maslin Nir, Audit Finds L.I. School Overbilled the State, *The New York Times*, 4/6/11, http://www.nytimes.com/2011/04/07/nyregion/07viscardi.html?_r=3&ref=specialeducationhandicapped, reported the audit's findings. The State Education Department's agreement with the findings, and the school's disagreement, were each reflected in the audit, respectively at 25–26 and at 27–37.

Myers and Ross, supra, at 214, offer the medieval English history of the attorney general's power to supervise charities. In New York, this power is reflected in its Executive Law § 175. Executive Law § 172-a provides an exemption from its registration requirements for legitimate religious organizations.

Nancy H. Cooper, Audit Report: District Inspector General for Audit, Southeast/Caribbean District, Report 98-AT-121-0002, Office of Inspector General, Department of Housing and Urban Development, 5/1/98, Appendix B, Summary of 203(k) Program Procedures, 14, lists the requirements of the 203(k) program. Spitzer announced his lawsuit against Helpline in Press release, Non Profit Group Named in Federal Housing Scam, website, Office of the Attorney General, 11/29/00, http://www.ag.ny.gov/media_center/2000/nov/nov29a_00.html, reported by Terry Pristin, Suit Alleges Major Housing Fraud Against U.S. by Brooklyn Charity, The New York Times, 11/29/00, B1. Criminal prosecution of participants in the scam was reported in Terry Pristin, 7 Are Charged In Scheme to Defraud Loan Program, *The New York Times*, 12/12/00, B3, c1; Terry Pristin, Papers Describe Alleged Plan to Bilk HUD, *The New York Times*, 12/13/00, B1; and Terry Pristin, 9 More Are Charged in Scheme to Defraud HUD Program, *The New York Times*, 12/14/00, B10, c1. The description of the distribution of the recoveries from the civil suit is unsourced, and from co-author Feldman's recollections, although notes in authors' files suggest its accuracy, including Letter from Daniel Feldman to Bertha Lewis, Executive Director, ACORN,

12/19/03. Terry Pristin, City Requests $160 Million to Fix Up Homes in Scandal, *The New York Times*, B6, 7/6/01; New York City Department of Housing Preservation and Development, website, Update on 203(k) Buildings, http://www.nyc.gov/html/hpd/html/buyers/update-203k.shtml; and Faculty Profile of Jerilyn Perine, Columbia School of International and Public Affairs website, http://www.sipa.columbia.edu/academics/directory/jp2784-fac.html, describe the partnership effort between New York City and the federal government to assist the victims of the program's failures.

Warnings about vulnerabilities in the 203(k) program by the staff of HUD's IG in 1997 appear in Audit Case Number 97-AT-121-0001, Office of the Inspector General, Department of Housing and Urban Development, 2/6/97, http://www.nytimes.com/packages/pdf/nyregion/20061102_HUD/2.pdf, iii. The direct quotations from the audit are from its pages 3, and 14–15. The 1998 audit of the program can be found at Audit Case Number 98-AT-121-0002, Office of the Inspector General, Department of Housing and Urban Development, 5/1/98, iii, http://archives.hud.gov/offices/oig/reports/internal/ig840002.pdf. IG Gaffney's credentials appear in the National Academy of Public Administration website, at Fellows Biographies: Susan Gaffney, http://www.napawash.org/fellows/fellows-biographies/susan-gaffney/. Her complaints about the HUD secretary are detailed in Legislative Information, Senate Government Affairs Committee, September 9, 1998, http://hsgac.senate.gov/090998_summary.htm, and in Matt Rees, Andrew Cuomo's Vendetta, WeeklyStandard.com, 5/17/99, Vol. 4, No. 33, http://www.weeklystandard.com/Content/Public/Articles/000/000/001/602lgzqm.asp. Her subsequent attribution of the failures of the 203(k) program appear in Terry Pristin, Metro Business Briefing: Cuomo Defends HUD, *The New York Times*, 12/20/00, B8, c5, http://www.nytimes.com/2000/12/20/nyregion/metro-business-briefing-cuomo-defends-hud.html?src=pm and Deborah Martinez, Cuomo housing program frozen, *Albany Times-Union*, 4/30/01, B1, http://www.highbeam.com/doc/1G1-157509708.html. The GAO had assessed the program's vulnerabilities and failures in Problems Persist With HUD's 203(k) Home Rehabilitation Loan Program, Report to the Chairman, Subcommittee on Housing and Community Opportunity, Committee on Banking and Financial Services, House of Representatives, GAO/RCED-99-124, 6/14/99, 3-4, 6, 22, http://www.gao.gov/archive/1999/rc99124.pdf. The GAO's follow-up report, Stanley Czerwinski, Problems Persist With HUD's 203(k) Home Rehabilitation Mortgage Insurance Program, Testimony Before the Subcommittee on Oversight and Investigations, House Financial Services Committee, GAO-01-1124T, 9/10/01, 1, http://www.gao.gov/new.items/d011124t.pdf, credited the HUD Office of the IG for its unheeded warnings in 1997 and 1998, and at pages 2 and 4 noted that HUD had in May 2000 adopted more stringent procedures.

GAGAS requirements for performance audits can be found at Government Accountability Office, Government Auditing Standards, 2011 Revision, 12/11, Section 7.05(4), http://www.gao.gov/assets/590/587281.pdf.

Chapter 11. Local Legislative Oversight

See Tip O'Neill and Gary Hymel, *All Politics is Local: And Other Rules of the Game*, Adams Media, Avon, 1995. An episode guide for *The Wire* is available at www.hbo.com/the-wire/episodes/index.html. The mandate for council oversight in New York City can be found in Section 12 of the New York City Charter.

ICMA, *County-Manager Form of Government*, Frequently Asked Questions, Washington: 2007.

Information on the City of Chester and the structure of its government is available at www.chestercity.com/council.cfm. Information on the size of local city councils was based on information on local government city websites, including: Chicago: www.cityofchicago.org/city/en/about/council.html; New York: council.nyc.gov; San Diego: www.sandiego.gov/citycouncil; Phoenix: phoenix.gov/citycouncil; and Philadelphia: www.phila.gov/citycouncil. For a discussion of council wars in Chicago, see, Gary Rivlin, *Fire on the Prairie: Chicago's Harold Washington and the Politics of Race,* Henry Holt & Co. 1992

Background on Fenty as a member of the council is from David Nakamura, "Cropp and Fenty Have Pursued Their Legislative Agendas by Opposite Means," *Washington Post,* 8/21/06. For a discussion of Fenty's electoral success, see Wikipedia at http://en.wikipedia.org/wiki/Adrian_Fenty#cite_note-2006g-22

Our discussion of the council investigation of Mayor Fenty's administration is based on the City Council's final report, Robert P. Trout and Gloria Solomon, Report of the Special Counsel to the Special Committee on the Investigation of Capital Projects of the Department of Parks and Recreation, 3/11/11. The report is the source of the language of the council resolution, at p. 19, the quote related to the "claimed failure of recollection"—found at p. 13—and the quote related to "the need for speed" found at p. 14. The impact of the investigation on Fenty's re-election bid—based, in part, on polling data—is discussed in Nikita Stewart and Jon Cohen, Poll shows D.C. Mayor Fenty getting more credit than support in primary race against Gray, *Washington Post,* 8/28/10. The results of the Gray-Fenty election are discussed in Tim Craig and Nikita Stewart, Gray decisively defeats Fenty in race for D.C. mayor, *Washington Post*, 9/15/10.

Allegations against Mayor Gray are described in Nikita Stewart, Vincent Gray campaign accepted cash donations above legal limit, review shows, *Washington Post*, 7/18/11 and Memorandum from Mary M. Cheh, Chairperson, Special Committee on Investigation of Executive Personnel Practices to Members of the Council of the District of Columbia, Report and Recommendations on the Committee's Investigation into the Executive's Personnel Practices, 8/24/11. Quotes related to the findings of the Council report on the Gray investigation are from pages 2 and 27.

Chapter 12. Local Auditors and Inspectors General

The opening quotes are from Wallace Sayre and Herbert Kaufman, *Governing New York City: Politics in the Metropolis,* New York: Norton, 1965 and William Lerach, "Blame Wall Street, Not Hard Working Americans, for the Pension Funds Fiasco," *Huffington Post,* 2/26/11 at www.huffingtonpost.com/william-s-lerach/wall-street-pension-funds_b_828598.html. The famous quote from the movie, Casablanca, can be found at www.imdb.com/title/#0034583/quotes.

For a discussion of the role of CAFRs and the role of the Single Audit, see, eg, Karen Tenance, Anatomy of a CAFR at www.gfoaaz.org and www.whitehouse.gov/omb/financial_fin_single_audit. As noted previously, the Yellow Book can be found on line at www.gao.gov/yellowbook.

Discussion of the role of the San Francisco controller is based on a review of materials, including the Government Barometer, on the office's website at www.sfcontroller.org

The charter requirement in New York that the comptroller audit all city departments on a four-year cycle can be found in Sec. 93 (c) of the New York City Charter

The appointment process and role of auditors and IGs in large cities and counties was based on a city-by-city and county-by-county review of the websites of the following cities and counties. Specifically, websites for the comptroller, auditor, IG, and/or Internal Audit division were reviewed, as were the most recent available budget documents for the city (to assess staffing and budget levels): New York: www.comptroller.nyc.gov; www.nyc.gov/doi; www.nyc.gov/omb; Los Angeles: www.controller.lacity.org; budget.lacity.org; Chicago: www.cityofchicago.org/city/en/depts/fin/provdrs/audit.html; chicagoinspectorgeneral.org; www.cityofchicago.org/city/en/depts/obm/provdrs/city_budg/svcs/budget_documents.html; Houston: www.houstontx.

gov/controller; www.houstontx.gov/legal/oig.html; www.houstontx.gov/budget; Phoenix: www.phoenix.gov/auditor; www.phoenix/gov/budget; Philadelphia: www.philadelphiacontroller.org; www.phila.gov/oig; www.phila.gov/reports/reports2.html; San Antonio: www.sanantonio.gov/cityauditor; www.sanantonio.gov/budget; San Diego: www.sandiego.gov/auditor; www.sandiego.gov/fm; Dallas: www.dallascityhall.com/auditor; www.dallascityhall.com/Budget; San Jose: www.sanjoseca.gov/auditor; www.sanjoseca.gov/budget; Detroit: www.detroitmi.gov/CityCouncil/LegislativeAgencies/AuditorGeneral/AboutAuditorGeneral.aspx; www.detroitmi.gov/CityCouncil/LegislativeAgencies/Ombudsman/FunctionsandPowers.aspx; www.detroitmi.gov/DepartmentsandAgencies/BudgetDepartment.aspx; San Francisco: www.sfcontroller.org; www.sfbos.org; Jacksonville: www.coj.net/city-council/council-auditor.aspx; www.coj.net/departments/inspector-general.aspx; www.coj.net/departments/finance/budget/budget-in-brief.aspx; Indianapolis: www.indy.gov/egov/city/oap; www.indy.gov/eGov/City/OFM; Austin: www.austintexas.gov/department/auditor; www.ci.austin.tx.us/budget/budget.htm; Columbus: auditor.columbus.gov; finance.columbus.gov; Fort Worth: fortworthtexas.gov/internalaudit; fortworthtexas.gov/budget; Charlotte: charmeck.org/city/charlotte/Budget/Documents/InternalAudit.pdf; charmeck.org/city/charlotte/budget; Memphis: www.cityofmemphis.orf/framework.aspx?page=145; www.cityofmemphis.org/framework.aspx?page=20; Boston: www.cityofboston.gov/auditing; www.cityofboston.gov/budget; Los Angeles County: auditor.lacounty.gov; www.lacountyfraud.org; ceo.lacounty.gov; Cook County: www.cookcountygov.com/portal/server.pt/community/auditor%2C_office_of_the/249/auditor%2C_office_of_the/346; www.cookcountygov.com/portal/server.pt/community/inspector_general/302/inspector_general; www.cookcountygov.com/portal/server.pt/community/budget_and_management_services,_department_of/252/budget_and_management_servicesw,_department_of; Harris County: www.co.harris.tx/us/auditor; www.hctx.net/budget; Maricopa County: www.maricopa.gov/internal_audit; www.maricopa.gov/budget; San Diego County: www.sdcounty.ca.gov/auditor; www.sdcounty.ca.gov/cao/oia.html; www.sdcounty.ca.gov/auditor/budinfo.html; Orange County: www.ocgov.com/ac; www.ocgov.com/audit; egov.ocgov.com/ocgov/Info%20OC/Departments%20&%20Agencies/Office%20of%20of%20Performance%20Audit%20Director; www.ocgov.com/financials/finance.asp; Miami Dade: www.miamidade.gov/ams; www.miamidadeig.org; www.miamidade.gov/budget; Dallas County: www.dallascounty.org/department/auditor/auditor.php; www.dallascounty.org/department/budget/budget.php; Riverside County: www.auditorcontroller.org; www.countyofriverside.us/government/budget andfinancial.html; San Bernardino County: www.sbcounty.gov/atc; www.sbcounty.gov; Wayne County: www.waynecounty.

com/commission/lag.htm; www.co.wayne.mi.us/commission/adminbudget.
htm; Clark County: www.clarkcountynv.gov/depts/internal_audit/pages/
default.aspx; www.clarkcountynv.gov/depts/finance/budget/Pages/default.aspx;
Tarrant County: www.tarrantcounty.com/eauditor; www.tarrantcoun-
ty.com/ebudget; Santa Clara County: www.sccgov.org/portal/site/fin/
agencychp?path=%2Fv7%2FFinance%20Agency%20(AGY)%2FController-
Treasurer%20Department%2FInternal%20Audit%20Division; www.sccgov.
org/portal/site/scc/chlevel3?path=%2Fv7%2FSCC%20Public%20Portal%2F
County%20Connection%2FBudget%20and%20Finance; Broward County:
www.broward.org/auditor; www.broward.org/budget; Bexar County: gov.bex-
ar.org/auditor; www.bexar.org/budget; Suffolk County: www.suffolkcountyny.
gov/Departments/Comptroller.aspx; www.suffolkcountyny.gov/Departments/
CountyExecutive/BudgetandManagement.aspx; Alameda County: www.
acgov.org/auditor; www.acgov.org/budget.htm; Sacramento County: www.
finance.saccounty.net/Auditor/InternalAudits.asp; www.budget.saccounty.net

For a discussion of the details of the Orange County bankruptcy, see
Mark Baldassare, *When Government Fails: The Orange County Bankruptcy,*
Berkeley: University of California Press, 1998.

Information on IGs in Houston, Philadelphia, and Miami is from
City of Houston, Executive Order 1-39 Revised, Establishment of Office
of Inspector General for Investigation of Employee Misconduct, 7/14/10;
City of Philadelphia, Office of the Inspector General, Annual Report 2009;
Miami Dade County Office of the Inspector General, Annual Report, 2008.
A history of corruption and response in Cuyahoga County and New Orleans
is detailed in Doing Well by Doing Good: Can Corruption Prevention and
Government Efficiency Strategies Help Turn Around Declining Cities?, 13
Government, Law and Policy Journal 78–86 (Winter 2011). For a discus-
sion of the referenda in Jefferson Parish and Palm Beach County, see, Mary
Sparacello, Kenner group endorses Jefferson Parish IG proposals, *The Times
Picayune,* 10/21/11 and Andy Reid and Marc Freeman, Palm Beach County
ethics referendum, schools tax leading in initial vote counts late Tuesday, *Sun
Sentinel,* 11/2/10. An excellent summary of the Bernard Kerik case—and
DOI's role in it—is found in Tom Robbins, "Rudy Giuliani and Bernie
Kerik: The Final Chapter," *Village Voice,* 1/19/10.

Much of the background information on Chattanooga is based on
recollections by author David Eichenthal, who served as City Finance Officer and Chair of the General Pension Plan Board. Information on pension
contributions and funding levels is generally from the City's Comprehensive
Annual Financial Reports (CAFRs), all of which are available on the city
website at /www.chattanooga.gov/finance/finance-division/cafr. A discussion
of efforts in the Corker Administration to improve performance can be

found in Bob Corker and David Eichenthal, "Applying Innovations in Mid-Sized Cities: 311 and Chattanooga's Results" in Erwin Blackstone, Michael Bognanno & Simon Hakim, eds., *Innovations in e-Government: Governors and Mayors Speak Out,* Lanham: Rowman & Littlefield, 2005.

Background on the beginnings of the local government pension crisis is from Mary Williams Walsh, "Some Cities Struggling to Keep Pension Promises," *New York Times,* 5/5/04; Deloitte, *Paying for Tomorrow: Practical Strategies for Tackling the Public Pension Crisis,* 2006; and U.S. Government Accountability Office, Defined Pension Benefits: Conflicts of Interest Involving High Risk or Terminated Plans Pose Enforcement Challenges, GAO 07-703, June 2007.

Background on the history of the Board's relationship with William Keith Phillips is discussed in detail in the minutes of the General Pension Plan—especially Meeting of the Trustees, City of Chattanooga General Pension Plan, 3/14/02 and in Edward Siedle, Report to the City of Chattanooga General Pension Plan: Investigation of Former Investment Consultant, 3/18/04.

Changes in the operations of the Pension Plan board are described in Duane W. Gang, "Pay Ends to Attend Pension Sessions, *Chattanooga Times Free Press,* 11/08/03. Coverage of the Siedle investigation and the decision to file a complaint can be found in Duane W. Gang, "Outside Firm Reviews Pension Consultants," *Chattanooga Times Free Press,* 4/28/04; Duane W. Gang, "City Uncovers Pension Loss: Officials file complaint alleging mismanagement by financial adviser cost fund $20 million," *Chattanooga Times Free Press,* 10/10/04; and Gretchen Morgenson and Mary Williams Walsh, "How Consultants Can Retire on Your Pension," *New York Times,* 12/12/04.

The settlement of the GPP's claim is described in Herman Wang, "Payment to City Ends Pension Fight," *Chattanooga Times Free Press,* 3/17/06. The GPP's reforms are discussed in a memo from David Eichenthal, in his files, Steps Taken by General Pension Plan to Address Issues Raised By Claim against Phillips Group, Paine Weber and Morgan Stanley, 2/7/05. Coverage of subsequent settlements involving Phillips are described in Marcy Gordon, Morgan Stanley paying $500K to settle SEC charges, *USA Today,* 7/20/09 and *In the Matter of William Keith Phillips,* Securities Exchange Commission, Administrative Proceeding File No. 3-13559, 7/20/09.

Chapter 13. Other Elected and Appointed Local Officials

The Report of the Independent Commission on the Los Angeles Police Department, 1991 (the so-called Christopher Commission Report) is available on line at www.parc.info. Chief Beck's comments are quoted from Tony Castro, Rodney King's March 3, 1991 traffic stop and beating turned LA into a riot zone . . . then changed it, *Daily News*, 3/2/11.

Different oversight structures in New York City government include www.nyc.gov/html/conflicts/home.html (New York City COIB), www. cityclerk.nyc.gov (New York City Clerk, for information on regulation of lobbying), and www.nyccfb.info (New York City Campaign Finance Board).

A discussion of the history of police corruption—and oversight—in New York can be found in Harold Baer and Joseph Armao, The Mollen Commission Report: An Overview, 40 New York Law School Review 73 (1995). Information about New York's Commission on Police Corruption can be found at www.nyc.gov/html/ccpc/html/about/about.shtml and information about the CCRB can be found at its website, www.nyc.gov/html/ccrb/home.html. A discussion of the various different models of civilian police oversight can be found in Police Assessment Resource Center (PARC), Review of National Police Oversight Models, February 2005 and is available at the PARC website at www.parc.info.

For a discussion of correction oversight issues, see Michael B. Mushlin and Michele Deitch, "Opening Up a Closed World: A Sourcebook on Prison Oversight," Pace Law Review, Vol. 30, No. 5, Fall 2010. In addition, the history of the New York City Board of Correction can be found on line at www.nyc.gov/html/boc/html/about/history.shtml.

Much of the discussion related to the public advocate and to the office's investigation of the NYPD response to officer misconduct relies on the recollections of one of the authors, David Eichenthal, who was the first chief of staff to the first-ever public advocate. For a review of the history and powers of the office of public advocate, see, Mark Green and Laurel Eisner, The Public Advocate for New York City: An Analysis of the Country's Only Elected Ombudsman, 42 New York Law School Review 1093 (1998). The provisions of the New York City Charter related to the public advocate's power to review complaints and to have access to records are sections 24(f) and 24(j).

For an informative discussion of the reduction of crime in New York City, see, Franklin Zimring, *The City that Became Safe: New York's Lessons for Urban Crime and Its Control*, New York: Oxford University Press, 2011. Data on CCRB complaints and crime in New York is from Letter from Public Advocate Mark Green to Attorney General Janet Reno, 8/18/97; Testimony of Public Advocate Mark Green, New York City Council Committee on Public Safety, 9/11/97; and Office of the Public Advocate, *Trend Analysis of Complaints Received by the New York City Civilian Complaint Review Board, 1992-1996*, 9/11/97.

The errant reference to "Giuliani time" is discussed in Lawrence Goodman, "3 Quit Louima Team After Remark Denial," *New York Daily News*, 1/28/98. Judge Lehner's trial level opinion can be found at *Green v. Safir*, 174 Misc. 2d 400, 664 NYS2d 232, Sup. Ct., NY Co. (10/14/97).

Data on both the *New York Times* and Quinnipiac polls is cited in Office of the New York City Public Advocate and The Accountability Project, Disciplining Police: Solving the Problem of Police Misconduct, 1/27/00. The report is also the source of the discussion of its findings.

The front-page *New York Times* coverage of the preliminary report consisted of Kevin Flynn, Public Complaints are Played Down Police Data Show, *New York Times*, 9/15/99. The change in disciplinary actions by the Police Department is discussed in a brief report issued by the public advocate and summarized in a press release, Office of the Public Advocate, Green Report Shows NYPD Punishment Rate Rises Significantly, 12/27/01. The report on the Diallo case is Office of the New York City Public Advocate, Report of the Public Advocate on the Police Commissioner's Decision to Decline to Proceed with Disciplinary Action against the Officers Involved in the Shooting of Amadou Diallo June 2001.

Chapter 14. The Role of the Press

The introductory comment by Thomas Jefferson came from his letter of January 16, 1787 to Edward Carrington, which can be found in *The Founders' Constitution*, Amendment I (Speech and Press), Document 8, Papers 11: 48–49, at http://press-pubs.uchicago.edu/founders/documents/amendI_speechs8.html. The introductory comment by Richard Nixon from December 11, 1972, on the Nixon Tapes, can be heard on Nixon Tapes: No Washington Post Reporters Allowed!, at http://www.youtube.com/watch?v=dHe8lYekBRM.

The entire script of the 1939 movie discussed in the opening paragraphs, *Mr. Smith Goes to Washington*, screenplay by Sidney Buchman, story by Lewis Foster, can be found at http://www.dailyscript.com/scripts/MrSmithGoesToWashington.txt. Other information about it can be found at the Internet Movie Database, at http://www.imdb.com/title/tt0031679/.

Percentages of respondents using various news sources come from The Pew Research Center's Project for Excellence in Journalism, *The State of the News Media 2011*, Press Alert: Woes Go Beyond Audience, Economics: Journalism Losing Control of Future, 3/14/11, http://stateofthemedia.org/2011/overview-2/press-alert/.

Sources of information on Nellie Bly, Jacob Riis, Lincoln Steffens, and Upton Sinclair include Nellie Bly, Muckraking and Social Reform, *Mod-

ern America, https://wikis.nyu.edu/ek6/modernamerica/index.php/Reform/
MuckrakingAndSocialReform; Brooke Kroeger, *Nellie Bly* (excerpts), http://
www.correctionhistory.org/rooseveltisland/bly/html/blackwell.html;   Carol
Quirke, Picturing the Poor: Jacob Riis's Reform Photography, 36 *Reviews
in American History* #4, 557-565, December 2008, Project Muse, Johns
Hopkins University Press, http://www.americanantiquarian.org/chavicread-
ings2011/quirke.pdf; The Shame of the Cities: Steffens on Urban Blight,
History Matters: The U.S. Survey Course on the Web, http://historymat-
ters.gmu.edu/d/5732/; Jon Blackwell, 1906: Rumble over 'The Jungle,'
http://www.capitalcentury.com/1906.html; and Gary Younge, Blood, Sweat
and Fears, The Guardian, 8/5/06, http://www.guardian.co.uk/books/2006/
aug/05/featuresreviews.guardianreview24.

Sources of information about and quotations from I.F. ("Izzy") Stone
can be found in Myra MacPherson, *All Governments Lie: The Life and
Times of Rebel Journalist I.F. Stone*, New York: Scribner 2006, 192–193;
I.F. Stone, Izzy on Izzy, A Word About Myself, *The Website of I.F. Stone*,
http://www.ifstone.org/biography.php; Jeff Cohen and Norman Solomon,
30-Year Anniversary: Tonkin Gulf Lie Launched Vietnam War, FAIR (Fairness and Accuracy In Reporting), Media Beat 7/27/94, http://www.fair.
org/index.php?page=2261; I.F. Stone, What Few Know About the Gulf of
Tonkin Incidents, *I.F. Stone's Weekly*, V. 12, No. 28, 8/24/64, page 1, http://
www.ifstone.org/weekly8-24-64.pdf; and About I.F. Stone, Nieman Foundation for Journalism at Harvard, website, http://www.nieman.harvard.edu/
NiemanFoundation/Awards/AwardsAtAGlance/IFStoneMedalForJournalis-
ticIndependence/AboutIFStone.aspx.

Robert D. McFadden, Clark R. Mollenhoff, Pulitzer Winner, Dies at
69, *The New York Times*, 3/4/91, http://www.nytimes.com/1991/03/04/obit-
uaries/clark-r-mollenhoff-pulitzer-winner-dies-at-69.html is a good source of
information about Clark Mollenhoff. Mollenhoff's "rules" can be found at
Seven Basic Rules for Investigative Reporting, Committee of Concerned
Journalists, http://www.concernedjournalists.org/node/162/.

Rachel Cooke, The Man Who Knows Too Much, *The Guardian*,
10/19/08,   http://www.guardian.co.uk/media/2008/oct/19/seymour-hersh-
new-yorker-reporter supports most of the discussion of Seymour Hersh,
including Richard Perle's characterization of Hersh. However, the obituary
of Sidney Korshak, Robert McG. Thomas Jr., Sidney Korshak, 88, Dies:
Fabled Fixer for the Chicago Mob, *The New York Times*, 1/22/96, http://
www.nytimes.com/1996/01/22/us/sidney-korshak-88-dies-fabled-fixer-for-
the-chicago-mob.html?src=pm, credits Hersh for much of the exposure of
Korshak's mob connections.

The best source for information about Woodward and Bernstein's work
investigating Watergate is probably the Woodward and Bernstein Water-

gate Papers, Web Exhibitions, Harry Ransom Center, University of Texas at Austin, http://www.hrc.utexas.edu/exhibitions/web/woodstein/post/. Tim Weiner's obituary of W. Mark Felt, Watergate Deep Throat, Dies at 95, *The New York Times*, 12/19/08, http://www.nytimes.com/2008/12/19/washington/19felt.html includes his admission that he was "Deep Throat." Edward R. Murrow and the Irresponsible Media of Today, *Daily Kos*, 12/6/10, http://www.dailykos.com/story/2010/12/06/926271/-Edward-R-Murrow-and-the-Irresponsible-Media-of-Today, explains the magnificent work of Edward R. Murrow.

Documentation for comments about *60 Minutes* comes from Howard Rosenberg, Keeping '60 Minutes' Ticking, *Los Angeles Times*, 2/23/94, http://articles.latimes.com/1994-02-23/entertainment/ca-26273_1_lowell-bergman; Suein L. Wang and Milo Geyelin, Getting Personal: Brown & Williamson has 500-Page Document Attacking Chief Critic, *Wall Street Journal*, 2/1/96, http://jeffreywigand.com/wallstreetjournal.php; Editorial, Self-Censorship at CBS, *The New York Times*, 11/12/95, http://www.nytimes.com/1995/11/12/opinion/self-censorship-at-cbs.html?pagewanted=all&src=pm; Marie Brenner, The Man Who Knew Too Much, *Vanity Fair*, May 1996, http://www.marie-brenner.com/PDF/TheManWhoKnewTooMuch.pdf; and Frank Rich, Journal; Smoking Guns at '60 Minutes,' *The New York Times*, 2/3/96, http://www.nytimes.com/1996/02/03/opinion/journal-smoking-guns-at-60-minutes.html?src=pm.

Discussion of Geraldo Rivera's work and career appears in Hal Kennedy, Introduction, A Guide to Willowbrook State School Resources at Other Institutions, Archives and Special Collections, College of Staten Island, http://www.library.csi.cuny.edu/archives/WillowbrookRG.htm; and in Richard Huff, Kvetching with Imus II—Geraldo Blasts Gumbel, New York *Daily News*, 4/7/95, http://articles.nydailynews.com/1995-04-07/news/17963546_1_geraldo-rivera-talk-bryant-gumbel.

The quotation from the Pew Center about Jon Stewart's *Daily Show* comes from The Pew Research Center's Project for Excellence in Journalism, Journalism.org, Journalism, Satire or Just Laughs? "The Daily Show With Jon Stewart," Examined, 5/8/08, http://www.journalism.org/node/10953. Bill Carter and Brian Stelter, In 'Daily Show' Role on 9/11 Bill, Echoes of Murrow, *The New York Times*, 12/26/10, http://www.nytimes.com/2010/12/27/business/media/27stewart.html?pagewanted=all, reports Stewart's role in the passage of federal legislation to assist 9/11 responders, as well as Mayor Bloomberg's comment crediting his effort.

The FCC report cited is Steven Waldman and working group, *The Information Needs of Communities: The Changing Media Landscape in a Broadband Age*, July 2011, http://transition.fcc.gov/osp/inc-report/The_Information_Needs_of_Communities.pdf or at http://books.google.

com/books?id=bLulzihSxPEC&pg=PA11&dq=especially+of+investigativ
e,+enterprise+and+beat+reporting&hl=en&sa=X&ei=9vNKT52IJpOQ0
QG-koSNDg&ved=0CDgQ6AEwAA#v=onepage&q=especially%20of%20
investigative%2C%20enterprise%20and%20beat%20reporting&f=false.
Information and quotations from that document appear especially on pages
5, 10–15, 18, 24, 34, 35, 43, 46–17, and 52.

Chelsea Ide and Kanupria Vashisht, Today's investigative reporters
lack resources, *The Arizona Republic*, 5/28/06, http://www.azcentral.com/
specials/special01/0528bolles-stateofreporting.html, provides the information cited from the study from the journalism school at Arizona State
University (now the Walter Cronkite School of Journalism) and the quotation from Bob Greene. Information about ProPublica can be found
at its website, ProPublica: Journalism in the Public Interest, at http://
www.propublica.org/about/. VoiceofSanDiego.org at http://www.voiceof-
sandiego.org/, MinnPost at http://www.minnpost.com/, and the Sunlight
Foundation at http://sunlightfoundation.com/, similarly provide information about those organizations. ProPublica's report on the New Orleans
Memorial Medical Center, Sheri Fink, The Deadliest Choices at Memorial, *ProPublica*, 8/27/09, can be found at http://www.propublica.org/topic/
deadly-choices-memorial-medical-center-after-katrina.

Matt Schudel's obituary, Muckraking N.Y. Reporter Dies At 66,
Washington Post, 12/23/04, http://www.washingtonpost.com/wp-dyn/arti-
cles/A21116-2004Dec22.html, provides information about the life of Jack
Newfield. Ed Koch's characterization of Newfield can be found at L.S.
Klepp, book review, *All the Best* by Edward I. Koch, *Entertainment Weekly*,
4/20/90, http://www.ew.com/ew/article/0,,20167667,00.html. Information about Wayne Barrett can be found in Richard Perez-Pena, The (Ex)
Voice of the Village, *The New York Times*, 2/25/11, http://www.nytimes.
com/2011/01/05/nyregion/05voice.html. Tom Robbins, in The Lush Life
of a Rudy Appointee, *The Village Voice*, 4/16/02, http://www.villagevoice.
com/content/printVersion/196333/, details the history of the Russell Harding scandal, including the quotations offered in the text. The quoted comment by US Attorney James Comey, however, was reported in Benjamin
Weiser, Ex-Chief of Housing Agency is Accused of Embezzlement," *The
New York Times*, 3/18/03, http://www.nytimes.com/2003/03/18/nyre-
gion/ex-chief-of-housing-agency-is-accused-of-embezzlement.html.   His
guilty plea and sentence was reported in Sabrina Tavernise, Ex-Housing
Chief Gets 63-Month Sentence, *The New York Times*, 7/22/05, http://
www.nytimes.com/2005/07/22/nyregion/22harding.html?ref=russella
harding.

The article by Jeff Gottlieb and Reuben Vives cited in the text, Is a City Manager Worth $800,000, appeared in the *Los Angeles Times*, 7/15/10, http://articles.latimes.com/2010/jul/15/local/la-me-bell-salary-20100715. Additional information about the prosecution of officials of the city of Bell in California can be found in Ruben Vives and Jeff Gottlieb, "3 Bell leaders to quit in pay scandal," *Los Angeles Times*, 7/23/10; Jeff Gottlieb and Corina Knoll, "Robert Rizzo, aide accused of conspiracy in Bell corruption scandal," *Los Angeles Times*, 3/31/11; Robin Abcarian and Geraldine Baum, "Los Angeles Times wins 2 Pulitzer Prizes," *Los Angeles Times*, 4/19/11; Jeff Gottlieb, Judge questions why Bell's former police chief isn't facing corruption charges, *Los Angeles Times*, 12/19/11, as well as in *People v. Rizzo*, Indictment, Superior Court of the State of California for the County of Los Angeles, Case No. BA382701 3/29/11.

Al Tompkins, *LA Times* Public Service Pulitzer winner combined traditional City Hall beat reporting with innovative digital storytelling, *Poynter*, 4/19/11, http://www.poynter.org/latest-news/als-morning-meeting/128504/la-times-public-service-pulitzer-winner-combined-traditional-city-hall-beat-reporting-with-innovative-digital-storytelling/ includes in its coverage of the affair how the *L.A. Times* itself made data about Bell's officials more accessible to its citizens. The website of the League of California Cities reports the enactment of the California law requiring disclosure of stipends paid to municipal officials for attending meetings at Governor Signs Second Bell Bill, Six Bills Remain in Legislature, 7/29/11, http://www.cacities.org/index.jsp?zone=locc&previewStory=28589.

Tom Robbins' stories on Russell Harding include "Party Harding: Lush-Living Rudy Aide Threw $22K Bash for Board Chairman," *Village Voice*, 4/23/02; "Scandal Repair: As Harding Probe Continues, Cleanup Costs Grow," *Village Voice*, 2/11/03; "Russell Harding's Vanity Fair: 'Voice' Trail Led to Charges," *Village Voice*, 3/18/03; and "Hard Time for Harding," *Village Voice*, July 19, 207/19/05

The EDHEC study to which the text refers comes from École des Hautes Études Commerciales Business School and was cited in the FCC report at page 203. David Simon's quoted comment appears in Richard J. Tofel, Why Corruption Grows in Our States, *The Daily Beast*, 5/24/10, http://www.thedailybeast.com/articles/2010/05/24/why-corruption-grows-in-our-states-fewer-reporters-and-remote-state-capitals.html.

The role of technology and its use by citizen journalists is discussed in Radley Balko, Tech-Savvy Occupy Protesters Use Cellphone Video, Social Networking to Publicize Police Abuse, *The Huffington Post*, 10/29/11, http://www.huffingtonpost.com/2011/10/29/occupy-protesters-armed-with-technology_n_1063706.html and Rebecca J. Rosen, So, Was Facebook Responsible for the Arab Spring After All?, *The Atlantic*, 9/3/11, http://www.theatlantic.com/technology/archive/2011/09/so-was-facebook-responsible-for-the-arab-spring-after-all/244314/.

Chapter 15. The Role of Public Interest and Other Nongovernmental Oversight Organizations and Participants

The introductory quotation by George Bernard Shaw comes from a special section in his 1903 play *Man and Superman* which he called "Maxims for Revolutionists," available at Bartleby.com, http://www.bartleby.com/157/6.html. Pamela Gilbert and Susannah Goodman, in their Chapter on the Resolution Trust Corporation starting at page 589. The other introductory quotation is attributed to Nicholas Johnson in Mark Green, ed., *Changing America: Blueprints for the New Administration*, New York: Newmarket Press, 1992, 603. John Grisham's *The Pelican Brief* was published in New York by Doubleday in 1992 (see http://www.randomhouse.com/book/72167/the-pelican-brief-by-john-grisham/9780385421980/); the 1993 Warner Brothers movie starred Julia Roberts and Denzel Washington (see http://www.imdb.com/title/tt0107798/).

Information on CU and the Bureau of Municipal Research can be found in Francis S. Barry, *The Scandal of Reform*, Piscataway, New Jersey: Rutgers University Press, 2009, especially at pages 60 and 69. The quotation from Andrew White, who had been president of Cornell University and US ambassador to Berlin, can be found in Volume III of the collection of issues of the magazine *The Review of Reviews*, American edition, ed. Albert Shaw, New York, January through July 1891, page 56, reviewing White's article On the Government of American Cities, http://books.google.com/books?id=MetwMY90xwEC&pg=PA56&lpg=PA56&dq=city+governments+worst+Christendom&source=bl&ots=uuqZZQPzWj&sig=x81ollsXoVmFuRBzsTk7ibXd0DE&hl=en&ei=yyt-TpjTA8Tk0QHd1qAF&sa=X&oi=book_result&ct=result&resnum=3&ved=0CC4Q6AEwAg#v=onepage&q=city%20governments%20worst%20Christendom&f=false; and also in Robert Caro, *The Power Broker*, New York: Alfred Knopf, Inc. 1974, page 60. Caro also, at pages 61–62, credits the work of the Bureau of Municipal Research for the first formal city agency budget in the United States. Donald C. Stone, in Birth of ASPA—A Collective Effort in Institution Building, 35 *Public Administration Review* 83–93, Jan.–Feb. 1975, explains how other institutions descended from the bureau. Press release, Citizens Union Calls for New Way on Redistricting Reform, 9/21/11, http://www.citizensunion.

org/www/cu/site/hosting/news_release/092111_release_redistricting.html;
Erin Einhorn, New Service from the civic website Gotham Gazette tracks
political cash in city government, *NYDailyNews.com*, 2/3/11, http://www.
nydailynews.com/ny_local/2011/02/03/2011-02-03_site_keeping_tabs_on_
cash_to_council.html; and Councilpedia: Keeping Track of City Officials,
published by the Citizens Union Foundation, http://www.councilpedia.org/
index.php?title=Main_Page supply information on the recent work of the
CU. The quotation commenting on the source of contributions to statewide
New York political campaigns in 2010 comes from Capitol Investments
2010: An Analysis of Campaign Spending in the 2010 New York Election,
January 2011, http://www.scribd.com/doc/46228722/NYPIRG-report, page
5, a report issued by CU in conjunction with the other organizations cited
in text.

Material on Common Cause was taken from locations on its website,
http://www.commoncause.org/site/pp.asp?c=dkLNK1MQIwG&b=4860183
and   http://www.commoncause.org/site/apps/nl/newsletter2.asp?c=dkLNK
1MQIwG&b=4773613, press releases therein listed for 10/5/11, 9/15/11,
8/3/11; and from Rosen, *Holding Government Bureaucracies Accountable*,
supra, pages 107–110.

Material on the LWV, similarly, comes from locations on its website,
press release, On 90th Anniversary, League of Women Voters Elects Elisabeth
MacNamara as New National President, LWV website, 6/15/10, http://www.
lwv.org/AM/Template.cfm?Section=Our_History&Template=/TaggedPage/
TaggedPageDisplay.cfm&TPLID=36&ContentID=1501; and state-by-state
search, LWV website, http://www.lwv.org/AM/Template.cfm?Section=Find_a_
Local_League. Its latest membership census is actually down from more than
200,000 in 1,100 chapters in 1998, Rosen, *Holding Government Bureaucracies
Accountable*, *supra* at 112). Samples of its listings of elected officials include
LWV of City of New York Education Fund, *They Represent You 2003: Direc-
tory of Elected Officials*, New York 2003, and now online, eg, LWV of City
of New York, *They Represent You*, LWV of City of New York website, http://
www.lwvnyc.org/TRY_find.html. Balancing Justice in New York, *Everyday
Democracy* website, 10/1/00, http://www.everyday-democracy.org/en/Arti-
cle.236.aspx reflects its roundtable discussions on the Rockefeller drug laws
in New York. Feldman and Benjamin, *Tales from the Sausage Factory*, New
York, SUNY Press 2010, 41 discusses its part in the campaign for "free
speech in shopping malls." James Odato, Fund Draws Call for Probe, *Albany
Times Union*, 10/30/09, http://www.timesunion.com/AspStories/storyprint.
asp?StoryID=859561 reported its inquiries in the Monserrate affair.

Grossman Publishers of New York published Ralph Nader's 1965
book, *Unsafe at Any Speed*. His lawsuit against General Motors is reported as

Nader v. General Motors Corp., 25 N.Y. 2d 560, 307 N.Y.S. 2d 647 (1970). Further information on Nader can be found in Rosen, *Holding Government Bureaucracies Accountable, supra*, pages 110–111; and Independent Lens, An Unreasonable Man: Ralph Nader—How Do You Define A Legacy?, http://www.pbs.org/independentlens/unreasonableman/raiders.html.

Ford Explorer Rollover.com provides Joan Claybrook's testimony to Congress on that scandal, at http://fordexplorerrollover.com/controversy/default.cfm; and Paul Pinkham, Ford settles 7 tire-related lawsuits in Florida, *The Florida Times-Union*, 4/30/02, http://jacksonville.com/tu-online/stories/043002/met_9277164.html covers the congressional response to it.

The *Citizens United* decision is reported at 130 S. Ct. 876, and Public Citizen's efforts to combat it are described at Public Citizens Presses to Overturn *Citizens United*, Public Citizen website, http://www.citizen.org/Page.aspx?pid=4788.

Sources of information about the various PIRGs discussed include PIRG campus chapters, US PIRG website, http://www.uspirg.org/about-us/pirg-campus-chapters; the state PIRGs, US PIRG website, http://www.uspirg.org/about-us/the-state-pirgs; What is PGPIRG?, PGPIRG website, http://pgpirg.tumblr.com/whatispgpirg; Stop Taxpayer Giveaways, Illinois PIRG website, http://www.illinoispirg.org/issues/stop-taxpayer-giveaways; press release, Red Light and Speed Cameras: Public Safety or Private Gain?, Illinois PIRG website, 10/27/11, http://www.illinoispirg.org/news-releases/stop-taxpayer-givaways-news/stop-taxpayer-givaways/red-light-and-speed-cameras-public-safety-or-private-gain; press release, Taxpayer Subsidies for Junk Food Wasting Billions, Illinois PIRG website, 9/21/11, http://www.illinoispirg.org/newsroom/more-news/more-news/taxpayer-subsidies-for-junk-food-wasting-billions; press release, Watchdog Group Raises Concerns Over Lack of Transparency for Proposed Commerce Authority, Arizona PIRG website, 2/16/11, http://www.arizonapirg.org/news-releases/advocacy/tax--budget-news/watchdog-group-raises-concerns--over-lack-of-transparency-for-proposed-commerce-authority; A History of Action in the Public Interest: 2000 to Present, U.S. PIRG website, http://www.uspirg.org/results/a-history-of-action-in-the-public-interest/2000-to-present; and Mission Statement, US PIRG website, http://www.uspirg.org/about-us/mission.

You can hear Lewis Black's comment about POGO at POGO Celebrates 30th Anniversary, video, 2011, http://www.pogo.org/about/30/30.html. Eric B. Kempen and Andrew P. Bakaj, Marshalling Whistleblower Protection, *Journal of Public Inquiry*, Spring/Summer 2009, page 6, http://www.ignet.gov/randp/sp09jpi.pdf quote Sen. Grassley's comment about Ernest Fitzgerald, also reported in the *Congressional Record* at 1 152 Cong. Rec. S1780 (daily ed. March 06, 2006). They also relate other aspects of Fitzgerald's story. The U.S. Supreme Court ruled on *Nixon v. Fitzgerald* at 457 U.S. 732 (1982), http://caselaw.lp.findlaw.com/cgi-bin/getcase. pl?court=us&vol=457&invol=731. Terry Cooper, *The Responsible Administrator*, San Francisco: Jossey-Bass 2006, page 222, reports Pentagon retaliation against Fitzgerald.

Introductory letter by Danielle Bryan, Executive Director, POGO Annual Report, 2010, page 1, http://pogoarchives.org/m/xp/2010ar.pdf, describes POGO's origins. Sources of information about POGO's recent work include POGO Celebrates 30th Anniversary, video, 2011, http://www.pogo.org/about/30/30.html, *supra*; POGO website, Impact, http://www.pogo.org/about/impact.html; Danielle Bryan, Changing the Debate About Public Service Contracting, 10/6/11, https://webmail.jjay.cuny.edu/owa/?ae=Item&t=IPM.Note&id=RgAAAABOvOyWRO8eQqInPlmaYqorBwCZx9lrAyiIQbeuzqDPMnfVADLpl1FnAACZx9lrAyiIQbeuzqDPMnfVADkqxPJ2AAAJ; Ben Freeman, Lydia Dennett, and DahnaBlack, Super Committee Under the (Foreign?) Influence, POGO, 10/6/11, http://pogoblog.typepad.com/pogo/2011/10/super-committee-under-the-foreign-influence.html; Michael Smallberg, Bailout Watchdog Questions All $5.8 Million of Simpson Thacher's Legal Fees, POGO, 9/29/11, http://pogoblog.typepad.com/pogo/2011/09/bailout-watchdog-questions-all-58-million-of-simpson-thachers-legal-fees-.html; Michael Smallberg, Newly Released Document Adds to the Mystery of the SEC's Dropped Case Against Deutsche Bank, POGO, 9/20/11, http://pogoblog.typepad.com/pogo/2011/09/newly-released-document-adds-to-the-mystery-of-the-secs-dropped-case-against-deutsche-bank.html; Ben Freeman, Defend America. Defend the Foreign Corrupt Practices Act, POGO, 9/20/11, http://pogoblog.typepad.com/pogo/2011/09/defend-america-defend-the-foreign-corrupt-practices-act.html; Adam Zagorin, And Who the Heck is "Terry A. Hogan"?, POGO, 9/2/11, http://pogoblog.typepad.com/pogo/2011/09/diplomatic-cover-did-the-state-dept-facilitate-extraordinary-rendition.html; Bryan Rahija, Pentagon Personnel Official Resigns Amid Whistleblower Allegations of Incompetence, POGO, 10/27/11, http://pogoblog.typepad.com/pogo/2011/10/pentagon-personnel-official-resigns-amid-whistleblower-allegations-of-incompetence.html; and POGO Annual Report, 2010, page 6, http://pogoarchives.org/m/xp/2010ar.pdf.

Information about Judicial Watch comes from David Korn, Klayman Watch, *The Nation*, 3/29/04, http://www.thenation.com/article/klayman-watch; Transcript, Bill Moyers Interviews Larry Klayman, PBS.org, 7/11/03, http://www.pbs.org/now/transcript/transcript_klayman.html; press release, U.S. Secret Service Forced to Release More White House Logs Detailing Abramoff Visits, Judicial Watch website, 7/7/06, http://www.judicialwatch.

org/news/2006/jul/u-s-secret-service-forced-release-more-white-house-logs-detailing-abramoff-visits; press release, Halliburton CEO Admits Cheney Knew of Alleged Fraudulent Accounting Policies, Judicial Watch website, July 2002, http://www.judicialwatch.org/halliburton-ceo-admits-cheney-knew-alleged-fraudulent-accounting-policies; and press release, Judicial Watch Announces List of Washington's "Ten Most Wanted Corrupt Politicians" for 2010, Judicial Watch website, 11/1/11, http://www.judicialwatch.org/news/2010/dec/judicial-watch-announces-list-washingtons-ten-most-wanted-corrupt-politicians-2010. Information about Citizens for Responsibility and Ethics in Washington ("CREW") comes from Ben Smith, Staffing up for congressional investigations, *Politico*, 11/18/10, http://www.politico.com/blogs/bensmith/1110/Staffing_up_for_Congressional_investigations.html; Linda Burstyn, The Most Feared Woman on Capitol Hill?, *Ms. Magazine*, Winter 2007, http://www.msmagazine.com/winter2007/2007-02-01-mostfearedwoman.asp; Matthew Boyle, CREW names 'most corrupt members of Congress,' critics raise questions, *The Daily Caller*, 9/20/11, http://dailycaller.com/2011/09/20/crew-names-%E2%80%98most-corrupt-members-of-congress%E2%80%99-critics-raise-questions/; press release, Rep. Weiner Must Resign, CREW, 6/13/11, http://www.citizensforethics.org/press/entry/crew-anthony-weiner-must-resign; and press release, Representative Rangel Must Resign, CREW, 11/16/10, http://www.citizensforethics.org/press/entry/crew-rangel-must-resign.

Rosen, *Holding Government Bureaucracies Accountable*, *supra* at 117-134; and Edward P. Richards, State Tort Claims Acts, Louisiana State University Law Center's Medical and Public Health Law website, http://biotech.law.lsu.edu/map/StateTortClaimsActs.html, respectively, discuss federal and state tort claims acts. Cases that Made a Difference, American Association for Justice website, 2011, http://www.justice.org/cps/rde/xchg/justice/hs.xsl/3618.htm provides some examples of the important oversight role played by personal injury attorneys.

New York's "Scaffold Law" is codified at New York Labor Law §§ 240 and 241. George M. Chalos, New York Labor Law 240: What Does It Really Mean?, 5/23/05, http://www.frc-law.com/files/pub_ny-labor-law-240.pdf; and Barry M. Temkin, New York's Labor Law Section 240: Has It Been Narrowed or Expanded by the Courts Beyond the Legislative Intent?, 44 *New York Law School Law Review* 45–68 (2000), relate some of its history. The cited decision illustrating its continued importance can be found at *Gilbert v. Albany Med. Ctr.*, 9 A.D.3d 643 (3d Dept. 2004). Reflections on OSHA's History, Department of Labor, Occupational Safety and Health Administration website, http://www.osha.gov/history/OSHA_HISTORY_3360s.pdf discusses the history of the federal OSHA. Information about New York's construction safety record comes from Glenn von Nostitz, Lives in the Balance: Immigrants and Workers at Elevated Heights at Greatest Risk in Construction, New York State Trial Lawyers Association, 6/05, http://www.nystla.org/nicecontent/documents/Lives%20in%20the%20Balance,%20rep%20with%20apps.pdf and from Glenn von Nostitz, New York's "Scaffold Law": An Essential Protection for Immigrant Construction Workers, New York State Trial Lawyers Association, 6/04, http://www.nystla.org/nicecontent/documents/Scaffold_Law_Protects_Immigrant_Workers.pdf.

The *qui tam* definition can be found at Duhaime.org website, http://www.duhaime.org/LegalDictionary/Q/QuiTam.aspx. Other information about *qui tam* comes from Gene De Santis and Reannon Froehlich, False Claims Acts, City, State, and Federal: Enlisting Citizens to Protect the Fisc, 13 *Government Law & Policy Journal* 64, New York State Bar Association, Winter 2011; press release, More Than $1 Billion Recovered by Justice Department in Fraud and False Claims in Fiscal Year 2008, Department of Justice website, 11/10/08, http://www.justice.gov/opa/pr/2008/November/08-civ-992.html; The False Claims Act—State Laws, Phillips and Cohen LLP's All-about-qui-tam.org website, http://www.all-about-qui-tam.org/statelaws.shtml; and Advisory Legal Opinion AGO 2011-10, Florida State Attorney General website, 6/16/11, http://www.myfloridalegal.com/ago.nsf/Opinions/0D99E807DB86E533852578B100789E26.

The characterization of IPSIGs is quoted from Stanley N. Lupkin and Edgar J. Lewandowski, Independent Private Sector Inspectors General: Privately Funded Overseers of the Public Integrity, *NY Litigator Journal*, Summer 2005, Vol. 10, No. 1, 6-19, http://www.iaipsig.org/nylit-newsl-spring05-lewandowki.pdf. Other information about IPSIGs comes from that article as well as from James B. Jacobs and Ellen Peters, Labor Racketeering: The Mafia and the Unions, *Crime and Justice: A Review of Research*, Vol. 30, University of Chicago, 2003, 239-240, 252, http://www.fclaw.com/article/Materials/Crime_and_Justice_2003.pdf; Ronald Goldstock, On the Origins and Operations of the Independent Private Sector IG Program, 13 *Government Law & Policy Journal* 59, New York State Bar Association, Winter 2011; and Navigant Consulting, The Role of Independent Private Sector Monitors in Federal Contracts, Federal Bar Association, Government Contracts Section, 4/28/11, http://fedbar.org/Image-Library/Sections-and-Divisions/Govt-Contracts/GovtContr-Reception-Apr-2011.pdf. Eric Feldman, Core Integrity Group LLC, in his Presentation at Annual Conference of Association of Inspectors General, The IG's Use of Independent Monitors to Enhance Government Oversight, Williamsburg, Virginia 10/14/11, questioned their value as compared with that of less expensive monitors. Ronald Calvosa, program manager, Office of the Port Authority Inspector

General, in his presentation at Northeast Conference on Public Administration, John Jay College, 10/28/11, defended and explained their now
widespread use. About IAIPSIGs, 2006, http://www.iaipsig.org/about.html,
includes the Code of Ethics of the international body, and explains the
standards of quality it expects.

The Administrative Procedure Act, 5 U.S.C. §§ 551-559, sets forth
the laws governing judicial review of agency action generally; and Rosen,
Holding Government Bureaucracies Accountable, supra at 117-134, explains
how citizens may challenge agency rulings in court.

Hartman v. Moore, 547 U.S. 250 (2006) updates the requirements
for citizen lawsuits against individual government officials under § 1981
of the Civil Rights Act, as earlier set forth in *Bivens v. Six Federal Agents,*
403 U.S. 388 (1971).

The Ochs Center study on job creation in coal plant construction is
Ochs Center for Metropolitan Studies, *A Fraction of the Jobs: A Case Study
of the Job Creation Impact of Completed Coal-Fired Power Plants between 2005
and 2009,* March 2011 at www.ochscenter.org/documents/fractionofthejobs.
pdf. The quote of the coal industry spokesperson appeared in Pam Sohn,
Ochs study: Coal-fired power plants bring few jobs, *Chattanooga Times Free
Press,* 4/2/11. The Ochs Center's study of Plant Washington is Ochs Center
for Metropolitan Studies, Energy Efficiency as an Alternative Strategy for
the Power4Georgians EMCs: Assessing the Economic Impact for Georgia
Residents and Businesses, March 2010 at www.ochscenter.org/documents/
PlantWashington.pdf.

Information related to the ownership and value of properties related to
the development of Plant Washington are based on data from the Washington County Assessors Office, for Parcel 124.011, Parcels 125.003, 125.003B,
125.003C and 125.003D accessed via Internet. The 2009 Tax Year Value
of the property on Mayview Road was $1,596,156 and the total land was
1251.42 acres.

Information on the membership of members of the Tarbutton family
on boards and commissions was based on the most recent online filings by
family members with the Georgia Ethics Commission that are required as
a result of their service on these boards at ethics.ga.gov/filer-information/
public-officials/.

Campaign contribution information was from online resources. State
contribution data can be found at ethics.georgia.gov/Reports/Campaign/
Campaign_ByName.aspx and federal contribution data is accessible at www.
fec.gov.

Information about the role of the Washington County Development
Authority and its membership was accessible on line on the Washington
County Website at washingtoncountyga.com/development-authority/. The

Development Authority's potential role in financing the plant construction is based, among other things, on published reports such as Heather Duncan, Plant Washington financing question, *Macon Telegraph*, 12/9/09.

Financial disclosure requirements in Georgia are at O.C.G.A. 21-5-50(b)(4) (2009). For a discussion of the indictment of Dwight Brown, see Brandon Wilson, EMC's Brown Indicted for theft, racketeering, *Marietta Daily Journal*, 1/7/11. Although the initial indictment was thrown out by a court order, Brown was subsequently re-indicted on the same and additional charges. Challenges to the second indictment were rejected and as of this writing, the case is pending. Janet Davis, Cobb judge upholds ex-Cobb EMC chief's indictment, *Atlanta Journal Constitution*, 1/5/12.

For documentation related to the nondisclosure of information to the Federal Energy Regulatory Commission, see, Cobb Electric Membership Corporation, 2010 Annual Report; Cooperative Energy Incorporated Petition for Authority to Sell Power at Market-Based Rates, December 21, 2007; Cooperative Energy Incorporated, FERC, Docket Nos. ER08-371-000 and ER08-371-001, February 26, 2008; Application of Mr. W.T. Nelson III for Authority to Hold Interlocking Positions Pursuant to Section 305(b) of the Federal Power Act, May 27, 2008; Order Authorizing Holding of Interlocking Positions, 123 FERC 62,216 (June 12, 2008); Cooperative Energy Incorporated, Docket Nos. ER08-371-000, ER08-371-002 Notice of Sales in Excess of 4,000,000 Megawatt Hours of Electricity, July 2, 2008.

For documentation related to the role of Dean Alford in Cobb Energy and the development of Plant Washington, see, Cobb County Superior Court Documents,   sca.cobbcountyga.gov/downloads/CourtPostings/CobbEMC-FindingsOfFact.pdf; Letter from C. Dean Alford to Karen Handel, 1/15/08; Kelly Brooks, Cobb EMC joins co-ops in plans to build own generating plant, *Marietta Daily Journal*, 1/18/08; Cobb Energy's financial statements accessed at ww.cobbemc.com/info/cobb_energy_financial_statements.shtml, including: Cobb Energy Management Corporation and Subsidiaries, Consolidated Financial Statements as of January 31, 2002 and 2001; Cobb Energy Management Corporation and Subsidiaries, Consolidated Financial Statements and Schedules Year Ended January 31, 2003; Cobb Energy Management Corporation and Subsidiaries, Consolidated Financial Statements and Schedules, Years Ended January 31, 2004 and 2003; Cobb Energy Management Corporation and Subsidiaries, Consolidated Financial Statements and Schedules, Years Ended January 31, 2005 and 2004 (Restated); Cobb Energy Management Corporation and Subsidiaries, Consolidated Financial Statements and Schedules, Years Ended December 31, 2005 and January 31, 2005.

For documentation on the business relationship between Brown and Alford, see, Certificate of Organization, Buster & Brown Properties, LLC, 4/3/06. For documentation related to the Department of Labor grant, see,

Federal Register, Vol. 73, No. 198, 10/10/08; U.S. Department of Labor, U.S. Department of Labor awards nearly $123 million in 4th round of President's Community-Based Job Training Grants, 1/16/09 at www.dol.gov/opa/media/press/eta/archive/eta20090068.htm; Letter from Chari Magruder, FOIA Coordinator, Division of Contract Servicers, U.S. Department of Labor, Employment and Training Administration to Stacy Richardson, Ochs Center, 5/4/10; and Statement of Work, The TCSG Construction and Energy Industry Initiative.

Cobb EMC's withdrawal of support for Plant Washington is described in Kim Isaza, 7 of 9 on EMC board voted down coal plant, *Marietta Daily Journal*, 1/26/12 at www.mdjonline.com/view/full_story/17293660/article-7-of-9-on-EMC%E2%80%88board-voted-down-coal-plant-?instance=home_news_bullets.

Alexis de Toqueville, *Democracy in America*, Book 2, Chapter 5, Of the Use Which the Americans Make of Public Associations in Civil Life, http://xroads.virginia.edu/~HYPER/DETOC/ch2_05.htm.

For a discussion of access to government information, see, eg, Pete Weitzel, The Steady March of Government Secrecy, *Nieman Reports*, The Nieman Foundation for Journalism at Harvard, Fall, 2004, http://www.nieman.harvard.edu/reports/article/100791/The-Steady-March-of-Government-Secrecy.aspx; States Failing FOI Responsiveness, National Freedom of Information Coalition, 10/07 http://www.nfoic.org/states-failing-foi-responsiveness: "The tools available to citizens to enforce their rights under state FOI laws are, with rare exceptions, endemically weak."

Chapter 16. Conclusion

Data on unemployment by state was accessed from the Bureau of Labor Statistics website at www.bls.gov.

David Brooks' discussion of American liberalism is from Where Are the Liberals?, *The New York Times*, 1/9/12.

The discussion of the economic imperative for oversight is largely based upon, and quotes at length from, David Eichenthal, Doing Well by Doing Good: Can Corruption Prevention and Government Efficiency Strategies Help Turn Around Declining Cities?, 13 *Government, Law and Policy Journal* 78–86 (Winter 2011), published in Albany, New York by the New York State Bar Association.

The discussion of the cautionary tale of a public servant that concludes the book is largely based on, and quotes at length from Daniel Feldman, Former assemblyman asks: Who Guards the Guardians?, *Legislative Gazette*, 12/6/11.

Name Index

Subject Index

321